The Blue Guides

Please write in with your comments, suggestions and corrections for the next edition of the Blue Guide. Writers of the most helpful letters will be awarded a free Blue Guide of their choice.

Umbria

Alta Macadam

BLUE GUIDE

A&C Black • London
WW Norton • New York

3rd edition 2000

Published by A & C Black (Publishers) Limited
35 Bedford Row, London WC1R 4JH

Maps and plans drawn by RJS Associates, © A&C Black

Illustrations © Peter Spells

A CIP catalogue record of this book is available from the British Library.

ISBN 0–7136–4973–9

Published in the United States of America by
WW Norton and Company Inc.
500 Fifth Avenue, New York, NY 10110

Published simultaneously in Canada by
Penguin Books Canada Limited
10 Alcorn Avenue, Toronto
Ontario M4V 3B2

ISBN 0–393–32016–2 USA

The author and the publishers have done their best to ensure the accuracy of all the information in Blue Guide Umbria; however, they can accept no responsibility for any loss, injury or inconvenience sustained by any traveller as a result of information or advice contained in the guide.

Cover photograph: bas relief by Agostino di Duccio on the Oratory of San Bernardino, Perugia. By Shelia Terry/Robert Harding Picture Library.

Title page illustration, Loggia del Bantitori, Piazza Marconi, Amelia.

Alta Macadam has been a writer of Blue Guides since 1970. She lives in Florence with her family (the painter Francesco Colacicchi and their children Giovanni and Lelia). Combined with work on writing the guides she has also been associated with the Bargello Museum, the Alinari photo archive and Harvard University at Villa I Tatti in Florence. As author of the Blue Guides to Rome, Venice, Sicily, Florence, Tuscany and Umbria, she travels extensively in Italy every year in order to revise new editions of the books.

Printed and bound in England by Butler & Tanner Ltd., Frome and London.

Contents

Maps and Plans

Introduction

Umbria, one of the 20 regions of Italy, lies at the very heart of the country. It is the only region on the peninsula without a sea coast. Although less well known to foreigners than its famous neighbour Tuscany, it has some of the most beautiful landscape to be found in the country as well as some of its most interesting towns. Its capital, Perugia, is a city of great antiquity which has numerous works of art. Gubbio, Spello, Todi and Spoleto remain among the most attractive and best preserved small medieval towns in Italy. Orvieto, with its magnificent cathedral has perhaps the most spectacular position of all the hill towns. Assisi is world famous as the birthplace of St Francis. Smaller, less well known towns but also of great interest include Bevagna, Montefalco, Trevi, Norcia, Amelia and Narni.

With an area of 8456 square kilometres, Umbria has only 850,000 inhabitants. The landscape is characterised by hills covered with small silver olive trees, chestnut woods and vineyards. The soil of Umbria is not particularly rich and so farmers have had to cultivate the fields of their smallholdings with extra care. A special feature of Umbria is Lago Trasimeno, the fourth largest lake in Italy, with its reedy shores and lovely islands. The Tiber river traverses most of the region: in its upper reaches tobacco is cultivated, while south of Perugia its valley widens out and passes beneath the town of Todi, often covered by a bluish mist off the river. In the south-west corner of Umbria, between the Tiber and Nera rivers, are isolated castles and villages amidst chestnut woods and farming country. Further east are the Monti Martani, pretty wooded hills dotted with villages and country churches. The exceptionally wide alluvial plain south-east of Perugia, known as the Valle Umbra is watered by numerous small rivers and is overlooked by the compact little hill towns of Trevi, Spello and Assisi. Here the beautiful Monte Subasio (1290m) is a protected area. In the south-east corner of Umbria is the lesser known Valnerina which follows the Nera river from its source in the high Monti Sibillini in the Marche down a pretty wooded valley, on the slopes of which are small villages and churches, towards Terni and the spectacular Marmore waterfalls. Nearby is the delightful Lago di Piediluco. Above Norcia is a remarkable solitary upland plain (1300m) known as the Piano Grande di Castelluccio, a protected area of great interest to naturalists.

Umbria takes its name from the Umbri, called *gens antiquissima* Italiae by Pliny the Elder. Of Indo-European origin, they inhabited an area considerably larger than present-day Umbria (including Romagna and part of the Marche). They settled here in prehistoric times and reached their moment of greatest cultural importance around the 5C–4C BC. The seven bronze 'Eugubian tables' still preserved in Gubbio include the most important known examples of the Umbrian language.

Umbria has a great variety of monuments from all periods of Italian history. Impressive Etruscan remains survive in Perugia, including the Arco d'Augusto, Porta Marzia and the Ipogeo dei Volumni. The walls of Amelia date from around the 5C BC. Prehistoric, Etruscan and Roman finds are displayed in the archaeological museums of Perugia and Orvieto. Some of the most remarkable Roman monuments north of Rome are to be found in Umbria. These can be seen at Assisi (Temple of Minerva), Narni (the Ponte d'Augusto), Bevagna (a mosaic, a temple and part of a theatre), Spello (several gateways and an amphitheatre), Todi and Spoleto. The ruined Roman towns of Carsulae and Ocriculum are archaeological sites of the greatest interest. Early Christian churches include San Salvatore in Spoleto and Sant'Angelo in Perugia, as well as the unusual little Tempietto di Clitunno.

The Gothic and Romanesque period is represented by churches, castles, town halls and abbeys all over Umbria, as well as by frescoes and sculptural works. The great Gothic cathedral of Orvieto is one of the most memorable sights in Italy, and the interior of San Fortunato in Todi, and the upper church of San Francesco in Assisi are important examples of Italian Gothic architecture. Romanesque churches of the 12C and 13C include San Silvestro in Bevagna, San Pietro and Santa Chiara in Assisi, and Sant'Eufemia in Spoleto. Lesser known churches which also represent this period include the Collegiata di Lugnano in Teverina and San Felice di Narco, and the pievi (parish churches) in the Monti Martani, as well as the abbeys of San Pietro in Valle (where the 12C frescoes are among the most important works in Italy of this date) and Sant' Eutizio. Splendid sculptured 12C façades include those of San Rufino in Assisi and San Pietro in Spoleto.

Of all the civic buildings erected in Umbria in the Middle Ages, the most impressive is Palazzo dei Consoli in Gubbio, begun in 1332, and attributed to Gattapone, perhaps the most ingenious Umbrian architect (who is also thought to have built the Ponte delle Torri in Spoleto). Other fine town halls are to be found in Orvieto (Palazzo del Popolo) and in Perugia (Palazzo dei Priori). Fine examples of military architecture include the 13C castle at Castiglione del Lago, and the splendid fortresses of Assisi, Spoleto and Narni, built for Cardinal Albornoz in the 14C.

The frescoes in the upper and lower churches of San Francesco in Assisi painted in the late 13C and early 14C to celebrate St Francis, by the greatest Italian painters of the time (Cimabue, Giotto, Simone Martini and Pietro Lorenzetti) deserve a place apart in the history of art. These churches also contain some of the best stained-glass windows to be found in Italy. Church treasuries of the greatest interest are preserved in Assisi (San Francesco) and Città di Castello (Museo del Duomo). Interesting early 15C frescoes of secular subjects in late Gothic style can now be seen again after restoration in Palazzo Trinci in Foligno.

The Renaissance produced isolated masterpieces in Umbria, such as the frescoes by Filippo Lippi in the Duomo of Spoleto, and the frescoes by Luca Signorelli in the chapel of San Brizio in Orvieto cathedral. Numerous frescoes and paintings by Perugino, the greatest Umbrian painter (1446–1523), and master of Raphael, can be seen in Perugia (notably in the Collegio del Cambio), Città della Pieve, and other towns. His pupils included Pinturicchio, who frescoed a chapel in Santa Maria Maggiore in Spello. Montefalco preserves some fine frescoes by Benozzo Gozzoli.

Gifted 15C–16C artists of the Umbrian school of painting, whose work can be seen almost exclusively in Umbria, include Pier Antonio Mezzastris, Nicolò di Alunno, Matteo da Gualdo, Francesco Melanzio, Tiberio d'Assisi and Bartolomeo di Tommaso of Foligno. The best comprehensive view of Umbrian painting is provided by the Pinacoteca Nazionale in Perugia.

Umbria also produced skilled woodworkers whose carvings can be seen in numerous churches all over the region. Agostino di Duccio carried out beautiful sculptural work on the façade of the Oratorio di San Bernardino in Perugia. One of the most remarkable Renaissance buildings in Umbria is the domed centrally planned church of Santa Maria della Consolazione in Todi.

Sixteenth- and seventeenth-century architecture, sculpture and painting can be seen in Santa Maria degli Angeli outside Assisi. The 17C and 18C in Umbria is perhaps best represented by the palaces of Foligno which contain pictorial decorations by Pietro da Cortona, Marcello Leopardi and Coccetti. Local architects of the 19C include Giovanni Santini. The region is particularly rich in late 18C and early 19C theatres, many of which have recently been restored; these can be found in Terni, Narni, Amelia, Spoleto, Norcia, Monteleone di Spoleto, Montecastello di Vibio, Orvieto, Trevi, Todi, Panicale, Città della Pieve and Bevagna.

An attempt has been made in this guide to include small and lesser known places of interest in order to give as comprehensive a picture as possible of the art and architecture of Umbria. These places will generally not be visited by those with little time at their disposal, but will be of interest to the more leisurely travellers. A comprehensive index of artists has also been provided to help those interested in their exploration of Umbria.

Umbria is now very well equipped with hotels and restaurants of all categories. In the last few years some delightful small hotels have been opened in historic palaces in the centre of towns or in lovely villas in the countryside (these are often classified in the official hotel lists as 'country house hotels' or 'historic residences' and listed separately). Local transport by bus or train is generally excellent. As in the rest of Italy, the best time to visit Umbria is in early spring or autumn. At Easter and in summer the more famous sights can be uncomfortably crowded. Assisi totally changes character out of season: in winter it remains one of the most fascinating and beautiful towns in Italy.

The 1997–98 earthquake

In the earthquake which hit Umbria and the Marche in September and October 1997 (with its epicentre at Colfiorito, Sellano and Nocera Umbra) 11 people died, 126 were injured and over 50,000 people were rendered temporarily homeless. Help was immediate and very efficiently organised by the Italian government, so that by December 1997 8822 families had been rehoused in the disaster zone in prefabricated villages as close as possible to their damaged homes. However, the earthquake continued to cause serious damage, with more violent tremors registered in March and April 1998, when the epicentre was near Nocera Umbra and Gualdo Tadino.

The exceptionally long duration of the earthquake meant not only that the inhabitants suffered greatly, but also that reconstruction was not able to commence as quickly as was originally hoped. It is now the work of the authorities to decide how work should proceed, but funds have been assured and there is a general feeling that everything possible is being done to restore peoples' lives to a situation of normality as quickly as possible. Because the earth tremors continued for so long the entire region was affected as a result of the heavy loss of income from tourism both in 1997 and 1998.

The earthquake wrought most harm in the eastern part of Umbria, leaving the western and southern districts virtually untouched. The greatest damage to historic monuments was caused in Assisi where in the upper church of San Francesco the vaults in two of the bays of the nave, with frescoes by Cimabue and attributed to Giotto, crashed to the ground. However, the famous St Francis fresco cycle on the walls below as well as the stained glass in the windows survived virtually untouched. The vaults were carefully reconstructed and the church reopened in late November 1999. So far two of the frescoes on the arch at the west end have been recomposed in situ from the shattered fragments. The Franciscan monastery (and treasury) is still closed for repairs, and the other important churches in Assisi are in the process of restoration: the Duomo (although restoration of the façade has been completed), Santa Chiara, and San Pietro. The little town of Nocera Umbra will have to be totally restored, and the monuments in Gualdo Tadino are all severely damaged. There was considerable destruction in the district around Colfiorito, Sellano has had to be temporarily abandoned, and some churches in the upper Valnerina were badly shaken. In Foligno, the Duomo and numerous other churches have had to be closed, and the Duomo of Trevi is also closed. The two most important churches in Bevagna were also badly shaken (San Silvestro and San Michele Archangelo) and other churches have also had to be closed there. Most of the churches in Montefalco are closed and the frescoes by Benozzo Gozzoli in the Museo Civico di Sna Francesco have been covered for restoration. The Duomo of Spoleto was also damaged (but has been kept open) and the Museo Diocesano is closed.

However, all the other most important monuments and museums of the region are open and undamaged. Indeed, many more have reopened since the last edition of this guide, including delightful local museums in Norcia, Bevagna, Trevi, Todi, Bettona, Deruta, San Feliciano, Montone and Cascia. The Galleria Nazionale dell'Umbria and the Museo Archeologico Nazionale in Perugia have both opened more rooms; the Pinacoteca Comunale in Città di Castello has reopened; more rooms are open in Palazzo dei Consoli in Gubbio, where a lovely park is now also accessible to the public; and restoration has been completed on the fascinating early 15C frescoes in Palazzo Trinci in Foligno which has finally reopened after many years' closure. In Orvieto the Signorelli frescoes in the Duomo can be seen again after their restoration, the Museo Claudio Faina has reopened, and the Torre del Moro can now be climbed. Underground rooms and Roman cisterns can be visited in Narni and Amelia thanks to the work of volunteers, and the theatre in Amelia has been restored.

It is to be hoped that visitors will now return to this beautiful and fascinating region of Italy where the people, despite the tragic times they have been through in 1997–98, are particularly hospitable and welcoming.

Acknowledgements

As for past editions of this guide I am firstly indebted to **Roberto Colacicchi** and **Raffaella Trabalza** who provided much generous help to me while I was travelling in Umbria. I was not only able to take advantage of their kind hospitality but also of their expert knowledge on numerous aspects of Umbria. I am extremely grateful to them for their friendship. I would also like to thank warmly Flavia Serego who gave me a lot of useful information, especially about gardens and hospitality. I also owe much to Jocelyn and Mark Tress, who have made Umbria their second home, and who helped me in many ways. My sister Helen Taylor shared part of the travelling with me and I am very grateful to her for her companionship and suggestions for improvements to the guide. I would also like to thank Giulio Mancini of San Cristoforo, near Amelia, Rino Polito of Norcia, Carlo and

Anna Bianconi of Norcia, and Maurizio Bravi of Narni, for their kind assistance.

The Umbrian tourist board was extremely helpful (special thanks to Lindijer Ineke), and local tourist offices all over the region, and in particular those of Terni, Orvieto (Danca Caccavello), Spoleto (Gilberto Giasprini), and Città di Castello.

How to use the Guide

The guide is divided into **chapters** which describe the main towns, with their immediate environs, and regions of Umbria, as well as certain areas known for their distinctive landscape. The routes dedicated to the major towns are organised into a number of walking itineraries, with separate descriptions for the major monuments and museums.

An exhaustive section at the beginning of the book lists all the **practical information** a traveller is likely to need in preparation for a visit to Umbria and while travelling. More detailed practical information, which includes public transport, is at the beginning of each chapter, or chapter section, and at the beginning of the description of each town. Information has been given both for those who visit the area by car and those who travel by public transport.

A small selection of **hotels** has been given at the beginning of each chapter, with their official star rating in order to give an indication of price. In making the choice for inclusion, generally speaking the smaller hotels have been favoured, those in the centre of towns, or in particularly beautiful rural situations. For further information, see under 'Where to stay' in the Practical information section.

Restaurants have also been indicated at the beginning of each chapter, and these have been divided into three categories which reflect price ranges in 1999: **A** indicates luxury-class restaurants where the prices are likely to be over 60,000 lire a head (and sometimes well over 100,000 lire a head). These are the most famous restaurants in Umbria and they usually offer international cuisine. **B** indicates first-class restaurants where the prices range from 50,000 lire and above. These are generally comfortable, with good service, but are not cheap. The third category, **C**, are simple trattorie and pizzerie where you can eat for around 25,000–40,000 lire a head, or even less. Although simple, and by no means 'smart', the food in this category, which often includes local specialities, is usually the best value. For further information, see under 'Restaurants' in the practical information section.

The **most important monuments or works of art** in Umbria have been highlighted in bold type throughout the text. The 'Highlights' sections on p. 13 singles out the major monuments which should not be missed.

Bold type has also been used in **churches** to differentiate the various parts of the building (i.e. the façade, south side, east end, important chapels, etc.) All churches are taken as being orientated to the east, with the entrance at the west end and the altar at the east end, and the south aisle on the right and the north aisle on the left.

In Perugia all the main monuments have been keyed (i.e. map 2) against the **town map** on p. 52, which is gridded with numbered squares, the first number refers to the map and the second to the square.

The **local tourist boards** (Servizio Turistico Territoriale, known as IAT) are usually extremely helpful and are the only way of securing up-to-date information on the spot about opening times and accommodation. Information offices, with their telephone numbers, are listed at the beginning of each chapter. On the town maps they are marked with the letter **i**, the symbol which is used on local signposts throughout Italy.

Opening times of museums and monuments have been given throughout the text (i.e. 09.00–14.00; PH 09.00–13.00), with the abbreviation PH showing times for Sundays and public holidays. The telephone numbers of the most important museums have also been listed. The times vary and often change without warning, and it is best to telephone first, or ask the local IAT tourist office on arrival about up-to-date times. For further information, see p. 32. Almost all churches close at 12.00 and do not reopen again until 15.00, 16.00, or even 17.00.

Although detailed town plans are provided, every traveller to Umbria, whether driving or using public transport, will also need a large-scale **map** of the region: the best are those produced by TCI (details on p. 27).

Abbreviations used in the guide:

ACI	Automobile Club Italiano
APT	Azienda di Promozione Turistica dell'Umbria (official local tourist office)
b.	born
C	century
c	circa (about)
CAI	Club Alpino Italiano
d.	died
ENIT	Ente Nazionale Italiano per il Turismo
fl.	floruit (flourished)
FS	Ferrovie dello Stato (Italian state railways)
IAT	local information office of the Servizio Turistico Territoriale, a subsidiary of the APT in Perugia
PH	public holiday
St and Sts	Saint and Saints
TCI	Touring Club Italiano
ProLoco	local tourist board

The terms *Quattrocento*, *Cinquecento* (abbreviated in Italy '400, '500), etc., refer not to the 14C and 15C, but to the 'fourteen-hundreds' and 'fifteen-hundreds', i.e. the 15C and 16C, etc.

Highlights

Etruscan buildings
Perugia (Arco d'Augusto, Porta Marzia, Ipogeo dei Volumni, Etruscan well). **Orvieto** (temple, underground caves and well-shafts, Crocifisso del Tufo necropolis and other tombs in the environs).

Roman buildings
Perugia (mosaic). **Assisi** (Temple of Minerva and sacred area, cistern in the Duomo, Roman house below Santa Maria Maggiore). **Bevagna** (mosaic, temple and part of the theatre). **Spello** (several gateways and amphitheatre). Narni (Ponte d'Augusto). **Todi** (niches). **Spoleto** (theatre, foundations of Sant'Ansano, Arco di Druso, Roman house, walls, Ponte Sanguinario). **Gubbio** (theatre). **Amelia** (walls, begun in 5C BC, and Roman cisterns). Colle Plinio (villa of Pliny the Younger, not yet open to the public). **Terni** (amphitheatre). Archaeological sites of the Roman towns of Carsulae, Ocriculum and Urbinum Hortense.

Archaeological collections (prehistoric, Etruscan and Roman material)
Perugia (Museo Archeologico). **Orvieto** (Museo Archeologico Nazionale, Museo Claudio Faina e Museo Civico). **Gubbio** (Sezione Archeologico in Palazzo dei Consoli). **Bevagna** (Museo della Città). **Spello** (collection in Palazzo Comunale Vecchio). **Assisi** (Museo Civico, Museo Capitolare). **Montefalco** (Museo Lapidario). **Terni** (Museo Civico in Palazzo Carrara). **Piediluco** (Roman statue in San Francesco). **Spoleto** (Museo Archeologico).

Early Christian churches
Spoleto (San Salvatore). **Perugia** (Sant' Angelo). Tempietto di **Clitunno**. **Terni** (San Salvatore).

Medieval towns
Assisi, Bevagna, Todi, Spoleto, Trevi, Gubbio, Spello, Narni.

Secular medieval architecture
Gubbio (Palazzo dei Consoli). **Spoleto** (Ponte delle Torri). **Orvieto** (Palazzo del Popolo). **Perugia** (Palazzo dei Priori, Via Bagliona, Sala dei Notari).

Military medieval architecture
Assisi (Rocca). **Spoleto** (Rocca Albornoz). **Narni** (Rocca). **Castiglione del Lago** (Castello). **Castello di Zocco**, Lago Trasimeno. **Gualdo Tadino** (Rocca Flea).

Romanesque churches and monuments
Perugia (Fontana Maggiore). **Bevagna** (San Silvestro). **Assisi** (San Pietro, Santa Chiara, façade of San Rufino). **Spoleto** (Sant'Eufemia). **Lugnano in Teverina** (Collegiata). **San Felice di Narco**. San Pietro in Valle. **Abbeys of Sant'Eutizio** and **Sassovivo** (cloister). Country churches (pievi) in the **Monti Martani**.

Gothic churches
Orvieto (Duomo). **Todi** (San Fortunato). **Assisi** (upper church of San Francesco).

Late 13C and early 14C frescoes
Assisi (upper and lower churches of San Francesco) by Cimabue, Giotto, Simone Martini, and Pietro Lorenzetti.

Renaissance buildings
Todi (Santa Maria della Consolazione). **Gubbio** (Palazzo Ducale). **Castel Rigone** (Madonna dei Miracoli). **Orvieto** (Pozzo di San Patrizio).

Renaissance frescoes, paintings, and sculptures
Spoleto (frescoes by Filippo Lippi in the Duomo). **Orvieto** (frescoes by Luca Signorelli in the Duomo). **Spello** (frescoes by Pinturicchio in Santa Maria Maggiore). **Montefalco** (frescoes by Benozzo Gozzoli in San Francesco and by Tiberio d'Assisi in San Fortunato). **Città di Castello** (paintings in the Pinacoteca Comunale). **Perugia** (paintings in the Galleria Nazionale dell'Umbria, frescoes by Raphael in San Savero, and sculptures by Agostino di Duccio on the façade of the Oratorio di San Bernardino).

Works by Perugino
Perugia (Collegio del Cambio, Galleria Nazionale dell'Umbria, San Pietro, San Severo, Sant'Agnese); **Corciano** (San Cristoforo); **Assisi** (Oratorio dei Pellegrini, Santa Maria degli Angeli); **Città della Pieve** (Oratorio di Santa Maria dei Bianchi, San Pietro); **Panicale** (San Sebastiano); **Trevi** (Madonna delle Lacrime); **Spello** (Santa Maria Maggiore); **Foligno** (Nunziatella); **Montefalco** (San Francesco); **Cerqueto** (parish church); **Bettona** (Museo Comunale).

18C and 19C theatres
Terni, Narni, Amelia, Spoleto, Norcia, Monteleone di Spoleto, Montecastello di Vibio, Orvieto, Trevi, Todi, Panicale, Città della Pieve, Bevagna and Citerna.

Stained glass windows
Perugia (San Domenico). **Assisi** (San Francesco). **Orvieto** (Duomo).

Woodcarvings
Perugia (Sala di Udienza del Collegio della Mercanzia and choir stalls in the Duomo, San Pietro, and Sant'Agostino). **Gubbio** (San Domenico). Cathedrals of **Todi**, **Orvieto** and **Spoleto**.

Museums with ceramic collections
Deruta (Museo Regionale della Ceramica); **Gubbio** (museum in Palazzo dei Consoli); **Torgiano** (Museo del Vino); **Todi** (Museo Comunale); **Perugia** (Galleria Nazionale dell'Umbria).

Church treasuries (and reliquaries)
Perugia (Galleria Nazionale dell'Umbria); **Orvieto** (reliquary in the Duomo and Museo dell'Opera del Duomo); **Città di Castello** (Museo Capitolare); Assisi (Treasury of San Francesco); **Spello** (Pinacoteca Civica); **Spoleto** (Pinacoteca Comunale).

Areas of particular natural beauty
Lago Trasimeno (and Isola Polvese), Monte Subasio, Valnerina, Monti Martani, Marmore waterfalls, Lago di Corbara, Monte Peglia, Oasi di Alviano, Valle Castoriana, Piano Grande di Castelluccio.

PRACTICAL INFORMATION

 Planning your visit

When to go

The best time to visit Umbria is in spring or autumn. In these seasons the countryside is at its best, covered with wild flowers in the spring and bright with orange and yellow leaves in the autumn. However, spring can be unexpectedly wet until well after Easter, and Easter itself should be avoided if possible as it is the most crowded time of year throughout Italy. Autumn is often drier and can be quite warm throughout October and even in early November. At the height of summer Umbria can be extremely hot. As in other parts of Italy Umbria is crowded with Italian school parties from March until early May. The special charm of a visit to Umbria in winter is that even the most famous sights (notably Assisi) can be totally deserted.

Passports

Pasports are necessary for all British and American travellers entering Italy. You are obliged to carry some means of identification with you at all times when in Italy. A lost or stolen passport can be replaced by the relevant embassy in Rome.

Italian tourist boards

General information can be obtained abroad from the Italian State Tourist Office (ENIT) who provide detailed information on Italy.

- **Canada** 1 Place Ville Marie, Suite 1914, Montreal ☎ 001 514 8867667, fax 514 392 1429.
- **Netherlands** Stadhoudestrade 2, 1054 ES Amsterdam, ☎ 003 120 6168244, fax 120 618 8515.
- **UK** 1 Princes Street, London WIR 8AY ☎ 020 7408 1254, fax 020 7493 6695.
- **USA** New York: 630 Fifth Avenue, NY 10111, Suite 1565 ☎ 001 212 2454822, fax 212 5869249. Chicago: 500 North Michigan Avenue, Suite 2240 Chicago 1, IL 60611 ☎ 001 312 6440996, fax 312 6443019. Los Angeles: 12400 Wilshire Blvd, Suite 550, CA 90025 ☎ 001 310-8201898, fax 310 8206357.

Tour operators

Among the many UK tour operators offering inclusive holidays to Umbria are the following:

Abercrombie & Kent, ☎ 020 7730 9600; fax 020 7730 9376.
Ace Study Tours, ☎ 01223 835055; fax 01223 837394.
Alternative Travel Group, ☎ 01865 315678; fax 01865 310299 which specialise in walking tours.
Citalia, ☎ 020 8686 5533; fax 020 8686 0328.
City Escapades, ☎ 020 8563 8959; fax 020 8748 3731.

CTS Travel, (☎ 020 7 637 1648; fax 020 7580 5675).
Headwater Holidays (Bass Travel) Ltd, (☎ 01606 813333; fax 01606 813334, which specialise in walking and biking holidays).
Inntravel, (☎ 01653 628811; fax 01653 628741 which specialise in walking holidays).
International Chapters Plc, (☎ 020 7722 9560; fax 020 7722 9140.
Italian Escapades, (☎ 020 8748 4999; fax 020 8748 6381).
Magic of Italy, (☎ 020 8748 4999; fax 020 8748 3731).
Prospect Music and Art Tours Ltd, (☎ 020 7486 5705).
Martin Randall Travel, (☎ 020 8742 3355; fax 020 8742 3355).
Specialtours, (☎ 020 7730 2297; fax 020 7823 5035).
Travelscene Ltd, (☎ 020 8427 8800; fax 020 8861 4154).

In Canada, *Artfocus au point* (☎ 514 937 6391, fax 514 933 5346) specialise in art and architectural tours of Italy.

Relevant web sites include *Let's roam Italy* (http://tqd.advanced.org/2838); *Italytour.com* (http://www.italytour.com/); and *Italy online* (http://www.in-italy.com/).

Maps

Although detailed town plans have been included in this book, it has not been possible, because of the format, to provide an atlas of Umbria adequate for those travelling by car. The maps at the end of the book are only intended to be used when planning an itinerary. The *Touring Club Italiano* publishes several sets of excellent maps: these are constantly updated and are indispensable to anyone travelling by car in Italy. They include the *Grande Carta Stradale d'Italia* on a scale of 1:200,000. This is divided into 15 sheets covering the regions of Italy: Umbria is covered on the sheet (No. D40) entitled *Umbria, Marche*. These are also published in a handier form as an atlas (with a comprehensive index) called the *Atlante Stradale d'Italia* in three volumes (the one entitled *Centro* covers Umbria). These maps can be purchased from the Italian Touring Club offices and at many booksellers; in London they can be purchased from *Stanfords*, 12–14 Long Acre, WC2E 9LP (☎ 020 7836 1321).

The *Istituto Geografico Militare* of Italy has for many years been famous for its map production (much of it done by aerial photography). Their headquarters are in Florence (10 Via Cesare Battisti). Their maps are now available at numerous bookshops in the main towns of Italy. They publish a map of Italy on a scale of 1:100,000 in 277 sheets, and a field survey partly 1:50,000, partly 1:25,000, which are invaluable for detailed exploration of the country, especially its more mountainous regions; the coverage is however, still far from complete at the larger scales, and some of the maps are out-of-date.

Money and banks

The monetary unit is the Italian *lira* (plural *lire*). There are coins of 50, 100, 200, 500 and 1000 lire, and notes of 1000, 2000, 5000, 10,000, 50,000, 100,000, and 500,000 lire. There are currently three sizes of 50 and 100 lire coins. Travellers' cheques and Eurocheques are the safest way of carrying money while travelling, and most credit cards are now generally accepted in the grander shops, hotels and restaurants (and at some petrol stations). However, many places in

Umbria are still reluctant to accept payment by any other means than cash. In the centre of the main towns there are cashpoint machines (ATMs) called Bancomat, and also automatic machines which change foreign bank notes. The 'Euro' introduced in 1999 is recognised as valid currency all over the country.

Banks are usually open Monday–Friday 08.20–13.20, 14.30–15.30 (or 14.45–15.45). They are closed on Saturday and public holidays, and close early (about 11.00) on days preceding national holidays. The commission on cashing travellers' cheques can be quite high. Money can be changed at exchange offices (*cambio*), in travel agencies, some post offices and main stations. Exchange offices are usually open seven days a week at airports and some main railway stations. At some hotels, restaurants and shops money can be exchanged (but usually at a lower rate).

Health

British citizens, as members of the EU, have the right to claim health services in Italy if they have the E111 form (available from all post offices). There are also a number of private holiday health insurance policies. First aid services (*pronto soccorso*) are available at all hospitals, railway stations, and airports. **Chemists** (*farmacie*) are usually open Monday–Friday 09.00–13.00, 16.00–19.30 or 20.00. On Saturdays and Sundays (and holidays) a few are open (listed on the door of every chemist). In all towns there is also at least one chemist open at night (indicated on the chemists' doors). For emergencies, ☎ 113.

Disabled travellers

Italy is at last catching up slowly with the rest of Europe in the provision of facilities for the disabled. All new public buildings (including museums) are now obliged by law to provide access for the disabled, and specially designed facilities. In the annual list of hotels published by the local IAT offices, hotels which are able to give hospitality to the disabled are indicated. Airports and railway stations provide assistance, and certain trains are equipped to transport wheelchairs. Access is allowed to the centre of towns (normally closed to traffic) for cars with disabled people, where parking places are reserved for them. For all other information, contact local IAT offices, *Chance* (☎ 045 8060110) or *Si...viaggiare* (☎ 06 23267504).

Getting there

By air

The nearest international airports to Umbria are in **Pisa** (220km north-west of Perugia), and in **Rome** (210km south-west of Perugia). There is a daily bus service (by *ACAP-SULGA*, ☎ 075 5009641) from Rome airport (Fiumicino) to and from Perugia (in 3.5 hrs). Direct flights from numerous cities in the USA as well as from Europe fly to Rome (Fiumicino). Rome's second airport (Ciampino) also operates charter flights from London Stansted. From Pisa airport there is a train or coach service to Florence which takes 1 hr, and from Florence there are frequent mainline trains to Rome (change at Terontola for Perugia).

The small airport near the centre of **Florence** (Amerigo Vespucci at Peretola) operates flights from other parts of Europe (including London Gatwick), and there is also an international airport at **Bologna**, across the Apennines in Emilia-Romagna. There is a small airport at Sant'Egidio, 12km from Perugia, which operates flights from Milan (☎ 075 6929447).

From the UK, direct air services are operated by *British Airways* (☎ 020 8897 4000) and *Alitalia* (☎ 020 7602 7111) from London daily to Pisa, Rome and Bologna airports. There are also flights from Manchester, Dublin and Glasgow to Pisa. *Ryanair* (☎ 0541 569569) operates from Stansted to Pisa and Ancona. *Meridiana* (☎ 020 7839 222) flies from Gatwick to Florence. Details of charter flights are available through travel agencies and listings sections in many of the national newspapers, especially the Sunday newspapers and the London *Evening Standard* and in *Time Out*. Scheduled services offer special fares which are available according to season; there are reduced youth fares. *Citalia* (☎ 020 8686 0677) has fly-drive schemes.

Air services **from the USA** to Rome are operated by *Alitalia* (☎ 800 223 5730), which flies non-stop from New York, Boston, Chicago and Los Angeles. Flights from New York to Rome are also operated by *Continental*, ☎ 800 231 0856, *Delta*, ☎ 800 241 4141 and *TWA*, ☎ 800 892 4141. *United*, ☎ 800 5382 929 operate between Washington DC and Rome. *British Airways*, *Air France*, *KLM* and *Sabena* offer flights connecting through London, Paris, Amsterdam and Brussels, and these are often more economical than direct flights.

By rail

From the UK, Florence can be reached by through train from Paris Lyon overnight (by sleeper); there are now frequent trains from London Waterloo through the eurotunnel via Calais to Paris Nord (in c 3 hrs).

For more information, contact *European Rail Ltd*, ☎ 020 7387 0444; fax 020 7387 0888. Italian state railways are represented in the UK by *Citalia*, ☎ 020 8686 0677; fax 020 8686 0328.

In the USA, information is available from CIT, ☎ 212 697 1394 (New York office), ☎ 310 338 8616 (Los Angeles office). In Canada, there are CIT offices in Montreal (☎ 514 8459101) and Toronto (☎ 416 927 7712).

In Italy, the main line from Milan via Bologna and Florence to Rome has a station at Terontola (although most of the fast trains do not stop here) on the branch line to Lago Trasimeno, Perugia, Assisi, Spello and Foligno. From the south, the main line between Rome and Florence has a station at Orte, for the line to Narni, Terni, Spoleto, Trevi and Foligno. Orvieto is on the main line between Florence and Rome (the slow trains all stop here, but only a few fast trains a day stop at Orvieto station). From the Adriatic coast there is a line from Ancona to Foligno, Spoleto and Terni.

Overnight car sleeper services run May–September once a week from Calais to Bologna (for information and booking, ☎ 02 72544350 or 051 6303589).

By coach

A coach service operates in two days between London (Victoria Coach Station) and Rome (Piazza della Repubblica) via Dover, Calais, Paris, Turin, Milan, Bologna and Florence, daily from June to September, and once or twice a week for the rest of the year. There is a reduction for students. Information in London from *Eurolines*, ☎ 01582 404511. In Florence, information from the SITA office, ☎ 055 214721.

There are long-distance coach services from Florence to Perugia and Assisi, and from Rome to Perugia.

By car

The easiest approaches by road are the motorways through the Mont Blanc, St Bernard, or Monte Cenis tunnels, over the Brenner pass, or along the south coast of France.

The A1 motorway from Milan and Bologna to Rome runs through Tuscany from Prato to Florence, the Valdarno, Arezzo, Valdichiana, Chiusi, and then traverses the western limit of Umbria past Orvieto. From the Valdichiana exit a fast *superstrada* leads east (entering Umbria at Lago Trasimeno) to Perugia. The Chiusi exit is also convenient for Lago Trasimeno and Città della Pieve. From the Orvieto exit two spectacular roads run east to Todi and at Orte there is an exit for a fast road to Narni and Terni.

An alternative approach to Umbria from northern Italy (avoiding the busy A1 motorway and the particularly difficult stretch with numerous tunnels and heavy traffic between Bologna and Florence), is the A14 motorway down the Adriatic coast. At the Cesena exit a fast superstrada (E45) leads south to Città di Castello and Perugia.

Umbria is often visited **from Tuscany**, which adjoins it to the north (see *Blue Guide Tuscany*). From Florence Perugia can be reached in under 2 hours (via the A1 motorway to the Valdichiana exit and from there by the superstrada). Umbria can also be easily reached from Cortona, just across the border in Tuscany. Another beautiful approach from Tuscany can be made from Pienza, Montepulciano, and Chiusi, a short distance to the west of Lago Trasimeno.

British drivers taking their own cars via any of the routes across France, Belgium, Luxembourg, Switzerland, Germany and Austria need the vehicle registration book, a valid national driving licence (accompanied by a translation, issued free of charge by the Italian State Tourist Office), insurance cover, and a nationality plate attached to the car. If you are not the owner of the vehicle, you must have the owner's written permission for its use abroad. A Swiss motorway pass is needed for Switzerland, and can be obtained from the RAC, the AA or at the Swiss border.

The continental rule of the road is to drive on the right and overtake on the left. The provisions of the respective highway codes in the countries of transit, though similar, have important variations, especially with regard to priority, speed limits and pedestrian crossings. Membership of the AA (☎ 01256 20123), or the RAC (membership enquiries and insurance, ☎ 01345 3331133; route information ☎ 01345 333222) entitles you to many of the facilities of affiliated societies on the Continent. They are represented at most of the sea and air ports.

Motorway routes to Italy from other parts of Europe
The main routes from France, Switzerland and Austria are summarised below.

Route 1 The direct motorway route from France, bypassing Geneva, enters Italy through the **Mont Blanc Tunnel** (toll; closed for repairs until at least the end of 2000). The road from Courmayeur to Aosta has not yet been improved. At Aosta the A5 motorway begins: it follows the Val d'Aosta. Just beyond Ivrea is the junction with the A4/5 motorway: the A5 continues south to Turin, while the A4/5 diverges east. At Santhia the A4 motorway from Turin is joined for Milan via Novara, or the A26/4 can be followed south via Alessandria, reaching the coast at Voltri, just outside Genoa. For Umbria there is a choice between the Autostrada del Sole (A1) from Milan or the Florence–Pisa motorway from Genoa. The latter route avoids the Apennine pass between Bologna and Florence which carries very heavy traffic and can be subject to delays.

Route 2 The most direct approach to Turin from France is through the **Monte Cenis Tunnel** from Modane in France to Bardonecchia. A road continues to Oulx where a motorway is under construction, via Susa to Turin, parallel to the old road. From Turin a motorway (A6) descends directly to the coast at Savona, or the motorway (A21, A26) via Asti and Alessandria leads to Genoa; either one connects with the coastal motorway for Pisa and Florence. Alternatively, the A4 motorway leads from Turin east to Milan for the Autostrada del Sole.

Route 3 The **coastal route from the South of France** follows the A10 motorway through the foothills, which has frequent long tunnels, to enter Italy just before Ventimiglia. The motorway continues past Alassio, Albenga and Savona (where the motorway from Turin comes in), to Voltri (where the A26 motorway from Alessandria comes in) and Genoa (with the junction of the A7 motorway from Milan). The coastal motorway continues beyond Rapallo and La Spezia past the resorts of Versilia, and at Viareggio it divides. The left branch (A11) continues via Lucca to Florence (and the Autostrada del Sole), while the coastal branch (A12) continues to Pisa and Livorno.

Route 4 The approach to Italy from Switzerland (Lausanne) is usually through the **Great St Bernard Tunnel** (toll; or by the pass in summer) which only becomes motorway at Aosta (see route 1, above).

Route 5 Another motorway route from Switzerland is via the **St Gotthard Tunnel** (opened in 1980) and Lugano. The motorway (A9) enters Italy at Como and continues to Milan where the Autostrada del Sole (A1) begins for central Italy.

Route 6 From Germany and Austria (Innsbruck) the direct approach to Italy is via the motorway over the **Brenner Pass**. The motorway (A22) continues down the Isarco valley to Bolzano and the Adige valley via Trento to Verona. Here the motorways fork west for Brescia and Milan, or east for Vicenza and Venice, or continue south via Mantua to join the A1 motorway just west of Modena for Florence and central Italy. A better approach to Umbria from the A1 motorway in Bologna is via the A14 motorway to Cesena, and from there via the E45 super-strada through Emilia Romagna and eastern Tuscany (Sansepolcro). It enters Umbria at Città di Castello and continues south to Perugia and Todi.

 ## Where to stay

Hotels

Hotels are classified by stars as in the rest of Europe. There are five official categories of hotels from the most expensive luxury ☆☆☆☆☆ hotels to the cheapest and simplest ✩ hotels. However, these categories are bound to disappoint many travellers: the categories are now established by the services offered (i.e. television in each room, private telephone, 'frigo-bar', etc) and often do not reflect quality. ✩✩✩✩✩ and ✩✩✩✩ hotels in some localities are not always on a par with hotels with the same designation in the rest of Europe. Travellers should note that there are now other categories of hotels (without stars) which are often extremely pleasant and reasonable: these are officially known as *residenze d'epoca, country houses* and *agriturismo.* While prices in these categories, and services offered vary greatly, these types of accommodation can often be the most attractive, especially to visitors not in groups. They are listed separately (under the above categories) in the hotel lists provided by the tourist offices (see below).

A small selection of all types of accommodation in Umbria has been given at the beginning of each chapter of the guide. In making the selection for inclusion, smaller hotels have been favoured, and those in the centre of towns, or in particularly picturesque rural situations, as well as those in historic buildings.

Each local tourist board (IAT, see above) issues a free list of hotels giving category, price and facilities. The Regione dell'Umbria also publishes annually a list of all the hotels, *residenze d'epoca, country houses,* youth hostels and campsites in Umbria in one booklet (free of charge), and in another booklet (also free of charge) they list all the *Agriturismo* accommodation available in Umbria. Local tourist offices help you to find accommodation on the spot; it is, however, advisable to book well in advance, especially at Easter and in summer. To confirm the booking a deposit is usually required (this can normally be made by using a credit card): you have the right to claim this back if you cancel the booking at least 72 hours in advance.

Hotels equipped to offer hospitality to the disabled are indicated in the APT hotel lists. There are now numerous agencies and hotel representatives in Britain and America who specialise in making hotel reservations (normally for ✩✩✩✩✩-star and ✩✩✩✩-star hotels only). **Accommodation services** from the UK are offered by *Accommodation Line Ltd.* ☎ 020 7409 1343; *The Italian Connection,* ☎ 020 7486 6890; and *Room Service,* ☎ 020 7636 6888.

Up-to-date information about hotels and restaurants can be found in numerous annual **specialised guides** to Italy. These include *Alberghi d'Italia,* a selection of ✩✩✩ hotels published by Gambero Rosso, *Alberghi e Ristoranti d'Italia* published by the Touring Club Italiano, and the red guide *Italia: Hotel–Ristoranti,* published by Michelin.

Every hotel has to declare its **prices** annually (and these are published in the local tourist offices' hotel lists, and cannot be exceeded). The total charge for the room (excluding breakfast) should be displayed on the back of the hotel room door, and in the foyer there should be a list of all the rooms in the hotel with their prices. Prices usually change according to the season, and can be considerably less in off peak periods. Hotels in the more famous towns of Umbria such as Assisi and Spoleto are bound to be a lot more expensive than hotels of the same category in the less well-known localities. In all hotels the service charges are included in the rates. You should beware of **extra charges** added to the bill. The drinks from the 'frigo-bar' in your room are extremely expensive (it is always best to buy drinks outside the hotel). Telephone calls are also more expensive if made from your room; there is usually a pay telephone (see p. 39) in the lobby which is the most economical way of telephoning (and more convenient than using the public telephones in the streets). Hotels are now obliged by law (for tax purposes) to issue an official receipt to customers: you should not leave the premises without this document.

Breakfast (which can be disappointing and costly) is by law an optional extra charge, although a lot of hotels try to include it in the price of the room. When booking a room, always specify if you want breakfast or not. If you are staying in a 2-star or 3-star hotel in a town, it is usually well worthwhile going round the corner to the nearest pasticceria or bar for breakfast. However, in the more expensive hotels some good buffet breakfasts are now provided. But even here the standard of the 'canteen' coffee can be poor: you can always ask for an *espresso* or *cappuccino* instead. There is a large supplement if you order breakfast in your room.

Historic residences

There is now a separate category of hotel (without stars) called a **residenza d'epoca** (an historic residence). These are in a building, or group of houses, of historic interest, often a palace, castle, villa, or monastery. Furnished in keeping with their period, they usually have only a few rooms, and sometimes offer self-catering accommodation. They are listed separately in the IAT hotel lists, with their prices, which vary greatly. They are usually comfortable and particularly attractive, especially for travellers not in a group. There are signs that more and more of these will be opened, although at present there are only seven in the whole of Umbria. Yet another category of hotel now exists known as a **country house**. These are very similar to the *residenze d'epoca*, but as the name implies they are in the country, and sometimes have self-catering facilities. At present there are 15 of these open in Umbria.

Agriturismo

Agriturismo, the rather unhappy term for farm holiday accommodation, is now well established throughout Italy. This is highly recommended for travellers with their own transport, and for families, as an ideal (and usually cheap) way of visiting Umbria. Accommodation is provided in rural buildings or farmhouses (*aziende agrituristiche*) in the countryside by the owners who usually have just a few rooms or apartments available for visitors. Often the farm produce is for sale, and regional specialities are served if there is a restaurant. Terms vary greatly from bed-and-breakfast, to self-contained flats. Some farms require a stay of a minimum number of days. Many have built swimming-pools for their guests, and some also offer recreational activities, especially horse-back riding. A 'star' system, similar to that used to classify hotels may soon be introduced, using ears of corn (from one to five depending on the facilities available). Agriturismo accommodation in Umbria is listed in an annual brochure issued (free) by the APT dell'Umbria, listing all the facilities available and prices. The local IAT hotel brochures also now include a section on agriturismo. *Umbria in Campagna*, 16 Strada San Cristoforo, Amelia (☎ 0744 988249; fax 0744 988459) is a group of farm owners who adhere strictly to the principle of offering agriturismo hospitality only on working farms (and they publish a catalogue).

For more information on this type of holiday contact *Agriturist Umbria*, 38 Via Savonarola, Perugia (☎ 075 32028), *Terranostra Umbria*, 10 Via Campo di Marte, Perugia (☎ 075 5009559), and *Turismo Verde Umbria*, 14 Via Campo di Marte, Perugia (☎ 075 5002953). Terranostra publish an annual guide to Agriturismo accommodation called *Vacanze e Natura*.

Religious organisations

Religious organisations sometimes run hostels or provide accommodation, particularly in Assisi. Visitors must stay for a minimum of two nights, and have to be in by 21.00 or 22.00 at night. These are listed in the annual hotel list published by the APT dell'Umbria, and information is provided by the local IAT offices.

Renting accommodation

Renting accommodation for short periods in Italy has recently become easier and better organised. The APT of Umbria publish a list of houses and apartments which can be rented in the region. Villas and farmhouses can also be rented for holidays through specialised agencies. Information can be obtained from ENIT offices abroad, and IAT offices in Umbria. Specialised agencies in the USA include: *The Parker Company Ltd*, 319 The Lynnway, Lynn, MA 01901 1810, ☎ 1 800 280 2811.

Camping

Camping is now well organised throughout Italy. An international camping carnet is useful. Campsites are listed in the annual hotel list published by the APT dell'Umbria, giving details of all services provided, size of the site, etc., and the local IAT offices also provide an up-to-date list. On some sites caravans and camper vans are allowed. The sites are divided into official categories, from the most expensive 4-star sites, to the simplest and cheapest 1-star sites. Their classification and rates charged must be displayed at the campsite office. Some sites have been indicated in the text, with their star ratings. It is advisable to book in advance.

Full details of the sites in Italy are published annually by the Touring Club Italiano in *Campeggi e Villaggi Turistici in Italia*. The Federazione Italiana del Campeggio have an information office and booking service at 11 Via Vittorio Emanuele, Calenzano, 50041 Florence (☎ 055 882391, fax 055 8825918).

Youth hostels

The Italian Youth Hostels Association (Associazione Italiana Alberghi per la Gioventù, 44 Via Cavour, 00184 Rome, ☎ 06 4871152, fax 06 4880492) has 61 hostels all over the country. They publish a free guide. A membership card of the AIG or the International Youth Hostel Federation is required for access to Italian Youth Hostels. Details from the Youth Hostels Association, Trevelyan House, 8 St Stephen's Hill, St Albans, Herts AL1 2DY, and the American Youth Hostel Inc, National Offices, PO Box 37613, Washington DC 20013-7613, USA.

The Umbrian regional office is at the Ostello della Pace, Via di Valecchia, Assisi (☎ 075 816767). In Umbria there are youth hostels at: Perugia (13 Via Bontempi); Assisi (*Fontemaggio*, Strada per l'Eremo delle Carceri, *Victor*, 102 Via Sacro Tugurio, and *Della Pace*, San Pietro Campagna); Gubbio (*Aquilone*, località Ghigiano); Magione (*Casa del Fanciullo*, 10 Via del Lavoro), and Poggiodomo (*Il Sentiero*, 2 Via del Colle). There are also hostels at Trevi (*Casa San Martino*, 4 Viale Ciuffelli); and Sigillo (*Ostello Centro di volo libero*, località Villa Scirca).

Getting around

By rail

The Italian State Railways (**FS**; *Ferrovie dello Stato*) run various categories of trains: **ES** (*Eurostar*), international express trains run between the main Italian and European cities, they have a special supplement (approximately 30 per cent of the normal single fare), although booking is no longer obligatory except on Friday and Sunday, there are first- and second-class carriages; **EC** and **IC** (**Eurocity** and **Intercity**), international and national express trains, with a supplement (but cheaper than the Eurostar supplement); **Espressi**, long-distance trains (both classes) not as fast as the *Intercity* trains. **Diretti**, although not stopping at every station, a good deal slower than *Espressi*. **Interregionali**, local trains stopping at most stations; **Regionali**, local trains stopping at all stations, mostly with second-class carriages only.

Tickets (valid for two months after the day sold) must be bought before the journey, otherwise a fairly large penalty has to be paid to the ticket-collector on the train. **In order to validate your ticket it has to be stamped at an automatic machine in the railway station before starting the journey (there is always a machine at the beginning of each platform and sometimes half-way up the platform).** If, for some reason, you fail to do this, try to find the ticket conductor on the train before he finds you. Once the ticket has been stamped it is valid for six hours for distances up to 200km, and for 24 hours for distances over 200km.

The most convenient way of buying rail tickets (and making seat reservations) is from a travel agent (but this is only possible through those who are agents for the Italian State Railways), as there are often long queues at the station ticket offices. Some trains charge a special supplement (see above), and on some seats must be booked in advance; when buying tickets you therefore have to specify which category of train you intend to take as well as the destination. Trains in Italy are usually crowded especially on holidays and in summer; and it is now always advisable to book your seat for long-distance journeys when buying a ticket for a *Eurocity* or *Intercity* train. There is a booking fee of 5000 lire and the service is available from two months to three hours before departure.

In the main stations the better known credit cards are now generally accepted, and there is a special ticket booth which must be used when buying a ticket with a credit card.

Fares and reductions In Italy fares are still much lower than in Britain. Children under the age of four travel free, and between the ages of four and 12 travel half price, and there are certain reductions for families. For travellers over the age of 60 (with Senior Citizen Railcards), the **Carta Res** (valid for one year) offers a 30 per cent reduction on international rail fares. The Inter-rail card (valid for one month), which can be purchased in Britain by young people up to the age of 26, is valid in Italy (and allows a reduction of 50 per cent on normal fares). In Italy the **Carta d'Argento** and the **Carta Verde** (which both cost 40,000 lire and are valid for one year) allow a reduction on rail fares for those over 60, and between the ages of 12 and 26. A **Chilometrico** ticket is valid for

3000km (and can be used by up to five people at the same time) for a maximum of 20 journeys. A **Eurodomino** ticket is valid for one month's travel in a number of European countries (for 3, 5 or 10 days).

You can claim reimbursement (on payment of a small penalty) for unused tickets and sleepers not later than 24 hours before the departure of the train. Bicycles are allowed on most trains (except *Eurostar* trains): a day ticket costs 5000 lire on slow trains, and 10,000 lire on *Intercity*, *Eurocity* and *Espressi*. A **Carta Blu** is available for the disabled, and certain trains have special facilities for them (information can be obtained from the main railway stations in Italy).

Timetables The timetable for the train services changes on about 26 September and 31 May every year. Excellent timetables are published twice a year by the Italian state railways (*In Treno*; one volume for the whole of Italy) and by Pozzorario in several volumes (*Nord e Centro Italia* cover Umbria). These can be purchased at news-stands and railway stations.

Left luggage offices are usually open 24 hours at the main stations; at small-er stations they often close at night, and for a few hours in the middle of the day.

Porters are entitled to a fixed amount (shown on noticeboards at all stations) for each piece of baggage, but trolleys are now usually available in the larger stations.

Restaurant cars (sometimes self-service) are attached to most international and internal long-distance trains. Also, on most fast trains, snacks, hot coffee and drinks are sold throughout the journey from a trolley wheeled down the train. At every large station snacks are on sale from trolleys on the platform.

Sleeping cars, with couchettes, or first- and second-class cabins, are carried on certain long-distance trains, as well as 'Sleeperette' compartments with reclining seats (first-class only).

Train services in Umbria are generally good, although most of the lines are secondary. Details of the services have been given in the text. Information about the state railways (*Ferrovie dello Stato*) can be obtained from the main railway station in Perugia (Piazza Vittorio Veneto), ☎ 1478 88088; or the railway sta-tion in Terni (Piazza Dante Alighieri), ☎ 1478 88088. A line between Città di Castello, Umbertide, Perugia, Todi and Terni is run by the *Ferrovia Centrale Umbra*: information is available from the station of Sant'Anna in Perugia (☎ 075 5729121) or the station in Terni (☎ 1478 88088).

By bus

Local country bus services are plentiful between the main towns in Italy, and offer an excellent alternative to the railways. It is difficult to obtain accurate information about these local bus services outside Italy. Details have been given in the text. The main bus companies operating in Umbria are: *Azienda Perugina della Mobilità (APM)*, località Pian di Massiano, Perugia (☎ 075 506781); *Società Spoletina di Imprese e Trasporti*, Via Flaminia, Spoleto (☎ 0743 212211); *Azienda Speciale Consorziale Trasporti Pubblici (ATC)*, 19 Piazza Europa, Terni (☎ 0744 59541); and *SULGA*, località Pian di Massiano, Perugia (☎ 075 5009641).

Town buses

Now that most towns have been partially closed to private traffic, town bus services (the details of which have been given in the text) are usually fast and efficient. You buy a ticket before boarding (at ticket machines, tobacconists, bars, newspaper kiosks, information offices, etc.) and stamp it in the automatic machine on the bus.

Taxis

Taxis (yellow or white in colour) are provided with taximeters; make sure these are operational before hiring a taxi. They are hired from ranks or by telephone; there are no cruising taxis. A tip of about 1000 lire is expected. A supplement for night service, and for luggage, is charged. There is a heavy surplus charge when the destination is outside the town limits (ask roughly how much the fare is likely to be). Women travelling alone in the evening are sometimes entitled to a reduced rate.

Driving in Italy

Umbria has an excellent network of roads, and drivers are strongly advised to avoid motorways and superstrade and use the secondary roads which are usually well engineered and provide fine views of the countryside. Buildings of historic interest are often indicated by yellow signposts (although there are long-term plans to change the colour to brown). White road signs sometimes indicate entry into a municipal area which is (confusingly) often a long way from the town of the same name. In autumn, winter and spring many of the roads in Umbria (especially between Perugia and Spoleto) can be covered with thick fog in the early morning or late afternoon. Hotels and restaurants are almost always clearly signposted (yellow signs). Information offices are marked with a yellow 'i' symbol throughout Italy.

Temporary membership of the *Automobile Club d'Italia (ACI)* can be obtained at the border or in Italy. They provide a breakdown service (*Soccorso ACI*, ☎ 116).

Motorways (autostrade)

Italy probably has the finest motorways in Europe, although in the last few decades too many have been constructed to the detriment of the countryside. Tolls are charged according to the rating of the vehicle and the distance covered. There are service areas on all *autostrade* (open 24 hours), and, generally speaking, the FINI cafés and restaurants are usually the best. Most *autostrade* have SOS points every two kilometres. Unlike in France, motorways are indicated by green signs (and normal roads by blue signs). At the entrance to motorways, the two directions are indicated by the name of the most important town (and not by the nearest town) which can be momentarily confusing: from Florence the motorway towards Umbria is signposted *Roma* (as opposed to *Milano*). The only motorway in Umbria is the A1 motorway (*autostrada del sole*) from Florence to Rome which skirts its western border, with exits at Valdichiana, Chiusi, Fabro, Orvieto, Attigliano and Orte. It is less wide than some of the more recent motorways and carries very heavy traffic (including numerous lorries, except on Sundays).

Superstrade are dual carriageway fast roads which do not charge tolls. They do not usually have service stations, SOS points, or emergency lanes. They are also usually indicated by green signs. In Umbria a superstrada (N75bis) connects the Valdichiana exit from the A1 motorway to Lago Trasimeno and Perugia. The superstrada (E45) from Cesena in Romagna to Orte in Lazio runs through the centre of Umbria past Città di Castello, Perugia, Todi, Terni and Narni. Another fast road (N75 and N3), dual carriageway in places, connects Perugia to Foligno and Spoleto.

Petrol stations are open 24 hours on motorways, but otherwise their opening times are: 07.00–12.00, 15.00–20.00; winter 07.30–12.30, 14.30–19.00. There are now quite a number of self-service petrol stations open 24hrs operated by bank notes (10,000, 50,000 lire) or credit cards. Unleaded petrol is now available all over Italy. Petrol in Italy costs more than in England, and a lot more than in America.

Car parking Not all towns have solved their traffic problems as successfully as Perugia, where several car-parks have been built below the old town, and connected to the centre by a series of escalators. However, almost every town in Umbria (as in the rest of Italy) has now taken the wise step of closing its historic centre to traffic (except for vehicles belonging to residents) which makes them much more pleasant to visit on foot. Access is allowed for hotels and the disabled.

On approaching a town, the white signs for *centro* (with a bull's eye) should be followed towards the historic centre. Car-parks are also usually indicated by blue **P** signs; where parking is a particular problem, the best places to park near the centre have been mentioned in the main text. Some car-parks are free, while others charge an hourly tariff. In some towns mini-bus services connect car-parks with the centre. With a bit of effort it is almost always possible to find a place to leave your car free of charge, away from the town centre. It is forbidden to park in front of a gate or doorway marked with a *passo carrabile* (blue and red) sign. Always lock your car when parked, and never leave anything of value inside it.

Car hire is available in the main towns and at Pisa, Florence and Rome airports. Arrangements for car hire in Italy can also be made through **Citalia**, **Alitalia** or **British Airways** (at specially advantageous rates in conjunction with their flights).

Rules of the road Italian law requires you to carry a valid driving licence when travelling. It is obligatory to keep a red triangle in the car in case of an accident or breakdown. This serves as a warning to other traffic when placed on the road at a distance of 50 metres from the stationary car. It is compulsory to wear seat-belts in the front seat of cars in Italy. Driving in Italy is generally faster (and often more aggressive) than driving in Britain or America. Road signs are now more or less standardised to the international codes, but certain habits differ radically from those in Britain or America. Unless otherwise indicated, cars entering a road from the right are given precedence (also at roundabouts). If a driver flashes his headlights, it means he is proceeding and not giving you precedence. In towns, Italian drivers are very lax about changing lanes without much warning. Some crossroads in small towns have unexpected 'stop' signs. Italian drivers tend to ignore pedestrian crossings. In towns, beware of motorbikes, mopeds and scooters, the drivers of which seem to think that they always have right of way.

The police (see p. 38) sometimes set up road blocks on country roads to check cars and their drivers: it is important to stop at once if you are waved down by a policeman at the side of a road and you must immediately show them your driving licence and the car documents.

Food and drink

Umbrian food

The standard of cuisine in Umbria is still fairly high, and generally better than that to be found in many other parts of Italy. The region is famous for the quality of its meat, in particular pork. Excellent *salumi*, cured pork meats including ham, sausages and salami are produced, especially around Norcia and the Valnerina. Pork butchers, known as *norcini*, are famous throughout Italy, see p. 207. *Porchetta*, roast suckling pig boned and stuffed with fennel, herbs, garlic, salt and pepper, is prepared all over Umbria. It is often sold from vans at local markets, and makes a delicious sandwich. The best beef comes from the cattle known as **Chianina**, raised near the Chiana river.

Umbria is also known for the high quality of its **olive oil** (see p. 177), produced all over the region, especially near Trevi, Lago Trasimeno and the Monti Martani.

The prized black truffles *(tartufi neri di Norcia*; see p. 217*)* found only in the districts of Norcia, Spoleto and the Valnerina are a delicacy often served on toasted bread as an hors-d'oeuvre, or as a condiment for pasta or risotto, or as a flavouring for meat, game, egg or fish dishes.

As an **hors-d'oeuvre**, *affettati* (cold cuts) are almost always available, with numerous types of excellent cured pork meat, such as salame, salted raw ham (*prosciutto crudo*), pig's liver sausage (*mazzafegato*), and cooked pig's neck, with garlic, salt and pepper *(capocollo)*.

Often *bruschetta*, toasted bread with fresh olive oil and garlic, and *crostini*, bread or toast topped with grated truffles, mushrooms, tomatoes, or chicken liver paste, will be served together with *affettati*.

First courses, as in the rest of Italy, include numerous **pasta dishes**. *Strangozzi*, or *strozzapreti*, are an Umbrian speciality, homemade thick spaghetti made with water and flour, and served with a sauce.

Tagliatelle or *fettuccine* are homemade noodles made with the addition of eggs, usually served with a meat sauce (*al ragù*). *Tagliolini* are a smaller thinner version of *tagliatelle*, and when served *al tartufo nero di Norcia*, oil and melted butter are used as a condiment, and they are generously flavoured with freshly grated black truffles.

Near Amelia *manfricoli*, homemade pasta made with water and flour, are traditionally served *all'arrabbiata*, with a spicy tomato sauce.

In Spoleto, a favourite pasta dish is *spaghetti col rancetto*, served with a tomato sauce prepared with diced bacon, onion, a garlic clove, and majoram. This dish is usually eaten with a sprinkling of *pecorino* sheeps' cheese (rather than parmesan).

Pappardelle al cinghiale are homemade noodles served with a rich sauce made from wild boar, tomatoes, red wine, onion, carrot, celery, and seasoned with juniper berries, sage, bay and parsley.

Lasagne and *cannelloni*, filled with ricotta cheese and spinach, are also served all over Umbria.

Gnocchi is fresh pasta made with potatoes and flour, usually served with a rich sauce (often made with mushrooms).

Polenta, a maize flour cake, can be a pasta dish (with a sauce) or an accompaniment to sausages, or game. Restaurants often offer various types of *risotto*, one of the best of which is flavoured with truffles. The rich warming vegetable soup called *acquacotta*, which is also made in Tuscany, is usually prepared in Umbria with potatoes, celery, onion and tomato sauce, and served with toasted bread and grated *pecorino* cheese, but there are numerous different versions of this nutritious traditional peasants' soup, which often has the addition of cooked greens and eggs.

Spelt (*farro*) is a grain which has been cultivated in this area since before the Roman era, and which has become particularly popular in the last few years as a nourishing genuine food (organically grown). The classic *minestra di farro* is simply spelt boiled in water with whole cloves of garlic, with the addition of finely chopped garlic when cooked. Spelt can also be cooked in a broth (*zuppa di farro*), made from a ham bone. In summer spelt is sometimes cooked in a tomato sauce with celery and carrots, with fresh olive oil added when it is cooked.

Lentils (*lenticchie*), another nutritious food, are cultivated at Colfiorito and on the high upland plain of Castelluccio (see p. 214). The classic *zuppa di lenticchie* is made with a lot of chopped celery and a clove of garlic, with fresh olive oil added at the end.

Wild mushrooms (*funghi*) are a delicacy in season. They are often best served grilled, but are also used in sauces as a condiment to pasta dishes. The best known varieties include *porcini* and *prataioli*, both found in May and June after rain. Numerous other varieties served all over Umbria include *sanguinacci*, *ovoli* and *prugnoli* (these last grow in April and May in the district around Spoleto).

Other local specialities can sometimes be offered on restaurant menus in season. These include a rare type of celery (*sedano nero*), which has a distinctive strong taste, cultivated on the plain below Trevi in October; snails *(lumache)* usually found after wet weather in May; and wild asparagus (*asparago salvatico*) which grows in May and June (and is delicious in omelettes).

Main courses. The quality of the **meat** in Umbria is usually particularly good, and is best grilled or roasted on the spit. **Chicken** (*gallina* or *pollo*) is served in numerous ways. In Orvieto *gallina ubriaca* is a dish which requires a lot of dry white wine. Pieces of chicken are added to a sauce of raw ham fat, a few ripe tomatoes and garlic, and then covered with white wine and cooked at a very low temperature for several hours.

Lamb (*agnello*) is also a speciality of Umbria, and it is usually best grilled. It can also be served *alla cacciatora*: there are various recipes for this dish which is cooked slowly over a low heat, some of which call for garlic and red wine. When ready, a sauce is usually added, made from well-chopped anchovies, garlic and rosemary amalgamated with a little vinegar.

Game (*salvaggina*), such as wood pigeon (*palombe* or *palombaccio*) is sometimes cooked *alla leccarda* (or *alla ghiotta*), that is roasted on a spit with a terracotta pot beneath to collect the juices in which the giblets are cooked with red wine, garlic, sage and rosemary (this sauce is then usually served as an accompaniment to the meat on *crostini*). Rabbit, pigeon, or game cooked in a spicy sauce with chopped onions, celery and carrots, with the addition of capers and sometimes mushrooms, is known as *salmì di cacciagione*. Game is also often cooked in a casserole with oil, onions, carrots, celery and herbs, with the addition of white wine and vinegar. Wild boar *(cinghiale)* which almost became extinct 100 years ago, is now found all over Umbria, and indeed causes great damage to local agriculture (the hunting season starts in November). It is sometimes prepared *alla cacciatora*: marinated in red wine, with parsley, bay, garlic, rosemary, onion, carrot, celery, sage and wild fennel. It is then cooked slowly at a low heat in a terracotta pot with oil, lard, hot spicy pepper, and a little tomato sauce.

Excellent **fish** is still served in the restaurants around Lago Trasimeno. These include carp *(carpa)*, pike *(luccio)*, grey mullet *(cefalo)*, and perch *(persico)*. Eels *(anguille)* are often served fried. The rich fish soup typical of Trasimeno called *tegamaccio* is prepared by lightly frying onions, garlic and parsley and then adding tomato conserve. The fish are then cooked very slowly in the same pan with the lid on, in a little white wine. *Regina in porchetta* is carp stuffed with lard, rosemary, fennel and garlic and cooked in the oven in a little olive oil. Trout *(trote)* found in the rivers of the Valnerina and Clitunno (and also raised on trout farms) are often served grilled or baked.

In and around Perugia **bread** is sometimes made with the addition of cheese in the form of a cake, especially at Easter time, and white pizza made with flour and water and cooked on a red-hot stove, known as *torta al testo* is traditionally filled with cheese, cooked greens or raw ham. *Pane nociato* is prepared especially near Città di Castello, when walnuts are added to the bread dough. In Orvieto *lumachelle* are delicious savoury rolls made with ham and cheese.

Excellent **cakes and biscuits** are made all over Umbria, and typical ingredients include almonds, candied fruits, pinenuts, chestnuts and walnuts. The *torciglione* or *serpentone* is a delicious cake in the form of a snake made with almond paste. The *torcolo* is made with eggs, flour, sugar and butter, flavoured with pinenuts and candied fruits. In Assisi *pane di San Francesco* and *biscotti Francescani* are hard cakes made with honey, currants, aniseed, pinenuts and vegetable oil. *Tozzetti* are biscuits made with almonds and aniseed. Typical carnival sweets known as *le frappe* or *i fiocchi* are still made in Spoleto, from flour and eggs, and lemon rind, fried in olive oil and then dipped in honey. The *crescionda* is a rich traditional cake cooked in the oven, usually made with eggs, milk, almond biscuits, lemon rind, bitter chocolate and a little flour. It can also contain apples, cinnamon and raisins. A speciality of Amelia are the delicious large, dried *candied figs (fichi)* prepared with almonds and cocoa, which are produced by the local firm Girotti and sold almost exclusively in the town. Excellent honey is produced locally all over Umbria.

Umbrian wines

The **wines** of Umbria are usually of good quality. White wine is made from *Trebbiano toscano*, *Grechetto* and *Malvasia* grapes, and red wine from *Sangiovese*, *Sagrantino* and *Ciliegiolo* grapes. The most famous white wine is produced around Orvieto, but is not now usually the best wine available (although the wine produced by the Antinori at Castello della Sala can be good). A good white wine produced at Torgiano is the *Torre di Giano*. Among the best red wines are *Montefalco* (especially those produced by Caprai, Antonelli, Rocca di Fabbri, Adanti and Scaccia Diavoli) and *Torgiano Rubesco*. Other DOC wines in Umbria are: Colli Altotiberini (red, white and rosé from the upper Tiber valley, particularly Umbertide); Colli Amerini (red, white and rosé) from the area around Amelia; Colli del Trasimeno (red and white) from the area around Lago Trasimeno, notably Castiglione del Lago, Città della Pieve and Corciano; Colli Martani (red and white) from near Montefalco; Colli Perugini (red, white and rosé) from near Perugia.

The deep red *Sagrantino* (which can be *passito* or *secco*) also produced around Montefalco and Bevagna is one of the most exceptional wines in Umbria. Grappa is now also produced in Umbria (by Lungarotti, Caprai, etc.). It is often well worth trying the wine from the local consortium (*Cantina Sociale*). All those interested in wine should not miss the Wine Museum in Torgiano. To visit the wine cellars of the estates which produce wine in the Orvieto district, contact the Consorzio Tutela Vino Orvieto Classico e Orvieto, 36 Corso Cavour, Orvieto, ☎ 0763 343790.

Restaurants

Restaurants in Italy are called *ristoranti* or *trattorie*; there is now usually no difference between the two, although a *trattoria* used to be less smart (and usually cheaper) than a *ristorante*. Italian food is usually good and not too expensive. The least pretentious restaurant almost invariably provides the best value. Almost every locality has a simple (often family run) restaurant which caters for the local residents; the decor is usually very simple and the food excellent value. This type of restaurant does not always offer a menu and the choice is usually limited to three or four first courses, and three or four second courses, with only fruit as a sweet. The more sophisticated restaurants are more attractive and comfortable and often larger and you can sometimes eat al fresco. They display a menu outside, and are also usually considerably more expensive. In all restaurants it is acceptable to order a first course only, or skip the first course and have only a second course. Note that fish is always the most expensive item on the menu in any restaurant.

In each chapter in the main text of the guide a small up-to-date selection of restaurants has been given, which is by no means exhaustive. The restaurants have been divided into three categories (**£££**, **££** and **£** to reflect current price ranges:

£££ Luxury-class restaurants where the prices are likely to be over 60,000 lire a head (and sometimes well over 100,000 lire a head). These are the most famous restaurants in Umbria and they usually offer international cuisine.

££ First-class restaurants where the prices are around 50,000 lire. These are generally comfortable, with good service, but are not cheap.

£ Simple trattorie and pizzerie where you can eat for around 25,000–40,000 lire a head, or less. Although simple and by no means 'smart', the food in this category, which often includes local specialities, is usually the best value.

Lunch is normally around 13.00 or 13.30, while dinner is around 20.00 or

21.00. Some restaurants still have a cover charge (*coperto*, shown separately on the menu) which is added to the bill (although this has officially been discontinued). Prices include service, unless otherwise stated on the menu. Tipping is therefore not strictly necessary, but a few thousand lire can be left on the table to convey appreciation. Restaurants are now obliged by law (for tax purposes) to issue an official receipt to customers; you should not leave the premises without this document (*ricevuta fiscale*).

Some of the best annual guides to eating in Italy (but only in Italian) are published by Gambero Rosso (**Ristoranti d'Italia**) and Slow Food Arcigola (**Osterie d'Italia**, a guide to cheaper eating). Specialised annual guides to restaurants (mostly in the £££ and ££ categories as described above) include the red Michelin guide (**Italia: hotel-ristoranti**); **I Ristoranti di Veronelli**, and **Alberghi e Ristoranti** (TCI).

Pizze (a popular and cheap food throughout Italy) and other excellent snacks are served in a *pizzeria, rosticceria* and *tavola calda*. Some of these have no seating accommodation and sell food to take away or eat on the spot.

Bars and cafés

Bars and cafés (*caffè* or *pasticcerie*) are comfortable and pleasant places to sit and have a snack. A selection of these in towns has also been given in the main text below. They are open all day, and most Italians eat the excellent refreshments they serve standing up. You pay the cashier first, and show the receipt to the barman in order to get served. In almost all bars, if you sit at a table you are charged considerably more (at least double) and are given waiter service (and you should not pay first). However, some simple bars have a few tables which can be used at no extra charge (it is always best to ask before sitting down). Black coffee (*caffè* or *espresso*) can be ordered diluted (*alto, lungo* or *americano*) or with a dash of milk (*macchiato*), or with hot milk (*cappuccino* or *caffè-latte*) or with a liqueur (*corretto*). In summer, iced coffee (*caffè freddo*) or iced coffee with milk (*caffè-latte freddo*) are served. A wide selection of soft drinks, wines and spirits are also available. A *pasticceria* (usually also a café) always sells the best cakes since they are made on the premises. Ice-creams are always best in a *gelateria* where they are made on the spot: bars usually sell packaged ice-cream only.

Take away food

For **picnics**, sandwiches (*panini*) are made up on request (with ham, salami, cheese, anchovies, tuna fish, etc.) at *pizzicherie* and *alimentari* (grocery shops). *Fornai* (bakeries) often sell delicious individual pizzas, bread with oil and salt (*focaccia* or *schiacciata*), and puff pastry topped or filled with cheese, spinach, tomato, salted anchovies, ham, etc; they also usually sell good sweet buns, rolls and cakes. Some of the best places to picnic in towns have been indicated in the main text of the guide below.

Museums, monuments and churches

The **opening times** of museums and monuments have been given in the text but they vary and often change without warning; when possible it is always advisable to telephone (numbers have been supplied) or to consult the local tourist office (IAT) on arrival about the up-to-date times. The opening times of state-owned museums and monuments are in the process of change: many museums and archaeological sites in Umbria are now open seven days a week (although if they have a closing day it is still usually Monday). However, there is no standard timetable and you should take great care to allow enough time for variations in the hours shown in the text when planning a visit to a museum or monument. Some museums in the larger cities now usually stay open on the main public holidays, and sometimes remain open in the evenings in summer. The APT dell'Umbria usually publishes an annual leaflet giving the opening times of all museums in the region.

Admission charges vary, but are usually between 4000 and 8000 lire. British citizens under the age of 18 and over the age of 60 are entitled to free admission to state-owned museums and monuments in Italy (because of recip- rocal arrangements in Britain): passport required. During Museum Week (the *Settimana per i Beni Culturali e Ambientali*) there is free entrance to all state- owned museums and others are specially opened: traditionally held early in December, for the last few years it has been held instead in March.

In recent years many local regional museums have been opened in Umbria which are of the greatest interest. Most of these are now administered by an organisation called *Sistema Museo*, and there is an information office in Perugia in the Rocca Paolina (Centro Servizi Museali, ☎ and fax 075 5732403).

Although they usually open very early in the morning (at 07.00 or 08.00), churches are normally closed for a considerable period during the middle of the day. Almost all churches close at 12.00 and do not reopen again until 15.00, 16.00, or even 17.00. Cathedrals and some of the larger churches (indicated in the text) may be open without a break during daylight hours. Smaller churches and oratories are often open only in the early morning, but it is sometimes possi- ble to find the key by asking locally. The sacristan will also show closed chapels, crypts, etc., and sometimes expects a tip. Some churches now ask sightseers not to enter during a service, but normally visitors not in a tour group may do so, provided you are silent and do not approach the altar in use. An entrance fee is becoming customary for admission to treasuries, cloisters, bell-towers, etc. Lights (operated by lire coins) have now been installed in many churches to illu- minate frescoes and altarpieces, but a torch and binoculars are always useful. Sometimes you are not allowed to enter important churches or religious sanctu- aries wearing shorts or with bare shoulders.

Annual festivals and local fairs

There are a number of **traditional festivals** in Umbrian towns which are of the greatest interest. When they are in progress the towns become extremely lively, and, apart from the central race or competition, numerous other celebrations take place at the same time. All the local festivals have been mentioned in the text, and the most important ones described in detail, but a summary is given below, in case you are able to choose a period in which to visit Umbria when some of them are taking place. They are particularly exciting events for children. Information from local IAT offices.

- **Castiglione del Lago**: *Coloriamo i cieli* (even years only), late April–beginning of May
- **Narni**: *Corsa all'Anello*, second Sunday in May
- **Assisi**: *Calendimaggio*, three days in early May
- **Gubbio**: *Festa dei Ceri*, 15 May
- **Gubbio**: *Palio della Balestra*, last Sunday in May
- **Orvieto**: *Festa della Palombella*, Whit Sunday
- **Orvieto**: *Corpus Domini*, Sunday in early June after Corpus Domini
- **Spello**: *Infiorate*, Corpus Domini (around late May/early June)
- **Bevagna**: *Mercato delle Gaite*, second half of June
- **Montefalco**: *Corso del Bove*, second half of June
- **Spoleto**: *Festival dei Due Mondi*, end of June–beginning of July
- **Piediluco**: *Festa delle Acque*, late June, early July
- **Città della Pieve**: *Palio dei Terzieri*, second Sunday in August
- **Foligno**: *La Giostra della Quintana*, second and third Sunday in September
- **San Gemini**: *Giostra dell'Arme*, end of September–beginning of October
- **Trevi**: *Palio dei Terzieri*, early October

Another special feature of Umbria are the **fairs and markets** held periodically:
Foligno: the festival of San Manno (14 and 15 September) and of San Feliciano (25 and 26 January).
Bevagna: *Mercato delle Gaite* in the last eight or ten days of June.
Perugia: for a week from 2 November.
Bastia Umbra: the *Mercatino Quattro Stagioni* is held on the first Sunday of each new season.
Montefalco: a fair of artisans' products in August.

Among **local products** which can sometimes still be found are **pottery** (Deruta, Torgiano, Gubbio, Gualdo Tadino, Orvieto, Ficulle and Città di Castello); **wrought-iron work** (Gubbio, Assisi, Città della Pieve and Norcia); objects in **copper** (Magione); and **textiles**, **embroidery** and **lace** (Perugia, Città di Castello, Montefalco, Marsciano, Assisi, Panicale, Castiglione del Lago and Isola Maggiore on Lago Trasimeno, and Orvieto).

Walking in Umbria

Hiking and walking has become more popular in Italy in recent years and more information is now available locally. There are numerous areas in Umbria ideal for walkers, although the area has still not been sufficiently mapped and paths are often not well marked, and sometimes peter out unexpectedly. The best area for hiking is in the Monti Sibillini on the border with the Marche. There are also some marked trails on Monte Subasio, Monte Cucco, and near Castelluccio, and above Lago Trasimeno, and in the Valnerina.

The local offices of the Club Alpino Italiano (CAI) and the World Wide Fund for Nature provide information. CAI offices in Umbria: Foligno, Via Piermarini; Perugia, 9 Via della Gabbiaia; Spoleto, 4 Via Pianciani (☎ 0743 220433); and Terni, 96 Via Roma. The *Delegazione Umbra of the World Wide Fund for Nature* is at 15 Via della Tartaruga, Perugia (☎ 075 65816).

Specialised guides include *Umbria–Le più belle escursioni* (Cori, CAI, 1995); *A piedi in Umbria* (Ardito, 1989); *Il Cammina Umbria* published in collaboration with the World Wide Fund for Nature (1989). There are also local guides to walking in Monte Cucco and the Valnerina. For the Parco Nazionale dei Monti Sibillini, there are guides by Alesi and Calibani (1992) and by Zanetti and Tonello (1993).

Maps are published by the Istituto Geografico Militare (see above), and by CAI (1:25,000), including paths on Monte Subasio, the Monti Martani, and the Parco Nazionale dei Sibillini. There is a map (1:50,000) of the footpaths in the Spoleto area (1989), and a series of maps (1:50,000) published by Kompass to various areas of Umbria including Lago Trasimeno.

Travel agents in Britain who specialise in walking holidays include *The Alternative Travel Group*, *Headwater*, and *Inntravel*, see p. 15–16 for details

Protected areas

Although only recently areas of great natural beauty have been designated parks in Umbria there are signs that more will eventually be done to protect these areas and open them up to walkers. Information from Parchi Regione Umbria, ☎ 075 5044356.

Mountain areas which have become regional parks include Monte Cucco (1566m) in the Appenines near Gubbio and Gualdo Tadino (park office, Villa Anita at Sigillo, ☎ 075 9177326); the small marshy area near Colfiorito (for information, ☎ 0742 332231), and, above Norcia, the Piano Grande di Castelluccio, on the edge of the Parco Nazionale dei Monti Sibillini (most of which lies in the Marche region). Information from the Casa del Parco, Norcia, ☎ 0743 817090.

Monte Subasio (1290m), above Assisi, is also now a protected area (for information ☎ 07 815181).

Other regional parks have been instituted in the lower Valnerina with the famous Marmore waterfalls, along the Tiber river near the Lago di Corbara and Oasis di Alviano, and around Lago Trasimeno.

Visiting with children

Umbria has a variety of sights which may be of special interest to children and may help to alleviate a day of undiluted Madonnas and museums. A golden rule when allowing a break for an ice-cream is to search for a *gelateria* (rather than a bar) where the locally produced ice-creams are generally excellent.

A few suggestions are given below of places that might have particular appeal to children, listed in the order of the routes into which the book is divided. These include some important monuments which are likely to give a clear impression of a particular period of art or architecture, a few museums, places of naturalistic interest, and the most exciting annual festivals. Detailed descriptions of all the places mentioned below are given in the main text (and can easily be found by reference to the index at the back of the book).

Perugia, Assisi and Lago Trasimeno

In **Perugia**: Rocca Paolina; Corso Vannucci; Sala di Udienza del Collegio del Cambio; San Severo; Oratorio di San Bernardino; Arco d'Augusto; Sant'Angelo; Convent of Beata Colomba or Sant'Agnese; the Roman mosaic; Archaeological Museum. **Environs of Perugia**: The Ipogeo dei Volumni; Torgiano wine museum; and *Città della Domenica*.
Assisi: Basilica of San Francesco (particularly the Upper Church, but this has been closed since the earthquake); Oratorio dei Pellegrini; Rocca Maggiore; Santa Chiara; Eremo delle Carceri; and Monte Subasio. *Calendimaggio* medieval pageant, and *Palio di San Rufino* (archery contest).
Lago Trasimeno: Boat trips to the Isola Maggiore and Isola Polvese; Hannibal's battle route at Tuoro; bathing in the lake (at Tuoro); Museo della Pesca, San Feliciano; walking and horse-riding; the castle of Castiglione del Lago; and the nature reserve on Monte Pausillo. *Coloriamo i cieli*, kite festival at Castiglione del Lago.
The *Palio dei Terzieri* at **Città della Pieve**.

The upper Tiber valley and Gubbio

Ethnographical Museum at Garavelle near **Città di Castello**, the castle of San Giustino.
Gubbio: Cable car to Sant'Ubaldo on Monte Ingino; Fontana dei Pazzi. The *Festa dei Ceri* and *Palio della Balestra*. In the environs of Gubbio: Gorge of Bottaccione. **Gualdo Tadino and environs**: Monte Cucco.

Central Umbria with Spoleto

Foligno: Palazzo Trinci. The *Giostra della Quintana*. Colfiorito; Monte Pennino. **Spello**.
Bevagna: Roman mosaic and other Roman remains; *Mercato delle Gaite*; Good Friday and Easter Day processions.
Montefalco: the tower of Palazzo Comunale (at present closed); San Francesco; *Corsa del Bove*.
Trevi: *Palio dei Terzieri*.
Spoleto: Ponte delle Torri; Rocca Albornoz (when restored); Roman theatre and archaeological museum; Roman house; *Festival dei Due Mondi*.
Fonti del **Clitunno**.

Cascia, Norcia and the Valnerina

Norcia: Piano Grande di Castelluccio.

Todi and Orvieto

Todi: Santa Maria della Consolazione.

Orvieto: funicular; Pozzo di San Patrizio; Duomo; Archaeological Museum. *Corpus Domini* procession. Monte Peglia.

Amelia, Narni and Terni
The walls of **Amelia**, the Roman cisterns, and the Teatro Sociale.
Environs of Amelia: Alviano Castle (with its ethnographical museum). Oasis of Alviano (bird sanctuary). Fossil forest of Dunarobba (with related exhibition at Avigliano Umbro).
Narni: the Rocca (when restored), and the *Corsa all'Anello*.
Environs of Narni: Roman remains of Otricoli.
Terni: Marmore waterfalls; Lago di Piediluco; Roman remains of Carsulae.
Environs of Terni: Sangemini: *Giostra dell'Arme*.

Golf courses in Umbria
An 18-hole golf course is being built at Antignola, south of Umbertide (designed by Robert Trent Jones). There is another 18-hole course at Ellera, 10km outside Perugia (☎ 075 5172204), and a nine-hole course at Panicarola, 26km outside Perugia (☎ 075 837582).

Theatres
Numerous small historic theatres in Umbria have recently been restored and reopened. These include the Teatro Sociale in Amelia, the Teatro della Concordia in Montecastello Vibio, the Teatro Cesare Caporali in Panicale, the Teatro Clitunno in Trevi, the Teatro Torti in Bevagna, and the Teatro Bontempelli in Citerna. Other theatres in the region with important seasons include the Teatro Morlacchi in Perugia, the Teatro Caio Melisso and Teatro Nuovo in Spoleto, and the Teatro Mancinelli in Orvieto and the Teatro Comunale in Todi. There are also theatres at Gubbio and Avigliano Umbro.

 Additional information

On arrival
In Umbria the Regional Tourist office is in Perugia: Azienda di Promozione Turistica (APT) dell'Umbria, 21 Via Mazzini, ☎ 075 575951; fax 075 5736828 (web-site: www.regione.umbria.it; e-mail: ente@regione.umbria.it).

Umbria is divided into sectors, each with a local tourist information office, called the Servizio Turistico Territoriale (IAT) which provide invaluable help to travellers on arrival: they supply a free list of accommodation (revised annually), including hotels, youth hostels and campsites; up-to-date information on museum opening times and annual events; and information about local transport. They also usually distribute, free of charge, illustrated pamphlets about each town, sometimes with a good plan, etc. The headquarters are normally open Monday–Saturday 08.00–14.00, but in the towns of particular interest there is sometimes a separate information office, which is also often open in the afternoon.

Information offices

- *APT di Perugia*, 21 Via Mazzini, Perugia, ☎ 075 575951; information office, 3 Piazza IV Novembre, ☎ 075 5736458.
- *IAT del Ternano* (for Narni, Terni, etc.), 5 Viale Battisti, Terni, ☎ 0744 423047.
- *IAT di Assisi*, Piazza del Comune, Assisi, ☎ 075 812534.
- *IAT della Valnerina-Cascia* (also for Norcia), 1 Piazza Garibaldi, Cascia, ☎ 0743 71147.
- *IAT dell'Alta Valle del Tevere* (for the upper Tiber valley), Piazza Costa, Città di Castello, ☎ 075 8554922.
- *IAT del Folignate-Nocera Umbra* (for Bevagna, Foligno, Montefalco, Spello and Trevi), 126 Porta Romana, Foligno, ☎ 0742 354459.
- *IAT di Gubbio*, 6 Piazza Oderisi, Gubbio, ☎ 075 9220693.
- *IAT di Spoleto*, 7 Piazza della Libertà, Spoleto, ☎ 0743 220311.
- *IAT dell'Orvietano*, 24 Piazza Duomo, Orvieto, ☎ 0763 341772.
- *IAT del Trasimeno* (for Lago Trasimeno and Città della Pieve), 10 Piazza Mazzini, Castiglione del Lago, ☎ 075 9652484.
- *IAT del Tuderte* (for Todi and environs), 6 Piazza Umberto I, Todi, ☎ 075 8943395; information office, 38 Piazza del Popolo ☎ 075 8942526.
- *IAT del Amerino* (for Amelia and environs), 1 Via Orvieto, Amelia, ☎ 0744 981453.

Crime and personal security

For all emergencies, ☎ 113. Help is given to British and American travellers in Italy, who are in difficulty, by the British and American consulates and the embassies in Rome. They will replace lost or stolen passports, and will give advice in emergencies. The nearest consulates to Umbria are in Florence: British Consulate, 2 Lungarno Corsini, Florence (☎ 055 284133); US Consulate, 38 Lungarno Vespucci, Florence (☎ 055 2398276).

Pickpocketing is a widespread problem in towns all over Italy: it is inadvisable to carry valuables in bags, and be particularly careful on public transport. Cash and documents can be left in hotel safes. It is a good idea to make photocopies of all important documents in case of loss. You are strongly advised to carry some means of identification with you at all times while in Italy, since you can be held at a police station if you are stopped and found to be without any.

There are three categories of **policemen** in Italy: *vigili urbani*, the municipal police (who wear blue uniform in winter and white during the summer and hats similar to London policemen); *carabinieri*, the military police who have local offices in every town and small village (and who wear black uniform with a red stripe down the side of their trousers); and the *polizia di stato*, state police (who wear dark blue jackets and light blue trousers).

Crime should be reported at once. A detailed statement has to be given in order to get an official document confirming loss or damage (essential for insurance claims). Interpreters are usually provided.

Opening hours and public holidays

Government offices usually work from 08.00–13.30 or 14.00 six days a week. Shops (clothes, hardware, hairdressers, etc.) are generally open from 09.00–13.00, 16.00–19.30, including Saturday, and for most of the year are closed on Monday morning. Food shops usually open from 08.00–13.00, 17.00–19.30 or 20.00, and for most of the year are closed on Wednesday afternoon. From mid-June to mid-September all shops are closed instead on Saturday afternoon.

The Italian national holidays when offices, shops and schools are closed are as follows: 1 January, 25 April (Liberation Day), Easter Monday, 1 May (Labour Day), 15 August (Assumption), 1 November (All Saints' Day), 8 December (Immaculate Conception), Christmas Day and 26 December (St Stephen). Each town keeps its patron saint's day as a holiday.

Telephones and postal services

There are numerous public telephones all over Italy in kiosks, bars, restaurants etc. These are operated by coins or telephone cards which can be purchased from tobacconists (displaying a blue **T** sign), bars, news-stands and post offices. Telephone numbers in Italy can have from four to eight numbers. **All numbers have an area code, which (since 1998) always has to be used (even for local calls).** Placing a local call costs 200 lire. Directory assistance (in Italian) is available by dialling 12. Numbers that begin with 800, called *numeri verdi*, are toll-free, but require a deposit of at least 200 lire. Most cities in the world can now by dialled direct from Italy (and international telephone cards are available). To make an international call to Italy, ☎ 39 and then the full area code (i.e. 075 for Perugia) followed by the number. To make a call from Italy to the U.K. ☎ 0044 then the area code and number.

Stamps are sold at tobacconists as well as post offices. Post offices are open Mon–Sat 08.10–13.25, although central offices in main towns are often open 08.10–18.00. The post offices in Perugia and Assisi now also stay open on public holidays (08.30–13.30).

Public toilets

There is a notable shortage of public toilets in Italy. All bars (cafés) should have toilets available to the public (generally speaking the larger the bar, the better the facilities). Nearly all museums now have toilets. There are also toilets in railway stations and bus stations.

Useful words and phrases

Although many people speak a little English, some basic Italian is helpful for everyday dealings. If you are able to say a few words and phrases your efforts will be much appreciated. See Food and drink section for relevant vocabulary.

good morning *buon giorno*
good afternoon/good evening *buona sera*
good night *buona notte*
goodbye *arrivederci*
hello/goodbye (informal) *ciao*
see you later *a più tardi*

yes/no *sì/no*
okay *va bene*
please/thank you *per favore/grazie*
today *oggi*
tomorrow *domani*
yesterday *ieri*
now *adesso*
later *più tardi*
in the morning *di mattina*
in the afternoon/evening *di pomeriggio/di sera*
at night *di notte*

what is your name? *come si chiama/ come ti chiami?* (informal)

railway station *stazione ferroviaria*
bus station *stazione degli autobus*
airport *aeroporto*
ticket *biglietto*
police station *ufficio di polizia/questura*
hospital *ospedale*
doctor *medico*

Monday *lunedì*
Tuesday *martedì*
Wednesday *mercoledì*
Thursday *giovedì*
Friday *venerdì*
Saturday *sabato*
Sunday *domenica*

spring *primavera*
summer *estate*
autumn *autunno*
winter *inverno*
my name is ... *mi chiamo ...*
I would like *vorrei*
do you have ...? *ha ...?/avete ...?* (plural)
where is ...? *dov'è ...?*
what time is it? *che ore sono?*
at what time? *a che ora?*
when? *quando?*
how much is it? *quanto è?*
the bill *il conto*
where are the toilets? *dove sono i gabinetti?*

do you speak English? *parla inglese?*
I don't understand *non capisco*
cold/hot *freddo/caldo*
with/without *con/senza*
open/closed *aperto/chiuso*
cheap/expensive *economico/caro*
left/right/straight on *sinistra/destra/ diritto*

dentist *dentista*
asprin *aspirina*
town council/town hall *Comune*
municipality/town hall *municipio*
old town (centre) *centro storico*
café (which sells cakes) *pasticceria/e*
ice-cream parlour *gelateria*

January *gennaio*
February *febbraio*
March *marzo*
April *aprile*
May *maggio*
June *giugno*
July *luglio*
August *agosto*
September *settembre*
October *ottobre*
November *novembre*
December *dicembre*

BACKGROUND INFORMATION

Umbria: an historical introduction
by John Law

The 'discovery' of Umbria

Umbria for long remained one of the regions of Italy little explored by foreign travellers, even in the age of the Grand Tour, and despite expanding tourism in the 19C. This was mainly because it lay off the principal routes chosen by pilgrims, antiquarians and connoisseurs heading for Rome and further south. Its rich heritage of medieval art and architecture was largely unacknowledged as long as taste was dominated by the classical: the legacies of Rome and the Renaissance.

Within the Papal States, the cities of Umbria acquired a provincial character; the aspirations of its larger cities for wide autonomy or statehood had ceased with the Renaissance, and the absence of the society and patronage associated with court life had encouraged noble families, intellectuals and artists to gravitate to major or capital cities like Rome or Florence. Protestants, liberals and supporters of Italian Unification viewed papal government with hostility, as reactionary and oppressive, dependent on *bastille*-type prison citadels in cities like Perugia, Narni and Spoleto. They also criticised the papal regime on social and economic grounds, in terms of absentee, grasping landlords, backward industries and an absence of exports other than a steady migration of people in search of better opportunities elsewhere in Italy or abroad. Umbria had to await Italian Unification (1860) before its railways were built. This retarded its economic growth and with it the development of the hotels and spas attendant on expanding tourism.

However, tastes and interests were changing even before the overthrow of papal rule and the expansion of the rail network. More adventurous and discerning travellers saw Umbria in sympathetic and even romantic terms. Off the beaten track, it was purer, more natural, more spiritual, more medieval than centres of long-acclaimed importance and growing popularity like Florence, Venice or Rome. One enthusiast was Thomas Trollope (1810–93) who published an account of his journey under the title *Travels in Central Italy or a Lenten Journey* in 1862. Another was Edward Hutton (1875–1969) who expressed his love of the area in his *Cities of Umbria*, first published in 1905 before running into many subsequent editions. Hutton's work was beautifully illustrated, as was another early guide for the discerning English-speaking public, Ada Harrison's *Some Umbrian Cities* (1925).

But the growing literature on Umbria was not merely a reaction to the more frequented resorts and cities of Italy. The legacy and shrine of St Francis of Assisi (1181–1226) had an increasing impact on travellers, Protestant and Catholic alike, who saw the saint and his immediate followers as representatives of a purer, revitalised Christianity. At the same time, appreciation grew for the art and architecture of the region, as seen in such cities as Perugia, Assisi and

Orvieto. The influence of John Ruskin (1819–1900) and the pre-Raphaelites ensured that the medieval period was no longer dismissed as primitive, superstitious, naive or quaint. Medieval sculptors, masons and painters became admired, not only for their craftsmanship, but also for their ability to express Christian belief in a pure and direct form. To such sympathetic eyes, even the Umbrian countryside, the *'Italia mystica'* of Edward Hutton, with its many shrines, hermitages and monasteries, could be viewed in spiritual terms. But Hutton expressed the fear that Umbria's special heritage and character were under threat from a modernising, industrialising and secular Italy.

Although Hutton wrote of an unspoiled, timeless Umbria the region had not been bypassed or unmarked by history. It has suffered natural disasters in the forms of earthquake, plague and disease. The flourishing Roman *municipium* of Carsulae on the Via Flaminia was abandoned after a serious earthquake. The whole region was hit by the Black Death (1348) and its successive outbreaks; Todi lost around half its population from plague in 1523. Malaria has only recently been eradicated, but depopulation continues, draining the inhabitants from the farms and smaller communities of the countryside.

Man-made disasters came in the form of wars and invasions. Terni's history is punctuated by moments of destruction: by Totila (546), by Frederick I Hohenstaufen (1174) and by Allied bombardment (1944).

Umbria's internal history was also frequently agitated and violent. This helps to explain why the present boundaries were stabilised only in the 20C. Moreover, the name 'Umbria' was not always used to denote the area. The name derives from the Umbri, an Italic tribe whose principal area of settlement stretched from the Tiber to the Adriatic, and therefore did not correspond with the present region. Their neighbours to the west, who occupied most of what is now Umbria, were the Etruscans whose civilisation was at its most influential from the 8C to the 5C BC. It was adopted by the Romans, and re-emerged in the works of local antiquarians in the 16C.

From Rome to Charlemagne

By the 3C BC both the Umbri and Etruscans had succumbed to Roman hegemony. This was marked by military defeat (the destruction of Etruscan Orvieto in 265 BC); colonisation (Spoleto, 241 BC); some redistribution of land; some instances of rebellion (Perugia, 40 BC). However, on balance Romanisation should not be seen in terms of wars of conquest and military rule. Neither the Umbrians nor the Etruscans were organised into centralised, unified states, and the advance of Roman influence and authority was piecemeal, with some cities like Gubbio first becoming allies of Rome. Many Umbrian cities showed their loyalty to Rome in the dark days of the Second Punic War and Hannibal's crushing defeat of Rome at Lake Trasimene (217 BC). Rome recognised Umbrian communities as self-governing *municipia* and extended its citizenship to their inhabitants. There was religious and cultural toleration; indeed Roman civilisation and religion were heavily indebted to the Etruscans. The whole process was expressed and encouraged by the construction of a network of roads, principally the Via Flaminia (220 BC).

Under Augustus (29 BC–8 AD) Umbria emerges as an administrative region for the first time—it was later joined to Tuscany under Diocletian (285–305). This eliminated a border which, in the absence of clear, natural frontiers, remained hard to draw throughout history.

Whatever its frontiers, Roman provincial organisation collapsed with the Roman Empire and the massive invasions of the Visigoths (5C) and the Ostrogoths (early 6C). On the road to Rome, central Italy became a battle-ground between the invaders and the Byzantine Empire whose emperors claimed the Roman succession and tried to uphold its authority and defend its territories in the west. Byzantine-led resistance was not without success. The emperor Justinian (527–65) sent armies under Belisarius and Narses to fight the Ostrogoths; in 552 Totila, King of the Ostrogoths, was defeated and killed. However, the Byzantines were less able to withstand the invasion of the Lombards later in the century; they captured Umbria and established a Lombard duchy in Spoleto in (570). Their ascendancy lasted up to the late 8C when the Franks intervened in Italy under Pepin III (714–68) and Charlemagne (742–814). Frankish rule over the duchy of Spoleto dates from 789.

Frankish intervention had been solicited by the papacy which tried to secure their loyalty by crowning Charlemagne as Emperor in Rome in 800. The papacy also sought Frankish recognition of papal lordship over central Italy. This claim, to govern as secular rulers (what came to be called the Lands of St Peter or the Papal States) was criticised and contested by lawyers, reformers, political thinkers and opponents of the papacy from the early Middle Ages to the 20C. In the first place, the papacy was anxious to secure itself from attack and political pressure. The popes also sought to control the agricultural land, the ports, the trade and pilgrim routes necessary to sustain the city of Rome. They were also anxious to establish their authority over other wealthy and influential churches and monasteries in central Italy. Lastly, the popes saw themselves as legitimate heirs to the temporal authority of the Roman emperors.

To strengthen its position, the papacy secured recognition of its claims from Frankish rulers, Pepin in 756 and Charlemagne in 774, 781 and 787. It also resorted to invention and forgery in the Donation of Constantine, an 8C docu-ment which purported to be the cession of temporal authority in the west to the papacy by the Emperor Constantine (306–27) in recognition of his conversion to Christianity and his miraculous recovery from illness. The validity of the grant was attacked in the Middle Ages by Roman lawyers hostile to papal pretensions, and its authenticity was demolished in the 15C by the humanist Lorenzo Valla (1407–57).

The weakness of Papal Rule

However, papal authority in the States of the Church for long remained stronger in theory than in practice. It was only with Innocent III (1198–1216) that an attempt was made to realise papal lordship, but for centuries after that papal rule remained intermittent. For example, in 1353 Innocent VI made the Spanish Cardinal Albornoz his representative in Italy, and a series of military and politi-cal successes appeared crowned by the issue of a constitution in 1357. That remained on the statute book until the 19C; its implementation proved much more difficult.

There are various reasons for the weakness of papal rule in the later Middle Ages: breaks in the succession (e.g. 1292–94); a prolonged absence from Italy

(1305–76); schism within the Church (1378–1418); challenges to papal authority from Church councils (e.g. the Council of Basle, 1431–49). Threats to papal rule also came from secular rulers. They included: the Hohenstaufen emperors Frederick I (1152–90) and Frederick II (1212–50); the Florentine Republic; Ladislas of Naples (1386–1414), Giangaleazzo Visconti, lord then duke of Milan (1378–1402). Papal rule in Umbria was also weakened by lords from within the Papal States, some of whom were also mercenary military leaders, or *condottieri*, and all of whom were anxious to defend and extend their lands. Some were native to Umbria like the Trinci of Foligno who ruled that and neighbouring cities from c 1300 to 1439, or Braccio de Montone (1368–1424) who established an ascendancy over Perugia in 1416. Others came from other papal provinces like the Montefeltro of Urbino who ruled Gubbio from 1387 to 1508, or Francesco Sforza who held Amelia briefly from 1434 to 1435.

The Rise of the Communes

A major reason why Umbria attracted the ambitions of foreign and native rulers, and a further reason for the intermittent nature of papal rule was the political, economic and military development of towns. As cities like Perugia, Spoleto, Todi and Orvieto still bear witness—even to the non-archaeologist—urban life in Umbria predates the Roman period by centuries. As throughout the Roman Empire, city life was equated with civilisation (*civis*, means citizen). The Etruscans and the Umbrians most often chose hill sites for reasons of security, health, availability of building stone and the economical use of agricultural land. Other cities owed their origin and development to river crossings or the road system (Foligno, Terni). If the majority of the population worked the land and if agriculture remained the major engine of the economy, towns were the centres of political, cultural and religious activity.

The spread of Christianity from the 2C was closely linked to the road system and the towns along it. The barbarian invasions damaged rather than destroyed the situation, but the collapse of central authority as represented by pope or emperor did not in the longer term prevent the revival of the towns in the 10C and 11C, in most cases on Etruscan, Umbrian or Roman sites. Gradually the town populations revived and economic activity recovered as local and then regional markets, and as centres of industry (construction, textiles, pottery).

Such developments created greater political and military muscle which in turn led towns and cities in Umbria to form associations or communes, to increase their privileges and seek greater self-government in the 11C and 12C. This period saw the communes of Umbria gradually extending their authority over the surrounding *contado* (county or jurisdiction) at the expense of lay and ecclesiastical landlords and smaller communities. Distant overlords, the emperors in particular, could challenge but not reverse this trend. Contemporary and later authorities probably exaggerate when they describe Hohenstaufen rule in towns like Montefalco in the 12C and 13C as a period of devastation.

Historians once enthused over the communes as early bourgeois republics, if not as democracies, which destroyed the power of local bishops and feudatories and developed the economy beyond a dependence on agriculture into trade and industry. Nowadays the communes tend to be viewed in a much more critical light. They were jealous of their own authority in matters of territory, jurisdiction and trade routes. The history of medieval Umbria is full of internecine disputes; the young Francis of Assisi (1181–1226) was captured when fighting for his city against its neighbour and arch-rival Perugia in 1202; later that city's acceptance of his preaching and his cult was grudging. The freedoms and privileges the cities enjoyed were not extended to subject communities and the rural population. Nor were the communes themselves in any sense democracies. Full political, legal and economic rights remained in the hands of an oligarchy of established families. When the *popolo* (the people) acquired a share in government in the 13C, they did not represent a democratic revolution, as their party name might suggest, but the arrival of new wealth.

The communes of medieval Umbria were small; the largest, Perugia, possibly reached 28,000 inhabitants at the peak of the population curve, c 1300. None was a major financial, industrial or manufacturing centre; the bulk of the population drew its wealth and support from the land. Moreover the feudal lords had not been destroyed as a class; magnate families resided in the cities, often behind private fortifications. They built up networks of clients and dependents. Their more aristocratic lifestyle appealed to aspiring members of the bourgeoisie, and their power and influence were sources of political and social instability. Indeed, faction stalked the internal history of the communes. There was no sense of legitimate opposition, and political and family rivalry could explode into street-fighting, murder and exile (as between the Oddi and the Baglioni of Perugia c 1500). Faction could also reflect and feed off conflicts on a larger scale, most notoriously between the pro-papal Guelphs and the pro-imperial Ghibellines, in 14C Orvieto for example. Such instability helps to explain why many of the communes of Umbria succumbed in the late medieval period to the hegemony or formal lordship (*signoria*) of prominent local families, like the Baglioni in Perugia or the Trinci in Foligno.

It would be wrong to conclude that the communal period was entirely one of disaster and failure; after all, this was the period that largely shaped the towns and cities of Umbria as they appear today. The communes defended themselves with circuits of walls. Hostile regimes and unruly families were punished by the reduction of their fortresses. Legislation was passed to stimulate the economy and protect the environment (such as the erosion of the cliffs on which Orvieto was built). The common interest, the public good, was expressed via the statute books and more obviously in the public buildings (*palazzi*) that housed the communal courts, council halls, treasuries and archives. Streets and squares were paved, bridges and roads constructed, markets established and wells and fountains installed—prized engineering marvels in the hill towns. The community witnessed the construction, enlargement and embellishment of its churches. The cathedral tended to take pride of place, but the importance of churches associated with religious orders (especially friars), parishes and local cults was also acknowledged. In Perugia, a university was founded in the 13C which soon acquired a formidable reputation for law.

But considerable and abiding their achievements, the communes of Umbria failed to retain the status of independent city states for long. Many of the reasons for this have been suggested above, but none of the communes had the resources to resist papal authority, set out in the Middle Ages but enforced in the Renaissance. Architecture can again prove very revealing. The great fortresses built by Cardinal Albornoz, such as those at Spoleto or Narni, signal an early attempt to secure papal rule. When Perugia rebelled against papal taxation in 1540, the forces of Paul III took the city, reduced its privileges, levelled the houses of the prominent Baglioni dynasty and began work on a citadel, the *Rocca Paolina*. The fortress lasted until 1860, and increasingly became a means and a symbol of oppression. When Thomas Trollope visited the city after its liberation from papal rule, he rejoiced at the destruction of that *bastille*-type structure.

Umbria and the Church

However, to see Umbria's history within the Papal States entirely in terms of oppression would be misleading. The spread of papal authority, particularly from the 15C, could be perceived as offering liberty and good government; when the warrior Cardinal Giovanni Vitelleschi overthrew the Trinci of Foligno in 1439 this was justified as bringing an end to tyranny. The reputation of despotic papal rule itself emerged late, in the 18C and 19C. Unrest and criticism were encouraged by the experiments and changes brought about by the Revolutionary and Napoleonic wars, when the continuity of papal government was interrupted. Only with the 19C is there evidence of active sedition and revolt (1831, 1848, 1859). Some concessions were made to reform, as in the early years of the pontificate of Pius IX (1846–78). More generally, papal government was distant and inefficient. Communes preserved their sense of identity and a degree of autonomy. Leading families, like the Geraldini of Amelia, could be flattered and advanced by papal favours and service. The construction of a large number of civic theatres in the 18C and early 19C suggests that social and cultural life was far from dead.

More positively, Umbria was of great religious significance to the Roman Catholic Church. It was converted to Christianity early, and its saints and martyrs remained closely associated with its towns and cities. Moreover, the region long remained a breeding-ground for religious revival led by men and women. St Benedict (480–550), the founder of western monasticism, was born at Norcia. His example later influenced St Francis, the reluctant founder of one of the principal mendicant orders of friars. An early disciple of Benedict was his sister, St Scholastica. The reputation of the Franciscan movement spread thanks to the example of a closer follower of Francis, St Clare of Assisi, founder of the Order of Poor Clares (1194–1255). Ideas central to the Catholic faith were strengthened in Umbria. St Francis and his followers elaborated the Nativity story, giving it its abiding appeal. The feast of **Corpus Domini** was inaugurated at Orvieto in 1264 after a local miracle concerning the Eucharist. Both events led to the foundation of the magnificent cathedral there (1290).

But not all religious activity supported the official Church. Orvieto was also associated with the Cathar heresy in the 13C. In 1260, Perugia was a starting-point for the penitential Flagellants whose extremism and anti-clericalism alarmed the Church. The mystical Franciscan poet, Jacopone da Todi (1230–1306), now venerated for his hymns, or lauds, to the Virgin, among them the **Stabat Mater**, was imprisoned for attacking the corruption of the papacy from 1298 to 1303. In the late 19C, count Enrico Campello (who came from the Spoleto area) led a movement to reform the Catholic Church which drew inspiration and support from the Protestant world; he was later persuaded to recant. Although he has a fine tomb at Campello, no cult survives.

The plethora of Umbrian saints and religious figures still attract both an international and a local following. St Benedict was declared patron saint of Europe in 1964 and Assisi has ecumenical appeal, but small towns like Montefalco proudly preserve shrines such as St Clare's (1268–1308), that still attract the devout. And such cults can also be seen as manifestations of an urban-orientated society that pre-dates Christianity. To this day, local patriotism, or campanilismo, can easily be detected, finding expression in such ceremonies as the Corsa dei Ceri at Gubbio. This part-religious, part-sporting event is held on 15 May in honour of St Ubaldo (1100–60), a local bishop who allegedly saved the city from Frederick I Hohenstaufen, but its origins may well be much older, like the city of Gubbio itself.

Place names in Italian towns and cities

Many of the place names in Italian towns and cities have ancient origins; the names assigned to public buildings, market-places, towers, bridges, gates and fountains frequently date to the Middle Ages. But the practice of formally naming all streets and squares began in the 19C. Frequently local—even parochial—patriotism determines the choice as the community celebrates its own history and its own political, literary, religious and scientific figures, as well as famous foreign visitors.

But the choice of place names can reflect wider issues, and events and figures from Italian national history are prominently represented. Thus a united republican Italy can be celebrated in terms of concepts (e.g. Via della Repubblica, della Libertà, della Vittoria), events (e.g. Via del Plebiscito recalling the vote that preceded a region uniting with the Kingdom of Italy in the 19C), or by drawing on the gazetteer of Italian rivers, mountains, seas and cities.

Broadly speaking the national figures and events chosen tend to be representative of four phases in recent Italian history. Probably the most emotive and frequently commemorated is the *Risorgimento* (the Resurgence), the movement that led to the unification and independence of Italy in the 19C; among the battles commemorated are: Custoza, Lissa, Solferino, Magenta, Montebello, Mentana. For some historians, Italy's entry to the First World War represents the final phase in the pursuit of national unity; the battles and campaigns between Italy, her allies and the Central Powers, are also frequently recorded in place names: the Isonzo; Monte Pasubio; Caporetto; Monte Grappa, the Piave; Vittorio Veneto. Opposition to Fascism and the ending of the Second World War are also commemorated in this way, as are the statesmen and events associated with the country's reconstruction, economic development and membership of the EU. Casualties in Italy's successful struggle against political terrorism (Aldo Moro, murdered by the Red Brigade in 1978) and the less successful war against organised crime (Alberto della Chiesa, killed by the Mafia in 1982) are also being honoured.

Largely censored and deleted from the record are the events and personalities closely linked to Fascism, Italy's empire and the reigns of the last two members of the House of Savoy, Vittorio Emanuele III (1900–46) and Umberto II (1946). However, the keen-eyed observer might be able to identify traces of Fascist insignia and the Fascist system of dating (1922, when Mussolini was invited to lead the government, is year 1) on public buildings and monuments, and some street names still recall territories once ruled from Rome (e.g. Istria, Dalmatia, Albania, Lybia).

Below is a selection of the more prominent figures and events from recent Italian history which the traveller is likely to encounter time and again.

People

ALFIERI, **Vittorio** (1749–1803), poet and dramatist.

BATTISTI, **Cesare** Italian patriot executed by the Habsburg regime in Trento, 12 July 1916.

CARDUCCI, **Giosuè** (1835–1907), patriotic poet and literary critic.

CAVOUR, **Camille** (1810–61), statesman and cautious architect of Italian unification.

CRISPI, **Francesco** (1818–1901), statesman.

FOSCOLO, **Ugo** (1778–1827), poet and patriot.

GARIBALDI, **Giuseppe** (1807–82), inspirational political and military leader in the Risorgimento.

GRAMSCI, **Antonio** (1891–1937), political thinker, Marxist, opponent of Fascism.

MANIN, **Daniele** (1804–57), Venetian patriot and statesman, defender of that city against Habsburg forces, 1848–49.

MARCONI, **Guglielmo** (1874–1937), electrical engineer and radio pioneer.

MARGHERITA **of Savoy** (1851–1926), wife of King Umberto I, noted for her piety, good works and cultural patronage.

MARTIRI DELLA RESISTENZA (or DELLA LIBERTÀ), opponents of Fascism and German occupation, 1943–45.

MATTEOTTI, **Giacomo** (1885–1924), socialist politician, assassinated by Fascists.

MAZZINI, **Giuseppe** (1805–82), leading republican figure of the Risorgimento.

OBERDAN, **Guglielmo** (1858–82), Italian patriot, executed by the Habsburg regime in Trieste.

RICASOLI, **Bettino** (1809–80), Florentine statesman, instrumental in securing Tuscany's adherence to the Kingdom of Italy in 1860.

SAFFI, **Aurelio** (1819–1890), man of letters and hero of the Risorgimento.

UMBERTO **I of Savoy**, King of Italy, 1878–1900.

VERDI, **Giuseppe** (1831–1901), prolific opera composer whose output was often associated with the cause of a united Italy. His surname could be read as the initials of *Vittorio Emanuele Re d'Italia*.

Vittorio Emanuele II of Savoy, King of Sardinia–Piedmont from 1849, King of Italy 1861–78.

Events

XI FEBBRAIO: 11 February 1929, formal reconciliation between the papacy and the Kingdom of Italy.

XXIX MARZO: 29 March 1943, armistice between Italy and the Allies.

XXVII APRILE: 27 April 1945, Benito Mussolini captured in northern Italy. The Fascist leader was quickly tried and executed on 28 April.

XI Maggio: 11 May 1860, Garibaldi landed with 1,000 men at Marsala (Sicily), launching the military campaign that led to the Unification of Italy.

XXIV Maggio: 24 May 1915, Italy enters the First World War.

II Giugno: 2 June 1946, referendum designed to favour a republican constitution.

XX Giugno: 20 June 1859, papal forces and their supporters violently suppressed a pro-Unification rising in Perugia.

XIV Settembre: 14 September 1860, the forces of the Kingdom of Italy entered Perugia.

XX Settembre: 20 September 1870, Italian forces enter Rome, overthrowing papal rule.

IV Novembre: 4 November 1918, proclamation of the armistice between Italy and Austria.

Further reading

J. Bentley, *Umbria* (London 1989).

J. Bentley, *Italy: the Hill Towns* (London 1990).

Lord Byron, *Selected Poems* (London 1996).

G.K. Chesterton, *St Francis of Assisi* (London 1923).

L. Duff Gordon, *The Story of Assisi* (1913).

L. Duff Gordon and M. Symonds, *The Story of Perugia* (1912).

G. Fauré, *The Land of St Francis of Assisi* (London 1924).

A. Harrison, *Some Umbrian Cities* (London 1925).

D. Hay (ed.), *The Longman History of Italy* (London 1980).

H. Hearder and D.P. Waley (eds.), *A Short History of Italy* (Cambridge 1962).

H. Hearder, *Italy: A Short History* (Cambridge 1990).

W. Heywood, *A History of Perugia* (London 1910).

E. Hutton, *The Cities of Umbria* (London 1905).

C. Lansing, *Cathar Heresy in Medieval Italy* (1998).

J.R.H. Moorman, *A History of the Franciscan Order* (Oxford 1968).

P. Partner, *The Lands of St Peter*.

J. Pemble, *The Mediterranean Passion* (Oxford 1988).

T.W. Potter, *Roman Rome* (London 1987).

A. Smart, *The Assisi Problem and the Art of Giotto* (1971)

J.H. Stubblebine, *Assisi and the Rise of Vernacular Art* (1985)

T. Trollope, *Travels in Central Italy or a Lenten Journey* (London 1862).

D.P. Waley, *The Italian City Republics* (London 1978).

D. Waley, *Medieval Orvieto* (1952).

J. White, *Art and Architecture in Italy 1250–1400* (London 1993).

THE GUIDE

Perugia, Assisi & Lago Trasimeno

PERUGIA
• • • • • • • • •

Perugia (population 129,000), capital of a province (6357 sq km), which comprises well over half of Umbria, has a booming economy. Disorderly suburbs with ugly tower blocks (especially prominent on the route from Florence and Siena) have sprawled on to the lower hills below the old town in the last 20 years or so. The historical centre, however, keeps its character and numerous tortuous streets climb up and down the oddly shaped hilly spurs of land (494m above sea-level and some 300m above the Tiber) on which the town is built. It is perhaps the most difficult town in Italy in which to get one's bearings. It has numerous

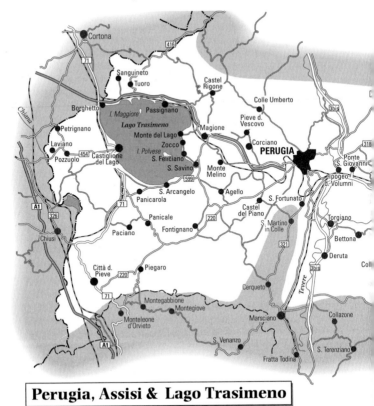

Perugia, Assisi & Lago Trasimeno

interesting monuments, including the Palazzo dei Priori on the delightful Corso, where the Pinacoteca has a magnificent display of Umbrian art. Lovely churches are situated on the edges of the hills.

The famous painter Pietro Vannucci was called 'Perugino' due to his long association with the town, and many works by him survive here, notably in the Collegio del Cambio. Students from all over the world come to Perugia to attend the famous Università per Stranieri (University for foreigners). Perugia was the first hill town in Italy to resolve its traffic problems in the 1980s: this was achieved by constructing car-parks connected to the historical centre (*cento storico*) by a series of escalators. However, if you come to the town by car the one-way system in the modern town at the foot of the hill is extremely confusing and the signposting very erratic.

Practical information

Information offices

IAT information office, Piazza IV Novembre (**map 6**), ☎ 075 5736458 and 075 5723327. Headquarters of the Azienda di Promozione Turistica dell'Umbria; 21 Via Mazzini, ☎ 075 575951.

Getting there

By train The main station is in a modern part of the town at Fontivegge (**map 12**), below the historical centre to the south-west. Frequent services from Foligno (with connections from Rome) and from Terontola (with connections from Florence). Bus nos 6, 7 & 9 for Piazza Italia (**map 7**). A private railway company (*Ferrovia Centrale Umbra*) operates two services from the Stazione Sant'Anna (**map 8**) and the Stazione Ponte San Giovanni (6km south-east) from Città di Castello and San Sepolcro, and from Terni via Deruta, Marsciano and Todi.

By air There is a small airport at Sant'Egidio, 12km east of Perugia, with daily flights from Milan.

Car parking The historic centre (on the highest hills) is closed to traffic on weekdays 07.00–13.30 and after 20.00, and from 17.00 on PH), but visitors can obtain permission to reach hotels within this area. Car-parks are clearly indicated on the approach roads: the most convenient one for visitors is in Piazza Partigiani (**map 8**), signposted from Via Cacciatori degli Alpi or Via Baldassare

Orsini. This huge two-storey underground car-park has an hourly tariff (special reduced tariff for overnight periods). From here escalators (described below) mount through the Rocca Paolina to Piazza Italia (**map 7**), in the centre of the city.

Another convenient car-park on several storeys (signposted from the railway station), also provided with escalators, is in **Viale Pellini** (**map 11**) with an hourly tariff (less expensive than Piazza Partigiani). On the approach to this car-park, off Via Arturo Cecchi, there is free car parking in **Piazzale della Cupa**, and on the other side of Via Arturo Cecchi, although it is not always easy to find space at these two car-parks. From Via Arturo Cecchi an escalator ascends to Viale Pellini, where more escalators continue up to emerge in Via dei Priori (**map 7**), which leads up to Corso Vannucci on the right.

There is also a car-park below the **covered market** (**map 7**) with a lift up to Piazza Matteotti (**map 7**).

By bus Bus services run by *APM*, Piazza Partigiani (**map 8**. ☎ 075 5731707, and 800 512141). For **city buses** from the railway station, see above. There is a wide network of **country buses** from Piazza Partigiani to the main towns of interest in Umbria, with frequent daily services: to Assisi in c 1hr (slower services via Santa Maria degli Angeli); to Spello (50mins) and Foligno (1hr 15mins); to Gubbio (1hr 10mins); to Deruta (30mins) and Todi (1hr 30mins); to Lago Trasimeno (Passignano 1hr, Tuoro 1hr 15mins, and Castiglione del Lago 1hr 15mins); to Città della Pieve (1hr 30mins) and Chiusi (1hr 40mins); to Torgiano (20mins) and Bettona (30mins). Services once a day to Norcia (2hrs 50mins); to Orvieto (2hrs 30mins); and Spoleto (1hr 30mins; better reached by train).

Long distance coach services operated by *Sulga* via the motorway to Florence (2hrs) and Rome (2hrs 30mins) and Rome Fiumicino airport.

 ### Hotels
✰✰✰✰✰ *Brufani*, 12 Piazza Italia, ☎ 075 5732541; fax 075 5720210. Opened as a hotel in 1883, it has comfortable old-fashioned public rooms with a panorama of the valley. Most of the 27 heavily carpeted bedrooms, which include five luxurious suites, are very quiet, also looking over the valley. However, this hotel, now one of a chain of six in Italy owned by Sina Hotels, is to merge with the Palace Hotel Bellavista next door (acquired by Sina in 1997) so that it will have a total of some 90 rooms. Ambitious renovations are planned (including the addition of a swimming-pool), which may unfortunately change the characteristic atmosphere.

✰✰✰✰ *La Rosetta*, 19 Piazza Italia, ☎ & fax 075 5720841. A solid old-fashioned hotel in a magnificent position at the beginning of Corso Vannucci. Cordial efficient staff. The 96 bedrooms, indifferently furnished, are quiet. It can be busy with groups. Good restaurant attached, and half- and full-board terms available.

✰✰✰ *Palace Hotel Bellavista*, 12 Piazza Italia, ☎ 075 5720741; fax 075 5729092. Next door to the Hotel Brufani, this lovely old-fashioned hotel, which retains its furnishings from the 1930s (including a period bar with a superb view over the valley and comfortable living rooms) has been bought by the Sina Hotels chain and is to be merged with the Brufani as a ✰✰✰✰✰ hotel (see above). At present it has 74 rooms, the quieter ones are those on the side away from the valley (since there is a busy road below the hotel on that side).

✰✰✰ *Fortuna*, 19 Via Bonazzi, ☎ 075 5722845; fax 075 5735040. In a lovely old palace in a very quiet position just off Corso Vannucci. A special feature is the terrace overlooking the old town and the valley beyond. On the third floor six rooms have their own little terraces. The furnishing is unimaginative and the desk staff could be more helpful.

** *Hotel Priori*, Via dei Priori, ☎ 075 5723378; fax 075 5723213. On one of the most characteristic old streets in the city, with a splendid large terrace for breakfast. Very simple decor and rather unfriendly staff.

** *Umbria*, 37 Via Boncambi, ☎ 075 5721203. In a lovely position on a narrow old street behind Palazzo dei Priori. The Iranian proprietor is making some renovations, but it is extremely simple. Four of the 17 rooms have views, and there are two family rooms. This is one of a group of nine small ** hotels in the old centre which are to club together to offer package deals to guests (the others include *Signa*, 9 Via del Grillo, ☎ 075 5724180).

Campsite

There is a campsite on Colle della Trinità: *Paradis d'Etè* ☆☆☆☆; to reopen 2000, ☎ 075 5179714. Il Rocolo ☆☆☆; open in summer, ☎ & fax 07 5178550.

Youth hostel

There is a youth hostel at 13 Via Bontempi (**map 2;6**, ☎ & fax 075 5722880).

Theatre and annual festivals

Teatro Morlacchi, Piazza Morlacchi (**map 6**) for prose and concerts. An international Festival of Jazz is held at the beginning of July. A large fair is held from 1 November for one week at Pian di Massiano. There is a small antiques fair in Perugia on the last Sunday of each month, and a fair of natural and organic products and traditional crafts on the first Sunday of each month. An international music fesival is held in the town in September.

Restaurants

£££ *Osteria del Bartolo*, 30 Via Bartolo, ☎ 075 5731561; ££ *La Piazzetta*, 3 Via Deliziosa, ☎ 075 5736012; *Il Falchetto*, 20 Via Bartolo, ☎ 075 5731775; *La Taverna*, 8 Via Streghe, ☎ 075 5724128; *La Rosetta*, 2 Via del Sette, ☎ 075 5720841; *Aladino*, 11 Via delle Prome, ☎ 075 5720938; *Giancarlo*, 36 Via dei Priori, ☎ 075 5724314; *La Bocca Mia*, 36 Via Ulisse Rocchi, ☎ 075 5723873; *Del Sole*, 28 Via Oberdan, ☎ 075 5735031; *Il Canto delle Sirene*, 4G Via Campo di Marte, ☎ 075 5055185, near the railway station (specialising in fish; with a good *tavola calda* adjoining).

£ *Il Cantinone*, 6 Via Ritorta, ☎ 075 5734430; *Dal Mi' Cocco*, 12 Corso Garibaldi, ☎ 075 5732511; *Cesarino*, 15 Via della Gabbia, ☎ 075 5728974; *Altromondo*, 11 Via Caporali, ☎ 075 5726157; *Bianca*, 13 Via Piantarose (Tre Archi), ☎ 075 5727132. The *Enoteca Provinciale*, 18 Via Ulisse Rocchi, has a wide selection of **Umbrian wines**.

Cafés

There are cafés with good snacks on Corso Vannucci, notably *Sandri*, at no. 32.

Picnics

Good places to picnic can be found near the churches of Sant'Angelo and San Pietro.

Market days on Tuesday and Saturday in Via Ercolano and (on Saturday) at Pian di Massiano.

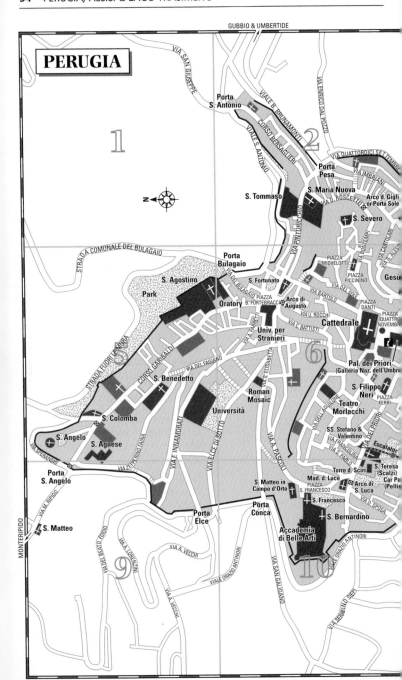

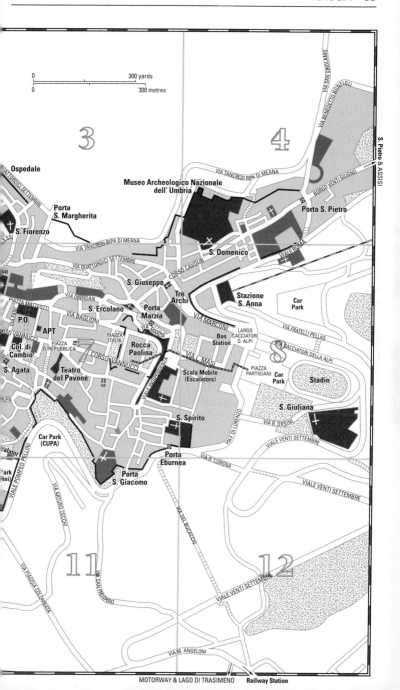

0

300 yards

0

300 metres

3

4

Ospedale

VIA SAN GIROLAMO

VIA BENEDETTO BONFIGLI

VIA TANCREDI RIPA DI MEANA

S. Pietro & ASSISI

Museo Archeologico Nazionale dell' Umbria

Porta S. Margherita

BORGO VENTI GIUGNO

Porta S. Pietro

S. Fiorenzo

VIA TANCREDI RIPA DI MEANA

VIA QUATTORDICI SETTEMBRE

S. Domenico

VIALE ROMA

S. Giuseppe

CORSO CAVOUR

VIA OBERDAN

Tre Archi

Stazione S. Anna

Car Park

PIAZZA MATTEOTTI

S. Ercolano

VIA BAGLIONI

Porta Marzia

VIA MARCONI

P.O.

APT

PIAZZA ITALIA

VIA MAZZA

LARGO CACCIATORI D. ALPI

Bus Station

VIA FRATELLI PELLAS

VIA CACCIATORI DELLA ALPI

Col. di Cambio

PIAZZA D. REPUBBLICA

Rocca Paolina

7

8

CORSO VANNUCCI

VIA L. MASI

PIAZZA PARTIGIANI

Car Park

Stadin

S. Agata

Teatro del Pavone

Scala Mobile (Escalators)

S. Giuliana

VIALE INDIPENDENZA

VIA B. ORSINI

VIALE POMPEO PELLINI

S. Spirito

VIA DI LORENZO

VIALE VENTI SETTEMBRE

Car Park (CUPA)

Porta Eburnea

VIA D. CORGNA

VIALE VENTI SETTEMBRE

ark ini)

Porta S. Giacomo

VIA ARTURO CECCHI

VIA DEL BULAGAIO

VIALE PIAGGIA COLOMBATA

VIA SAN PROSPERO

11

12

VIALE VENTI SETTEMBRE

VIA M. ANGELONI

MOTORWAY & LAGO DI TRASIMENO   **Railway Station**

History

Perusia was one of the 12 cities of the Etruscan Confederation and it submitted to the Romans under Q. Fabius in 310 BC. Its ancient walls of irregular blocks of travertine with seven gates were built probably at the end of the 2C BC. In the civil war between Octavian (Augustus) and Mark Antony, L. Antonius, brother of the triumvir, was besieged in Perusia in 41–40 BC. Famine compelled the city's surrender; but one of its citizens, Gaius Cestius, in panic set fire to his own house, and the flames spread, razing all Perusia to the ground. Augustus rebuilt the city and called it *Augusta Perusia*. It is said to have been besieged by Totila in 547, and saved by the wisdom of its bishop, St Herculanus. In 592 it became part of the Lombard duchy of Spoleto, and after the restoration of the Western Empire its history is one of obscure and intricate wars with neighbouring towns in which it generally took the Guelf side.

The first despot was one of the Raspanti ('scratchers'; the nickname of the burghers), named Biordo Michelotti (1393), who murdered two of the noble family of the Baglioni, became leader of the Florentine army, and allied himself with Gian Galeazzo Visconti. The city passed to the latter family, and afterwards to Braccio Fortebraccio (1416–24), the famous *condottiere* and a wise governor. Perugia subsequently suffered from the rivalry between the Oddi and Baglioni families. When the Baglioni got the upper hand, they in turn quarrelled, until the day (14 August 1500) when all their leaders were massacred as the result of a conspiracy, with the exception of Gian Paolo, who revenged himself upon the murderers. Pope Paul III seized the town in 1535 and built the Rocca Paolina (see below). From then onwards Perugia was ruled by a papal governor.

In 1809 it was annexed to the French Empire, and it was called *Perouse* by the French; in 1815 it was restored to the Church. In 1859 the papal Swiss Guards occupied the city after an indiscriminate massacre, but a year later they were expelled, and a popular insurrection all but destroyed the Rocca Paolina. The British 8th Army entered Perugia on 20 June 1944.

Etruscan Perugia

Perusia and Orvieto (Volsinii Veteres) were the two important Etruscan cities in the Umbrian region west of the Tiber. Perugia thrived in particular towards the end of the Etruscan period, in the 4C and 3C BC. The city retains part of its Etruscan walls and gates, most notably the Porta Marzia and Arco d'Augusto. There is a remarkable well, built to supply water for the entire population in the 3C BC in Piazza Danti. The 'Cippo di Perugia', found near Perugia in 1922 and displayed in the Museo Archeologico, is a travertine cippus with a 151 word inscription, one of the longest texts known in the Etruscan language. Other important local Etruscan material can be seen in this museum, including recent finds from the Cutu tomb at Monteluce. On the outskirts of the town there are a number of vaulted Etruscan tombs including the Ipogeo dei Volumni one of the most impressive burial places known of this period (regularly open to the public), and the Ipogei of San Manno and Villa Sperandio.

Art

Perugia was the chief centre of the splendid Umbrian school of painting, which was formed in the 12C. By the 15C it had became independent of Siena and Florence, and produced such masters as Gentile da Fabriano, Ottaviano Nelli, Niccolò da Foligno (L'Alunno), Matteo da Gualdo, Bartolomeo Caporali, and Benedetto Bonfigli (c 1420–96), the first great Perugian painter. His immediate follower was Fiorenzo di Lorenzo (1445–1522), but the greatest Perugian painter was Pietro Vannucci (1446–1523), born at Città della Pieve, but called *Perugino*. Although Raphael was his most famous pupil, he had a profound influence on numerous subsequent painters of the Umbrian school including Pinturicchio (Bernardino di Betto; 1454–1513), Andrea d'Assisi (*L'Ingegno*), Tiberio d'Assisi, Francesco Melanzio of Montefalco, Lo Spagna, Bernardino di Mariotto, Eusebio da San Giorgio, Domenico and Orazio Alfani, and Giannicola di Paolo. The city also produced especially skilled woodworkers who carved numerous beautiful choir stalls which still survive in many churches of the city, and whose work culminated in the exquisitely panelled Sala della Mercanzia.

The Rocca Paolina and Via Bagliona

The approach to Perugia from the west or from the main station is by Via Venti Settembre (**map 12**), which winds uphill towards the old city. Off Largo Cacciatori degli Alpi (**map 8**), with its monument to Garibaldi by Cesare Zocchi (1887), is **Piazza Partigiani** (**map 8**), where there is a two-storey underground car-park (signposted). From the car-park the stadium is conspicuous beside the 13C–14C church of **Santa Giuliana** (**map 8**), with a graceful 14C campanile, and two cloisters (13C and 14C; now incorporated in a military hospital).

A series of escalators (and some steps), opened in 1983, lead up from the car-park to the centre of the city; beyond Via del Circo they cross the huge vaulted foundations of part of the **Rocca Paolina** (**map 7**), a fortress built by Antonio Sangallo the Younger at the command of Paul III to dominate the Perugians who had rebelled against his salt tax. A whole medieval district, including the ruins of the old Baglioni mansions, was vaulted over for this *bellissima e inutilissima opera*. Much of it, including the upper part on the site of the present Piazza Italia (see below), was destroyed by the Perugians in 1860 in anger against the papal rulers.

The escalators emerge at a crossing where the subterranean **Via Bagliona**, an ancient road, descends past remains of medieval and Renaissance dwellings (some built on Etruscan foundations), and the huge brick vaults built by Sangallo to sustain the fortress above. Only some of the buildings, including the 13C towers and houses of the Baglioni family, are identified, but the succession of tall scenographic vaults and huge shadowy rooms produces a remarkable atmosphere. The area to the right of the road formed part of the defence works of the fortress, with embrasures in the bastions for the cannon, and the huge cisterns here provided water.

Via Bagliona emerges on Via Marzia beneath the splendid Etruscan **Porta Marzia** (**map 7**; 3C–2C BC), carefully re-erected in its present position by Sangallo. It is decorated on the external façade by a few worn sculptures in dark stone.

The subterranean road continues from the escalators up to the left past several plans of the Rocca, and the last flight of escalators ends beneath the portico of Palazzo della Provincia (1870; now the Prefettura, whose front bears the Perugian griffin in bronze), on **Piazza Italia** (**map 7**), flanked by imposing buildings. Behind the Prefettura is the charming little terraced **Giardino Carducci** which has a view extending from Monte Amiata to the summits of the central Apennines, with Montefalco, Assisi, Spello, Foligno and Spoleto in the distance. Corso Vannucci begins at Piazza Italia.

Corso Vannucci and Palazzo dei Priori

The exceptionally wide and undulating **Corso Vannucci** (**map 7**), is at the centre of the old city, and it provides a magnificent setting for the *passeggiata* at dusk when it is even more crowded than at other times. It is named in honour of Perugia's greatest painter, always known as 'Perugino'. Towards the far end is the long curving façade of **Palazzo dei Priori** (**map 6,7**), one of the largest and most magnificent town halls in Italy. It stretches as far as Piazza IV Novembre, which has the oldest façade (described on p. 64). The Palazzo was built by the local architects Giacomo di Servadio and Giovannello di Benvenuto (1293–97), and enlarged and completed by 1443 (restored in the 19C and again in 1990). It houses the Collegio del Cambio, the Collegio della Mercanzia, municipal offices, and the Galleria Nazionale dell'Umbria, and beneath it runs Via dei Priori. The front, on the Corso, has castellations above two rows of Gothic three-light windows placed unusually close together. On the ground floor are a series of arches on either side of the high archway over Via dei Priori, and the elaborately decorated main portal.

Palazzo dei Priori

Collegio del Cambio

The façade on the left of Via dei Priori (and the bell-tower) incorporates a medieval tower and was added in the same style in the 15C. Here (at no. 25) is the entrance to the hall and chapel of the Collegio del Cambio (**map 7**), which has a main portal with bas-reliefs and polychrome terracotta tiles in the arch, flanked by two smaller doorways. The wooden doors are fine works by Antonio Bencivenni da Mercatello. The guild of money-changers played an important part in the public administration of the city, and passed judgement in law suits concerning financial disputes. It was founded before 1259 and still functions as a charitable institution. Since 1457 it has been housed in these rooms in Palazzo dei Priori, adapted by Bartolomeo Mattioli and Lodovico d'Antonibi.

The entrance (open 09.00–12.30, 14.30–17.30; PH 09.00–12.30. 7 Jan–28 Feb 08.00–14.00; PH 09.00–12.30; closed on Mon from Nov–Feb; ☎ 075 5728599) is through the **Sala dei Legisti** which became the property of the Collegio dei Legisti in 1613. The fine walnut benches were carved by Giampietro Zuccari in 1615–21. The beautifully decorated **Sala di Udienza del Collegio del Cambio** is one of the best preserved rooms of the Renaissance in Italy, famous for its **frescoes** by **Perugino**, perhaps his masterpiece. The work was carried out, with the help of pupils, including Andrea d'Assisi, and possibly also Raphael, in 1498–1500 (although a final payment was made to Perugino in 1507).

Perugino

The first great Umbrian painter, Pietro Vannucci, was born in Città della Pieve in 1446. He was called Perugino by his Florentine contemporaries because of his Umbrian background, but may not have visited Perugia until 1475. He spent his formative years in Florence in the workshop of Verrocchio with Leonardo da Vinci and his work shows the influence of Botticelli and Piero della Francesca. Famous in his lifetime, he was called to Rome in the 1480s to paint *Christ giving the keys to St Peter* in the Sistine chapel. His elegant graceful figures and spacious luminous landscapes greatly influenced his famous pupil Raphael. He has always been well known in England: in 1776 Oliver Goldsmith mentioned him in *The Vicar of Wakefield*. There are numerous paintings by him in the Galleria Nazionale dell'Umbria, and altarpieces by him in the city in the churches of San Pietro, Sant'Agnese, and San Severo. Other works by him can be seen all over Umbria, from his earliest dated work in the parish church of Cerqueto near Lago Trasimeno, to works in churches in Assisi, Spello, Foligno, Montefalco, Trevi, Panicale, Corciano, and in the museum at Bettona.

The frescoes here illustrate the ideal combination of Christian virtues with Classical culture in a scheme drawn up by the Perugian Humanist, Francesco Maturanzio. The ceiling has beautiful grotesques and medallions with pagan divinities. On the right of the portal is the figure of *Cato*, symbol of *Wisdom*. On the left wall is a lunette with *Prudence* and *Justice* seated above six standing figures of Classical heroes (all named). On the pilaster is a fine self-portrait by Perugino. The second lunette has the figures of *Fortitude* and *Temperance* seated above Classical heroes; the figure of Fortitude has been attributed to Raphael, then only 17 years old.

On the end wall, *Transfiguration* and *Nativity*, and on the right wall, the *Eternal Father* in glory above 12 figures of *Prophets* and *Sibyls*, perhaps the most successful composition in the room. The remarkable figure studies here include *Daniel*, thought to be a portrait of Raphael. The beautiful carved and inlaid woodwork is by Domenico del Tasso (1492) and Antonio Bencivenni da Mercatello (1508). In the niche is a gilded statue of *Justice* attributed to Benedetto da Maiano.

The **Cappella di San Giovanni Battista** is entirely frescoed with stories from the life of St John the Baptist by Perugino's pupil, Giannicola di Paolo (1515–18). The altarpiece is also by him. The woodwork is by Antonio Bencivenni da Mercatello.

The **Sala di Udienza del Collegio della Mercanzia**, is entered at no. 15 in the Corso (on the right of the main portal, see below). It is open 09.00–13.00, 14.30–17.30; PH 09.00–13.00; 1 Nov–19 Dec, and 7 Jan–28 Feb 08.00–14.00 except Mon (Wed and Sat also 16.00–19.00); PH 09.00–13.00; ☎ 075 5730366. The merchants' guild (still a charitable institution) has been housed here since 1390. Founded before the 13C, it was the most important guild in Perugia in the 14C. The vault and walls are entirely panelled with splendid carving and intarsia work, carried out during the early 15C by unknown craftsmen, showing Northern European influence.

Galleria Nazionale dell'Umbria

The main portal of Palazzo dei Priori was erected in the 14C and is beautifully carved. The outer pilasters, borne by lions, display the Perugian griffin, and in the lunette there are copies (made in 1993) of statues of Perugia's patron saints. The doors are original. The entrance hall has fine vaulting and a large 15C safe.

Stairs (or a lift) lead up to the third floor with the Galleria Nazionale dell'Umbria (**map 6,7**), founded in 1863 and moved here in 1879. It is the most important surviving collection of Umbrian paintings, and one of the finest galleries of paintings in Italy. It was reopened in 1997, but since the mezzanine floor was damaged in the 1997 earthquake some of the paintings there have been moved downstairs and the arrangement is therefore temporary.

Open every day 09.00–19.00 except the first Monday of the month. At certain periods, the gallery is only open 09.00–13.00 on PH. ☎ 075 5741247.

The **Sala Maggiore** was the hall of the the Consiglio Generale del Comune. It has been divided by screens into two halves: on the left are Rooms I–III (the present arrangement is to change). The carved, polychrome wooden statue of *Christ deposed* dates from the early 13C, and the detached frescoes from the convent of Santa Giuliana, and the churches of Santa Elisabetta alla Conca and San Francesco al Prato from the 14C. The bronze group of four fantastic animals and the remarkable bronze nymph (1278), both usually attributed to the circle of Giovanni Pisano, are restored **sculptures from the Fontana Maggiore** (see p. 62). The **sculptural fragments** by **Arnolfo di Cambio** (1278–81) were made for another public fountain.

The **Umbrian paintings of the late 13C** include a tabernacle with the *Madonna and Child* and stories of the *life of Christ;* a dossal by the Maestro di Farneto, a painted *Crucifix with St Francis in adoration*, and *Deposition, Entombment* and three *Saints*, all by the **Maestro di San Francesco** (1272); dossals by the Maestro di San Felice di Giano, and Vigoroso da Siena (signed and dated 1291), a tabernacle with painted doors by the Maestro della Sala dei Notari, and more 13C Crosses including one by the Maestro della Croce di Gubbio, painted on both sides.

Room IV displays **14C painting and sculpture**. The three *Saints* from the lateral doorway of Palazzo dei Priori are by Ambrogio Maitani. The exquisite *Madonna and Child* is by **Duccio di Buoninsegna**; Marino di Elemosina,

Madonna and Child with angels and saints; Ambrogio Maitani, a polychrome wooden statue of the *Madonna and Child*; a 14C Cross painted on both sides; Meo di Guido da Siena, a polyptych; works by the Maestro di Paciano and the Maestro dei Dossali di Montelbate; a detached fresco of the *Crucifixion* by Lorenzo Salimbeni; a polyptych from Pietralunga by Ottaviano Nelli; a dossal by a 14C painter from Spoleto; a stained-glass window of the Crucifixion; a painted Cross by the Giottesque school; a *Madonna and Child* with the *Crucifixion* by Puccio Capanna; a *Madonna and Child* by the Maestro della Madonna di Perugia; *Mary Magdalen and seven Saints* by the Maestro di Verucchio (Francesco di Rimini?).

The famous *polyptych of Sant'Antonio* is a splendid Renaissance work by **Piero della Francesca** (painted for the monastery of Sant'Antonio in Perugia probably around 1466–68). On either side of the *Madonna and Child* are *Sts Anthony of Padua* and *John the Baptist*, and *Sts Francis* and *Elizabeth of Hungary*. Above is an exquisitely painted *Annunciation* and, in the predella, *Miracles of St Anthony, St Francis* and *St Elizabeth*.

Room V contains works by Bartolo di Fredi and Taddeo di Bartolo (including the polyptych of *St Francis*). Room VI has three handsome doorways dated 1673 and works by **Gentile da Fabriano**, a *Madonna and Child* (an early work from San Domenico); a *Crucifix* by Lorenzo Salimbeni; and a 15C cassone in pastiglia. Room VII has works by Giovanni Boccati (called Giovanni di Pier Matteo), from Camerino (fl. 1445–80), including a very ruined *Pietà* (signed and dated 1479) and the *Madonna 'del Pergolato'*. Room VIII displays works by Bicci di Lorenzo. Rooms IX and X contain works by Bartolomeo Caporali, and Benedetto Bonfigli (including the beautiful *Gonfalon of St Bernardine of Siena*, dated 1465, an *Annunciation* with the charming figure of *St Luke*, and an *Adoration of the Magi*) and L'Alunno.

Room XI displays the *Miracles of St Bernardine of Siena*, eight exquisite small panels painted in 1473 with remarkable architectural details. They almost certainly decorated two sides of a niche which may have housed a statue of St Bernardine. Their attribution has been under discussion for a long time, and some scholars believe Perugino and possibly Francesco di Giorgio Martini were involved in their execution. This room also contains a terracotta high relief of the *Madonna and Child*, and a stone *Madonna* (c 1475), both by Agostino di Duccio. The painting of the *Adoration of the Magi* from the church of Santa Maria dei Servi is by Perugino, and that of the *Adoration of the Shepherds* by Bartolomeo Caporali.

Room XII has a case of Deruta ceramics dating from the 16C–18C. The **Cappella dei Priori** (Room XIII) was built in 1442–50. The majolica pavement is a modern reconstruction of one dated 1455. The carved stalls also date from the 15C. The **frescoes** of the lives of *Sts Ercolano and Louis of Toulouse*, the patron saints of Perugia, are by **Benedetto Bonfigli** (1454).

Room XIV displays an exqusite bronze bas-relief of the *Scourging of Christ* by **Francesco di Giorgio Martini**.

Room XV (the other part of the Salone, see room 1 above) has a number of fine works by **Perugino** including *St Jerome*, a lunette fresco of the *Adoration of the Shepherd*, the *Pala di Andreana Signorelli*, the *Transfiguration*, and *Mourners at the foot of the Cross* (on either side of a carved 15C German Crucifix), an *Ecce Homo* (1494), and *Pietà*. The *Pala di Santa Maria dei Fossi* is by Pinturicchio

(1495). The putti are by the workshop of Raphael. Below a painting of *God the Father*, is an *Entombment* by Cavalier d'Arpino, a copy of Raphael's *Deposition*, in the Galleria Borghese in Rome.

Room XVI has works by Sebastiano Conca and Giuseppe Maria Crespi.

The collection formerly exhibited in the *mezzanine* (at present closed) includes works by Valentin de Boulogne, Gian Domenico Cerrini, Luigi Pellegrino Scaramuccia, Pietro da Cortona (the *Birth of the Virgin* signed and dated 1643), Sassoferrato, Ludovico Mazzanti, Giovanni Odazzi, Sebastiano Conca, Francesco Trevisani, Corrado Giaquinto and Benedetto Luti. An early 17C German equestrian model in wood was made for a monument to Orazio Baglioni. The Carattoli collection, left to the gallery in 1894, includes portraits and a tiny landscape attributed to Paul Brill.

The collection also includes a beautiful *Madonna with angels and saints*, with a *Miracle* and the *Death of St Nicholas* in the predella (part of a triptych) by **Fra Angelico**, a *Madonna and Saints* by Benozzo Gozzoli (1456), both restored in 1999, and fine works by Eusebio da San Giorgio, Fiorenzo di Lorenzo, Lippo Vanni and Domenico di Bartolo.

The **16C works** not yet on view include paintings by Domenico di Paride Alfani, Giannicola di Paolo, Raffaellino del Colle, and Marcello Venusti. **Seventeenth century works** still to be arranged include paintings by Orazio Gentileschi, Pierre Subleyras and Antonio Amorosi. The sculpture includes a bronze statuette of a female allegorical figure attributed to Vincenzo Danti and a marble bust of Marcantonio Eugeni attributed to Francesco Mocchi. There is a good collection of **church silver** including 14C croziers, and a silver gilt chalice and paten, and reliquaries, all by Cataluccio di Pietre da Todi.

On the first floor (reached by two flights of stairs) is the **Sala del Consiglio Comunale** (sometimes unlocked on request; glass window in the door). The original bronze **lion** and **griffin** from the exterior of the palace (see below) have been placed here. On the inside, in a lunette above the carved portal, is a fresco of the *Madonna and Child with angels* commissioned from Pinturicchio in 1486 (his first documented work, and restored in 1998). For a long time this room was known as the Sala del Malconsiglio, named after the ill-advised consent of the Perugians to spare the lives of the English soldiers of Sir John Hawkwood (the famous *condottiere* who died in 1394 and was known in Italy as Giovanni Acuto), by whom they were later defeated in 1366.

The Fontana Maggiore

The Corso rises to end at the delightful **Piazza Quattro Novembre** (map 6), on a slope, with the famous **Fontana Maggiore** (restored in 1994–99). The fountain, one of the most important Romanesque monuments in Europe, was designed in 1278 by Fra' Bevignate, a Silvestrine monk who lived in Perugia. At the centre of the town, it is its main fountain, at the end of an aqueduct from Monte Pacciano, some 5km long and specially built by the Venetian hydraulic engineer Boninsegna. It has two polygonal marble basins decorated with exquisitely carved reliefs and statuettes by Nicola Pisano and his son Giovanni, which follow a carefully worked out scheme celebrating the glory of Perugia (each of them explained by a Latin inscription).

The lower basin has 25 double reliefs, separated by columns. Beginning on the side facing Palazzo dei Priori, the first 12 reliefs illustrate the *Labours of the Months* (with their signs of the zodiac):

January has two seated figures beside an open fire, the man holding a chicken and chalice, and the woman a loaf of bread and a wine jug.

February shows a fishing scene.

March a traveller extracting a thorn from his foot (derived from the Roman figure of the *spinario*) and a man pruning a tree.

April is represented by two garlanded Roman figures bearing branches and cornucopia.

May has a charming chivalrous scene with two figures on horseback: a lady with a falcon pursued by a knight with a bunch of roses.

June has a harvest scene with peasants reaping and scything.

July shows peasants at threshing time.

August is represented by a man and a woman with baskets picking figs.

September depicts the grape harvest.

October shows a man pouring wine into a barrel, while another one is repairing a barrel.

November shows ploughing and sowing.

December the butchering of a pig.

Beyond a relief of a lion and griffin, symbols of the town, are four double reliefs illustrating the Liberal Arts:

Grammar and *Dialectic*, with two seated female figures, one teaching a young pupil, and the other holding two serpents.

Rhetoric and *Arithmetic*, with scholars in attendance.

Geometry, taking measurements with a compass.

Music, with bells and a psaltery.

Astronomy and *Philosophy*, the two highest Arts, are both crowned and enthroned.

Beyond a double relief with two fine eagles, are scenes from the Old Testament: *Temptation* and *Expulsion from Paradise*; *Samson and the lion*, and *Samson and Delilah*.

The relief with a seated lion and a young lion (or puppy) being beaten is an allegory demonstrating the virtues of punishment.

The next panel depicts *David and Goliath* (the giant is shown dead), and the next *Romulus* and *Remus*, both seated and holding falcons.

The panels with the *Wolf feeding the twins* and the Roman Vestal Virgin *Dea Silvia* holding a large basket, are both copies.

The last relief illustrates two fables of Aesop: the *Crane and the Wolf* (the crane is extracting a bone caught in the wolf's throat), and the *Wolf and the Lamb*, showing the wolf on a rock about to devour a lamb.

The 24 statuettes around the upper basin (most of them by Giovanni Pisano) depict personifications of cities, personages from the Old Testament, saints and contemporary figures:

Perugia is shown enthroned holding a cornucopia, *Chiusi* presenting ears of corn, and *Trasimeno*, fish.

St Herculanus was bishop of Perugia in AD 547 and became her patron saint.

The *Traitor Cleric* opened the doors of the town to the enemy during Totila's seige in 547.

St Benedict is shown with two angels and his disciple Fra' Mauro kneeling.
St John the Baptist (holding a lamb); *King Solomon*; *David* holding a psaltery; *Salome* (with the splendid head of St John the Baptist); and *Moses*.
The next figure is a portrait of *Matteo da Correggio*, Podestà in 1278 (the date of the construction of the fountain).
The *Archangel Michael* has a fine classical head.
Euliste, shown holding a scroll, was the legendary founder of Perugia.
The figure of *Melchisedec* was substituted by a copy by Guglielmo Ciani in 1858.
The figure of *Ermanno da Sassoferrato*, Capitano del Popolo in 1278, is another portrait.
Victory is represented by a female figure holding a palm, and, beyond the bearded *St Peter* holding a key, is the *Roman Church*, an allegorical female figure holding a model of a church (the face is a modern substitute).
The seated crowned figure of *Rome* is a copy made in 1949.
Beyond *Theology*, a fine robed figure looking up to the sky, is *St Paul* holding a sword and a scroll.
The last two figures represent the *Cleric of St Laurence* and *St Laurence*, patron saint of the town, dressed as a deacon with a finely embroidered dalmatic.
The simple basin above supports three graceful bronze female figures holding an amphora thought to represent the three Virtues, also by the circle of Giovanni Pisano (to be replaced by a copy: the original is displayed in the Galleria Nazionale).

Sala dei Notari

In the piazza is the main façade of **Palazzo dei Priori** (see above), with copies of the bronze Perugian griffin and the Guelf lion, bearing chains, carried off from the gates of Siena by the Perugians after a victory at Torrita in 1358. The latest suggestion about the sculptures is that the wings of the griffin were added before 1281 to an Etruscan body and the new lion made at that time. To the right is a portico of three arches with fine medieval capitals, probably from the church of San Severo, destroyed to make room for the palace.

A charming flight of steps leads up to a Gothic portal, the entrance to the huge **Sala dei Notari** (open 09.00–13.00, 15.00–19.00; closed Mon except in June – Sept), one of the most impressive rooms in Italy, with remarkable vaulting. It was originally used for popular assemblies, and later as an audience hall by notaries of the city. It is now used for concerts and lectures. After 1860 Matteo Tassi covered the walls with the painted coats of arms of the podestà of the city from 1297 – 1424, but the most interesting decoration (difficult to see) is high up on the spandrels of the arches which bear frescoes of Old Testament scenes and fables by a close follower of Pietro Cavallini (1297).

On the opposite corner of the Corso is the mutilated **Palazzo del Collegio dei Notari** (15C), with attractive windows.

The Duomo

Along the upper side of the piazza is the flank of the **Duomo** (map 6), dedicated to San Lorenzo (closed 12.00–16.00), a Gothic building of the 15C, orientated towards the west with an unfinished façade on Piazza Danti.

Exterior The exterior of the south side, overlooking the fountain, has Gothic windows and 14C marble geometrical decoration. Here is an exterior pulpit buil for St Bernardine in 1425, a doorway by Galeazzo Alessi (1568), and a bronze statue of Pope Julius II, by Vincenzo Danti (1555, the year of the Pope's death). The elegant Loggia di Braccio Fortebraccio, of four arches on octagonal travertine columns, was built in 1423.

Interior The dark interior, imposing rather than harmonious, with aisles equal in height to the nave, has columns painted in imitation of impossible marble. Surrounded by a little altar, on a pillar of the nave, is the highly venerated *Madonna delle Grazie*, a beautiful painting attributed to Giannicola di Paolo. Above the west door, in an elaborate frame, is the *Madonna and Child with the patron saints of Perugia*, by Giovanni Antonio Scaramuccia (1616).

At the beginning of the south aisle, beside the tomb of Bishop Baglioni (d. 1451), attributed to Urbano da Cortona, is the **Cappella di San Bernardino**, closed by a fine wrought-iron screen (15C). It contains a magnificent *Descent from the Cross*, one of the best works of Barocci (1569), and a stained-glass window by Costantino di Rosato and Arrigo Fiammingo. The carved bench dates from the same time (1565).

The **baptistery** has carved marble decoration of 1477, a fresco of the *Baptism of Christ* by Domenico Bruschi (1876) and, above, stained-glass with the *Eternal Father*, also by Bruschi. The large wooden *Crucifix* is a 17C work by Christophe Fournier. The **Chapel of the Sacrament** is attributed to Galeazzo Alessi (the painting of the *Pentecost* by Cesare Nebbia is temporarily exhibited on the high altar). Since its restoration in 1994, the lovely *Pala di Sant'Onofrio* (the *Madonna enthroned with four saints and an angel musician*) by Luca Signorelli has been placed here. Beyond, on the nave wall, is the *Martyrdom of St Sebastian* by Orazio Alfani.

South transept. On the altar is Giovanni Baglione's *Martyrdom of St Stephen*. In the chapel to the right of the choir, there is an altarpiece by Francesco Appiani (1784). The bishop's throne (1520) and stalls of intarsia work by Giuliano da Maiano and Domenico del Tasso (1486–91) in the **choir** caught fire in 1985 and one-third were lost. The rest were removed for restoration and part has been completed and returned (sometimes shown on request by the sacristan). A painting of the *Pentecost* by Cesare Nebbia is temporarily exhibited on the high altar (see above).

In the chapel to the left of the choir is Ippolito Borghese's *Assumption* (1624). In the north transept is a 16C wooden *Crucifix*. In the north aisle are bas-reliefs (*Pietà* and *Eternal Father*) by Agostino di Duccio, and a gonfalon painted by Berto di Giovanni (with a lunette above by Giannicola di Paolo).

In the **Cappella del Santo Anello**, at the west end of the aisle, the supposed marriage ring of the Virgin Mary is preserved, stolen from Chiusi by the Perugians. It is kept in a chased and gilded reliquary (1498–1511) by Bino di Pietro and Federico di Francesco Roscetto, under 15 locks and is exhibited only on 29 and 30 July. The altarpiece of the *Marriage of the Virgin* is by Jean Baptiste Wicar (1825). The fine intarsia bench is by Giovanni Battista Bastone (1520–29).

In the **sacristy** (which has been closed for many years for restoration), on the right side of the choir, are frescoes of the *Life of St Laurence* by Giovanni Antonio Pandolfi da Pesaro (1578) and inlaid cupboards by Mariotto da Gubbio (1494–97). Here another door leads into the **cloister** which has antique and medieval sculptural fragments beneath the portico. Beyond is another cloister with four pretty loggias.

The **Museo dell' Opera** has also been closed for many years. It was founded in 1923 and contains works of art from the cathedral. The paintings include the *Redeemer and saints*, by Lodovico di Angelo and works by Meo di Guido, Bartolomeo Caporali, Andrea Vanni and others. There is also a valuable collection of illuminated manuscripts, breviaries, missals, graduals and antiphonals, as well as gold and silver reliquaries and other vessels.

At the end of Piazza IV Novembre is the 13C **Palazzo del Vescovado**, which has been rebuilt several times. Nearby is the bell-tower of the cathedral (1606–12), which replaced an octagonal Gothic campanile that was pulled down in 1462.

Via del Sole, San Severo and the Etruscan Well

From Piazza Danti on the upper side of the Duomo, **Via del Sole** (**map 6**) leads up into an ancient part of the town, the Rione di Porta Sole. Via delle Prome forks left to Piazza Rossi Scotti, where there is a fine view of an unspoilt valley. Below, near at hand, is Via Pinturicchio and a stretch of walls, and on the extreme right, the campanile of Santa Maria Nuova. To the left, the 18C façade of Palazzo Gallenga Stuart is conspicuous, and, on the edge of the hill, Sant'Agostino with its small octagonal tower. In the distance, on the skyline, is the pyramidal cupola of Sant'Angelo, and, to the left, Porta Sant'Angelo.

In the piazza is a fine, large palazzo housing the **Biblioteca Comunale Augusta** which owns a good collection of manuscripts and incunabula. Beside the church of **Sant'Angelo della Pace** (closed; by Galeazzo Alessi) steps lead down to Via Bartolo.

Via del Sole continues up to **Piazza Michelotti** (**map 6**), the highest point of the city (494m), built on the site of the medieval castle, and now surrounded by 17C houses. From the far right corner of the piazza an arched passageway leads downhill; to the left, a stepped lane leads up and then down beneath Gothic arches to emerge in the secluded Piazzetta Raffaello, with a few ilexes in a quiet corner of the old town. Here is the church of **San Severo** (**map 2**). According to tradition, in the 11C Camaldulensian monks built here, on the site of a temple of the Sun, a convent and church dedicated to Severus, Bishop of Ravenna. Both were rebuilt in the 15C, and in 1748–51 the church (now deconsecrated and usually closed) was given its present form. One chapel of the 15C church survives (entrance by the inconspicuous door to the right usually kept ajar: 10.30–13.30, 14.30–16.30 or 18.30; Sat & Sun 14.30–17.30; ☎ 075 5733864), with a celebrated **fresco** by **Raphael** (c 1505; his earliest work of the kind; restored in 1976), representing the *Holy Trinity with saints*. Having been called to Rome to begin work on the *Stanze* in the Vatican, he left it unfinished and beneath, in 1512, Perugino, already in decline, painted six other saints. The seated statue of the *Madonna and Child* in terracotta dates from the 15C or early 16C.

Nearby, in Via Bontempi, is the Etruscan **Porta Sole** (or Arco dei Gigli), mentioned by Dante. There are numerous short, narrow medieval streets worth exploring in this area. In Via Alessi is the church of **San Fiorenzo** (**map 3**), rebuilt in 1770, which contains a gonfalon by Benedetto Bonfigli. In Piazza Piccinino, which adjoins Piazza Danti (see above), is a Renaissance well-head (with the arms of the Sorbello family) and the church of the Compagnia della Morte by Bino Sozi (1575).

At no. 18 Piazza Danti is the entrance to an **Etruscan Well** (admission as for San Severo, see above), beneath Palazzo Sorbello. The well, at least 35m deep and some 5.6m in diameter, was constructed in the 3C BC and could contain about 430,000 litres of water, enough to supply all the inhabitants. From a window the remarkable vault constructed with blocks of travertine can be seen. Steps lead down past the seeping walls to a bridge over the well.

Via dei Priori and the Oratorio di San Bernardino

Via dei Priori (map 6) is an attractive old medieval street which descends steeply from Corso Vannucci through Palazzo dei Priori. In Via della Gabbia (right) medieval houses incorporated in Palazzo dei Priori can be seen. On the left is the church of **Sant'Agata**, which has been closed as a result of earthquake damage in 1997. It was built in 1290–1314 and preserves interesting remains of frescoes, including a *Crucifixion* by the late 14C Umbrian school.

Further on, on the right, is the grandiose Baroque church of **San Filippo Neri** (map 6), with a façade by Paolo Marucelli (1647–63). This church was also damaged in the earthquake. The high altarpiece completed by Pietro da Cortona (with the collaboration of Ciro Ferri) in 1661 has been kept in the first chapel off the south side since its restoration, as repair work is due to begin at the east end. It represents the *Immaculate Conception*, and the Virgin has a huge dragon beneath her feet. The frescoes in the nave (1762) are by Francesco Appiani, and those in the cupola (1730) by Francesco Mancini (where the four *Evangelists* are by Giovanni Andrea Carlone, 1668).

Via della Cupa diverges left. It leads down under several arches past (right) Via Deliziosa (where at no. 17 Perugino is supposed to have lived; plaque) to the Etruscan walls. Steps lead down to a little public park.

Via dei Priori continues down to another small piazza in which is the delightful miniature apse, surmounted by a bell-cote, of the church of **Santi Stefano e Valentino** (map 6). A chapel was founded here in the 10C, and the cosy interior now has two aisles, one of the 12C and one of the 14C. It contains 12C–13C fresco fragments, a painting of the *Madonna and saints* by Domenico Alfani, and a copy made in 1911 of a triptych by Alunno.

On Via dei Priori, beside the entrance to the escalators which descend to the car-parks in Viale Pellini and off Via Arturo Cecchi, is the church of the Scalzi (1718, by Alessandro Baglioni), closed indefinitely since the earthquake. Next to it rises the **Torre degli Sciri**, the only tall medieval tower (46m) left in Perugia (there were once some 500 towers in the town).

Beyond an archway in Via dei Sciri (left) is the handsome portal of the **Oratorio della Confraternità dei Disciplinati di San Francesco**. The interior (closed for restoration) contains 17C stuccoes and paintings by Giovanni Antonio Scaramuccia (1611). Beyond is a delightful little piazzetta surrounded by a medley of medieval buildings and the church of the **Madonna della Luce** (map 10), with an elegant façade of 1512–18. In the tiny interior the ceiling has a lovely circular fresco of the *Holy Father* by Giovanni Battista Caporali and a gilded wooden high altar with a fresco of the Madonna and saints by Tiberio d'Assisi.

The **Arco di San Luca** or Porta Trasimena, a gate opened in Etruscan times, has a fine tall Gothic archway. On the right of the Madonna della Luce is another church (closed) dedicated to **San Luca** by Bino Sozi (1586), owned by the Knights of Malta, whose headquarters is next door in a 15C palace with handsome square windows.

Beyond is the peaceful Piazza San Francesco, surrounded by green lawns. The **Oratorio di San Bernardino** (map 10) was erected by order of Fra Angelo del Toscano, the year after St Bernardine's canonisation in 1450 in commemoration of his preachings here in the piazza on numerous occasions between 1420 and 1440. The beautiful **façade**, rich in polychrome marbles, was decorated in 1457–61 with exquisite **bas-reliefs** by **Agostino di Duccio,** the most important 15C sculptural work in the town. In the lunette *St Bernardine* is shown in glory surrounded by angels, and in the tympanum is *God the Father*. Four little tabernacles bear statues of the *Angel Gabriel* and *Virgin Annunciate* and *Sts Louis of Toulouse and Ercolano*. Below the lunette are bas-reliefs with scenes of the *miracles of St Bernardine*. Around the portal, flanked by green marble pilasters, are six delicately carved panels illustrating Franciscan virtues: on the left, from top to bottom, *Charity, Poverty* and *Chastity*, and on the right from top to bottom, *Justice, Mortification* and *Obedience*. Six more panels on the outer face of the arch have beautiful groups of *angel musicians*.

In the stark **interior**, with pretty vaulting, a fine 4C early Christian sarcophagus from the crypt of San Francesco al Prato next door, serves as high altar. It was the tomb of Beato Egidio of Assisi, the third companion of St Francis who died in 1262. On the right are two more works from San Francesco: a good 16C copy by Orazio Alfani of Raphael's famous painting of the *Deposition* (now in the Galleria Borghese in Rome) which was commissioned for the Baglioni chapel in that church, and a gonfalon of 1464 by Benedetto Bonfigli showing the *Madonna protecting Perugia from the plague* of the same year. The pavement tomb of Fra Angelo del Toscano (d. 1453) has been placed on the left wall, it may also be by Agostino di Duccio. Behind the east end is the Oratory of Sant'Andrea which has a fine ceiling (1558).

The adjoining convent is now the seat of the Accademia delle Belle Arti, a 16C foundation. The **Museo dell'Accademia di Belle Arti** (closed since the earthquake; ☎ 075 5726562) has a fine Gipsoteca with one of the best collections in Italy of plastercasts of famous sculptures including the *Three Graces* by Antonio Canova (donated by the sculptor in 1820), and four rooms of paintings and prints (mostly 19C).

The large 13C church of **San Francesco al Prato** has a façade of unusual design (rebuilt in 1927). The church (where concerts are given in the summer) has suffered from landslides since the 18C, and, now it is open to the sky at the east end, is inhabited by birds. Beyond is the charming little 14C church of **San Matteo in Campo d'Orto** (closed) with a very tall façade, on top of which is a bell-cote. From here Via Pascoli winds downhill (with the new building of the University prominent across the hillside) to Via Sant'Elisabetta (see p. 70).

Via delle Volte and Piazza Cavallotti

The picturesque medieval **Via delle Volte** descends from Piazza IV Novembre to the former church of the **Maestà delle Volte** (1567–90), now closed. The handsome late 16C façade is by Bino Sozi. Inside is a beautiful fresco of the *Maestà* by an unknown 14C artist who is named after this work, the Maestro della Maestà delle Volte. The cupola has fine decorations by Niccolò Pomarancio (1568). Outside is a Gothic arch and a 13C tower-house on the corner of the pretty Via Antonio Fratti.

Via delle Volte continues downhill under a remarkably high-flying arch to **Piazza Cavallotti**. Excavations beneath the piazza have revealed foundations of Roman houses and a Roman road (sometimes open in the summer). In the adjoining Piazza is **Teatro Morlacchi** (**map 6**) built in 1780 by Alessio Lorenzini.

Arco d'Augusto

The Arco d'Augusto and Piazza Fortebraccio

From Piazza Danti behind the cathedral (see above) the narrow old **Via Ulisse Rocchi**, formerly Via Vecchia, so called to distinguish it from the Via Nuova which runs parallel, now Via Bartolo, descends steeply north to the so-called **Arco d'Augusto** (**map 6**), a noble gateway in which three periods of civilisation are represented. The Etruscan lower part dates from the 3C–2C BC; the upper part, with the inscription '*Augusta Perusia*', was added after 40 BC. It is flanked by two trapezoidal towers, one of which had a graceful Renaissance loggia added to it in the 16C.

Outside the arch is the busy **Piazza Fortebraccio** where numerous roads meet. It is dominated by **Palazzo Gallenga Stuart** which has a colourful façade built in 1740–58 by Pietro Carattoli based on a design by Francesco Bianchi. It was given a new wing in harmony with the 18C palace in 1935–37, and is now the seat of the Università per Stranieri.

The **Università per Stranieri** (**map 6**) was founded in 1925 for the promotion of Italian language, literature and culture abroad. In 1931 the university received a gift of $100,000 from the American F. Thorne Rider, to enlarge it. It contains a library (70,000 volumes) of Italian, English, French and German books. The university is open to students of all nationalities, and is one of the best known places in Italy for studying the Italian language. On the left of the Arco d'Augusto is the church of **San Fortunato** (closed), rebuilt in the 17C.

Via Pinturicchio, named after the artist who lived here, leads east out of the piazza to the 14C church of **Santa Maria Nuova** (**map 2**). The organ in the **interior** dates from 1584. On the second south altar is a gonfalon (in very poor condition) by Benedetto Bonfigli with a view of Perugia and its towers in the background. In the chapel to the right of the apse is a wooden sarcophagus of Braccio I Baglioni (1479). In the apse there are some fine carved stalls (1456). In the chapel to the left of the apse are frescoes by Vasari's ancestor, Lazzaro Vasari.

On the second north altar, there is a copy of a *Madonna and saints* by Perugino, made by Giuseppe Carattoli in 1822. In a chapel at the west end is a 16C fresco of the *Madonna enthroned*.

Near the church is the **Porta Pesa**, so called from the time when produce brought in from the country was weighed here. About 500m further on is the **Madonna di Monteluce**, which has a rose window and a double portal (13C) in its façade, and contains a marble tabernacle by Francesco Ferrucci (1487). Adjoining it is the Policlinico, the hospital of Perugia, whose buildings are spread over the east part of the Colle di Monteluce.

In the other direction from Piazza di Fortebraccio steps lead down beside the University for Foreigners to Via Goldoni which leads west into Via Sant'Elisabetta. Here, beyond the span of a narrow footbridge (once a 13C aqueduct), a modern building of the University (on the right) covers a monochrome **Roman mosaic (map 6)** (2C), with the story of Orpheus charming the wild beasts (open 08.00–20.00; Sat 08.00–13.00; closed PH). The main buildings of the **University**, founded in 1307, are in Via Fabretti (**map 5,6**) in what was once a monastery of Olivetan monks, who were suppressed by Napoleon. From Via Sant'Elisabetta Via Pascoli (left) winds up to the south-west past fields to Piazza San Francesco (see above).

Corso Garibaldi and the church of Sant'Angelo

From Piazza Fortebraccio (see above) the long, narrow **Corso Garibaldi (map 5)**, a peaceful medieval street, leads up out of the town along a spur towards Porta Sant'Angelo. It is lined with fine old houses and a number of convents. The park of Porta Sant'Angelo is just beyond the houses off the right side of the Corso. A short way along on the right is the church of **Sant'Agostino (map 5)**. It has an attractive pink and white chequered **façade**. In the18C **interior** by Stefano Canzacchi the first south chapel is a fine 16C architectural work by Francesco di Guido di Virio da Settignano with delicately carved details in pietra serena. On the altar is a fresco of the *Madonna delle Grazie* by Giannicola di Paolo. In the apse, the **choir** is finely carved and inlaid by Baccio d'Agnolo (1502). On the north side, beyond a chapel showing the influence of Sanmichele, the second chapel has an early 16C fresco of the *Madonna enthroned between two saints*, and the first chapel has frescoes by Pellino di Vannuccio (1387), including a *Crucifixion* and a *Nativity*.

The **Oratory of the Confraternity of Sant'Agostino** is entered from the piazza (it is sometimes shown on request by the sacristan of Sant'Agostino). It was beautifully decorated in the 17C, and has paintings by Mattia Battini, Giulio Cesare de Angelis and Bernardino Gagliardi.

The Corso continues uphill for some way past interesting houses. Opposite no. 126, with an outside staircase, Via del Canerino leads right to a little park outside the walls with a view over the valley. A short way beyond, Via della Pietra leads left to the former monastery of **San Benedetto** (now used as offices by the Regione), with a pretty little cloister and well. The church (admission sometimes on request) has a 16C majolica pavement, probably of Deruta manufacture.

On the right of the Corso, beyond the Benedictine convent of Santa Caterina (no. 179), the last building (no. 191) before the arch is the **Convent of Beata**

Colomba (ring for access). The Dominican nuns show the cell of the Blessed Colomba of Rieti (1467–1501) in which is a remarkable painting of *Christ carrying the Cross*, delicately painted in tempera on a very thin cloth, attributed to Lo Spagna. Also here are a charming 15C painting of the saint, and mementoes including her carefully preserved and labelled clothes, etc. In the church of the convent (to the left of the entrance), above a colourful scagliola altar is an interesting painting of *Christ and St Thomas*.

Just beyond the arch the delightful little church of **Sant'Angelo** (map 5) can be seen on the right, at the end of Via del Tempio. It is preceded by a pretty lawn with cypresses, in a peaceful corner of the town. The church is a remarkable circular building derived from Roman models, erected in the 5C as a temple dedicated to St Michael Archangel. In the beautiful **interior** the rotunda has a drum supported by a ring of 16 splendid **Roman columns** of different heights and varying materials. There were formerly four chapels forming a Greek-cross plan: only the semicircular Cappella del Crocifisso and one rectangular chapel survive. The drum was reduced in height in the 14C and the building restored in 1948. The altar is supported by a Roman column. A few frescoes survive from the 14C and 15C, and above a Roman pedestal is the *Madonna del Verde* (transferred to canvas), a 14C work.

Steps lead down from the garden past orchards to **Porta Sant'Angelo** (restored in 1989) rebuilt in 1326 by Lorenzo Maitani, with a tower of a castle built by Fortebraccio. Outside the gate beautiful countryside reaches up to the well-preserved medieval walls providing a remarkably unspoilt approach to the town. Nearby is the 13C church of **San Matteo degli Armeni**, with interesting 13C frescoes restored in 1998. Beyond, on a little hill, the **convent of Monte Ripido** (map 9) can be seen, founded in the 13C, with an 18C library.

In Corso Garibaldi a lane opposite Via del Tempio (see above) leads up to the **convent of Sant'Agnese** (map 5; ring for access, 09.00–11.00, 15.00–18.00). One of the sisters will show visitors a chapel with a fresco by Perugino of the *Madonna and Sts Anthony Abbot and Anthony of Padua*. Another delightful fresco by Eusebio da San Giorgio may not be viewed since it is in part of the convent which is occupied by a closed order.

Piazza Matteotti and Sant'Ercolano

Below Corso Vannucci, and parallel to it, is the long **Piazza Matteotti** (map 7), built in part on the foundations of Etruscan walls. Here is the impressive **Palazzo dell'Università Vecchia** built in 1453–1515 by Gasparino di Antonio and Bartolomeo Mattioli da Torgiano, seat of the University until 1811. Next to it is **Palazzo del Capitano del Popolo** (1472–81), another fine Renaissance palace, by Gasparino di Antonio and Leone di Matteo (1472–81). Both of these palaces are now occupied by the law courts.

An archway leads out on to a terrace (used as a street market) above the large produce **market** (1932; now partly closed and in a sad state), reached by stairs or lift. From here medieval arches some 15m high against the walls can be seen. A 14C loggia above them is being restored. There is a fine view from the terrace with the large church of San Domenico prominent on the right.

The church of the **Gesù** dates from 1571, although the upper part of the façade was completed in 1934. It contains frescoes by Giovanni Andrea Carlone (1621) and a carved ceiling. At the north end of the piazza is a characteristic narrow old street, **Via Volte della Pace**, which rises beneath a 14C portico. Opposite the law courts is the post office, built in 1913 by Osvaldo Armanni.

From Piazza Matteotti Via Oberdan descends and (left) the stepped Via Ercolano continues to curve under the Etruscan **Porta Cornea**, later the Gothic Arco di Sant'Ercolano. The polygonal church of **Sant' Ercolano** (**map 7**) is a very unusual building dating from 1297–1326 with tall, blind arcading, preceded by a double staircase (1607). The good Baroque interior (in very poor condition) follows the lines of the octagonal Gothic structure. It contains frescoes by Giovanni Andrea Carlone (1680) and in the apse is a good copy of an altarpiece by Perugino, and paintings by Mattiuccio Salvucci. A well-preserved Roman sarcophagus serves as the high altar. Above, Via Marzia skirts the Rocca Paolina and Porta Marzia, both described on p. 57, with the escalators that connect Piazza Partigiani with Piazza Italia.

Viale Indipendenza (**map 7**) is reached from Piazza Matteotti by Via Oberdan and Via Ercolano (see above). From here Corso Cavour descends past the flank of the old stone church of **San Giuseppe** (formerly Santa Croce) which contains a fresco of the *Madonna and saints* in a niche by the school of Bonfigli and a painting of the *Madonna of the Misericordia with St Sebastian*. The neo-classical **Tre Archi** (1842) were built beside a smaller arch in the Etruscan and Roman walls.

San Domenico

Beyond, in a small piazza with a 15C well-head is San Domenico (**map 8,4**), the largest church in Perugia (122m in length). It was founded in 1305 and rebuilt, after the collapse of the vaulting, by Carlo Maderno in 1632. The façade is unfinished. Part of the Gothic structure can be seen on the exterior. The Gothic campanile by Gasparino di Antonio (1464–1500) was lowered in the 16C.

Interior The interior is dominated by the huge stained-glass window at the east end. South aisle. In the fourth chapel, a relic of the earlier church, is a beautiful marble and terracotta dossal by Agostino di Duccio (1459) and his pupils, recomposed and finished later. It includes four statues in carved niches, and a seated statue of the *Madonna and Child* flanked by two kneeling angels in the lunette above. The frescoed decoration was carried out by Bernardo di Girolamo Rosselli da Firenze (1532). The painting around the statue of the *Madonna of the Rosary* is by Domenico Bruschi (1869). By the side door is a funerary monument with the terracotta effigy of Guglielmo Pontano (1555).

Chapels at the east end. In the second chapel on the right of the choir, there are 14C votive frescoes and an altarpiece of the *Martyrdom of St Peter Martyr* by Bonaventura Borghesi (1705). In the first chapel on the right of the Choir, there are vault frescoes by a follower of Taddeo di Bartolo, and a Gothic *Monument to the Blessed Benedict XI* (d. 1304) by the early 14C Umbrian school. On the right pilaster of the choir, there is a monument to Elisabetta Cantucci with a bust by Alessandro Algardi (1648). The high altar dates from 1720. The huge stained-glass **window** (23 x 9m) bears the signatures of Fra Bartolomeo di Pietro da Perugia and Mariotto di Nardo, and the date 1411, but it is thought that the upper part is a later work. It is the largest stained-glass window in Italy, except for those in the Duomo of Milan. The carved and inlaid choir stalls date from 1476.

On the left pilaster of the choir is the funerary monument of the Danti family, with a bust of the sculptor Vincenzo by Valerio Cioli. In the first chapel on the left of the choir, the vault has very ruined frescoes attributed to Allegretto Nuzi. The altarpiece of the *Circumcision* is by Giuseppe Berrettini. The tomb (1429), with the effigy of Bishop Benedetto Guidalotti, and two reliefs of female virtues, is attributed to Urbano da Cortona. The second chapel to the left of the choir has votive frescoes. In the north transept is an elaborate organ, begun in 1660.

North aisle. The fifth chapel has important fresco fragments (very damaged) attributed to the late 14C Umbrian school; in the fourth chapel, the altarpiece of the *Madonna and Child with two saints* is by Giovanni Lanfranco. The third chapel has a gonfalon painted by Giannicola di Paolo (1494); and the first chapel, a 17C wooden *Pietà* showing the influence of Michelangelo, and a detached 14C fresco in a tabernacle (removed). The marble font dates from the 14C. Benedict's robes are preserved in the sacristy.

Museo Archeologico Nazionale dell'Umbria

The convent of San Domenico now houses the Archivio di Stato and the Museo Archeologico Nazionale dell'Umbria (**map 4**; open every day, 09.00–19.00; PH 09.00–13.00; ☎ 075 5727141). The museum consists of two collections: the Etruscan-Roman section was founded in 1790 and housed in the University from 1812–1936; in 1946 the contents were installed here. The Prehistoric Collection, one of the most important of its kind, was founded with the collection of Giuseppe Bellucci, and was first exhibited in 1937. Since 1952 it has been combined with the Etruscan-Roman collection and displayed here. Special exhibitions sometimes remain on display for some years.

The fine **large cloister** has recently been restored. It was begun in 1455 by Leonardo Mansueti and completed in 1579. On display here are an inscription of the Augustan era, found in 1970 near Perugia, and four cippi with inscriptions set up in honour of Augustus when he authorised the rebuilding of Perugia. In a room off the cloister there is a sarcophagus with the myth of Meleagar dating from the early 2C AD, possibly by the Master of the column of Marcus Aurelius, found at Farfa Sabina, and a puteal (well-head) of the 2C AD with reliefs of Sabines, also from Farfa. Also here is a display of material found in the Cutu family tomb discovered in 1983 at Monteluce di Perugia. The tomb, in use from the Etruscan to the Roman period (3C–1C BC), contained a sarcophagus and 50 cinerary urns, some with polychrome decoration. Another room is to be opened to display all the Cutu material.

Off the third walk of the large cloister a room displays the restored **bronze statue of Germanicus** found (in numerous fragments) outside the walls of Amelia in 1963 and the subject of a long and complicated restoration. This splendid colossal statue represents a Roman prince of the Giulia Claudia family, with his elaborate armour including a finely decorated breast-plate. The head is a remarkably fine posthumous portrait.

A corridor on the right of the upper level of the large cloister leads to the **small cloister**. A room on the right, and one walk of the cloister, contains the collection of Mariano Guardabassi (1823–80) of Etruscan and prehistoric objects.

The prehistoric collection

Beyond, the prehistoric collection is displayed. Of particular interest are the discoveries made in 1928–29 at the site of Belverde, near the foot of Monte Cetona (see *Blue Guide Tuscany*). Off a corridor (with a view at the end of Assisi and

Monte Subasio, beyond orchards and fields, and a didactic display) are eight small rooms, topographically arranged with objects of flint and pottery illustrating the development of civilisation in Central Italy, from the Palaeolithic to the Neolithic Age. Other rooms to the right are used to exhibit restored works, including a bronze bench from Gubbio (2C BC), 6C BC finds from Spello, and a little cinerary urn of Annia Cassia (Augustan period).

At the other end of the corridor, steps lead up to the **salone**, which contains a fine display (starting with the right-hand cases) relating to the Bronze Age. It includes axes, daggers and other implements, objects in copper and bronze; material from the caves of Belverde; vases, some with geometrical decoration, bone implements, agricultural tools, bronze shields and discs, armlets, articles of household use and adornment, and a fine bronze sword. From the windows are good views of Perugia.

The Etruscan-Roman collection
At the foot of the steps and to the right is another corridor where the Etruscan-Roman Collection begins. In the first case in the corridor are Villanovan finds (8C BC) from recent excavations at Monteluce. The chronological order of the display continues in the rooms off the corridor to the left: room 1 contains a stele with the representation of two warriors (from Monte Gualandro) and an archaic sphinx from Cetona. Room 2. The large stone sarcophagus from the Sperandio necropolis north of Perugia was discovered in 1843. Made in Chiusi around 500 BC, the unusual front panel may represent a victorious return from battle (or perhaps a family moving to colonise a new part of the country). The circular cippus has fine bas-reliefs. Rooms 3 and 4 contain **bronzes** from Castel San Mariano, found in 1812 and dating from the 6C BC. These include beautiful plaques in relief which formerly decorated chariots. Room 5 contains bronzes from the necropolis of Monteluce (6C–4C BC), also found in the 19C, and red- and black-figure vases. In room 6 (the last room) there are 5C–4C BC bronzes from the necropolis of Frontone, and red-figure vases.

In the corridor are two more cases of material found near Perugia (Palazzone necropolis and Ponte San Giovanni) including a ceramic fragment with letters of the alphabet (6C BC?). On the other side of the corridor are the last five rooms (7–11) overlooking the small cloister. At the end of the corridor is a cippus in travertine, with the celebrated **Inscription of Perugia** of 151 words, one of the most important monuments of Etruscan epigraphy. Room 7 contains two red-figure vases of the 5C BC found near Perugia, and finds from the necropolis of Santa Giuliana. Room 8 has Hellenistic material from tombs near Perugia and bronzes from the necropolis of Santa Giuliana. In room 9 are finds from the tomb of Bettona, dating from the 2C BC up to the time of Tiberius; jewellery and bronzes, including a large bronze shield probably from Pila. Room 10 displays bronzes from the Crocifisso del Tufo necropolis in Orvieto, and room 11 contains a votive hoard from Colle Arsiccio, dating from the Archaic period up to the time of Constantine. The bronzes include an elongated stylised figurine of the 3C–2C BC. In the corridor is a terracotta statuette of a seated divinity, signed by the artist.

San Pietro
Corso Cavour leads to (300m) **Porta San Pietro**, which has a lovely outer façade by Agostino di Duccio and Polidoro di Stefano (1473). Beyond the gate, Borgo XX

Giugno continues along a narrow ridge for another 400m to the Benedictine church of San Pietro (beyond map 4), which has a graceful polygonal Gothic tower (rebuilt in 1463) crowned with a spire, a characteristic feature of the city and visible for many miles around.

The church belonged to a convent (the buildings are now used by the University's Faculty of Agriculture), founded at the end of the 10C by the monk Pietro Vincioli, who became the first Abbot. At the end of a short avenue is the portal which leads into the **courtyard**, both built by Valentino Martelli in 1614. Under the portico on the left is the entrance to the church. The carved doorway dates from the late 15C and has a lunette of the *Madonna with two angels* by Giannicola di Paolo. Two Romanesque arches with 14C–15C frescoes have been uncovered from the old façade of the basilica.

Interior The dark basilican interior (closed 12.00–15.00; lit on request), with ancient marble and granite columns, was transformed in the early 16C. It is entirely decorated with paintings of particularly high quality (but many of them are in very poor condition). The red and white tiled floor dates from 1614, and the fine carved and gilded ceiling from c 1554. In the nave are 11 large canvases by l'Aliense (1592–94). On the west wall are frescoes transferred to canvas by Orazio Alfani and Leonardo Cungi.

South aisle. At the beginning of the aisle is a *Madonna and two saints* attributed to Eusebio da San Giorgio and an *Assumption* by Orazio Alfani. Between the first and second altars: Giacinto Gemingnani, *Miracle of the Column*; second altar, Cesare Sermei, *Miracle of St Mauro* (1648). Between the second and third altars: Ventura Salimbeni, *David and angels*; third altar, Eusebio da San Giorgio (attrib.), *St Benedict*; Ventura Salimbeni, *Procession of St Gregory the Great*.

The fine **Chapel of St Joseph** (light on the left) was decorated in 1857 by Domenico Bruschi. The altarpiece is a copy from Raphael by Carlo Fantacchiotti. Above the door is an early 16C fresco, and on the right wall, a *Holy Family* by the 16C Florentine school. On the wall of the aisle is an amusing painting by François Perrier of *Samson*. On the wall opposite, there is a *Pietà* by the school of Sebastiano del Piombo. Above a door are three small paintings: the *Madonna and the young St John with a female saint*, attributed to Bonifacio Veronese, and two saints, copies from Perugino by Sassoferrato. Opposite, there is a *Virgin* by Giovanni Domenico Cerrini. On the aisle wall is a *Resurrection* by Orazio Alfani. Above the sacristy door are three small paintings by Sassoferrato and, opposite, Cerrini's *St John the Baptist*.

The **sacristy** (opened on request) has numerous interesting small paintings, including *five saints* by **Perugino** (1496; *St Scolastica*, stolen in 1916, was returned here in 1993), *St Francesca Romana and the angel* attributed to Spadarino, and a *Head of Christ* by Dosso Dossi. A fragment survives of the Deruta majolica pavement (1563). The bronze *Crucifix* is by Alessandro Algardi. The intarsia work is by Giusto da Fiesole and Giovanni da Incisa (1472). Also displayed here are illuminated choir-books (15C–16C).

In the **choir** are stone pulpits with reliefs by Francesco di Guido (1521) and thrones by Benedetto da Montepulciano (1556). The 16C high altar bears a ciborium of the early 17C. The **stalls**, among the finest in Italy, are richly inlaid and carved by Bernardino Antonibi and Stefano Zambelli, with numerous assistants (1526). A door (usually locked), at the end of the choir, inlaid by Fra Damiano (1536), a brother of Stefano, leads out onto a balcony from which there is a wonderful view of Assisi and Spello. The autograph of the poet Carducci (1871) is indicated.

At the end of the north aisle is a *Pietà with two saints* by Fiorenzo di Lorenzo (1469). The **Vibi chapel** was built in 1507 by Francesco di Guido. It contains a marble tabernacle attributed to Mino da Fiesole and, above, a lunette of the *Annunciation* frescoed by Giovanni Battista Caporali. In the nave there is a copy by Sassoferrato of Raphael's *Deposition*. The **Ranieri chapel** is also by Francesco di Guido. On the left wall is *Christ on the Mount* by Guido Reni. On the nave wall, Sassoferrato's, *Judith* is displayed opposite *Sts Peter and Paul* by the school of Guercino. In the 18C **Cappella del Sacramento** are three paintings by Vasari. In the nave is Eusebio da San Giorgio's, *Adoration of the Magi*; the *Assumption* by Orazio Alfani is on the third altar and on the second altar is a wooden *Crucifix* of 1478. Between the second and first altars there is a *Pietà*, a late work by Perugino.

The former **convent** buildings include a large cloister and a staircase by Francesco di Guido and a small cloister by Galeazzo Alessi (1571). Outside the refectory is a lavabo by Benedetto Buglioni (1488). There is a recently planted **botanical garden** beyond the cloisters run by the Faculty of Agriculture (open on request).

From the **Giardino del Frontone**, on the other side of the road, there is another fine view in the direction of Foligno. Outside the **Porta San Costanzo**, dating from 1587 when the Roman road was diverted and the old medieval gateway was enclosed within the boundaries of the hanging garden of the monastery, is the church of San Costanzo (1143–1205), partly rebuilt and decorated by Leo XIII, who was Bishop of Perugia before his election to the Holy See in 1878.

BEYOND PERUGIA

There are many interesting places within the immediate environs of Perugia. The Ipogeo dei Volumni is one of the most impressive Etruscan tombs known (although it is unfortunately in very unattractive surroundings now). Torgiano is well worth visiting for its fine wine museum, and Deruta has a large new museum dedicated to ceramics, for which the town is famous. Corciano is a pretty medieval hill town.

Practical information

Information offices
IAT di Perugia, 3 Piazza IV Novembre, Perugia, ☎ 075 5736458. A tourist office is open in the Commune of Corciano (☎ 075 5188255)

Getting there
Ipogeo dei Volumni is in the unattractive busy suburb of **Ponte San Giovanni**, about 5km east of Perugia. By **car** the Ipogeo is not simple to find: it is best reached from the old road to Foligno which starts outside Porta San Costanzo beyond the church of San Pietro. Just before Ponte San Giovanni (also reached by an exit from the Perugia *superstrada*) the entrance to the tomb is right beside a railway crossing. By **bus** from Perugia (Largo Cacciatori degli Alpi) there is an

infrequent service, about three times a day for Ponte San Giovanni; the driver will stop at the tomb on request.

Torgiano is 14km south of Perugia (**bus** from Piazza Partigiani in about 35mins).

Deruta is 5km south of Torgiano. **Buses** from Piazza Partigiani in Perugia (30mins). The Ferrovia Centrale Umbra from the Stazione Ponte San Giovanni in Perugia to Terni has a station at Deruta (about 5km from the centre).

Corciano, 10km west of Perugia, is on the old road to Magione and Lago Trasimeno (N75bis) which leaves Perugia near the railway station. It can also be reached by the superstrada for Lago Trasimeno which has an exit for Corciano.

Hotels

Torgiano ☆☆☆☆☆ *Le Tre Vaselle*, ☎ 075 9880447; fax 075 9880214. Owned by the Lungarotti family who produce wines (now among the best known in Umbria)

on their extensive estate here, and also run the Wine Museum. It is a large hotel in a number of buildings in the centre of the peaceful little village, with numerous facilities, including outdoor and indoor swimming-pools, gym, sauna and congress centre, as well as a restaurant.

Castel del Piano 14km west of Torgiano, officially categorised as *agriturismo*, *Villa Aureli*, ☎ 075 5140444; fax 075 5149408. A grand country villa, with lovely apartments to rent (see p. 115).

Casaglia about 3km east of Perugia towards Ponte San Giovanni: ☆☆ *Stella*, 47 Via dei Narcisi, which has a good restaurant, ☎ 075 6920089.

Restaurants

Casaglia £ *Stella*, see above. At **Torgiano**, £££ *Le Tre Vaselle*, see above.

Corciano £££ *Ottavi*, 10 Anita Garibaldi, Località San Mariano (near Strozzacapponi), ☎ 075 774718.

The Ipogeo dei Volumni

The Ipogeo dei Volumni (open 09.30–12.30, 16.30–18.30; winter 09.30–12.30, 15.00–17.00; PH 09.30–12.30, ☎ 075 393329), one of the finest Etruscan tombs known, is in a very disappointing setting, right beside the railway crossing and the Perugia bypass. Discovered in 1840, it dates from somewhere between the second half of the 2C and the mid 1C BC. There is a splendid display of Etruscan urns, mostly in travertine, found in the nearby necropolis of Palazzone on either side of the very steep flight of stairs down to the entrance to the tomb, beside which is the huge travertine slab which served as a door. On the right-hand door post is an Etruscan inscription relating to the construction of the tomb.

The tomb itself is in the form of a Roman house with atrium, tablinum, and two wings. The ceiling of the atrium imitates a wooden roof, and above the entrance are two dolphins and a shield in relief. At the end is the tablinum with a Medusa's head carved in the ceiling. Here are six cinerary urns in travertine covered with stucco containing the ashes of the Volumni family. In the centre is that of Arunte Volumnio with the figure of the defunct on a bed resting on a plinth with two winged demons. The urn, in the form of a seated lady in the Roman style, is that of the daughter of Arunte. The seventh urn, in marble, is later and imitates the form of a building. It bears an inscription in Latin and Etruscan of the early Imperial era. The side cells are empty but two of them have coffered ceilings with Medusa heads hewn out of the rock, and one of the cells on the right has two owls in relief.

There is another Etruscan tomb in the western suburb of Perugia known as **Ferro di Cavallo**, where the little church of San Manno is situated (it has remains of 13C frescoes). The **Ipogeo di San Manno** (owned by the Knights of Malta; admission only with special permission), has a spacious vault faced with travertine slabs and an arched ceiling. The Etruscan inscription states that this tomb belonged to the Precu family. There is a large children's amusement park called **Città della Domenica** in the vicinity.

The **Ipogeo di Villa Sperandio** (also privately owned), in Via Sperandio outside Porta Sant'Angelo (see p. 71), is another vaulted Etruscan tomb discovered in 1900.

Torgiano

Torgiano, is a pleasant small village situated between the Tiber and Chiascio rivers, famous for its wine. Simple traditional pottery is also made here (still sold in a few potteries on the outskirts). At the upper end of the Corso is the church with a detached campanile. It contains numerous devotional statues, including the *Assunta*, fully robed. On the left side are a *Deposition* by Felice Pellegrini (1588), and a *Pentecost* signed by D. Finitia Gabrielis.

At no. 11 in the Corso, beside a wine shop and a pretty garden, is a **Wine Museum** (open 09.00–13.00, 15.00–18.00; summer 09.00–11.00, 15.00–19.00; ☎ 075 9880200) owned by the Fondazione Lungarotti. The exhibits are excellently displayed and labelled (also in English) in the cool cellars of the 17C Palazzo Baglioni. This particularly interesting collection displayed in 20 rooms illustrates the history of wine. To the left room I illustrates the origins of viticulture, with archaeological material including an Attic kylix from Vulci and Roman amphorae. Room II shows documents relating to wine in the Middle Ages. Rooms III and IV are devoted to the cultivation of vines, including agricultural tools and a wine-press. Downstairs room V illustrates wine-making.

The production of Vin Santo is shown in room VI and the craft of cask-making in room VII. In room VIII (behind room IV) are documents relating to legislation and the commerce of wine. Rooms IX and X contain handicrafts made in Torgiano. Rooms XI–XIII have a fine display of Italian majolica (including Faenza, Montelupo and Deruta ware). Beyond room XIV, which illustrates the importance of wine in mythology, stairs lead up to the last six rooms which contain waffle irons (*cialde* were always eaten with Vin Santo), engravings from the 17C–20C, ex libris decorated with vines and books on agriculture, etc.

On the west side of the Tiber and the Todi road is **San Martino in Campo** where a chapel called La Madonnuccia contains frescoes by the school of Perugino.

Deruta

Deruta, situated on a low hill (218m), is famed for its majolica which is still made in great quantity in modern factories in the new town below and sold in numerous shops in the old town.

The former convent of San Francesco now houses the **Museo Regionale della Ceramica** (open July, Aug, & Sept 10.00–13.00, 15.30–19.00; April, May and June, 10.30–13.00, 15.00–18.00; Oct–March 10.30–13.00, 14.30–17.00 except Tues. ☎ 075 9711000). The museum, with an impressive modern display on three floors, has recently been opened to illustrate the history of the production of Deruta ceramics from the 14C to the 19C.

On the ground floor (room 1) earthenware domestic pottery and (room 2) 20C painted majolica are displayed, and (room 5) 14C archaic majolica. On the first floor room 6 displays the majolica pavement of the church of San Francesco in Deruta (1524). The second floor has the most interesting exhibits, with Renaissance works in room 8, including lustre ware and painted plaques with sacred images (room 10). Deruta ware produced in 1920–50 from the Milziade Magnini collection (displayed in their attractive original show-cases made in the 1930s) is displayed in room 13, and (room 14) pharmacy jars and albarellos (15C–19C). The huge deposits can be seen from balconies on all three levels of the building.

The church of **San Francesco** contains 14C and 15C frescoes.

The **Pinacoteca** in Palazzo Comunale was reopened in 1999 (adm. as for the Museo della Ceramica). It contains works by Baciccia and L'Alunno (*Madonna and Child*, 1453, and a gonfalon). A beautiful detached **fresco** dated c 1478 from the church of San Francesco by Fiorenzo di Lorenzo has a view of Deruta with *Sts Roch and Romano* (the head is attributed to Perugino). Later works include portraits by Antonio Amorosi (1660–1736) and two small works by Francesco Trevisani.

The church of the **Madonna di Bagno**, 3km outside the town, on the Todi road, has a remarkable collection of 17C and 18C ex votos in majolica.

Corciano

The picturesque and well-kept medieval village of Corciano, which now has only about 100 families, has well-preserved walls and a 13C castle. There is a car-park outside the walls near the large church of **San Francesco** (ask locally for the key) which contains a small collection of paintings, including a *Madonna enthroned with Saints* by Melanzio and a late 16C wooden polychrome statue of *St Bernardine*. Steps lead up to the main street which passes a piazza (recently modernised) in front of the town hall, which was the summer residence of the Della Corgna dukes (adm. on request). It has a painted 16C wooden ceiling by the school of Zuccari.

The road continues up (the buildings of interest are marked with discreet ceramic signs) past the tiny **Palazzo dei Priori** and a garden with four terracotta busts of poets by Francesco Biscarini (1860). Beyond is **Santa Maria** with an isolated campanile built in 1864 onto a medieval tower. The church contains a very unusual gonfalon by Benedetto Bonfigli, with the *Madonna of the Misericordia* and a view of Corciano below, and (over the high altar) a late work by Perugino (*Assumption*; 1513). A little further up the hill is the chapel of **San Cristoforo**, with a little museum next door relating to rural life (for admission enquire at the Comune).

At **Pieve del Vescovo**, 2km north of Corciano, is a huge conspicuous 14C castle (now in an abandoned state) restored in the 16C by Galeazzo Alessi when the wall and monumental windows were added.

Further north is **Colle Umberto I**. Nearby (not signposted), off the new fast road to Umbertide, is the **Villa di Colle del Cardinale** with a splendid gateway. The villa is now owned by the state but is not yet opened to the public (☎ 075 5741273). It was built in 1580 to a design by Galeazzo Alessi for Cardinal Fulvio della Corgna, and is especially interesting for its very fine 16C **garden**.

ASSISI

• • • • • •

Assisi, on a commanding spur of Monte Subasio (360–505m), is a little medieval town (population 3000) which has retained its beautiful rural setting with olive trees and cultivated fields reaching right up to its walls. St Francis of Assisi, one of the most fascinating characters in history, founded his Order here. In the great Basilica begun two years after his death, the story of his life provided inspiration to some of the greatest painters of his time including Cimabue, Giotto, Simone Martini and Pietro Lorenzetti. The impressive and moving frescoes here are among the most important works of art in Italy. In this century Assisi has become one of the most famous religious shrines in the world; it is uncomfortably crowded in spring and summer when it is given over to the reception of hundreds of thousands of visitors (four to five million people visit Assisi every year). In the winter months the town, which is slowly becoming depopulated, retains its quiet medieval character: at this time its famous Basilica, as well as its Roman remains, beautiful churches and picturesque streets can be appreciated to the full.

It was one of the worst-hit towns in the earthquake in 1997 and the upper church of San Francesco was the most seriously damaged monument of major importance in the whole region. The vaults in two bays of the nave, with frescoes by Cimabue and attributed to Giotto crashed to the ground. The upper church had to be closed but was reopened in November 1999, after the vault and façade had been beautifully restored. The lower church was closed for just two months, but no serious damage was found. Other badly damaged churches in the town include San Pietro, San Rufina, and Santa Chiara. Most of the gates were also severely shaken and are still covered with scaffolding. However, life for the inhabitants of the town is now more or less back to normal and the shops have been reopened. The Istituto Serafico, on Viale Marconi at the entrance to the town, founded in 1871, which houses and educates young blind people with severe handicaps, had to be evacuated in 1997 and is still operating in a prefabricated village installed beside the damaged building.

Practical information

Information office

IAT, Piazza del Comune, ☎ 075/812534.

Getiing there

By car The prettiest approach is by the direct straight road (N147) from Perugia via Bastia Umbria which provides splendid views of the pale pink-and-grey stone buildings of Assisi beneath its ruined castle, as it runs through the fields at its foot. It climbs up round the northern spur of the hill on which the huge convent around the church of San Francesco is built. At a junction beneath the walls, Viale Marconi continues left for the car-park (A) nearest to San Francesco outside Porta San Pietro, while Viale Vittorio Emanuele skirts the walls in the opposite direction to the other car-parks.

Car parking The movement and parking of vehicles within the walls are limited to certain times of the day. Visitors are strongly advised to leave their cars outside the walls, but the only large free car-park (with facilities also for campers) is at the cemetery off Viale Albornoz (connected to the centre by minibus 'B'). Another small free car-park is near the Istituto Serafico, off Via

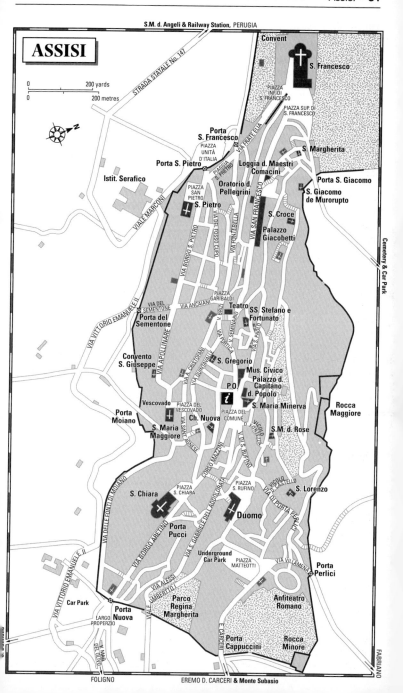

ASSISI

S.M. d. Angeli & Railway Station, PERUGIA

0   200 yards
0   200 metres

STRADA STATALE No. 147

Convent

S. Francesco

PIAZZA INF. DI S. FRANCESCO

PIAZZA SUP. DI S. FRANCESCO

Porta S. Francesco

VIA FRATE ELIA

S. Margherita

PIAZZA UNITÀ D'ITALIA

Porta S. Pietro

Porta S. Pietro

PIAZZA S. PIETRO

Loggia d. Maestri Comacini

Porta S. Giacomo

Istit. Serafico

PIAZZA SAN PIETRO

Oratorio d. Pellegrini

S. Giacomo de Murorupto

VIALE MARCONI

S. Pietro

VIA DEL FOSSO CUPO

VIA SAN FRANCESCO

S. Croce

Palazzo Giacobetti

VIA BORGO S. PIETRO

VIA FONTEBELLA

Cemetery & Car Park

VIA DEL SEMENTONE

PIAZZA GARIBALDI

VIA ANCAIANI

Teatro

VIA BRIZI

VIA SEMINARIO

SS. Stefano e Fortunato

Porta del Sementone

VIA VITTORIO EMANUELE II

VIA APOLLINARE

VIA PORTICA

VIA S. PAOLO

Convento S. Giuseppe

VIA A. CRISTOFANI

VIA SAN RUFINO

S. Gregorio

Mus. Civico
Palazzo d. Capitano d. Popolo

Vescovado

PIAZZA DEL VESCOVADO

P.O.

S. Maria Minerva

Rocca Maggiore

Porta Moiano

Ch. Nuova

PIAZZA DEL COMUNE

VICOLO S. FORTEZZA

S.M. d. Rose

S. Maria Maggiore

VIA SANT'AGNESE

CORSO MAZZINI

VIA DI S. RUFINO

PIAZZA S. RUFINO

S. Lorenzo

S. Chiara

PIAZZA S. CHIARA

Duomo

VICOLO CASTELLO

VIA DI PORTA PERLICI

VIA DELLE FONTI DI MOIANO

VIA BORGO ARETINO

VIA S. GABRIELE DELL'ADDOLORATA

Porta Pucci

Underground Car Park

PIAZZA MATTEOTTI

VIA VILLAMENA

Porta Perlici

VIA VITTORIO EMANUELE II

Car Park

VIA ALESSI

VIALE UMBERTO I

Parco Regina Margherita

Anfiteatro Romano

LARGO PROPERZIO

Porta Nuova

VIA DEL COLLE

Porta Cappuccini

Rocca Minore

FOLIGNO

EREMO D. CARCERI & Monte Subasio

VIA E. CARCERI

FABRIANO

Vittorio Emanuele II.

The three most central car-parks (signposted 'A', 'B' and 'C', all with an hourly tariff) are in **Piazza Unità d'Italia** (**A**), limited space, outside **Porta Nuova** (**B**), with an escalator up to Via Borgo Aretino (and minibus service 'A' via Santa Chiara to Piazza del Comune), and the underground car-park in **Piazza Matteotti** (**C**), with minibus service 'A' to Piazza del Comune. There is another car-park near **Porta Moiano**, with an hourly tariff, with minibus service 'B' to San Francesco, Santa Chiara and Piazza del Comune.

By rail At Santa Maria degli Angeli, 5km south-west of the town on the Terontola – Perugia –Foligno branch line (slow trains only). From Perugia (25mins); from Terontola (c 1hr). Bus c every half hour from the station to Piazza Matteotti via Largo Properzio and Piazza Unità d'Italia.

By bus and coach There are frequent bus services run by *APM* (☎ 075 5731707) from Perugia (50 mins). Long-distance coaches (run by *Sulga*, ☎ 075 5009651) terminate in Piazza San Pietro once a day from Florence (2hrs 40mins) and twice a day from Rome Tiburtina (3hrs).

Buses run from Piazza Matteotti to Santa Maria degli Angeli, via the railway station, every half hour (c 20mins).

Getting around

Town buses Two circular minibus services (**A** & **B**, see above) run through the town, and provide excellent views.

There are numerous bus services to and from destinations in the environs and Umbria and Tuscany, including Gubbio, Foligno and Spello, Bettona, Cannara and Bastia Umbra.

Bus services run from Santa Maria degli Angeli to Norcia, Cascia and Siena.

Hotels
☆☆☆☆ *Subasio*, 2 Via Frate Elia, ☎ 075 812206; fax 075

816691, open all year, and the only ☆☆☆☆ hotel in the town. Opened in 1868 it still has an old-fashioned atmosphere and décor and is the closest hotel to the Basilica of San Francesco. It has some suites, but since it has 70 rooms it also takes groups. It has a good terrace restaurant (half-board or full-board terms).

☆☆☆ *Umbra*, 6 Via degli Archi, ☎ 075 812240; fax 075 813653. A pleasant small secluded old-established hotel just off Piazza del Comune (25 rooms; the ten overlooking the plain are the largest), with spacious public rooms and several small terraces. Meals are served under the pergola in the charming little garden in warm weather.

☆☆ *Pallotta*, 4 Via Santa Rufina, ☎ & fax 075 812307. A family-run hotel in a very quiet part of the town, with just seven rooms (all with bathrooms), most of them with charming views. Solidly converted ten or so years ago with anti-seismic refinements, it has a tiny public room in a tower with a remarkable panorama of the town. Breakfast is not usually available but the same family run an excellent simple restaurant next door.

There are many other hotels in Assisi, some of which close in winter, and numerous **convents** and **monasteries** of every nationality also provide hospitality (minimum stay two nights; list and information from the IAT office).

In the environs On Monte Subasio, at Armenzano (12km east of Assisi) ☆☆☆☆ *Le Silve*, ☎ 075 8019000; fax 075 8019005.

Youth hostels
Della Pace, 177 Via di Valecchie, San Pietro Campagna, ☎ 075 816767, a particularly good hostel. Also **Fontemaggio**,Via Eremo delle Carceri, ☎ 075 813636 and *Victor*, 102 Via Sacro Tugurio, ☎ 075 8065562;

Campsites
☆☆☆ *Internazionale*, 110 Via San

Giovanni Campiglione, ☎ 075 813710 (open April–Oct);

✸✸ *Fontemaggio*, 8 Via Eremo delle Carceri, ☎ 075 813636.

Restaurants
**£££ *Da Alberto (Medioevo)*, 4 Via Arco dei Priori, ☎ 075 813068; *San Francesco*, 50 Via San Francesco, ☎ 075 812329. **££ *La Fortezza*, 26 Vicolo della Fortezza, ☎ 075 812418. **£ *La Rocca*, 27 Via Porta Perlici, ☎ 075 816467; *Pallotta*, 4 Via San Rufino, ☎ 075 812649.

Pasticceria
Bar Sensi, 14 Corso Mazzini.

Picnics
Beautiful picnic places can be found in the vicinity of Assisi. On Monte Subasio, above the Hermitage of the Carceri on the road across the summit towards Collepino, or on the road along the side of the hill (signposted San Benedetto); or on the hillside around the Rocca Maggiore.

Market day is on Saturday in Piazza Matteotti.

Note You are not allowed inside churches in Assisi in shorts or with bare shoulders.

Festivals
Annual festivals connected with St Francis with processions and liturgical ceremonies are held in Easter Week, Ascension Day, Corpus Domini, 22 June (Festa del Voto), 1–2 August (Festa del Perdono), 12 August (Festa di San Rufino), 11 August (Festa di Santa Chiara), 3–4 October (Festa di San Francesco), and at Christmas. A medieval pageant (when the town divides into two parts) known as the 'Calendimaggio' is held on the first Thursday, Friday, and Saturday after 1 May to celebrate the arrival of spring. An Antiques Market is also held in late April and early May.

History

An Umbro-Etruscan settlement here became the important Roman town of Asisium. Sextus Propertius (c 46 BC–c AD 14), the elegiac poet, was probably a native of Assisi, and his house is supposed to have been that discovered beneath the church of Santa Maria Maggiore. The town was evangelised by St Rufino, who was martyred here in 238. Later, under the dominion of the Dukes of Spoleto, it became a republic in 1184. It was famous in the 12C as the birthplace of St Francis. It flourished from the 13C, but at the end of the 14C was captured by Perugia, and from then until the 16C it was involved in numerous wars with neighbouring towns in the struggle between the Guelfs and the Ghibellines. It passed to the church in the 16C. After the Council of Trent it lost much of its religious significance as the shrine of St Francis.

In 1786 Goethe described his walk up to Assisi from Santa Maria degli Angeli when he 'turned away in distaste from the enormous substructure of the two churches on my left, which are built one on top of the other like a Babylonian tower, and are the resting-place of St Francis', in order to proceed directly to the temple of Minerva, the 'first complete classical monument' he had ever seen.

In 1818 the coffin of St Francis was rediscovered and a new interest in the saint developed. Assisi has become increasingly famous as a centre of pilgrimage in this century: in 1982, the anniversary of the saint's birth, some five million pilgrims visited Assisi.

St Francis of Assisi

St Francis of Assisi (1181–1226) was the son of a rich merchant, Pietro Bernardone, the husband of Pica (perhaps de Bourlemont, a Provençal). He was baptised Giovanni, but his father, who at the time was trading in France, called him Francesco. At the age of 24, after a year's imprisonment at Perugia, followed by an illness, he changed his way of life. He gave all he had to the poor, looked after the sick, and led a humble, exemplary life. He extended his devotion to animals and birds. As he was praying in San Damiano he heard a voice telling him to 'Rebuild my Church', and in the Chapel of the Porziuncola he heard the command 'Freely you have received, freely give'. He retreated with some followers to a stable in Rivotorto, and then settled in a hut around the Porziuncola. He and his companions also stayed on Monte Subasio in prayer and meditation.

In May 1209 he obtained from Pope Innocent III the verbal approval of his Order founded on a rule of poverty, chastity and obedience. He preached his gospel in Italy, Spain, Morocco, Egypt (1219), where the Sultan Melek-el-Kamel received him kindly, and in the Holy Land. In 1221 the Franciscan Rule was sanctioned by Pope Honorius III, and three years later Francis himself retired to La Verna. On 14 September 1224 he had a vision of a seraph with six wings and found on his own body the stigmata or wounds of the Passion. He returned to Assisi and died at the Porziuncola on 3 October 1226. St Francis was canonised on 16 July 1228 and became a patron saint of Italy in 1939. The Franciscan Order has various divisions: the first, a religious order divided into four families (Friars Minor, Conventuals, Capuchins and Tertiary Religious Order); the second, the Poor Clares, and the third, a secular Order of Tertiary lay brothers.

St Clare (Chiara), the daughter of a rich family, disciple of St Francis, and foundress of the Poor Clares, was born at Assisi in 1194, and died in her own convent in 1253.

Among famous painters who came to work here in the basilica of San Francesco in the 13C–14C were Cimabue, Giotto, Pietro Lorenzetti and Simone Martini. In the 15C Andrea d'Assisi (L'Ingegno) and Tiberio d'Assisi, both pupils of Perugino, were born here. Other native artists include Dono Doni (d. 1575) and the painter and architect Giacomo Giorgetti (1603–79). Cesare Sermei (1581–1668) worked here most of his life.

The Basilica of San Francesco

The two-storeyed Basilica di San Francesco, the principal monument to the memory of St Francis, contains a magnificent series of frescoes.

On his death St Francis was interred in the church of San Giorgio, now included as a chapel in the Basilica of Santa Chiara. A fund for a memorial church was started in April 1228, and its foundation stone was laid by Pope Gregory IX the day following the canonisation ceremony. Frate Elia, close friend and follower of St Francis and Vicar-General of the Franciscans, took an active part in the construction of the church and it is thought that he may himself have been the architect; the work has also been attributed to Filippo da Campello, Giovanni della Penna

The Basilica of
San Francesco

and Lapo Lombardo. The lower church was soon ready and on 25 May 1230 the
tomb of St Francis was transferred there. The completed church was consecrated
by Innocent IV in 1253. The beautiful tall campanile dates from 1239.

- **Opening times** The lower church is open 06.30 to dusk in summer but is
  closed 12.30–14.00 in Jan & Feb. The east end of the lower church is illuminated from 09.00–12.30, 14.00–17.00; otherwise the lighting is poor and it
  is difficult to study the frescoes in the other chapels in detail (binoculars are
  useful). On public holidays the lower church can only be visited 14.00–16.00
  (when the frescoes are illuminated), although the tomb of St Francis is open all
  day. The light upper church, reopened after restoration, is normally open at the
  same times except that it opens around 08.00, and should, if possible, be visited at different times of day.

The colonnaded **Piazza Inferiore di San Francesco** was laid out in the 15C. At
the far end is the huge convent, beside the entrance to the lower church which,
because of the sloping terrain, has no façade, and a double flight of steps (rebuilt
in 1731) which leads up to the lawn in front of the upper church.

The huge **convent** (now a missionary college; no admission, damaged in the
earthquake) is supported by massive tiered vaulting and buttresses built by
Sixtus IV in the 15C, conspicuous on the approach to the town from below.
Beside the convent entrance is the former **oratorio di San Bernardino**, with a
Renaissance double door, a graceful Lombard work of 1459–72 (now used as an
information office for the Basilica).

Lower church

The **lower church of San Francesco** has a Renaissance **porch** by Francesco
di Bartolomeo da Pietrasanta (1486–87) which protects its Gothic **portal** (1;
1271). Beneath the rose window is a tiny fresco of *St Francis*. The wooden doors
were carved in the late 16C. On the wall to the left is a 16C frescoed lunette and
a 14C tomb.

Interior The dark interior, lit by stained-glass windows, resembles a huge crypt
with Gothic vaulting and low arches. Its form is that of a Tau cross (**T**); the
narthex and side chapels were added at the end of the 13C. It has a wonderful old
pink and white marble pavement. In the entrance transept or narthex are frescoes by Cesare Sermei and Girolamo Martelli (1646); the latter also decorated the

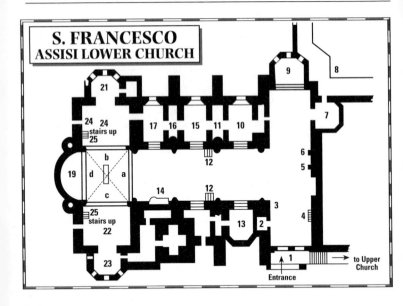

little chapel of San Sebastiano (**2**). On the wall beyond (**3**) is a *Madonna enthroned with saints* by Ottaviano Nelli (1422). On the opposite wall (**4**) is a 13C funerary monument of a member of the Cerchi family with a huge porphyry vase. Beneath it to the left is the tomb of Andrea Gabrielli (d. 1638) with his portrait by Cesare Sermei.

Beyond a 15C Cantoria (**5**), with 17C decoration, is the **tomb of John of Brienne** (**6**), King of Jerusalem and Emperor of Constantinople, friend of St Francis and a Franciscan Tertiary, who was present at the canonisation ceremony of the saint. The two carved angels are particularly fine. The frescoes in the last part of this transept are by Cesare Sermei. In the **Cappella di Sant'Antonio Abate** (**7**), now the Chapel of the Holy Sacrament, are two 14C tombs. The picturesque cloistered cemetery (**8**; 1492) is usually closed.

The **Cappella di Santa Caterina** (**9**) was decorated in 1367 for Cardinal Albornoz who found a temporary resting-place here before his body was transferred to Toledo. The chapel was designed by Matteo di Gattapone and the frescoes of the story of the *life of St Catherine* are by Andrea de' Bartoli. The fine stained-glass window dates from c 1320. From the transept there is access to the **Cappella di Santo Stefano** (**10**), with stories from the *life of St Stephen* by Dono Doni (1574), and 14C stained-glass. In the little **Cappella di San Lorenzo** (**11**), beyond, are frescoes by Andrea de' Bartoli.

Nave. The floor slopes down towards the altar. Here are the oldest **frescoes** (1253) in the basilica, damaged when the side chapels were opened. The *Passion* scenes (right wall), the *Life of St Francis* (left wall) and the geometric decoration of the rib vaulting are all attributed to an anonymous artist, known as the Maestro di San Francesco. On either side of the nave a staircase (**12**) descends to the **crypt** (services are held here throughout the day), opened in 1818 when the stone coffin of St Francis was rediscovered (it had been rendered inaccessible in the 15C as a precaution against Perugian raids). The neo-classical form of the crypt was altered in 1932. Around the tomb are grouped the sarcophagi of the saint's four faithful companions: Fra Leone, Fra Angelo, Fra Masseo, and Fra Rufino.

North side. The **Cappella di San Martino** (**13**) contains a very fine cycle of **frescoes** by Simone Martini (c 1312–15) illustrating the story of *St Martin*. The chronological order of the scenes starts on the lower register (left side): *St Martin divides his cloak*; *Christ appears to the saint in a dream*; (right side) *investiture by the Emperor*; *the saint renounces the sword*. Upper register: (left) *the saint resuscitates a child*; *meditation of the saint*; (right) *Mass at Albenga*; *the saint is honoured by the Emperor*. In the vault: two scenes of the *Death of the saint*. Above the entrance arch, Cardinal Gentile da Montefiore, who commissioned the frescoes, is shown kneeling before the saint. On the intrados are paired saints in niches. Simone Martini may also have designed the beautiful stained glass in this chapel. Beneath the third north bay (**14**) is a Cosmatesque tribune with a fresco of the *Coronation of the Virgin* by Puccio Capanna (c 1337).

South side. The **Cappella di Sant'Antonio da Padova** (**15**) has stories of the *Life of St Anthony* by Cesare Sermei (1610). The stained-glass windows date from c 1317. Beyond the **Cappella di San Valentino** (**16**) with the pavement tomb of Friar Ugo of Hartlepool (d. 1302) is the **Cappella della Maddalena** (**17**) with worn Cosmatesque panels and frescoes (c 1309) of the *Life of St Mary Magdalene*, thought to be by **Giotto**, with the help of assistants including Palmerino di Guido. Left wall: *Supper in the house of the Pharisee, Raising of Lazarus*. Right wall: *Noli me Tangere, Journey of St Mary Magdalene to Marseilles* and *the miracle of the Princess and her newborn child found alive on a rock in the middle of the sea*. In the lunettes: *the saint with angels, receiving the clothes of the hermit Zosimus*, and *kneeling before a priest*, and *her soul ascending to Heaven*. In the vault, with stars on a blue ground, are tondi with figures of the *Redeemer*, *St Mary Magdalene*, *Lazarus* and *St Martha*. The rest of the decoration consists of figures of saints. The stained-glass, with scenes of the life of the saint, predates the frescoes.

The pretty **high altar** (**18**), consecrated in 1253, is directly above the tomb of St Francis, which can be seen through a grille. The **east end** of the church (usually well illuminated, for times see above) has beautiful and well-preserved frescoes executed in a carefully worked out scheme relating to St Francis: above the altar are the *Franciscan Virtues* and *the Glory of the Saint*, and in the transepts *the Childhood* and *Passion of Christ*. The decoration, which replaces earlier frescoes here by the Master of San Francesco and Cimabue, was begun in the south transept and Cappella di San Nicola c 1306, continued in the central cross vault (c 1315) and terminated in the north transept (c 1320).

The cross-vault above the altar, known as the 'Quattro Vele', contains four celebrated **frescoes** representing allegories of the three Virtues of St Francis: *Poverty* (a), *Chastity* (b), and *Obedience* (c); and his *Triumph* (d), richly decorated in gold. Traditionally attributed to Giotto, they are now ascribed to an Umbrian pupil known as the Maestro delle Vele from these frescoes, and to a Tuscan follower of Giotto, possibly Stefano Fiorentino. In the **apse** (**19**) a *Last Judgement* by Cesare Sermei (1623) replaces a *Glory of Angels* by Stefano Fiorentino. The beautifully carved stalls were completed by Apollonio da Ripatransone (1471).

South transept (**20**). In the vault and on the end wall are large scenes of the

Childhood of Christ, traditionally attributed to Giotto but now thought to be by assistants working under his direction, including an artist known as the 'Maestro di San Nicola'. On the right wall the *Crucifixion* may be by the hand of **Giotto** himself. Next to it is a *Madonna enthroned with four angels and St Francis* by **Cimabue**. This survives from the earlier fresco decoration of c 1280 in this part of the church, and the figure of St Francis is one of the most famous representations of the saint. The tomb of five companions of St Francis bears their portraits by Pietro Lorenzetti. To the left of the door, half-length figures of the *Madonna and Child* with two King-Saints, and (on the end wall), five saints including one traditionally thought to be St Clare, all by **Simone Martini**.

The **Cappella di San Nicola (21)** is decorated with **frescoes** of the *life of St Nicholas* attributed by some scholars to **Giotto** and by others to his assistants, including one called from these frescoes the Maestro della Cappella di San Nicola, and Palmerino di Guido. Above the tomb of Giovanni Orsini (d. 1292/4) is a frescoed tripytch of the *Madonna and Child* between *St Nicola* and *St Francis* attributed to the hand of Giotto. The glass is contemporary with the frescoes.

North transept (**22**). The vault and walls are covered with moving frescoes of the *Passion* by **Pietro Lorenzetti** (c 1320), including a large *Crucifixion* (damaged in the 17C) and a *Descent from the Cross*. On the left wall is a charming *Madonna and Child with Sts Francis and John the Evangelist*. In the **Cappella di San Giovanni Battista (23)** there is a frescoed triptych of the *Madonna and Child with Sts John the Baptist and Francis* also by **Pietro Lorenzetti**. The central panel of stained-glass is attributed to Jacopo Torriti.

Beyond a door (**24**) in the south transept steps lead down past the vaulted apse to the **chapterhouse** (c 1240) with a fresco of the *Crucifixion* by Puccio Capanna (c 1340). Here are exhibited reliquaries of St Francis, including his chalice and paten, clothes, etc., and a horn and staff of office presented to him by Sultan Melek-el-Kamil. Also displayed here is a habit which belonged to St Francis, and the Rule of the Franciscan Order sent to the saint by Pope Honorius III in 1223.

Stairs (**25**; closed since the earthquake) lead up from both transepts to a terrace outside the apse of the upper church overlooking the **Cloister of Sixtus IV**. Here a door leads into the **Sala Gotica**, which houses the **Treasury** (there are views of the countryside from the windows). Its contents have been exhibited in various countries of the world since the earthquake, but it will be reopened here when restoration of the convent is completed. It is normally open from Easter to October, 09.30–12.00, 14.00–18.00 except Sun, but is closed from Nov to March. Though several times despoiled it still contains precious treasures.

In the entrance is the magnificent Flemish **tapestry** of St Francis, presented by Sixtus IV in 1479. Also here, **altar-frontal** (1473–78) presented by Sixtus IV in 1478. The figures of the *Pope kneeling before St Francis* are by Antonio del Pollaiolo, and the frieze above attributed to Francesco Botticini. In the main hall, the first cases contain a 12C Processional Cross and a 13C painted *Crucifix* by a follower of Giunta Pisano; on the wall there is an Umbrian *Crucifix* (c 1220–40). Cases 10–12 contain a reliquary of St Andrew (c 1290), presented by Nicholas IV; a panel painting of *St Francis* (1265–75); and a sinopia of the head of *Christ* from the Upper Church.

On a raised platform in the centre are displayed a silver gilt reliquary presented by Queen Joanna of Burgundy in the 14C; a *Madonna and Child*, a 13C ivory of French workmanship; and the illuminated missal of St Louis of Toulouse (French, 1260–64). On the left wall there is a sinopia of *St Martin* by Simone Martini from the Lower Church; a tabernacle designed by Galeazzo Alessi and made by Vincenzo Danti (1570), and medieval ceramics found in Assisi in 1968. Case 17 contains a silver gilt **chalice of Nicholas IV** (c 1290) by Guccio di Mannaie, with a portrait of the Pope in enamel. Cases 18–25 contain 14C–16C reliquaries and Crosses, including a 14C Venetian Cross in rock-crystal with enamels. On the platform more reliquaries are displayed and Crosses of the 16C–17C. At the end of the hall there is 18C and 19C church silver, and on the wall, there are paintings by Tiberio d'Assisi (*Crucifix and Saints*) and Lo Spagna (*Madonna enthroned*).

The room beyond was opened in 1986 to display the **Mason Perkins Collection** of paintings (some of them recently restored) left to the Convent by the art historian, collector and dealer, Frederick Mason Perkins (1874–1955), particularly interesting as an example of a private collection formed in Italy in the first half of the 20C. It includes works by Mariotto di Nardo, Lorenzo Monaco (*Madonna of Humility*), Pier Francesco Fiorentino, Lorenzo di Nicolò, Ortolano (*St Sebastian*), the Maestro di San Martino alle Palme (portable triptych), Segna di Bonaventura, Taddeo di Bartolo (*St Elizabeth of Hungary*), Pietro Lorenzetti (*Madonna and Child*), and Bartolo di Fredi.

The upper church

Two more staircases continue up from the terrace to the transepts of the upper church of San Francesco (since the earthquake only accessible from outside the lower church from the west end). The tall light interior provides a strong contrast to the lower church. The façade is described below. The architectural unity of this remarkable 13C Gothic building is enhanced by its contemporary frescoes and stained glass. It shows a close affinity to Northern Gothic churches, and may be the work of a French or even an English architect. The superb **frescoes**, carried out probably from 1277 to 1300, are by the greatest artists of the day, including **Cimabue**, Jacopo Torriti, and probably Giotto, together with anonymous masters. They follow a carefully worked out scheme which illustrates the importance of St Francis in his role as an intermediary between man and God. Two bays of the vault and an arch at the west end, all of them covered with important frescoes, fell to the ground in the earthquake. They have all been carefully reconstructed, and a small part of the frescoes recomposed from the shattered fragments.

In the transept, crossing and apse are the earliest frescoes (c 1277) with scenes from the life of the *Virgin*, the *Apostles* and the *Apocalypse*. They are very damaged and have lost their colour, taking on the appearance of negatives, for reasons still not fully explained. North transept. Scenes from the Apocalypse by Cimabue, and a dramatic Crucifixion are situated here. In the **crossing** the vault is decorated with the four Evangelists, also by Cimabue (one of which, *St Matthew*, fell to the ground in the earthquake). In the **apse** are scenes from the *Life of the Virgin* by an anonymous northern painter (finished by Cimabue). The Papal throne also dates from the 13C and is probably the work of Roman sculptors. The stalls date from 1501. South transept. The frescoes, with scenes from the life of Sts Peter and Paul, and another *Crucifixion*, were begun by an anonymous northern painter, and continued by Jacopo Torriti and assistants of Cimabue.

Nave. In the two **upper registers**, between the windows, are frescoes (difficult to see) of stories from the Old Testament (south wall) and New Testament (north wall), commissioned on the election of the first Franciscan pope, Nicholas IV, in 1288. Many of them have been damaged over the years. These were all ascribed by Vasari to Cimabue, but are now generally thought to be in part by pupils of Cimabue, and in part by painters of the Roman school, including Jacopo Torriti. Giotto is also now considered by some scholars to have been involved in some of the scenes; if this is so these would be his earliest works in the basilica.

The chronological order of the scenes follows the upper register, starting on the south side in the fourth bay with the *Creation of the World* and *Creation of Adam*, and continuing to the first bay, and then follows the middle register starting in the fourth bay with the *creation of the Ark*. The two remarkable scenes in the second bay of *Isaac blessing Jacob* and *Esau before Isaac* are attributed to the Maestro di Isacco, now usually identified with Giotto. The New Testament scenes on the north side of the church start on the upper register of the fourth bay with the *Annunciation*, and continue to the first bay with the *Baptism of Christ*. The story continues in the middle register at the fourth bay with the *Marriage at Cana* and ends in the first bay with the *Maries at the Sepulchre*.

On the **inner façade** are two scenes of the *Pentecost* and *Ascension* and Sts Peter and Paul. Two of the frescoes of saints on the arch have been painstakingly recomposed since they were shattered in the earthquake, and the arch reconstructed. In the **vault** of the first bay of the nave are the *four Doctors of the Church*, now usually attributed to Giotto (the one nearest the rose window, with St Jerome, fell to the ground in the earthquake), and in the third bay, *the Redeemer, the Virgin, St John the Baptist* and *St Francis*.

The **lower register** of frescoes in the **nave** are the famous scenes from the *Life of St Francis*, traditionally thought to be early works by Giotto and assistants (c 1290–95), but not attributed to Giotto by all scholars.

Giotto

Giotto di Bondone (1266/7–1337) was born in the Mugello, north of Florence. A pupil of Cimabue and friend of Dante, his painting had a new monumentality and sense of volume which had never been achieved in medieval painting. His figures are given an intensely human significance. He was famous as a great painter amongst his contemporaries. His most famous fresco cycle (and the only one to survive intact) is the one at the Cappella degli Scrovegni in Padua (1303–05). Giotto received commissions for other Franciscan fresco cycles in Rimini and Padua, both now lost, and in the Bardi chapel of Santa Croce in Florence. Although his fame is largely derived from his work at Assisi, documentary evidence is lacking about his work here. The frescoes are generally dated in the last decade of the 14C, and it seems that he worked in the Lower Church some 20 years later (although also here there are various attribution problems and differing theories about dates). Vasari was the first to attribute this *St Francis* cycle to Giotto, but throughout the 20C art historians have debated whether he was in fact involved and if so into which period of his activity they fall. A close study of the 28 scenes (recently well restored) reveals that several different hands were at work here.

The story of the saint begins on the **south wall**, in the fourth bay:

1. The young saint is honoured in the piazza of Assisi by a poor man who lays down his cloak before him
2. St Francis gives his cloak to a poor man (with a panorama of Assisi in the background)
3. The saint dreams of a palace full of arms
4. The saint in prayer in San Damiano hears a Voice exhorting him to 'Rebuild My Church'
5. The saint renounces his worldly goods in front of his father and the Bishop of Assisi
6. Innocent III dreams of the saint sustaining the Church
7. Innocent III approves the saint's Order
8. The saint appears to his companions in a Chariot of Fire
9. Fra Leo dreams of the throne reserved for the saint in Paradise
10. The expulsion of the Demons from Arezzo
11. The saint before the Sultan offers to undergo the Ordeal by Fire
12. The saint in Ecstasy
13. The saint celebrates Christmas at Greccio

West wall:

14. The saint causes a fountain to spring up to quench a man's thirst
15. The saint preaches to the birds

North wall:

16. The Death of the Knight of Celano as foretold by the saint
17. The saint preaches before Honorius III
18. The saint appears to the friars at Arles
19. The saint receives the Stigmata
20. The death of the saint and his funeral
21. The apparition of the saint to the Bishop of Assisi and Fra Augustine
22. Girolamo of Assisi accepts the truth of the Stigmata
23. The Poor Clares mourn the dead saint at San Damiano
24. Coronation of the saint
25. The saint appears to Gregory IX in a dream
26. The saint heals a man, mortally wounded, from Ilerda
27. The saint revives a devout woman
28. The saint releases Pietro d'Alife from prison

The medieval **stained glass** is the most important in Italy. The earliest windows are those in the apse (c 1253), probably by German artists. The glass in the south transept and nave is attributed to the Maestro di San Francesco and French masters.

The **façade**, with a beautiful rose window and a fine Gothic portal, overlooks a green lawn. It had to be heavily restored after the earthquake, but work was completed in 1998.

Via San Francesco and Piazza del Comune

From the lawn in front of the upper church of San Francesco, Via San Francesco leads towards the centre of the town. On the right is the 19C Oratorio dell'Immacolata Concezione. Next to it the Capuchin monks opened a museum in 1972 relating to the Indians of Amazonia. Beyond is **Palazzo Bernabei**, built by Giacomo Giorgetti after 1646. Further up, on the left (no. 14) is a 13C house known as the **Loggia dei Maestri Comacini**. From here a stepped alley (Vicolo di Sant'Andrea) leads up through a quiet medieval district of the town towards Porta San Giacomo (described at the end of this route).

Beyond, on the left, is the long pale terracotta-coloured façade of **Palazzo Vallemani** with handsome windows and an elaborate balcony. The rooms on the piano nobile have 17C painted decoration. It is the seat of the Biblioteca Comunale, and there are plans to move the **Pinacoteca Comunale** here (formerly displayed in Piazza del Comune). The collection was inaugurated in 1912, and contains numerous detached frescoes from street tabernacles and oratories in the town (many of them in poor condition).

The contents include interesting fragments of **frescoes** detached from Palazzo del Capitano del Popolo, including 13C Gothic scenes with knights on horseback and representations of the seasons, and a *Madonna* enthroned in a painted niche, attributed to the bottega of Giotto; an early 14C fragment of the *Crucifixion* with figures kneeling at the foot of the Cross; and a fragment of the *Prayer in the Garden* attributed to Pace di Bartolo. There is also a charming fragment of the *Child with St Francis* by Puccio Capanna, and the *martyrdom of St Stephen and three armed men* (14C), a lunette by l'Ingegno, and 15C votive frescoes including a scene of *St Julian murdering his parent*. The good frescoes attributed to Tiberio d'Assisi were detached from the Castello di San Gregorio. **Paintings** include a painted Cross attributed to the Maestro Espressionista di Santa Chiara (perhaps Palmerino di Guido), a standard of the *Madonna of the Misericordia* (with St Biagio enthroned behind) by l'Alunno, and works by Giacomo Giorgetti, Dono Doni, and Cesare Sermei.

On the right, beyond a palace built in 1883 with terracotta decoration round the windows and doorway, is the **Oratorio dei Pellegrini**, a relic of a 15C hospital where pilgrims used to be lodged. The worn fresco on the façade is by Matteo da Gualdo, who also painted the delightful frescoes inside on the altar wall. The vault and side walls were decorated in 1477 by Pierantonio Mezzastris with stories from the life of *St James* including the *Miracle of the two hens resuscitated in order to proclaim the innocence of a young pilgrim who had been unjustly accused*, and the *Miracle of a hanged man supported by the saint, and found alive by his parents*. On the left wall are two stories from the life of *St Anthony Abbot: the saint receiving some camels who have journeyed alone to bring provisions to the monks*, and *the saint distributing alms to the poor*. The inner façade has figures of three saints, once thought to be early works by Perugino but now considered by some scholars to be by l'Ingegno.

On the left (no. 81) is the 16C Palazzo Bartocci-Fontana (being restored), and opposite, the **Portico del Monte Frumentario** with seven columns. The frescoes by followers of Giotto have all but disappeared. This was one of the first public hospitals in Italy (founded in 1267). Next to it is a public fountain attributed to Galeazzo Alessi.

From the top of Vicolo Frondini there is a good view of the plain. The road now passes beneath an arch in the Roman circuit of walls, to Via del Arco del Seminario. The huge building of the former Missionary college on the left has a handsome loggia crowned by a balcony, built by Attilio Cangi in 1911. Opposite is the high red-and-white stone wall of the former monastery of **Sant'Angelo di Panzo**, with a fresco by Girolamo Marinelli (heavily restored in 1993 by a Japanese artist). Further on, on the right, is **Palazzo Rossi**, attributed to Galeazzo Alessi, with a balcony over its portal and, in a little piazza, the *Teatro Comunale Metastasio* (now a cinema) built in 1836 by Lorenzo Carpinelli. Via Fortini and Via Portica continue steeply up, with a view ahead of the Torre del Popolo and dome of San Rufino. On the right a pastry shop has a beautifully carved portal attributed to Franceschino Zampa (c 1470).

Opposite is the entrance to the **Museo Civico** (or Foro Romano and Archaeological Collection; open daily 10.00–13.30, 14.30 or 15.30–17.00 or 18.30; ☎ 075 813053) arranged in 1933 in a crypt, all that remains of the church of San Niccolò founded in 1097. It retains a delightfully old-fashioned atmosphere. The collection, formed in 1793 by the Accademia Properziano del Subasio, consists of Umbrian and Roman material found in Assisi and environs. The works are numbered and a hand-list is lent to visitors.

On the left there is a Roman sarcophagus and a cinerary urn of the 2C AD. On the right is a fragment of a funerary stele (1C AD). Beyond the entrance to the corridor (see below) are a number of urns (1C BC–1C AD) from a necropolis. Against the far wall are two statues dating from the 1C AD, and, on the left wall, a fragment of a seated female statue (1C AD). In the last part of the room are finds made in 1864 in a Roman house near the piazza, including interesting fresco fragments.

A corridor, with Roman paving stones and a drainage channel, lined with Roman inscriptions and funerary stelai, leads into an area first excavated in 1836. Once thought to be the forum of the Roman city, this is now usually interpreted as a **sacred area** at the centre of the city in front and below the so-called Temple of Minerva (see below). This consisted of a paved piazza surrounded on three sides by a colonnade (which has now almost totally disappeared): the corridor runs along the upper side of the piazza past a rectangular platform thought to be an altar or a base for votive statues. Aligned with this, to the right, is another rectangular structure of the 1C AD, well preserved with an inscription relating to the statues of the Dioscuri which once stood here. The main corridor continues past stairs which led up to the temple and remains of a monumental fountain which once decorated the piazza. At the end of the corridor the bases of two columns from the portico survive and on the end wall are remains of Roman buildings thought to have been shops.

In Via Portica is a pretty public fountain, reconstructed in 1926 and a little pulpit carved by Niccolò da Bettona (1354). The beautifully shaped **Piazza del Comune** is the centre of the town. It is above the site of a Roman piazza, once thought to be the forum, but now usually identified as a sanctuary around the Temple of Minerva. The excavations can be seen in the Museo Civico (see above), which include the altar and statue base in front of the temple (their positions have been outlined in white marble in the pavement of the present piazza).

The so-called **Temple of Minerva** has a perfectly preserved pronaos of six Corinthian columns on plinths which support a low tympanum, and a flight of travertine steps rises up between the columns. The building dates from sometime between the 1C BC and the Augustine age, and may have been dedicated to the

Dioscuri. It was particularly admired by Goethe when he visited Assisi in 1786, as it was the first Classical building he had ever seen. The cella was transformed in 1539 into the church of Santa Maria della Minerva and given a Baroque interior by Giacomo Giorgetti in 1634. It has 18C statues and paintings by Martin Knoller, Antonio Maria Garbi, and Francesco Appiani.

The very tall **Torre del Popolo** was erected in the 13C. At its base is a relief of 1348 showing various measures. Next to it is the 13C **Palazzo del Podestà**, reconstructed in the 16C. A neo-Gothic building (1927) by Silvio Gabrielli and Ruggero Antonelli (decorated inside by Adalberto Migliorati) served as a post office. It is now being restored as the new seat of the IAT information office. Next to it steps lead up to a tabernacle with a fresco of the Madonna del Popolo by a local follower of Simone Martini.

Opposite the temple is the 16C Palazzo Bonacquisti (now a bank) and the rest of this side of the piazza is occupied by **Palazzo Comunale** and **Palazzo dei Priori**. An open archway has its vault decorated with pretty grotesques (1556). The **Pinacoteca Comunale** here has been closed since the earthquake, and there are plans to move the collection to Palazzo Vallemani in Via San Francesco (see above).

The delightful fountain in the piazza was designed in 1762 by Giovanni Martinucci. Beneath the Arco dei Priori a road descends to the **Chiesa Nuova** (being restored) built on the supposed site of the house which belonged to the parents of St Francis. In the piazza are two bronze statues of them (1984) and a *Madonna and Child* in majolica tiles (1927). The handsome centrally planned church dates from 1615, and contains contemporary frescoes, and stuccoes of 1769. The two chapels on either side of the entrance have monochrome frescoes attributed to Cesare Sermei. In the chapel on the right are frescoes attributed to Vincenzo Giorgetti and an 18C altarpiece, and in the sanctuary, the high altarpiece and frescoes are by Cesare Sermei. In the chapel on the left, the altarpiece is by Andrea Polinori and the frescoes by Giacomo Giorgetti. In the pilaster is a tiny cell where St Francis is supposed to have been imprisoned by his father (the wooden statue of the saint here dates from the 17C). A door leads out to an alley with an oratory of the 13C indicated as the birthplace of the saint.

From Piazza del Comune, Via San Paolo leads past the church of **San Paolo** (closed), founded in 1071, next to the door of a Benedictine priory. Beyond the two-storeyed 14C Confraternity of Santo Stefano, the stepped Vicolo di Santo Stefano descends past a tabernacle with a worn fresco of 1363 by Pace di Bartolo to a little garden with a view of the valley. Here in 1995 a tiny medicinal herb garden or **Giardino dei Semplici** was planted, laid out on the traditional design of a cross within a circle, with plants documented before the 15C. Inspired by medieval monastic gardens, it contains aromatic plants, and those used domestically (for dyes, preserves, condiments, moth repellants, etc.), or for curative purposes, or used to decorate altars. It is run by the Assisi Nature Council (☎ 075 813521).

Here is the picturesque church of **Santo Stefano** with a bell-cote and pretty apse, in a peaceful corner of the town. The simple little church has interesting old vaulting above the presbytery and contains a very ruined fresco of the early 14C. Via San Paolo continues beyond an arch over the road down to the Renaissance Palazzo Locatelli, now the seat of the Opera Casa Papa Giovanni.

Beyond the huge Palazzo Spagnoli (1925) Via Metastasio continues past the entrance gate to the monastery of **San Giacomo de Murorupto** (closed 12.00–15.30). It has a picturesque cloister and Romanesque church.

Via San Giacomo leads down past Casa Tini with architectural fragments in its façade to the old **Porta San Giacomo** in the 14C walls. On the left the stepped Vicolo Sant'Andrea descends beneath a wide arch to a picturesque and quiet part of the town around the little churches of Santa Margherita and Sant' Andrea. There is a splendid view of the upper church of San Francesco from here; the lawn is reached by another flight of steps.

The Duomo ~ San Rufino

From Piazza del Comune, Via San Rufino leads up to the charming, quiet **Piazza di San Rufino**, with its wall

Vicolo Sant'Andrea

fountain of 1532, on the site of a Roman terrace which may have been the Roman Forum. It provides a splendid setting for the **Duomo** (San Rufino). Tradition relates that a chapel was built here c 412 to house the relics of St Rufino, the first bishop of Assisi, martyred in 238. A church, which occupied the site of the present piazza, was built by Bishop Ugone c 1029. The **campanile**, which stands over a Roman cistern, and the crypt (described below) survive from this building. The church was rebuilt in 1140 by Giovanni da Gubbio (who also raised the height of the campanile). The **façade** (restored since the earthquake) has rectangular facing between its doors which are decorated with intricate carvings. Above a gallery are three lovely rose windows, the central one with good carved symbols of the Evangelists and telamones. It was heightened with a Gothic blind arch before the church was consecrated in 1253.

Interior The interior (almost totally inaccessible since the earthquake) was transformed by Galeazzo Alessi in 1571. At the beginning of the north aisle a little door gives access to a well-preserved Roman cistern with a barrel vault beneath the campanile. The statues on the west wall of Sts Francis and Clare are by Giovanni Duprè and his daughter Amalia (1881–88). At the beginning of the south aisle is the font at which St Francis and St Clare were baptised. The Emperor Frederick II may also have been baptised here in 1187 (at the age of three). It is surrounded by a terracotta tabernacle of 1882. On the altar is Berto di Giovanni's, *Standard of St Joseph*.

The **Cappella del Santissimo Sacramento** was built in 1663 on a design by Giacomo Giorgetti, with paintings in fine frames by Giovanni Andrea Carlone, and an oval in the vault by Giorgetti. On the last altar in this aisle, with stuccoes by Agostino Silva, is an altarpiece of *Christ in glory with saints* by Dono Doni. St Rufino is buried beneath the high altar in the **presbytery**. On the right and left altars are a *Deposition* and *Crucifixion* both by Dono Doni. The choir stalls were inlaid by Giovanni di Piergiacomo da Sanseverino. North aisle. The black stucco statues of *Prophets*, and the stucco decoration of the altars is by Agostino Silva (1672). On the fourth altar is a wooden *Crucifix* (1561) and on the second altar, designed by Giacomo Giorgetti, is an altarpiece by Francesco Appiani.

From the south aisle a door leads into a corridor where the outside wall of the church can be seen. Here are displayed numerous lapidary fragments from the 11C church, and 17C paintings including works by Cesare Sermei. In the sacristy (1907, by Carlo Gino Venanzi) are paintings by Giacomo Giorgetti, Cesare Sermei and Martin Knoller.

From the corridor there is access to the **Museo Capitolare** (at present closed). It contains detached frescoes by Puccio Capanna from San Rufinaccio in Assisi, triptychs by l'Alunno and Matteo da Gualdo, works by Dono Doni and Cesare Sermei, and a standard of the *martyrdom of St Catherine of Alexandria* and *St Giacomo and Anthony Abbot* by Orazio Riminaldi (1627).

From a little door in the piazza (right of the façade) steps lead down through a Carolingian cloister (restored), with a well, to the entrance to the **crypt** of the 11C church (also at present closed) discovered in 1895. It has primitive vaulting and Ionic capitals, and in the apse are scant remains of the original frescoes. Nearby is a Roman wall and a channel which led to the reservoir (see above). The handsome Roman sarcophagus (3C AD), with reliefs relating to the myth of Diana and Endymion, was used as the tomb of St Rufino.

In front of the church Via Santa Maria delle Rose leads through a pretty district of the town past the ancient church of **Santa Maria delle Rose**, while Via di Porta Perlici continues uphill. On the left the stepped Vicolo del Castello leads up past a gate in front of a little garden with cypresses and a tabernacle protecting a fresco by Cola Petruccioli (c 1394) which belonged to the Confraternità di San Lorenzo.

Rocca Maggiore

The steps emerge on a road which continues up to the Rocca Maggiore (open daily 10.00–dusk, ☎ 075 815292) which dominates the town. There are wonderful views to the north and east towards the wooded Monte di San Rufino and gorge of the Tescio, and of the other citadel, known as the **Rocchiciola** (no admission), erected by Cardinal Albornoz in 1367, with the walls enclosing the picturesque little borgo of Perlici. In the other direction is the plain in front of Assisi. The hill was fortified in ancient times and the castle rebuilt in 1365 by Cardinal Albornoz. The entrance is beside a circular tower added by Paul III in 1538. The inner keep is surrounded by a high wall with slits for marksmen. From the courtyard is access to the kitchen, storerooms and (on the floor above) the dormitory. A walkway leads to a polygonal tower (torch necessary), from which there is a remarkable view of the Basilica of San Francesco.

Via di Porta Perlici (see above) continues uphill from San Rufino through two arches and then continues right with fine views of the wooded hills behind Assisi to end at the 14C Porta Perlici. To the right, Via dell'Anfiteatro Romano follows the form of the **Roman Amphitheatre** (1C AD) past the Fonte di Perlici (13C) and a public fountain erected in 1736. To the south is the large **Piazza Matteotti**, with a bus station, and a large underground car-park. The **Parco Regina Margherita** here was laid out in 1882 by Alfonso Brizi and planted with ilexes, elms and cedar trees.

Santa Chiara

Corso Mazzini, the busiest street in the town, leads out of Piazza del Comune past several 16C–17C palaces. Beyond the Portella di San Giorgio, a medieval gateway on the line of the Roman walls, is **Piazza Santa Chiara** with a beautiful view of the valley and hillside behind with the Rocca. The polygonal fountain was built in 1872 on a design by Attilio Cangi.

Here is the splendid red and white Gothic basilica of **Santa Chiara** (undergoing a radical restoration after severe earthquake damage), built in 1257–65. The simple **façade** has a portal flanked by high reliefs of two lions beneath a splendid rose window and a tympanum. The great flying buttresses that span one side of the piazza were added in 1351; beneath them are remains of a medieval public fountain. The campanile is the tallest in Assisi. On this site was the church of San Giorgio where St Francis was first buried, and his canonisation ceremony took place (his body was transferred to San Francesco when the church was completed). The present church was begun in 1257 as the shrine of St Clare, who was also first buried in San Giorgio in 1253.

Interior The dark interior (closed for restoration) has stained-glass windows in the apse by Francesco Moretti (1897–1925). Off the south side of the nave are two chapels on the site of the former church of San Giorgio. Preserved in the **Oratorio del Crocifisso** is the painted *Crucifix* (late 12C) that spoke to St Francis at San Damiano. At the end, behind a grille, are a triptych by Rinaldo di Ranuccio (c 1270) and reliquaries of St Francis and St Clare, pointed out by a veiled nun from the closed order of the Poor Clares. In the **Cappella del Sacramento** are charming frescoes (on the entrance wall) of the *Annunciation*, *Nativity*, *Adoration of the Magi*, and *St George* by Pace di Bartolo, and (on the left wall) a frescoed polyptych of the *Madonna and saints* by Puccio Capanna beneath scenes of the *Passion*. Outside the chapel, steps lead down to the **crypt** built in a neo-Gothic style in 1851–72 where St Clare is buried.

In the south transept are interesting frescoes (in poor condition; and very difficult to see as they are high up) with scenes of the *Apocalypse* and *Life of Christ* and, below, the *Death and Funeral of St Clare*, attributed to a close follower of Giotto known from these frescoes as the Maestro Espressionista di Santa Chiara, sometimes identified with Palmerino di Guido. Above the altar is a painting of *St Clare* with eight stories from her life, also attributed to the Maestro di Santa Chiara. Above the High Altar is a painted Cross dating from before 1260, and in the cross vault a *Madonna and Child with saints* by a Giottesque master (c 1337). In the north transept, high up at the top of the walls, are 13C frescoes of scenes from *Genesis* in two registers. Below is a 14C fresco of the *Nativity*. On the altar is a *Madonna and Child* (c 1265) also attributed to the Maestro di Santa Chiara. The huge **Convent of Santa Chiara** (closed order) is built on the right side of the church. It was enlarged in the 14C and 16C.

Via Borgo Aretino leads out of the piazza away from the centre of the town beneath the 13C Arco di Santa Chiara. The Borgo, with fine views of the church and convent of Santa Chiara, ends at the 14C Porta Nuova.

From Piazza Santa Chiara, Via Sant'Agnese leads downhill. Beyond steps (left) which descend to Porta Moiano in the walls, near a medieval public fountain, the road ends in Piazza del Vescovado with a few trees and a 16C fountain. A delightful palace here with a tall façade bears the name of its first proprietor Ignatio Vannola (gonfalon of the town in 1625) and a lion sleeps above the ingenious door. The church of **Santa Maria Maggiore** has a simple pink and white chequered façade with a good wheel window (1163). Half a Roman marble fountain basin has been placed above the doorway The interior (at present closed) has 14C–17C fresco fragments and a crypt dating from the 9C. Behind the pretty campanile there is a good view of Santa Chiara.

Below the church is a **Roman house** (admission only with special permission from the Soprintendenza Archeologica in Perugia), with interesting wall-paintings, which may have belonged to Sextus Propertius. Next door is the courtyard of the Palazzo Vescovile .

From the upper end of Piazza Santa Chiara the pretty medieval **Via Bernardo da Quintavalle** leads past the church of **San Gregorio** (closed) with a very damaged fresco on the exterior, to Piazza Garibaldi. This piazza can also be reached by Via Antonio Cristofani which leads out of the centre of Piazza del Vescovado. From Piazza Garibaldi the picturesque **Via Fontebella** continues down to Porta San Francesco past the Fonte Marcello (1557) and the Hotel Giotto, opened in 1900.

Via Giovanni di Bonino leads out of Piazza del Vescovado downhill to Via Sant'Apollinare in which the Benedictine monastery of **San Giuseppe** is situated. It incorporates the two façades of San Paolo and Sant'Apollinare which stand beside each other, and a campanile with a domed top. The wide Via Borgo San Pietro continues downhill with a view ahead of the campanile of San Pietro past the modern buildings of the Pro Civitate Christiana founded in 1939, with a library and gallery of modern religious art.

The road ends in the piazza with a view of the plain in front of the 12C abbey church of **San Pietro**, closed for restoration since 1997. The fine **façade** (covered for restoration) has a portal, guarded by two lions, and three large rose windows. The **interior** has interesting vaulting and a raised sanctuary beneath an unusual brick dome. There are several Gothic arcaded tomb recesses in red and white marble, and in the north transept frescoes by Pace di Bartolo.

The Eremo delle Carceri and Monte Subasio

A road (well-signposted) from Porta Cappuccini at first passes ugly new buildings before narrowing and zig-zagging up the lower slopes of Monte Subasio (4km) to the entrance gate of the **Eremo delle Carceri**, open 06.30–18.00 (or 19.30 in summer). A short walk (300m) leads to the forest hermitage in a remarkably secluded and peaceful spot (790m), nestled in a ravine covered with thick woods of ilexes and oaks. Here St Francis and his followers would come at times to live as hermits in caves, and in 1426 St Bernardine founded a convent here. Beyond the entrance to the monastery is a triangular terrace (inhabited by doves) with two wells, overlooked by the little buildings (no admission) of the convent with the refectory and dormitory, where four friars now live.

Ahead a door leads in to the **Cappella di San Bernardino** with a 15C *Crucifixion with St Francis* and a tiny 13C French stained-glass window. The **Cappella di Santa Maria delle Carceri** has a worn fresco of the *Madonna and Child with St Francis* by Tiberio d'Assisi. A tiny and very steep flight of steps leads down to the **Grotto of St Francis**, a cave where the saint had his bed hollowed out of the rock. A miniature doorway leads out to another terrace; above the door is a worn fresco of St Francis preaching to the birds. In the ravine iron bars support an ancient ilex tree on which birds are supposed to have perched to receive his blessing. A bridge leads over the ravine past a little bronze statue of the saint by Vincenzo Rosignoli (1882), and other statues by F. Bacci (1998) into the lovely woods where walks can be taken. From the bridge there is a good view back of the hermitage buildings. The exit is indicated up steps past the little Cappella della Maddalena; a path continues round the back of the monastery to the entrance gate.

From the hermitage a wide road, signposted Collepino, is open from 07.00–18.00 (07.00–20.00 in summer) for the summit of **Monte Subasio** (7km; 1289m), now a protected regional park which includes the Altipiano di Colfiorito, Monte Pennino, and the territory of Nocera Umbra, Foligno and Spello (administered by the Comunità Montana Monte Subasio at Valtopina). The mountain has a characteristic shape, with its gentle lower slopes covered with woods and a bare summit. The views are magnificent and include, on a good day, the chain of the Apennines. This is a pleasant cool spot to picnic in summer, although many of the fields are fenced to provide pasture for animals. In spring cowslips and wild hellebores grow here. There are a number of marked paths: maps published by Minerva (*Assisi: carta del Territorio*) and Club Alpino Italiano of Foligno (*Carte dei sentieri del Subasio*). One footpath is signposted from Porta Cappuccini in Assisi.

From the summit the road continues down to Collepino which is above Spello (see p. 163). Another road above the Carceri (signposted San Benedetto and Assisi) provides an alternative, but longer route back to Assisi. It leads along the side of the hill through woods past numerous picnic places, with views down to the plain. The road is surfaced but extremely narrow, and passes the abbey of **San Benedetto** founded c 1051, but abandoned by the monks in 1391. In 1945 it was returned to the Benedictines of San Pietro, who have restored it, and the 11C church survives. The road then descends steeply with fine views ahead of Assisi beneath its Rocca.

San Damiano and Rivotorto

A road (signposted) leads downhill from Viale Vittorio Emanuele near Porta Nuova to **San Damiano** (also reached on foot by a pretty lane from Porta Nuova). Here in 1205 St Francis renounced the world, and St Clare died in 1253. It was a Benedictine priory documented in 1030, and it was restored in 1212. St Francis stayed here on a number of occasions. Lord Lothian (Peter Kerr) left the convent to the Franciscans in 1983 and it can be visited (10.00 – 18.00). In front of the church is an arcaded courtyard with votive frescoes. To the right is the entrance to the **Cappella di San Girolamo** with a fine *Madonna and Saints* by Tiberio d'Assisi (1517). The adjoining **Cappella del Crocifisso** has a venerated wooden Cross of 1637.

The little **church** has a vaulted single nave with 14C frescoes showing St Agnes, St Francis in prayer before the Crucifix (a damaged scene), St Francis throwing down his money in front of the priest, and (on the west wall) the figure of the father of St Francis threatening the saint with a stick. The **monastery** can also normally be visited, including the 15C cloister which has a vestibule frescoed by Eusebio da San Giorgio (1507).

A road continues downhill (keep right; just over 2km) to the plain, as far as the conspicuous church of **Rivotorto** with its campanile crowned by a short spire. It is named after a stream which runs down from Monte Subasio and passes in front of the church. The Franciscan convent here is being restored (ring at the door beside the campanile for admission to the church). The **church** was built in 1600–40 over a hovel where St Francis came to live in 1208. After the earthquake of 1853 the church was reconstructed in neo-Gothic style, but the 19C decorations have recently been eliminated. The restored hut survives in the middle of the church. Twelve paintings of the *Life of St Francis* by Cesare Sermei have been removed from the church during restoration work.

Off the avenue which leads from the church towards Santa Maria degli Angeli there is a British Military Cemetery.

Santa Maria degli Angeli

A road leads from below the walls of Assisi down to the plain and the conspicuous domed basilica of Santa Maria degli Angeli (5km from Assisi, frequent bus service). It is open 05.45–12.30, 14.00–dusk. It is now surrounded by an unattractive small suburb. Visited by thousands of pilgrims because of its associations with St Francis, it has all the usual characteristics of a famous holy shrine. It has an ugly monumental approach, laid out in 1950, with flagstaffs and incongruous trees, and a car park for the numerous coach tours which stop here.

The church was designed in 1569 by Galeazzo Alessi and built by Girolamo Martelli, Giacomo Giorgetti, and others, and finished in 1679. It was rebuilt after an earthquake in 1832 by Luigi Poletti except for the fine **cupola** and apse which survive from the 16C church, and the side chapels, decorated in the late 16C–18C. The unattractive **façade** is by Cesare Bazzani (1928). The church was built on a place which belonged to the Benedictines, known as the Porziuncola, where St Francis and his companions first came to live in simple huts and where, in a little chapel, he founded his Order. The church was built to cover this little 11C oratory (Cappella della Porziuncola), and other chapels used by St Francis. This was the meeting-place of Sts Francis and Dominic, and here St Francis died.

Interior After earthquake damage, some of the side chapels are still closed, but the Porziuncola has been restored. The decorations in the side chapels, mostly commissioned between 1590–1630, are interesting works of this period. South side. The first chapel contains an altarpiece of *St Anthony Abbot* by Giacomo Giorgetti; the *Miracle of the Saint* (left wall) by Anton Maria Garbi, and paintings in the vault by Francesco Appiani. The second chapel was decorated by Cesare Sermei in 1602 and the wrought-iron gate dates from 1700. The altarpiece of the *Baptism of Christ* is by Giacomo Giorgetti. Third chapel: altarpiece of the Birth of the Virgin by Cristoforo Roncalli, and frescoes of the *Presentation in the Temple* and *Marriage of the Virgin* by Antonio Circignani. The fourth chapel was decorated by Baldassarre Croce in 1602–03. The fifth chapel contains an altarpiece of the *Nativity* by Domenico Pace (1830).

South transept. In the right chapel there is an altarpiece by Francesco Appiani and a 15C statuette of the *Madonna and Child* (formerly in the tabernacle on the roof of the Chapel of the Porziuncola). The elaborate altar of San Pietro is decorated with stuccoes by Giovanni Reinhold (1675). Above the door into a corridor (see below) is an *Annunciation* by the bottega of Federico Barocci. In the **crossing** are four frescoes in the pendentives by Francesco Appiani.

The little **Cappella della Porziuncola** stands beneath the cupola. It is a simple rustic hut built of stone (the pretty geometrical decoration of the roof was discovered during restoration in 1998). Over the wide entrance is a fresco of the *Pardon of St Francis* by Nazareno Friedrich Overbeck (1829) and a neo-Gothic tabernacle of 1832. In the simple interior the splendid altarpiece (removed for restoration) of the *Life of St Francis*, the only known work by Ilario da Viterbo (1393), decorates the east wall. On the exterior are remains of 15C frescoes and an inscribed stone recording the burial-place of Pietro Cattani, companion of St Francis (d. 1221). On the pretty east end is a fine fresco of the *Crucifixion* attributed to Perugino (heavily restored in 1830).

The tiny **Cappella del Transito** concealed behind the entrance to the chancel (right) was built over the cell where St Francis died. Through the fine wrought-iron gate frescoes of the first companions of St Francis by Lo Spagna can be seen and a statue of the saint by Andrea della Robbia (removed for restoration). The girdle of St Francis is preserved in a glass case. On the outside wall is a fresco of the *Death and Funeral of St Francis* by Domenico Bruschi (1886).

North transept. The Oratorio del Sacramento was opened in 1984 on the left side of the presbytery. It has a gilded wooden altarpiece (1691). The 18C altar in the transept in polychrome marbles incorporates a wooden *Crucifix* by a northern artist of c 1530. North aisle. In the fifth chapel there is an altarpiece of the *Madonna of the Rosary* by Domenico Maria Muratori and paintings by Baldassare Orsini and Carlo Morelli. The fourth chapel was decorated in 1603 by Simeone Ciburri. The third chapel (1602) contains an altarpiece of the *Deposition* by Baldassarre Croce and, in the vault, a *Resurrection* by Ventura Salimbeni, and good stucco work. In the second chapel there is an altarpiece of *St Francis receiving the Stigmata* by Giacomo Giorgetti and (left) *The Verification of the Stigmata*, also by him. The vault was decorated by Cesare Sermei. The first chapel contains 18C works by Benedetto Cavallucci and Anton Maria Garbi.

From the south transept a door leads into a corridor. Ahead is the **sacristy** with fine carved cupboards of 1671. The **crypt** is also entered off the corridor (for admission, ask in the sacristy: open only for services). It was excavated in 1968 beneath the high altar to reveal remains of the first Franciscan convent, and contains a beautiful enamelled terracotta altarpiece by Andrea della Robbia. Also off the corridor is access to a portico which leads past a garden of the thornless roses of St Francis which bloom annually in May. The bronze statue of the saint with a lamb is by Vincenzo Rosignoli (1916). The **Cappella delle Rose**, a barrel-vaulted chapel built by St Bonaventura over the cave of St Francis, has beautiful frescoes by Tiberio d'Assisi. Beyond the grille are frescoes of the *Redeemer* (in the vault) and, around the altar, *St Francis and his companions*, also by Tiberio.

Another corridor leads past a garden with a fig tree, recalling another episode in the life of St Francis, to the **Cappella del Pianto** restored in 1926. A corridor leads back towards the church past a room with old pharmacy jars and the cloister of the convent.

The **museum** has been closed for restoration. It has a small collection of paintings including a Portrait of St Francis, by an unknown master, known as the Maestro di San Francesco, a *Crucifix* by Giunta Pisano, another portrait of the saint by the school of Cimabue, and a detached fresco of the *Madonna enthroned* attributed to Pierantonio Mezzastris. There is also a display of church vestments and a delightful missionary museum. The pulpit from which St Bernardine preached, in a room near the entrance to the museum, is shown on request. A staircase leads up to the **Convent of St Bernardine of Siena** with cells, including that of St Bernardine.

BEYOND ASSISI

The immediate environs of Assisi, with the places associated with St Francis, and the beautiful hill of Subasio are described on pp 98–101. The places in this section are further out of the town, some of them in lovely countryside, and all of them little visited. An interesting small local museum has recently been opened in Bettona, and outside Collemancio is the Roman site of Urbinum Hortense in beautiful countryside.

Practical information

Information office
IAT di Assisi, ☎ 075 812534.

Getting there
Buses from Assisi (run by *APM*) to Bastia Umbra, Cannara and Bettona.

 **Hotels**
Bastia Umbra
☆☆☆☆ *Progetto La Villa*, ☎ 075

8010011; fax 075 8010574; ☆☆☆ *Lo Spedalicchio* (at Ospedalicchio), ☎ & fax 075 8010323 and *Turim*, ☎ 075 8001601; fax 075 8001723.

San Gregorio (8km north)
☆☆☆ *Castel San Gregorio*, ☎ 075 8038009; fax 075 8038904.

Petrignano d'Assisi
☆☆☆ *Poppy Inn*, ☎ 075 8038002; fax 075 8039255.

Bettona
Across the valley from Assisi to the south-west is the peaceful little village of **Bettona**, the ancient **Vettona**, surrounded by thick olive groves, with a fine view from its low hill (355m) which has been preserved from unattractive new buildings. On the western approach the road passes an Etruscan tomb (signposted left of the road) and the remarkable golden-coloured Etruscan walls. In the attractive piazza with a fountain is **Palazzo del Podestà** and **Palazzo Biancalana**, where the **Museo Civico** has been arranged in six rooms (open every day Tues – Sun

10.30–13.00, 14.30–17.00; summer 10.30–13.00, 15.00–19.00, ☎ 075 987306).

An outside staircase leads up to the entrance to Palazzo del Podestà. In the first room are two paintings by Perugino painted for the church of Sant'Antonio in Bettona, and an altarpiece of the *Adoration of the shepherds* with a predella showing stories from the life of San Crispolto, the most important work of Dono Doni. There is also a processional standard by the bottega of Alunno, and a 16C ceramic statue of *St Anthony of Padua*. Room 2 has three detached frescoes, including a charming *St Michael Archangel* by Fiorenzo di Lorenzo, and the *Trinity* and *St Roch* by Tiberio d'Assisi. The chapel has a scagliola altar frontal, and the last room has 18C Deruta ware. There are also a few pieces of furniture and an interesting collection of small wooden Umbrian coffers (15C–16C).

Below the fountain is the church of **San Crispolto** (the first bishop of Bettona) with a pyramidal campanile. To the right of the church is the restored cloister, and (beyond glass doors) a covered passageway leads out on to the hillside with a view of the town and its walls. The other church in the piazza, **Santa Maria Maggiore**, has been closed indefinitely. Opposite the church is the **Oratory of Sant'Andrea** (for admission ask at the Museum) where an interesting large fresco of the *Passion of Christ* was discovered in 1987 and attributed to the school of Giotto (1394).

At **Passaggio**, nearby, is the former abbey of San Crispolto, with a fine crypt perhaps dating from the 11C, and the 18C Villa del Boccaglione.

Cannara and Collemancio

Further east, on the Topino river, is **Cannara**. In the church of **San Francesco** is a painting of the *Madonna and Saints* by Nicolò Alunno. There is an interesting collection in the **Municipio** of detached frescoes and finds from Urbinum Hortense (see below).

Collemancio, to the west, amidst olives and oaks, is a pretty little village with a path around the outside of the walls, recently cleared. The church of San Bernardino has ex voto frescoes showing miracles of the saint and, next door, Santo Stefano has fine vaulting and devotional statues (including St Roch). By the public gardens a rough road (unsignposted) leads up to (500m) the unenclosed site of **Urbinum Hortense** on a little hill with splendid views of the beautiful surrounding countryside. This was a Roman municipium, and the remains include a Republican temple basement and baths. Wild thyme, chicory and lichen grow among the ruins. Across the valley is **Limigiano** with remains of a castle and the Romanesque church of San Michele.

Bastia Umbra and Petrignano

On the plain to the west of Assisi is **Bastia Umbra**, which was important for its **castle** in the Middle Ages, remains of which can still be seen. In the church of **Santa Croce** are works by Tiberio d'Assisi, Nicolò Alunno, and Cesare Sermei.

A byroad leads north to **Petrignano**, where there is a detached fresco by the school of Perugino in its church, and **Rocca Sant'Angelo**, a castle in a splendid position above the Chiascio valley. At the top of the hill, outside the castle walls, is the convent of **Santa Maria della Rocchicciola**, founded in the 13C. In the church are 14C frescoes in the apse, a *Crucifix* painted by Matteo da Gualdo, and frescoes by Bartolomeo Caporali and Lo Spagna.

LAGO TRASIMENO

Lago Trasimeno is a lake which has preserved its natural beauty to a large extent. It is surrounded by low fertile hills covered with olive groves and vineyards, and reeds grow on its shores. It has picturesque lakeside villages, and three lovely islands. The colour of its waters changes constantly according to the weather, and it is subject to sudden storms in winter. From a distance it provides one of the most breathtaking views in Umbria (particularly from the hills around Cortona).

Lago Trasimeno is the largest lake on the Italian peninsula, and the fourth largest lake in Italy, with a circumference of about 53km. It is 257m above sea-level and has an average depth of 4.9m. It has an abundant supply of fish (eels, carp, tench, perch, shad, and pike) which are still caught by a few fishermen from flat-bottomed boats using round nets attached to wooden piles driven into the water. The shores of Lago Trasimeno have been inhabited since the Palaeolithic era, and by 507 BC it was under the rule of Lars Porsena, king of Chiusi. It is famous as the site of the resounding victory of Hannibal over the Romans in 217 BC on its northern shores (described at Tuoro, see below).

Its central position on the borders of several warring communes meant that it was often used as a battlefield in the Middle Ages when numerous castles and fortified villages were built on its shores or on the neighbouring hills. In the 12C it came under the dominion of Perugia. Up until the 16C it was surrounded by thick woodlands, famous as hunting grounds. Attempts have been made to regulate the level of the lake since Roman times, when the first outlet was constructed. Leonardo da Vinci produced a study in 1503 in which he proposed linking the lake to the Chiana, the Arno and the Tiber.

Up until the end of the 19C the lake was constantly subject to flooding, and the swamplands on its shores caused malaria epidemics. In the 18C and 19C there were various proposals to drain the lake, but in 1896 a new outlet was constructed, next to the Roman one, which finally solved the problem of flooding. In the 20C work has had to be carried out to try to ensure that the lake will not dry out in years of drought, as its level is constantly diminishing because of the formation of peat. The first public boat service on the lake was inaugurated in 1905.

Practical information

Information offices
IAT del Trasimeno, 10 Piazza Mazzini, Castiglione del Lago (☎ 075 9652484).
Passignano: Pro Loco, 36 Via Roma.
Tuoro: Pro Loco information office in the main piazza, ☎ 075 825220.
Paciano, Pro Loco ☎ 075 830186.
Panicale information office, ☎ 075 837581.

Getting there
By car There is a good **road** round the shore of the lake, described below: the prettiest stretch is between Monte del Lago and Castiglione del Lago, as the north shore is disturbed by the *superstrada* (which connects Perugia to the A1 motorway) which runs between the old road and the lake. However, the *superstrada* has relieved Passignano and Magione of much heavy traffic.
By bus There are services (*ASP*) from Perugia to Castiglione del Lago, Tuoro and Passignano.
By rail There is a railway station at Castiglione del Lago on the old

Florence – Rome line (a few slow trains a day from Florence in 1hr 40mins – 2hrs). Railway station at Tuoro and Passignano on the branch line from Terontola to Perugia and Foligno (slow trains from Perugia to Passignano in c 30mins).

By boat Services are run by *APM* (Azienda Perugina della Mobilità, Località Pian di Massiano, ☎ 075 827157). There is a regular service throughout the year (c nine times daily) from Passignano via Tuoro to the Isola Maggiore (and vice versa) in c 30 minutes. The last boats from the Isola Maggiore to Tuoro and Passignano in the evening leave at 18.45, 19.45 or 20.20, according to the season. From 1 May to the end of September there are more services from Tuoro to the Isola Maggiore (10 mins) on public holidays. From 1 April–30 September services at least eight times a day also from Isola Maggiore to Castiglione del Lago (and vice versa) in 30 minutes. On public holidays in April and daily from May to the end of September, services from San Feliciano 12 times a day to the Isola Polvese (and vice versa). From 1 July to the end of September there is a service between the Isola Polvese and the Isola Maggiore.

Hotels
Isola Maggiore
✰✰✰ *Da Sauro*, ☎ 075 826168; fax 075 825130. Just 12 rooms in a simple little house beyond the end of the only street on this beautiful peaceful island. This has been a delightful place to stay, with a good restaurant, since it was opened in 1964 by Sauro, a fisherman on the lake (whose wife and son also work here). For the timetable of the boat service from Passignano or Tuoro, see above.
San Feliciano
✰ *Da Settimio*, ☎ 075 8476000, with a good restaurant. On the lakeside in this quiet little village, Settimio, formerly a fisherman on the lake, and his wife have run this simple small hotel for many years. Their son and daughter-in-law now help to continue the family tradition.
Panicale
✰✰✰ *Le Grotte di Boldrino*, ☎ 075 837161; fax 075 837166. A family run hotel in a handsome 19C palace in the old town. Eleven rooms, most of them with views over the countryside, rather eccentrically furnished but comfortable with nice bathrooms. Restaurant (££), with local specialities, in the over-restored medieval cellars below, or in the garden in summer. Half-board terms available.
Monte del Lago
✰✰ *Da Santino*, ☎ 075 8400130; fax 075 8400188.
Castiglione del Lago
✰✰✰ *Miralago*, 6 Piazza Mazzini, ☎ 075 951157; fax 075 951924.
Castel Rigone
✰✰✰✰ *Relais La Fattoria*, ☎ 075 845322; fax 075 845197.

For other accommodation near the lake, see also p. 115.
Paciano
Country house hotel, *Locanda della Rocca*, ☎ 075 830236 & fax 075 830155. In a lovely old house in the centre of the village, owned by the Buitoni pasta family, with five rooms and a restaurant. Reasonable terms.

There are numerous *agriturismo* hotels near the lake (list provided by the IAT in Castiglione del Lago), including *Poggio del Sole*, near Sanfatucchio outside Castiglione del Lago, ☎ 075 9680221 or 075 9589678, which is extremely well run and has a swimming-pool. Reasonably priced apartments to rent.

There are also numerous **self-catering flats and holiday houses** to rent in the vicinity of the lake (detailed information from the IAT in Castiglione del Lago).

Campsites
Sites near the lake are open from 1 April

to 30 September. ✩✩✩✩ *Villaggio Italgest*, Sant'Arcangelo, Magione, ☎ 075 848238; ✩✩✩ *Kursaal*, Viale Europa, Passignano, ☎ 075 828085; *Punta Navaccia*, Tuoro, ☎ 075 826357; *Badiaccia*, Castiglione del Lago, ☎ 075 9659097; Cerquestra, Monte del Lago, ☎ 075 8400100. ✩✩ *Europa*, Passignano, ☎ 075 827405. There are a number of ✩ sites on the lakeside at San Feliciano, Castiglione and Torricella.

Restaurants

Many restaurants serve fish from the lake.

Panicarola £££ *Il Bisteccaro*, 15 Via Trasimeno, ☎ 075 9589327.

Isola Maggiore ££ *Da Sauro* (see above).

Passignano ££ *Del Pescatore*, 5 Via San Bernardino, ☎ 075 827165.

San Savino ££ *Da Massimo*, 16 Via dei Romani, ☎ 075 8476094.

San Feliciano £ *Da Settimio* (see above), Via Lungolago.

Castel Rigone £ *Locanda del Galluzzo* at Trecine, ☎ 075 845352.

Castiglione del Lago £ *La Cantina*, 89 Via Vittorio Emanuele, ☎ 075 9652463; £ *Il Lido Solitario*, Via Lungolago (pizzeria), ☎ 075 951891.

● There are beautiful places to **picnic** all round the lake and on Isola Polvese and Isola Maggiore.

● There is a **market** on Wednesday at Castiglione del Lago.

● **Swimming** in the lake is permitted in various localities including Tuoro, Passignano and Castiglione del Lago. There are also facilities for wind-surfing and sailing.

● **Hiking and horseback riding facilities** have recently been introduced in the area surrounding the lake. These include marked tracks and paths (red and white CAI signposts). Detailed information with illustrated guides and maps from the IAT in Castiglione del Lago.

● A **festival** of kites *Coloriamo i cieli* is held biennially (even years) at Castiglione del Lago for three days at the beginning of May.

The islands

The lovely **Isola Maggiore**, with a circumference of c 2km and some 100 inhabitants, mostly fishermen, is the only island on the lake connected to the shore by a regular boat service throughout the year (see above). It has no cars.

It was visited in 1211 by St Francis of Assisi. Near the landing-stage is the delightful brick-paved street, Venetian in character, with some 15C houses, and several simple restaurants. The craft of lace-making was introduced to the island in 1904 by Elena Guglielmi and still survives here. At the north end (left) of the street a path leads to the 12C church of **San Salvatore** (restored in 1972). A path continues round the shore of the island with beautiful views across the lake.

At the south end of the island a 14C Franciscan church and convent were incorporated in the **Castello Guglielmi**, a Romantic mock-Gothic pile designed and built by the Roman senator Giacinto Guglielmi in 1885–91. It has been abandoned since 1960 and in the last ten years or so has fallen into ruin, but a custodian who lives in the village is usually here to show visitors what is left of the ground floor. It has a remarkable atmosphere of faded decadence. The church and two cloisters (from one of which there is a beautiful view of the lake) are in a derelict state, as are the kitchens, pantries, old billiard room and theatre. There seems little hope that the crumbling ruins can ever be saved. In the romantic overgrown garden a little children's play-house survives.

Nearby, on the highest point of the island next to the cemetery, is the church of **San Michele Arcangelo** surrounded by olive groves. It was founded before 1200 and restored in 1998. It contains 14C–15C frescoes, some attributed to Bartolomeo Caporali, and a painted Cross also by him (the custodian of the castle sometimes has the key).

Isola Minore, once renowned for the skill of its fishermen, was abandoned by the end of the 16C and is now privately owned.

Isola Polvese (c 69ha; reached by boat in summer from San Feliciano; see above) is the largest island on the lake and it has the most beautiful vegetation. It had five churches and 200 inhabitants in the 14C when the castle was built, but it was abandoned by the 17C because of malaria. Acquired in 1972 by the Province of Perugia, it has been a protected area since 1974, of the greatest interest for its birdlife. To the right there is access to a little beach (with a bar and restaurant open in summer), and to the left a path leads to the impressive remains of the 14C castle near poplars, tamarisk, and cypresses. Fruit trees grow inside its walls.

A beautiful path leads round the shore of the island in c 1hr. The sound of the birds which nest in the reeds is remarkable: they include grebes, coots, cormorants, bitterns, kites, kingfishers and ospreys. Ilexes, willows, oaks and ash grow around the edge of the island, with olives and cypresses in the centre. Another path runs across the centre of the island, near which are the ruins of a 12C Olivetan monastery.

Castiglione del Lago

Castiglione del Lago (304m) is the most important place on Lago Trasimeno. It is situated on a small promontory planted with olive trees jutting into the west side of the lake, which is dominated by its magnificent castle. It was inhabited in Etruscan and Roman times, and in the Middle Ages its fortress was contended by Perugia and Cortona, the inhabitants always taking the side of Cortona. In 1247 Frederick II reconstructed the castle. The Baglioni family of Perugia ruled the town after 1490: Machiavelli was a guest here of Gianpaolo Baglioni, as was Leonardo da Vinci who drew the castle in 1503. In the 16C Ascanio Della Corgna married Giovanna Baglioni, and, as nephew of Julius III, became Marquis of Castiglione. He was a famous *condottiere*, his military achievements culminating in the victory at the battle of Lepanto.

The little town has an interesting plan, with two parallel main streets ending in the gardens in front of the castle at the edge of the promontory. It is best to park outside Porta del Rondò at the top of the hill, or below the walls (from which steps lead up through Palazzo Della Corgna). In **Corso Matteotti** on the left is the church of **Santa Maria Maddalena** built in 1836–60 on a plan by Giovanni Caproni. The pronaos dates from 1868, and the tall campanile from 1893. In the centrally planned interior are frescoes by Mariano Piervittori (1850) and, on the left altar, *Madonna and Child* by Eusebio da San Giorgio. From Piazza Mazzini Via Vittorio Emanuele continues past a palace (no. 51) with good terracotta decoration, and the parallel Via del Forte leads past the church of **San Domenico**, with a 17C interior and an 18C wooden ceiling.

The two main roads end in Piazza Gramsci with a view of the lake. Here is **Palazzo Della Corgna**, approached by a double ramp and with an L-shaped plan. A 13C tower house was incorporated into a hunting-lodge by the Baglioni in the 16C, and in 1560 Ascanio Della Corgna rebuilt the palace, probably using Vignola as architect, and surrounded it with fine gardens (now diminished). The building was damaged by fire in 1824 and restored in 1934. The **interior** is open daily April–Oct 09.30–13.00, 16.00–19.30; winter on weekends only 10.00–16.00, ☎ 075 96581; the ticket includes admission to the castle; and there is a cumulative ticket *'Museo Aperto'* for museums and monuments in Paciano and Panicale (see below), and Città della Pieve (see p. 115). The palace has numerous 16C frescoes, many of them by Niccolò Circignani, known as Il Pomarancio. In the **entrance hall** is a ceiling fresco by Pomarancio of the *Judgement of Paris*, and mythological scenes. In the room to the right is the *Fall of Phaeton*, and the *four Seasons*. The next room has scenes from the *Aeneid* by Pomarancio and Giovanni Antonio Pandolfi. Another room has scenes of Hannibal in Italy, including the *Battle of Trasimene*. Beyond a vestibule with the *Rape of Proserpine* by Pomarancio, is the studio of Della Corgna, with his coat of arms, and scenes from the life of Julius Caesar. Beyond the Hall of the Gods, with more frescoes by Pomarancio, is the **main hall** with frescoes by Giovanni Antonio Pandolfi and Pomarancio illustrating various episodes in the life of the great general. The geometric decorations are by Cesare Nebbia.

From the studio of Della Corgna a door leads out to steps which descend to a long, narrow, fortified **passageway** with an old wooden roof and stone floor, which leads to the impressive **castle**. Many times destroyed and reconstructed, it was largely rebuilt by Frederick II in 1247, probably on a design by Frate Elia of Cortona, when it became one of the most impregnable fortresses in Europe. Its interesting plan is an irregular pentagon with walls following the slope of the hillside and four angle towers. The triangular keep is 39m high. Its fortifications were strengthened by Ascanio Della Corgna who was also a military architect. From the battlements there are excellent views down to the lake. The walls enclose the ruins of an ancient chapel and an open-air theatre.

A chapel in the hospital in the piazza (formerly the Convent of Sant'Agostino) has a fresco of the *Madonna* attributed to Giovanni Battista Caporali or Giovanni Spagna.

The Montepulciano road which leads west from Castiglione passes close to several villages on the old Etruscan road which linked Chiusi to Cortona, including **Pozzuolo**. Here Palazzo Moretti (1667) is now the property of the Comune, and the church dates from 1783. Nearby at Laviano, on the Tuscan border, St Margaret of Cortona was born in 1247. A little church in the here dates from c 1000. To the north at **Petrignano**, the church of Sant'Ansano (rebuilt in the early 19C) contains an altarpiece attributed to Andrea della Robbia and a wooden Ecce Homo (early 18C). Montepulciano, further west beyond the A1 motorway is described in *Blue Guide Tuscany*.

South of Pozzuolo are the Etruscan settlements of **Gioiella** and **Vaiano** at both of which tombs have been unearthed. At Vaiano the 17C parish church was renovated in 1740, and in the church of Santa Lucia is a fresco of the *Madonna enthroned* by the school of Perugino.

North-west of Castiglione is **Piana** with a neo-classical church by Giovanni Caproni (1809).

A road follows the shore of the lake north from Castiglione along the shore of the lake, and then diverges right from the Arezzo road for **Borghetto**, a pretty little fishing hamlet with a good view of Castiglione. Only one angle tower survives from its 15C castle. To the north is **Monte Gualandro** (442m) and its castle, owned by the Montemelini, where Frederick II is thought to have stayed in 1246. The road passes under the superstrada and climbs up with a good view of the lake to continue towards Tuoro (keep right). It passes the old customs house, **La Dogana**, with a portico, which marked the boundary between the Grand-ducal lands of Tuscany and the Papal States. Plaques recall travellers who have passed this way including Michelangelo, Galileo, Goethe, Stendhal, Byron and Hans Christian Anderson.

The road descends to a plain on the edge of the lake, enclosed by hills, which was the site of the battlefield where Hannibal routed the Romans in 217 BC. At that time the lake reached further inland.

On a corner is a signpost (right) for the first stopping-place in an interesting **Itinerary of the Battle of Lago Trasimeno** (marked by white signposts: *Percorso Storico Archeologico della Battaglia*) which can also be followed by car. Maps and explanatory panels are provided (if somewhat erratically) as well as viewing platforms above the battlefield. There is an information office in Tuoro. A rough road (temporarily closed) leads past a farm and the **Pieve di Confini** (being restored) dating from 1165, which was once one of the most beautiful Romanesque churches in the area. The portal with interesting carvings survives. Just beyond is the first platform (Sosta no. 1) which has an excellent view of the lake and its islands, but is only just above the superstrada.

Hannibal and the Battle of Trasimeno

The famous Battle of Trasimeno took place during the Second Punic War. Hannibal marched over the Alps into Italy with his Carthaginian army, which included some elephants and an estimated 6000 horses. In the early hours of the morning of 24 June 217 BC the Roman consul Flaminius (who built the road still named after him), with some 25,000 soldiers, was ambushed by Hannibal and his 40,000 soldiers, who had encamped on the surrounding hills, as he rashly marched through the fog along the edge of the lake here. The massacre lasted only a few hours as the Romans were taken completely by surprise. Flaminius died in the encounter and about 15,000 of his men, trapped between the hills and the lake, died or were taken prisoner; the others fled and eventually returned to Rome. Hannibal is thought to have lost only about 1500 soldiers. The dead were burned in ustrina, remains of which have been found in the area. The Roman prisoners were killed but Hannibal let those from other Italic tribes go free to demonstrate his goodwill towards them. However, the Umbrian cities remained faithful to Rome at this crucial point in her history when her supremacy was severely threatened. The Romans who were able to escape found refuge in Perugia, and Hannibal was unable to take Spoleto in his attempt to reach Rome. Byron, in the fourth canto of *Childe Harold's Pilgrimage* evokes the terrible battle scene and then records the tranquillity of the lake in his day in a description which is still apt today:

> *Far other scene is Thrasimene now;*
> *Her lake a sheet of silver, and her plain*
> *Rent by no ravage save the gentle plough;*
> *Her aged trees rise thick as once the slaine*
> *Lay where their roots are;*

On the other side of the main road (left) a single track road leads inland. At the beginning of a cypress avenue is Sosta no. 3. Beyond Sosta no. 4 the road climbs uphill past another stopping-place (near a necropolis where soldiers' tombs and the base of a funerary monument have been found) to the hamlet of **Sanguineto** whose name, as recorded by Bryon ('a name of blood from that day's sanguine rain'; canto IV *Childe Harold's Pilgrimage*) commemorates Hannibal's victory. A road continues right (keep right) and descends to another stopping-place (Sosta no. 6) where there is a platform which provides the best view of the battlefield in a natural amphitheatre.

The byroad continues (keep right) and becomes paved as it enters (by a back road) **Tuoro sul Trasimeno** on a low hill, now set back from the lake. Palazzo del Nardo (or del Capra) is supposed to have been built on Roman remains. There is a small private museum here illustrating the production of olive oil. A road descends towards the lake, and, on the modern Via Cartaginese (right; unsignposted) a column from the Roman Forum was set up in 1961 to mark the edge of the lake in Roman times. Some of Hannibal's troops are thought to have been stationed near here. The main road continues down to the lakeside district of Tuoro. Here is a landing-stage for the ferries to Isola Maggiore (see above), a bathing lido and several restaurants. An open-air sculpture park known as the Campo del Sole has columns of pietra serena carved by various sculptors in 1985–88.

The old road for Passignano continues past a fortified house (above the road to the left) known as **Mariottella** (1541) and a byroad outside Tuoro leads inland to **Vernazzano** whose medieval castle defended the north shore of the lake. One leaning tower survives. Just before Passignano an avenue leads up to the 18C villa of **Pischiello**, built by Uguccione Bourbon di Sorbello.

Passignano sul Trasimeno is a little resort on the side of the lake, and the head-quarters of the boat services for the islands. It also has moorings for private boats, as well as bathing beaches, hotels and restaurants. Passignano was the Roman *Passum Jani* and during the Middle Ages it was contested between warring communes. By the mid-13C it had come under the control of Perugia, and at that time the fortress was built. In the early 20C it had important seaplane construction works and it was bombed in the Second World War. From Piazza Garibaldi, in front of the landing-stage (built in 1967), several narrow lanes lead up to the remains of the castle with a triangular 14C tower in an old fortified district.

Castel Rigone

The road for Magione continues along the side of the lake off which a byroad forks left, where there are good retrospective views of the lake for Castel Rigone, a pleasant little hill resort in a beautiful position on Monterone (653m) with wonderful views. The **Madonna dei Miracoli** is a fine Renaissance church (1494). The portal, with a relief in the lunette, is by Domenico Bertini of Settignano (1512). Above is a prettily carved rose window. In the attractive interior are (south side) a delightful 16C statue of *St Anthony Abbot and his pig*, and (second altar) a *Madonna of the Rosary* by Bernardo di Girolamo Rosselli. The **high altarpiece** is a copy made in 1644 of the original *Epiphany* by Domenico Alfani, seized by the Florentine militia of Ferdinando II in 1643. The splendid gilded wooden frame by Bernardino di Lazzaro dates from 1528 (and the predella and lunette are original). On the choir arch are two tondi with Prophets, also by Alfani. The choir stalls date from 1619 and the paintings in the vault are by Giovanni Ellero (1930).

In the chapel to the right of the sanctuary is a carved *Crucifix* in front of mourning figures painted by Papacello (a bas-relief depicts a miracle connected with the *Crucifix*). Also here is a 17C painting of the *Deposition*. In the other pretty chapel left of the sanctuary (with a 16C grille) is the *Madonna dei Miracoli* to whom the church is dedicated. The painting is surrounded by a finely carved wooden frame and numerous ex votos. On the second north altar is a fresco of the *Assumption* and *Coronation of the Virgin* by Giovanni Battista Caporali and pupils. The organ dates from 1878. Remains of the castle and an old 15C hospice survive.

Magione

The main road from Passignano continues alongside the superstrada to a fork; on the left the road climbs up towards Magione. It passes a turning for **Montecolognola** (410m) where the inhabitants of Magione built a castle in 1293 (restored in the 15C), which has well preserved walls. In the parish church are 14C–16C frescoes, an *Annunciation* in Deruta majolica (1460), and a fresco by the Futurist painter Gherardo Dottori. There is a magnificent view of the lake.

Magione was the birthplace of Fra' Giovanni da Pian di Carpine, one of the first followers of St Francis, who in 1246 travelled to Karakorum to convert the successor of Genghis Khan. He wrote a history of Mongolia used by later travellers to the East, including Marco Polo. The main road passes (left) steps up past a war memorial to the neo-Gothic town hall, and (on the main road) a monumental 19C building. On the opposite side of the main road is the church of the **Madonna delle Grazie** with a good fresco of the *Madonna enthroned* attributed to Andrea di Giovanni da Orvieto (1371), in the apse. The Corso (Via Memorabile) or Via XX Settembre lead downhill towards the castle. In Via XX Settembre is the parish church of **San Giovanni** frescoed at the east end by Gherardo Dottori in 1947 when it was reconstructed after war damage. Nearby is the four-square **Castello dei Cavalieri di Malta**, with a fine courtyard by Fieravante Fieravanti (c 1420). The castle, beautifully kept, is still owned by the Knights of Malta (and is now usually open in summer for guided visits, Thur 10.00–13.00; weekends 16.00–19.00; for information, ☎ 075 8479261). A hospital of the Knights Templar existed in Magione in the 11C–12C, parts of which survive here.

On the hillside to the north is the isolated 13C **Torre dei Lombardi**, which was damaged by earthquake in 1846 and has been propped up by scaffolding for many years. A byroad leads south-east from Magione into the hills above the lake and the little fortified villages of **Montesperello** (a castle was built here before 997) and **Montemelino**.

The beautiful road which continues round the lake to the west of Magione passes **Torricella**, once an important posting-stage, and now with a number of campsites. **Monte del Lago**, with remains of its 14C castle (recently damaged by new buildings), juts into the eastern side of the lake. The road follows the lake past the picturesque **Castello di Zocco** (no admission) in a group of pine trees. On the site of a Franciscan convent, it was built c 1400 and was one of the most important fortresses on the eastern side of the lake. Abandoned some 50 years ago, it is now in a ruined state, but preserves its walls with five towers and an ancient chapel.

Fishing in Lago Trasimeno

The lake has long been famous for its fish, which include eel (*anguilla*), carp (*carpa*), tench (*tinca*), perch (*persico*), shad (*agone*), pike (*luccio*), and grey mullet (*cefalo*). Some 30 per cent of the fresh water fish caught in Italy come from this lake. Traditional methods of fishing here are well illustrated in the fishing museum (reopened in a new building in 1997) at San Feliciano, the centre of fishing on the lake and where the first fishing cooperative was set up.

In past centuries most of the fishermen used *barche volanti* and had a particularly hard life working for the owners of certain areas of the lake or the banks along its shores. The only exception were the *vallaioli* of San Feliciano who were both proprietors and fishermen and who in summer would work in simple huts on the shore to harvest the reeds. Eels were caught in cane mats (*arelle*) placed on the muddy bottom of the lake. Until the 17C very unusual fish traps constructed out of stacks of sticks and known as *tori* were used all over the lake: it may be that the name of Tuoro was taken from these. Certain parts of the shore known as *porti* were kept as reserves to attract the fish and here fishing was limited.

As early as 1342 fishing rights on the lake were regulated, and in 1566 Pio V issued strict rules about fishing and taxes on the catch. The fish was sold to fishmongers and transported from the lake by horse and cart to various parts of Umbria (the farthest place they reached, since it had to be sold in a few hours, was Todi). An arrangement also grew up whereby the fishermen and peasants who cultivated the fields around the shore of the lake would exchange each others produce several times a week (without payment passing hands).

The traditional and complicated methods of fishing changed in the 1950s when artificial fibre was introduced in the manufacture of nets and the boats were first powered by outboard motors. For a short period at this time many peasants left the surrounding countryside and set up as fishermen hoping to make a more profitable living. The boats on the lake still have a flat keel and the characteristic nets (or *tofi*) or fish-traps (used specially for eels) are designed in concentric circles and fixed to wooden piles which stick out of the water. The fishing industry has been given incentives recently, and the lake is being restocked with pike and eel. About 150 professional fishermen still work here.

Fish is served in numerous restaurants all round the lake, and typical dishes include *regina in porchetta*, carp stuffed with lard (or ham), rosemary, fennel and garlic and cooked in the oven with a little olive oil, and *tegamaccio* a fish stew cooked slowly in tomato conserve and white wine. Eels are usually cut up and fried or baked in pieces, and tench and perch filleted and fried in breadcrumbs.

San Feliciano, named after St Feliziano of Foligno who came here in AD 220, is now an attractive little village with a harbour for fishing boats. Some of the inhabitants work the reeds which abound in this part of the lake. The **Museo della Pesca** (open 10.00–12.30, 15.00–18.30 except Mon; ☎ 075 8479261) was moved to a new larger building on the side of the lake in 1997. It has a very interesting display illustrating the work of the fishermen on the lake over the centuries, and the delightful exhibits include boats and fishing equipment from the past. There is a regular boat service in summer from San Feliciano to the Isola Polvese (see above).

Oasi della Valle

The lakeside road continues to a crossroads with the San Savino road. Here is the building of the Consorzio del Trasimeno and entrance to the protected area known as the Oasi della Valle (open Tues–Sun 10.00–13.00, 15.00–18.00; 3000 lire; ☎ 075 8476007). There is a small museum with explanatory panels illustrating the history of the emissaries of the lake, and identifying its flora and fauna. Close by is the subterranean emissary from the lake built by the Romans, some 7300 metres long, and several times reopened. This carried excess water from the lake to prevent flooding, via the Caina torrent and the Nestore and Tiber rivers. Walkways lead across the outlet constructed in 1896, and nearby is another emissary built in 1421–23 by Braccio Fortebraccio of Montone to stabilise the water level. A walkway built above the reeds leads in about 10 minutes out to a hide on the water where a great number of birds can be seen, including kingfishers and herons, who nest here. In spring numerous migratory birds from Africa come here. Visitors can also take an excursion on an electric boat along the shore of the lake on Sat and Sun at 15.30 and 16.30 (10,000 lire; the trip, for a maximum of 15 people, lasts about 45 minutes). The oasis has been run by the conservation society known as *Legambiente* since 1989.

San Savino, stands on a little hill with remains of a walled castle, first built in 1006 with a tall triangular keep.

The road now goes uphill and there are splendid views across fields and reedy marshes down to the lake with the Isola Polvese and the promontory of Castiglione del Lago beyond. **Monte Buono** had another important 11C castle (now transformed); nearby is the abandoned church of **Santa Rufina** (10C). Beyond the little church of **Santa Maria delle Ancaelle** (closed), a late Romanesque building with traces of frescoes and a 14C painting of the Umbrian school, above the road to the left, in a fine position, is the **Badia di Sant'Arcangelo**, a former abbey which flourished in the 14C. The views of the lake are magnificent. Another byroad leads to the **Castello di Montalera** (487m) on a hill planted with ilexes. The castle, which had great strategic importance in the Middle Ages, was restored as a residence in 1534 by Braccio Baglioni.

Panicale

A byroad from the Montalera turning leads up through Casalini and Lemura to the picturesque little medieval village of Panicale on a hill with one of the best views of the lake from its old walls (13C–14C). It has Etruscan origins and was allied to Tuscany up until the 13C. It was the birthplace of the remarkable painter Tommaso Fini, known as Masolino da Panicale (1383–c 1440), master of Masaccio. The famous 14C *condottiere* Giacomo Paneri, called Boldrino di Panicale, was also born here. The attractive **Piazza Umberto I** (with the local tourist office, ☎ 075 837581) was built on a slope so that the rainwater would be collected in the well, replaced since 1473 by the present lovely fountain. Here is the massive fortified flank of the 17C **Collegiata** with a very dark interior (light at west end and in some of the chapels). It contains a lovely painting of the *Adoration of the Shepherds* attributed to Giovanni Battista Caporali (in the last chapel on the north side), and in the apse a 15C fresco (light behind the 16C wooden Crucifix).

A road continues uphill under an arch to the tiny piazza in front of the charming little **Palazzo del Podestà** (partly 14C), with a bell-tower added in 1769, at the top of the hill, where there is a fine view of the lake.

The local tourist office (see above) provides guided visits every day to the theatre and church of San Sebastiano (at 10.15, 11.15, 15.15 and 16.15; more frequently in summer). The **Teatro Cesare Caporali**, reached from Piazza Umberto beneath a vaulted passageway, is named after the famous poet born here in 1530 or 1531. It was built at the end of the 18C (restored in 1991), and has a backcloth painted by Mariano Piervittori and stuccoes by Alceste Ricci. Outside the walls, in a less attractive part of the village, is the church of **San Sebastiano** with two frescoes by Perugino: the *Martyrdom of St Sebastian* is particularly beautiful, but the *Madonna and Child* was damaged when it was detached.

A winding road leads west to **Paciano**, another well-preserved little medieval village in a fine position, with a 14C castle. It is particularly peaceful and well kept. Just below Piazza della Repubblica, beyond an arch, the church of **San Giuseppe** (reconstructed in the 18C) preserves the gonfalon of the Comune, a *Madonna of the Misericordia* dating from c 1460 and attributed to the school of Bonfigli or to Fiorenzo di Lorenzo. Above it is a little **parish museum** (open July–Sept 10.00–13.00; if closed ring at no. 12 or ☎ 075 830120) opened in 1994 in the Sala della Confraternità del Santissimo Sacramento which has an unusual fresco of the *Crucifixion* by Francesco di Città della Pieve (1452), by some considered to be the master of Perugino. The museum contains a miscellany of objects from churches in the parish, including two 15C panels of saints from a triptych, 17C reliquaries, church silver, 18C statues of the *Madonna* (the clothes carefully restored by the local inhabitants), and a few Etruscan finds.

The little 17C church of **San Carlo Borromeo** nearby is usually closed. Below it there is a lovely well.

Outside the village and below it are the churches of **San Sebastiano**, which contains a fresco of the *Martyrdom of St Sebastian* (1496) and the **Madonna della Stella** (1572) with frescoes by Silla Piccinino (1579).

Outside Porta Perugina the Panicale road leads uphill to **Ceraseto** where the church of Santissimo Salvatore (restored in 1998) has a fresco of *Christ enthroned between Sts John the Baptist and Peter*, attributed to Giovanni Battista Caporali (c 1510). Above the village in woods is the **Torre d'Orlando**, part of the earliest castle of Paciano (restored and privately owned).

On **Monte Pausillo** there is a nature reserve (picnic places) with deer and wild boar and interesting birdlife.

Close to the lake is **Panicarola** where an Iron Age necropolis has been found. The parish church is built on foundations of a pagan temple. On the approach to Castiglione del Lago (which is clearly seen ahead) is the **Santuario della Madonna della Carraia** built in 1661–63 (the cupola was rebuilt in 1856). On the left bank of the Pescia torrent is the 17C **Torre di Pescia**, with a 19C wing (reconstructed after war damage).

CITTÀ DELLA PIEVE AND ENVIRONS

Città della Pieve, in a beautiful position (508m) above the Val di Chiana, with a distant view of Lago Trasimeno, is a well-kept little town with attractive streets worth exploring. Since the 13C most of its buildings have been built in red brick, which give the town its characteristic appearance. Apart from its works by Perugino, who was born here, it is particularly interesting for its 18C and early 19C architecture.

Practical information

Information offices

Ufficio Turistico Comunale, Piazza del Plebiscito, ☎ 0578 299375. IAT del Trasimeno, Castigione del Lago, ☎ 075 9652484.

Getting there

By bus (*ASP*) from Perugia.
By rail The nearest railway station (8km) is at Chiusi on the main line between Florence and Rome.
Car parking near Sant'Agostino, otherwise with an hourly tariff within the walls.

Hotels
Città della Pieve
✩✩✩ *Vannucci*, Viale Vanni, ☎ 0578 299572; fax 0578 298063. In a pleasant position close to the centre of the town, between the churches of San Francesco and Santa Lucia. It has 32 rooms, a garden and a restaurant.

In the environs
Piegaro
✩✩ *Da Elio*, Località Osteria, ☎ 075 8358017; fax 075 8358005, with restaurant.

Castel del Piano
Villa Aureli, ☎ 075 5140444; fax 075 5149408. Officially categorised as *agriturismo* this is a grand country villa on the edge of an uninteresting little town. It is surrounded by a large estate with fine trees, where sheep are grazed, and a handsome formal garden with solid squares of yew, parterres of box hedges and citrus trees in pots. Two flats are available for rent by the week on the first and second floors. They preserve their delightful original 18C furnishings and are extremely spacious and comfortable with splendid views and charming majolica floor tiles made in 1925. The villa is lovingly kept and has been carefully restored since 1948 by the present owner Leonardo di Serego Alighieri who still lives here. There is a small swimming pool in a converted irrigation tank below the garden wall. Good red and white wine is produced in the cellars here.

Between **Pietraia** and **Bagnaia**, *Poggiolo*, località Poggio della Corti, ☎ 075 695236. An *agriturismo* in a 19C villa surrounded by a park run by a young couple. Rooms and flats to rent.

There is another *agriturismo*, further east at **San Biagio della Valle:** *Torre Colombaia*, ☎ 075 8787381. This is a large estate with a 19C hunting lodge and is in splendid wooded countryside. Rooms or apartments available (meals also provided). A delightful place, with simple but well-furnished accommodation of varying size, some in the hunting lodge 'folly' itself. Ideal for large family holidays.

Restaurants
Città della Pieve:
£ **Serenella**, 28 Via Fiorenzuola (off Via Veneto), ☎ 0578 299683, family-run trattoria of particularly good value; £ *La Silvana*, Corso

Vannucci, ☎ 0578 298311;
££ Da Bruno, Corso Vannucci, ☎ 078 298108.
Pasticceria *Stefanini*, Piazza del Plebiscito.

Market on Saturdays.

Annual festival
The *Palio dei Terzieri*, an archery contest preceded by a parade in period costume, is held here on 15 August and the following Sunday. On the Sunday nearest 21 June, *L'Infiorata*, a flower festival.

History

Etruscan in origin, Citlà della Pieve was later a Roman settlement. In the Middle Ages the town was controlled by Orvieto until 1198 when it was taken by Perugia, against whom the inhabitants rebelled for many centuries. In 1446 the great painter Pietro Vannucci, known as Perugino, was born here, and in 1568 Antonio Circignani, called Pomarancio, son of Niccolò, also known as Pomarancio.

The main brick-paved street, named after Perugino, leads into the town from the north past a medieval well and several picturesque streets. Next to the handsome **Palazzo Vescovile** (c 1780), by Andrea Vici, is the church of **Santa Maria dei Bianchi**, by Andrea Cini. It contains 18C decorations by Giovanni Miselli and Stefano Cremoni. In the sacristy is a fresco of the *Presentation in the Temple* by Antonio Circignani (Pomarancio). It adjoins the **Oratorio di Santa Maria dei Bianchi** (open 10.30–12.30, 15.30–dusk; if closed ring at no. 42 or ask locally for the custodian). This contains a fresco of the *Adoration of the Magi* by Perugino (1504; restored in 1984) with Lago Trasimeno in the background. It was painted in 29 days and copies of two letters from Perugino, found here in 1835, are displayed on the walls: he at first proposes 200 florins as a suitable fee, but then suggests reducing it to 100 florins since he is a native of the town, but after discussions with the confraternity finally agrees to an even more modest sum. The confraternity, founded in the 13C, still operates as a charitable institution (the robes of the brothers are displayed here).

Next door is the 14C **Casa Canestrelli** and, opposite, **Palazzo Giorgi-Taccini** with a neo-classical façade by Giovanni Santini.

Duomo

Via Vannucci ends in Piazza Plebiscito in front of the Duomo, begun at the beginning of the 17C above the ancient church of Santi Gervasio e Protasio. The façade incorporates 9C–10C sculptural fragments. The campanile was designed by Andrea Angelelli in 1738.

The **interior** contains some particularly fine works. South side. The first altar contains a 16C sculptured Crucifix attributed to Pietro Tacca; the second altar contains a *Madonna and Child with saints*, a beautiful painting by Domenico di Paride Alfani (1521). In the **apse** is a *Madonna in glory with saints* by Perugino, and paintings of the Madonna (right) by Giannicola di Paolo and (left) by Salvio Savini. The frescoes above are by Pomarancio.

In the **Chapel of the Holy Sacrament** are frescoes by Giacinto Boccanera (1714) and a painting of the *Blessed Giacomo Villa* by Giacinto Gemignani. In the **Chapel of the Rosary**, there is a *Madonna* by Salvio Savini and a wooden sculpture of the *Madonna* attributed to Giovanni Tedesco. The font of 1548 is by

Master Giovanni of Montepulciano. In the north transept is a *Madonna del Carmine*, by Antonio Pomarancio. North side. The second altar contains Antonio Pomarancio's, *Marriage of the Virgin* (repainted in the 18C), and on the first altar is Perugino's *Baptism of Christ*.

The small cathedral **museum** (open at weekends or on request) contains 16C–19C reliquaries and church silver, paintings, books and vestments. In the courtyard is archaeological material including Etruscan urns.

The splendid **Torre Civica**, next to the Duomo's façade, was erected in the 12C, re-using travertine from an older building, and heightened in the 15C. Opposite the tower is the 14C **Palazzo dei Priori** (renovated in the 19C). On the corner of Via Vannucci is the large **Palazzo Della Corgna** (open in summer every day 10.30–12.30, 17.00–19.00; or by request at the tourist office), built by Ascanio Della Corgna on his nomination as governor of the town in 1550, probably designed by Galeazzo Alessi. On the ground floor the Sala delle Muse has a fine ceiling frescoed by Niccolò Pomarancio. Other frescoes on the stairs and first floor are Salvio Savini (1580). There is a pretty view from the terrace. At the foot of the stairs is a curious sandstone obelisk, thought to be a sundial of ancient origin, formerly in the convent of San Francesco.

In Piazza Plebiscito is the neo-classical **Palazzo Cartoni** (1845, by Giovanni Santini) and, opposite, a little house (with a plaque) on the site of the house which may have belonged to Perugino's family.

Via Vittorio Veneto leads out of the piazza; in Via Roma (right) is the 16C **Palazzo Bandini**, perhaps by Galeazzo Alessi. Beyond the former church of **Sant'Anna** (1752) is the **Rocca**, erected in 1326 by Ambrogio and Lorenzo Maitani, with four angle towers. It is connected to Porta Romana by a stretch of 13C walls. In Piazza Matteotti is the church of the **Gesù** with a façade by Andrea Vici (late 18C).

Beyond, across Largo della Vittoria, is the church of **San Francesco** which has a 13C brick façade. In the interior (first altar on the south side), there is a *Madonna enthroned* by Domenico Alfani, and (first altar on the north side), *Descent of the Holy Spirit* by Antonio Pomarancio. Next door is the entrance to the **Oratorio di San Bartolomeo** (open 10.00–12.00, 16.00–19.00), with a large fresco of the *Crucifixion*, known as the *'Pianto degli Angeli'*, by Jacopo di Mono del Pellicciaio (1384). Viale Vanni continues to the church and monastery of **Santa Lucia**, which is surrounded by ilexes. The centrally planned church (left unfinished) is by Clemente Moghini (1774).

Via Roma (see above) leads out through Porta Romana and past the interesting church dedicated to **Beato Giacomo Villa** (1687–1717) to the church of **Santa Maria dei Servi** (left; usually locked; for admission apply to the custodian of the Oratorio di Santa Maria dei Bianchi), founded in the late 13C and transformed in the 18C when it was decorated with stuccoes. It preserves remains of a *Deposition* by Perugino frescoed in 1517.

From Piazza Plebiscito, Via Garibaldi leads south-west past the grandiose **Palazzo della Fargna** (now the town hall), begun in the early 18C. In the piazza here is the **Teatro degli Avvaloranti** (due to reopen shortly after a lengthy restoration), built in 1830 by Giovanni Santini (the backcloth by Mariano Piervittori, c 1870 has been lost). Via Garibaldi continues past Palazzo Baglioni (1780) to the church of **San Pietro** (usually closed) founded in the 13C and restored in 1667, and again in the 19C. It contains a ruined fresco (detached and mounted on canvas), by Perugino and assistants, of *St Anthony Abbot between*

Sts Paul the Hermit and Marcellus (to be restored). From the terrace here there is a fine view of the Val di Chiana.

Outside Porta Sant'Agostino (at the beginning of Via Vannucci) is the former church of **Sant'Agostino** with an interior dating from 1789, now used for conferences. It contains attractive side altars with 17C–18C paintings, recently restored. From the well in Via Vannucci, Via Santa Maria Maddalena leads north past the exceptionally narrow Vicolo Baciadonne to the church of **Santa Maria Maddalena** (c 1780 by Andrea Vici) which contains a 14C fresco of the Crucifixion attributed to Jacopo di Mino del Pellicciaio.

Beyond Città della Pieve

The road from Città della Pieve to Perugia (N220) is separated from Lago Trasimeno (described on p. 113–114) by the low hills on its southern shore, but it passes numerous small fortified villages whose histories are intimately connected with that of the lake. The road which leads south from Città della Pieve has a wide view over the Val di Chiana. The Perugia road soon bears left and winds down through woods with a good view of Città della Pieve on the left.

Piegaro, built on a wooded hill above the River Nestore, is of Roman origin. In the 13C Venetian exiles set up a glass industry here which flourished until the beginning of the 19C. A road leads south to Montegabbione, see p. 243. **Tavernelle** has a pretty piazza and the church of the Santissima Annunziata (1578). Outside the village are lignite mines used for a large electrical plant which supplies energy to Rome. A byroad leads left to the **Santuario della Madonna di Mongiovino**, a centrally planned church begun in 1513 on a design by Rocco da Vicenza. It contains frescoes by Nicolò Pomarancio and Arrigo Fiammingo. Above is **Mongiovino Vecchio**, where there is a fine medieval castle (restored in 1968) on the site of a Roman castrum. Panicale, closer to the lake, is described on p. 113.

Outside Tavernelle a byroad leads south to **Castiglion Fosco** with remains of its castle (1462). The church of Santa Croce (restored in 1823) contains 16C paintings and an 18C Crucifix, and the church of San Giovanni Battista a 16C painted wooden statue of the *Madonna and Child*. A minor road leads east through Collebaldo to **Pietrafitta** which has one tower left of its medieval castle, and the former **Abbazia dei Sette Frati**, a Benedictine foundation. To the south-east is the abandoned castle of Cibottola.

The main road for Perugia continues from Tavernelle to a turning (signposted) for **Fontignano**, on low ground, where Perugino died of the plague in 1523. Before reaching the modern church, the little chapel of the Annunziata (with two cypresses) contains a (disappointing) fresco of the *Madonna and Child* attributed to Perugino. (Ask for the key at the bar next to the church.) There is a photo of Perugino's *Adoration of the Shepherds* formerly above the arch which was detached in 1848 and bought by the Victoria and Albert Museum in London in 1895 (and is now in the National Gallery). The little funerary monument here dates from 1703. **Agello** is prominent on a hill to the left of the road. It is thought that some Roman soldiers fled here after Hannibal's victory on Lago Trasimeno. It was famous for its castle (restored with an incongruous bell tower), from which there is a fine view. The main road, now almost continuously built up, leads past **Montefreddo**, near Bagnaia, a villa interesting for its garden with a cypress avenue, terraces, and fountains (for adm. by appointment ☎ 075 774172). Just beyond is a turning for **Castel del Piano** (see p. 115).

The upper Tiber Valley & Gubbio

CITTÀ DI CASTELLO

Città di Castello is a pleasant little town with two very fine musuems, the Museo del Duomo and the Pinacoteca Comunale. In the upper Tiber Valley, on the border with Tuscany, is the attractive little village of Citerna, and the impressive Castello Bufalini at San Giustino, now owned by the state, which is partially open to the public. The Tiber Valley south of Città di Castello is described on pp. 129–132.

Città di Castello (population 38,000) is the most important town in the fertile upper Tiber Valley. It flourished in the High Renaissance under the rule of the Vitelli, when it gave employment to many famous artists, among them Raphael, Signorelli and the Della Robbia. It has been noted for its printing industries since the 16C. It retains much of its walls, although certain sections are in need of restoration.

Practical information

Information office
IAT dell'Alta Valle del Tevere, Logge Bufalini, Piazza Costa, ☎ 075 8554922 and 075 8554817.

Getting there
By railway Città di Castello is on the *Ferrovia Centrale Umbra* line from Perugia to Sansepolcro.
Car-parking There is a car-park on Viale Nazario Sauro, with escalators (temporarily out of order) to the Duomo.

Hotels
☆☆☆☆ *Tiferno*, 13 Piazza San Francesco, ☎ 075 8550331; fax 075 8521196. A comfortable old-established hotel opened in 1895 in a large palace in the centre of the town, with a good restaurant.
☆☆ *Umbria*, Via dei Galanti (off Via Sant'Antonio), ☎ 075 8554925; fax 075 8520911. A simple little hotel, but good value.

In the environs *Villa Pia*, ☎ 075 8502027; fax 075 8502127, at Lippiano opened in 1998/9, and officially categorised as a 'country house' hotel. Well run by a Welsh couple who live here, in a lovely old villa on the edge of the village, surrounded by a charming garden (with a swimming-pool). It is in a superb position on the border with Tuscany, best reached from Monterchi. It has a good restaurant (booking only) specialising in fish, presided over by the owner who was a chef at a leading London hotel. The villa, which has 13 bedrooms, is particularly suited to families and bookings are usually taken for one or two weeks. Half-board prices per person per week range from Lire 1,000,000–1,200,00 depending on the season.
Citerna ☆☆☆ *Sobaria*, 2 Via della Pineta, ☎ 075 8592118; fax 075 8593410.

Campsites
☆☆☆ *La Montesca* (open May–October), ☎ 075 8558566.
There are numerous holiday apartments for rent in the surrounding countryside (information from the IAT office).

Restaurants
££ Tiferno (see above); **Il Bersaglio**, 14 Via Orlando, ☎ 075 8555534.

£ Amici Miei, 2 Via del Monte, ☎ 075 8559904 (with a set menu, but very good value); **Adriano Due**, Piazza Che Guevara, ☎ 075 8556909; **Il Fiore**, 19 Via Don Milani, ☎ 075 8522149; **Trattoria Lea**, 38 Via San Florido, ☎ 075 8521678 (very good value; family run); **La Carabiniera**, 55 Via San Florido, ☎ 075 8559035.

Monte Santa Maria Tiberina
£ Oscari, ☎ 075 8570110.

Citerna **£ Belvedere**, 66 Corso Garibaldi, ☎ 075 8592148.

Fraccano, on the Fano road, **££ Da Meo**, ☎ 075 8553870.

Shopping
Handwoven linens can be purchased at the **Laboratorio della Tela Umbra** in Piazza Costa and at **Busatti**, Piazza San Francesco.

Market days on Thursdays and Saturdays (in Piazza Gabriotti).

Annual festival
An annual Chamber Music Festival is held here at the end of August and beginning of September. There is a truffle festival in the town on the second weekend in November.

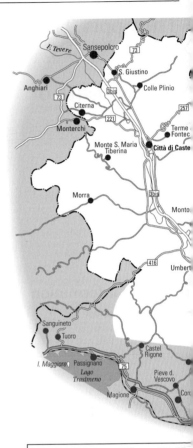

The upper Tiber Vall

History

In the Pleistocene era the valley was submerged by the great Lago Tiberino, a lake which stretched as far as Terni and Soleto. The region was later inhabited by elephants, hippopotamuses and rhinoceros. The presence of man here has been traced since the Stone Age. The inhabitants are still called **Tifernati** after the Umbrian town of **Tifernum** on this site. The Roman municipality of **Tifernum Tiberinum** was mentioned by Pliny the Younger who had a villa nearby, remains of which have been found in a locality called Colle Plinio. By the 6C it was the seat of a bishopric, and in the Middle Ages, as a free commune, it was contested between Perugia and the Church. The Vitelli family held the lordship in the 15C and 16C, and four of their palaces remain in the town. The firm of Scipione Lapi was famous for its book production here at the beginning of the 20C.

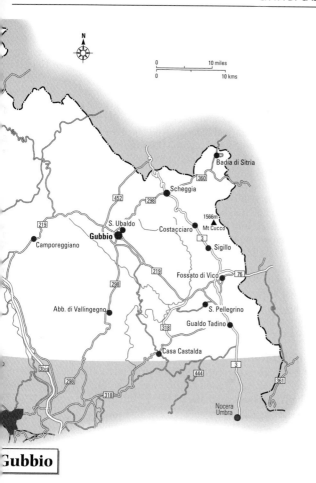

Gubbio

The Duomo

From the car-park off Viale Nazario Sauro a path leads through the walls to two short flights of escalators (out of order at the time of writing) which emerge in the **public gardens** on the site of a defensive tower destroyed in 1480. The monument to Vittorio Emanuele is by Vincenzo Rosignoli (1906).

Beyond is the **Duomo**, given a bizarre appearance by its half-finished façade begun in 1632–46. Of ancient foundation, it was rebuilt by St Florido who became bishop in 580, and again in the 11C and 14C. It had to be reconstructed after earthquake damage in 1458 and was consecrated in 1540. It is thought that Elia di Bartolomeo Lombardo and his son Tommaso were involved as architects. The splendid round **campanile** (seen from behind) dates from the 11C, and has a Gothic upper storey and a conical roof. The Gothic north portal has two beautifully carved panels dating from 1339–59 representing *Justice* and *Mercy*.

Interior The interior (closed 12.00–17.00 on weekdays, and 13.00–15.00 on PH) has fine Corinthian pilasters gilded in the 19C. The panelled wood ceiling was made by local craftsmen in 1697. It incorporates two paintings of angels by Tommaso Conca, and *St Florido in Glory* attributed to a follower of Giacinto Brandi. South side. In the third chapel there are works by Giovanni Battista Pacetti (**Lo Sguazzino**) born at Città di Castello in 1593, including a view of the town. In the fourth chapel, rebuilt in 1789 on a domed Greek-cross plan, is an **altarpiece** by Rosso Fiorentino, commissioned to show *Christ in Glory between the Madonna and St Anne*, *Mary Magdalene*, and *Mary the Egyptian*, and below a group of figures representing the populace. Although restored in 1983, the picture is very dark. In the fifth chapel are paintings by the local 17C painters Bernardino Gagliardi and Virgilio Ducci.

The crossing and **dome** are frescoed by Tommaso Conca (1795–97) and the four *Evangelists* in the spandrels are by Ludovico Mazzanti (1751). The two wooden cantorie have 16C carving by Alberto di Giovanni Alberti (called Berto). A door on the right leads into the **sacristy**, off which a little room contains a remarkable large frescoed lunette of the *Ecce Homo and four saints* dating from the 16C, discovered in 1968 (and shown on request). The **choir** is frescoed by Marco Benefial (1747–49) and the stalls are by Alberto di Giovanni Alberti from a design by Doceno and Raffaellino del Colle (1533 and 1540). The third north chapel is decorated by Bernardino Gagliardi, and the first chapel has works by Nicolò Pomarancio. In the **lower church**, on the site of the ancient crypt, the patron Saints Bishop Florido and Amanzio are buried in an ancient sarcophagus. There is a 15C fresco of St Florido in a side chapel.

The Museo del Duomo

On the right of the façade is the entrance (through an interesting 14C courtyard) to the Museo del Duomo (or **Museo Capitolare**), beautifully arranged in fine 14C–15C vaulted rooms (open 10.30–13.00, 15.00–17.00 or 18.00, ☎ 075 8554705).

Ground floor. The case at the right-hand end of the salone displays the magnificent **silver treasure of Canoscio**. This consists of 25 plates and utensils used during the celebration of the Eucharist, found while ploughing a field near Canoscio (in the district) in 1935. They are remarkable examples of early Christian art of the 6C.

The chronological order of the arrangement continues in the small room off the corridor ahead with a silver and gilded **altar-frontal** with carvings showing the figure of Christ blessing, surrounded by the symbols of the Evangelists and scenes from the life of Christ. According to tradition it was presented to the cathedral by Pope Celestine II in 1142. In the corridor is a wooden statue of the seated *Madonna and Child* by a 14C Umbrian artist (removed for restoration).

In the second small room off the corridor is an exquisite episcopal **crozier** attributed to Goro di Gregorio (c 1324), and an unusual little marble basin dating from the 16C. The paintings include *St Florido*, attributed to Giacomo di Ser Michele Castellano (1412), a *Madonna enthroned* in a Renaissance frame, dating from 1492, showing the influence of Signorelli, and an *Annunciation* by Francesco da Tiferno.

The other cases in the **salone** display liturgical objects dating from the 12C–19C including processional crosses, thuribles, reliquary boxes, chalices, paxes and an agate and silver gilt cross made by a Florentine goldsmith in the 15C. At the end of the salone is a 16C painted wooden reliquary and a *Madonna and Child with the young St John* by Pinturicchio. On the stairs is an unusual stone statue of *St Sebastian* (15C), two well-painted putti (fragments) attributed to Giulio Romano, and a fine Tuscan 15C wooden Crucifix (removed for restoration).

Upper floor. In the first room, a 17C painting of *St Bonaventura*, bozzetti by Ludovico Mazzanti, and *Rest on the Flight into Egypt* attributed to Tommaso Conca. In the second room there are 16C–18C liturgical objects and bozzetti by Ermenegildo Costantini (1731–91). The third room has 18C reliquaries and 17C–19C vestments.

Piazza Gabriotti and Piazza Matteotti

In **Piazza Gabriotti** (where a market is held on Thursdays and Saturdays), beyond the flank of the cathedral, is the fine **Palazzo Comunale** (or dei Priori) begun by Angelo da Orvieto in 1322 but left unfinished. It is constructed in sandstone with lovely two-light windows, and a well-designed vaulted entrance hall and stairway. Beneath an archway a short alley leads to Via del Modello from which the splendid round campanile of the cathedral (described above) can be seen. Opposite Palazzo Comunale is the 14C **Torre Civica** (open 10.00–12.30, 15.00–17.00 except Mon). A rickety old, narrow staircase ascends to the top from which there is a good view.

Corso Cavour, leads out of Piazza Gabriotti beneath a pretty 14C loggia. It has some interesting palaces and, above a covered market, an 18C printing works (which can be visited on request). On the right is **Palazzo del Podestà** (now the seat of the Pretura), also by Angelo da Orvieto, and finished by 1368. The façade, rebuilt by Nicola Barbioni in 1687, faces **Piazza Matteotti**, in which an elaborate 19C building is now the seat of a bank.

In the adjoining Piazza Costa is the **Laboratorio della Tela Umbra** (open 09.00–12.00, 15.00–17.30 except PH), founded in 1908 by Baron Leopolo Franchetti, where you can see weavers at work on 17C looms, demonstrating this traditional Umbrian skill. A private museum illustrating the history of Umbrian hand-weaving is open 10.00–12.30, 15.00–18.30, closed Mon; ☎ 075 8559071.

San Francesco and Piazza Garibaldi

Via Angeloni leads out of the piazza up to Piazza San Francesco (also called Piazza Raffaello Sanzio) where there is a monument commemorating the fall of the Papal government in 1860 by Elmo Palazzi. The church of **San Francesco** is situated here, built in 1273 and with a fine 18C interior. The **Vitelli chapel** (off the north side, damaged in the earthquake in 1997) was built by Giorgio Vasari and contains an altarpiece by him. The beautiful entrance gate (1566) is by a local craftsman and the stalls date from the 16C. Beyond an altar with a very darkened terracotta of *St Francis receiving the stigmata* by the Della Robbian school, the fourth north altarpiece is a copy of Raphael's *Marriage of the Virgin* commissioned for the church in 1504 and removed by Napoleon in 1798 (now in the Brera Gallery in Milan). Off the south transept is a chapel with a carved wooden 15C group of the *Pietà*.

From the piazza, Via degli Albizzini leads to **Piazza Garibaldi** with the large **Palazzo Vitelli a Porta Sant'Egidio**, now owned by a bank and used for concerts. It was built in 1540, perhaps on a design by Vasari, for Paolo Vitelli, with decorations by Cristoforo Gherardi and Prospero Fontana. It has a beautiful garden façade overlooking a large garden with a grotto (in need of restoration), statues, and a little hillock planted with ilexes. At the far end of the garden (on Via San Bartolomeo) is a palazzina decorated with frescoes. Also on Piazza Garibaldi is the 15C **Palazzo Albizzini** (open 09.00–12.30, 14.30–18.00; PH 09.00–13.00; closed Mon) which houses the **Collezione Burri**, a collection of works donated to the city in 1982 by the local artist Alberto Burri (1915–95). An even larger collection of his works can be seen in a huge warehouse on the outskirts of the town, see below.

Via San Bartolomeo leads to Via Giulianelle which is the seat of the Biblioteca Comunale. The **Museo Civico** (open 09.00–13.00, 15.00–19.00 except Sat afternoon and PH) is also here, containing an archaeological collection relating to the Tiber Valley (including fossils from the Pleistocene era).

The convents near Via XI Settembre

From Piazza San Francesco (see above) Via Angeloni leads to a crossroads at the beginning of Via XI Settembre. On the corner of Via dei Lanari is the convent of the **Clarisse Murate** (a closed order, no admission), with a fine entrance which preserves its wooden doors. Attached to the convent is the church of **San Giacomo** (entered from Via XI Settembre; key at the convent on request). The interior has pretty stucco decoration, and from a side door the little cloister can be seen.

Via Sant'Andrea leads left from Via XI Settembre to the church of **San Giovanni Decollato** (closed) which contains frescoes by the school of Luca Signorelli. The piazza here has been named after the ghetto on this site from 1390–1592. Via della Fraternità leads to the convent of the **Clarisse Urbaniste** (a closed order, no admission), which has remains of frescoes in the entrance hall. Their church, **Santa Cecilia**, has a large enamelled terracotta lunette of the *Epiphany* by the Della Robbian school, and the cloister dates from the 15C. In Via Sant'Angelo, also off Via Sant'Andrea, is the church of **San Michele Arcangelo** where there is a high altarpiece of the *Madonna and Child with saints* by Raffaellino del Colle.

Via XI Settembre continues east past the large 16C **Palazzo Vitelli a San Giacomo**. Opposite, at no. 21 is another convent of the **Clarisse** (or **Cappuccine**), also a closed order but accessible to visitors, next to the church of **Santa Veronica**. On request (08.30–17.00 or 18.00) one of the 21 nuns who still live here and cultivate the convent orchard show visitors the lovely cloister, recently restored, with two wells and herringbone paving, and a charming little museum arranged in a room off the cloister dedicated to St Veronica Giuliani (1660–1727) who lived in this convent for 50 years and was canonised in 1839. The exhibits include ceramics and objects used in the convent, as well as St Veronica's possessions, and a letter in her hand. On the other side of Via XI Settembre is the plain façade of **Santa Maria delle Grazie**, with a Renaissance portal. It was rebuilt in 1587 and contains a cast of the *Assumption* by Andrea della Robbia, and, in a chapel off the south side, a fresco (restored in 1996) of the *Transition of the Virgin* attributed to Ottaviano Nelli. On the north side is a chapel dedicated to the Madonna delle Grazie. It is named after a highly venerated altarpiece, the only known work signed and dated 1456 by Giovanni di Piamonte, who worked with Piero della Francesca. It is kept in an elaborate cupboard and exhibited only on 2 February and 26 August.

The Pinacoteca Comunale

In the southern part of the old town, in Via della Cannoniera, is the entrance to **Palazzo Vitelli alla Cannoniera**, seat of the Pinacoteca Comunale (open daily except Mon 10.00–12.30, 15.00–17.30; in summer 10.00–13.00, 14.30–18.30, ☎ 075 8520656), the most important collection of paintings in Umbria after the Pinacoteca in Perugia. The palace was built for Alessandro Vitelli in 1521–32 by Antonio da Sangallo the Younger and Pier Francesco da Viterbo. It was restored by Elia Volpi and donated to the town by him in 1907. The municipal gallery was founded in 1860–66 and was first exhibited here in 1912.

The stairs are decorated with frescoes attributed to Cola dell'Amatrice and Cristofano Gherardi (called Il Doceno).

First floor. Some of the rooms on the first floor also have 16C vault decorations by Doceno. Room I is dominated by a beautiful painting of the *Madonna and Child enthroned* (*a Maestà*) by an anonymous late 13C artist named from this work the Maestro di Città di Castello. It has recently been exquisitely restored. Also displayed here is a *Madonna and Child* by Spinello Aretino. Room II has a *Madonna* by Andrea di Bartolo, a tripych by Antonio Alberti, and early 15C choir stalls. Room III contains a *Madonna and Child*, by Antonio Vivarini, and the exquisite **reliquary of St Andrew** by the bottega of Lorenzo Ghiberti (1420), with two statuettes in gilded bronze by the master's own hand. Room IV. The striking *Head of Christ with signs of the Passion* is variously attributed to the Flemish school (Giusto di Gand?), to a follower of Piero della Francesca of the late 15C Umbrian school, or Cosimo Rosselli. Also here is a *Madonna and Child with two angels* by Neri di Bicci (or his bottega), and a 16C standard with the *Madonna della Misericordia*. The large *Coronation of the Virgin* in Room V is by the bottega of Domenico Ghirlandaio.

Room VI. The *Standard with the Creation of Eve and the Crucifixion of Sts Roch and Sebastian* is a beautiful but very damaged work by Raphael. In Room VII there are two paintings by the local artist Francesco Tifernate and a sacristy cupboard in poplar wood with walnut inlay by Antonio Bencivenni (signed and dated 1501). Rooms VIII, IX and X have remains of painted decoration by Doceno, and the salone (XI) also has decorations by Doceno and Cola dell'Amatrice.

Ground floor. Room XII displays a beautiful painting of the *Martyrdom of St Sebastian* by Luca Signorelli, probably painted in the last years of the 15C. Room XIII contains works derived from Signorelli, and Room XVI works by Raffaellino del Colle. Steps lead down to the loggia which has a small collection of sculpture, including a Sienese marble relief of the 14C showing the *Baptism of Christ* and Della Robbian works. Room XVII contains Mannerist works. A door leads out to the garden, where the very fine garden façade of the palace can be seen, which has remarkable graffiti decoration (1532–35) by Doceno, probably on a design by Vasari. The last two rooms (XIX and XX) contain works awaiting restoration and 19C paintings.

Behind the palace, in Via Oberdan, is the church of **San Domenico** a very dark Gothic church (1271–1424) which contains interesting 15C frescoes. On the right side of the nave, in a chapel with two Gothic arches dedicated as a war memorial, is a 15C Sienese fresco of the *Crucifixion*, and in the last chapel on the right are more 15C frescoes. At the east end of the nave, on the right and left sides, are two Renaissance altars which used to contain a *Crucifixion* by Raphael (now in the National Gallery in London) and the *Martyrdom of St Sebastian* by Signorelli (now in the Pinacoteca). The fine choir stalls are by Manno di Benincasa (1435).

Via Signorelli and Corso Vittorio Emanuele (right) lead to the church of **Santa Maria Maggiore** which has an interesting vaulted interior. Dating from 1505 it is thought to be the work of Elia di Bartolomeo Lombardo. On the walls and in the niches remains of 15C frescoes alternate with modern works.

On the outskirts of the town, c 1.5km along the old road to Perugia, in the **ex Seccatoi del Tabacco**, a warehouse once used for drying tobacco, is the **Collezione Burri**, another exhibition of works by Alberto Burri, donated by him to the city in 1990 (open at the same times as the Burri collection in Palazzo Albizzini, see above, ☎ 075 8554649). Beyond, at **Garavelle** (2km from the town), is an interesting **local ethnographical museum** (open 09.00–12.00, 14.00 or 15.30–17.00 or 18.30 except Mon, ☎ 075 8552119) in an old farmhouse. The ornithological collection, model railways, and two steam engines built in 1930, are not at present on view.

THE UPPER TIBER VALLEY

On the road to Fano (N257) the first turning on the right leads past the 19C **cemetery** designed by Emilio De Fabris to the **Terme di Fontecchio**, a spa, whose alkaline sulphurous waters were known in Roman times. The 19C thermal building was designed by Guglielmo Calderini (season Mar–Dec, ☎ 075 8520614).

Further on the Fano road climbs the hill of Belvedere planted with cypresses and pine trees and passes the **Santuario della Madonna del Belvedere**, a centrally planned octagonal building with a dome. It was constructed in 1668–84 by Antonio Gabrielli, a local architect and his pupil Nicola Barbioni. The unusual semicircular façade has a portico and two cylindrical bell-towers. The interior has numerous statues and stuccoes and over the high altar is a venerated image in terracotta of the *Madonna and Child*. The view of the Tiber Valley is magnificent.

Across the Tiber from Città di Castello is the sumptuous **Villa La Montesca** which is surrounded by a fine park, built in 1880 by Florentine architects for Baron Leopoldo Franchetti. For admission, enquire at the tourist office in Città di Castello. The **Eremo di Buonriposo**, was traditionally thought to have been founded by St Francis near a spring. It is now privately owned (admission on request), with a picturesque little cloister and a 17C chapel.

This byroad continues up to **Monte Santa Maria Tiberina**, a well preserved medieval village in a beautiful position (688m) overlooking the upper Tiber Valley. From the 11C this was the citadel of the Del Monte family whose burial chapel is in the Pieve of Santa Maria. A tower of the castle survives.

For other places of interest in the Tiber Valley to the south, see pp. 130–132.

San Giustino and Colle Plinio

On the northern border of Umbria, reached by two roads which run due north of Città di Castello, is **San Giustino** a busy little town in the centre of which is the impressive **Castello Bufalini**, surrounded by massive walls. The medieval fortress here was strengthened in 1480 and donated by the comune of Città di Castello in 1487 to the Bufalini family, feudal lords of the area, so that they could complete the defence works designed by Giovanni and Camillo Vitelli. It is rectangular with corner towers and battlements and was surrounded by a star-shaped moat. In the 16C Giulio Bufalini transformed the castle into a fortified villa, as his residence. He added the delightful loggia and courtyard which show the influence of Vasari. He also designed the beautiful Italianate **garden** between the walls and the moat, which has recently been restored. It was laid out on a geometrical design with box hedges, and a *ragnaia* for trapping birds (where the hedges used to be some 5–7 metres high; only a line of holm-oak trees survives from this part of the garden), and a maze (which has been preserved). Plantations of olives and oak trees were added later in the 16C. In the early 18C the garden was redesigned with French parterres, espaliered roses and dwarf fruit trees, as well as fountains and grottoes. Later, numerous ilexes, cypresses and magnolia trees were planted.

Eight rooms in the interior are frescoed by Cristofano Gherardi (Il Doceno) (1537–54), and a small part of the collection of paintings begun by Cardinal Giovanni Ottavio in the 18C survives, as well as some 17C and 18C furniture. The castle was sold by the Bufalini family to the state in 1989 and restoration work is still in progress, but the ground floor is usually open on weekends, July–Oct 10.00–13.00, 15.30–19.00, ☎ 075 8569977.

There is an interesting medieval building beneath the priest's house near the modern church.

A byroad (signposted Calalba) leads south out of the town and passes **Villa Magherini Graziani**, with a loggia, dating from 1616, now owned by the comune of San Giustino, but in a neglected state. Beyond the villages of Celalba and Pitigliano, just across an iron bridge, an unsignposted road leads left for the excavations of the Roman villa of **Colle Plinio** which can be seen behind a fence on either side of the road, but are not open to the public. The site, first excavated in the 1970s, has revealed remains of a villa built in the early 1C AD by Granio Marcello, which was inherited by Pliny the Younger (recognised as being his by the brick stamps found here). So far traces of a wine cellar and baths have been found, but other parts of the villa extended over the hillside. This byroad continues to run alongside the wall which surrounds the large neglected garden of the 17C **Villa Capelletti** (closed), beneath which more Roman structures have been found.

A very twisty mountainous road (N73bis) climbs from San Giustino through beautiful scenery via Bocca Trabaria (1049m), the pass between Umbria and the Marche, to Urbania and Urbino.

Off the Sansepolcro road is **Cospaia** which became a tiny Republic in 1440 when it was omitted by mistake from the territory around Sansepolcro, ceded by Pope Eugenius IV to the Florentine Republic. It remained independent until 1826. This was the first place in Italy where tobacco was cultivated (in 1575). The road enters Tuscany just before Sansepolcro, described in *Blue Guide Tuscany*.

Citerna

North-west of Città di Castello, off the Arezzo road, is Citerna, on a wooded hilltop on the border between Umbria and Tuscany. It was founded in Roman times, and reconstructed in the 7C–8C. Damaged by an earthquake in 1917 and in both World Wars, it is now a delightful peaceful village with fine walls and brick buildings, well-restored and well-kept.

Corso Garibaldi, named after the hero who spent three days here in 1849, leads up through the village from the entrance between two gate posts surmounted by fir cones. On the left, by no. 35, a yellow sign indicates a picturesque **medieval passageway** with a wooden roof and arches which runs along the side of the hill. **Casa Prosperi** (no. 41), now the property of the Church (ask locally for the key), contains a monumental carved 16C fireplace in pietra serena. Opposite is **Palazzo Vitelli**.

Beyond the town hall is the church of **San Francesco** (1316; rebuilt in 1508). It contains delightful gilded wooden altars. By the second right altar is a frescoed niche with the *Madonna and Child with Sts Michael and Francis and two angels* by Luca Signorelli and his workshop (in poor condition, but restored as far as was possible). It is thought to be a late work (1522–23), possibly with the help of Papacello. The two altars in the south transept have a Della Robbian frieze with cherubs' heads, and *Christ in glory with Sts Francis and Michael* with six lovely angels in the frame, by Raffaellino del Colle. The choir has pretty 16C stalls. Here are a *Madonna and angels and saints* by the 16C Umbrian school, a 14C statuette of the *Madonna and Child* in terracotta, and a crowded *Deposition* by a certain Alessandro Forzorio from Arezzo (1568; recently restored). In the left transept is a *Deposition* by Pomarancio, and in an elaborate wooden altar, *Madonna and St John the Evangelist*, by Raffaellino del Colle, in a beautiful landscape on either side of a 14C wooden Crucifix. At the sides are *Sts Jerome and Francis* and, above, the *Annunciation*. In a niche, seated Della Robbian statue of *St Anthony Abbot*. The organ dates from 1828. A *Holy Family* attributed to the school of Raphael also belongs to the church.

On the opposite side of the Corso is another vaulted medieval passageway. Beyond an arch over the road is the little Piazza Scipioni with a fountain (kept dry in winter) and three lime trees, and a view over the Tiber valley beyond the Belvedere park where deer run wild.

Above to the left is the church of **San Michele Arcangelo**, built in the 18C. It contains (third right chapel) a *Crucifixion* by Pomarancio and a bell dated 1269 and (second left chapel) a Della Robbian *Madonna and Child* with angels in polychrome terracotta. To the left of the church, by the bell-tower of San Francesco, is the **Teatro Bontempelli**, a delightful little theatre, recently restored. Via della **Rocca** leads in the other direction past solidly built houses to the Rocca, destroyed in the Second World War, except for a fine circular brick tower which can be seen beyond orchards from the damaged walls where there is a little fountain (1970) commemorating St Francis, who probably came here in 1224. The view of the upper Tiber Valley takes in Anghiari and La Verna, Sansepolcro and Monte Subasio.

About 2km south of Citerna is Monterchi in Tuscany, where you can see Piero della Francesca's famous fresco of the *Madonna del Parto*, described in *Blue Guide Tuscany*.

UMBERTIDE

This chapter takes in the pretty district around the upper Tiber Valley south of Città di Castello (described on p. 119). Umbertide has some churches of interest, but the most attractive place to visit in the area is the lovely hill town of Montone where a delightful local museum has recently been opened. Outside Morra the oratory of San Crescentino was frescoed by Luca Signorelli and assistants.

Practical information

Information office
APT dell'Alta Valle del Tevere, Citta di Castello, ☎ 075 8554817. At **Montone:** Associazione Montone in Umbria, 4 Via San Francesco, ☎ 075 9306215.

Getting there
By car Umbertide is 35km from Perugia and is reached by car from the E45 super-strada (for Cesena) which follows the Tiber north.

By rail The *Ferrovia Centrale Umbra* runs from Perugia (Stazione Sant'Anna) to Sansepolcro and has a station at Umbertide.

Hotels
Umbertide
☆☆ *Capponi*, Piazza XXV Aprile, ☎ 075 9412662; fax 075 9413803, with a very good restaurant.

Montone ☆☆☆ *La Locanda del Capitano*, 7 Via Roma, ☎ 075 9306521; fax 075 9306455. Opened in 1996 in an old house in the centre of this beautiful quiet little hill town. Just eight rooms simply furnished with local-ly made wrought-iron beds, and a rather more pretentious restaurant. *Chiostro di San Francesco*, ☎ 075 9306215; or 075 9306247, has simple but comfortable rooms to let by the week in the cloisters of San Francesco, in a superb position at the top of the town with very fine views.

Pietralunga
☆☆☆ *Candeleto*, ☎ & fax 075 9460083, with restaurant.

Coltavolino *Jacopo Fo*, Strada San Patrignano, Mulino Capuzzola 12, ☎ 075 9229914; fax 075 9229911, *Agriturismo* accommodation. Also *Il Covone*, Ponte Pattoli (near the Tiber) in a lovely 19C villa. The owners are extremely hospitable (☎ 075 694140).

Ronti, near Morra, *Palazzo Terranova*, ☎ 075 8526046; fax 075 8570083, was opened in 1998/9. Officially rated as a 'country house' hotel it offers luxury-class accommodation in the category of a ☆☆☆☆☆ hotel (prices range from 580,000 lire to 1,200,000 lire for a double room per night, bed and breakfast). It is a reconstructed 18C house in a magnif-icent secluded position with fine views, surrounded by land which is being planted with trees and provided with terraced gardens. The interior, lavishly decorated, has eight sumptu-ous bedrooms with large bathrooms (one with a sauna). The hospitable English owners live here and guests are looked after in grand style and with professional efficiency. Facilities are provided for families with chil-dren. A restaurant (booking only) was opened in 1999, and a swimming-pool is under construction, and exten-sions are planned.

Restaurants
Umbertide
£ *Capponi*, see hotel above. Good value.

Montone ££ in the two hotels: *La Locanda del Capitano*, see above), and *Fortebraccio*, 11 Via dei Magistrati, ☎ 075 9306215, and *Taverna del Verziere*, Via dell'Ospedale, ☎ 075 9306512. £ *Le Fonti*, 25 Via Bologni, ☎ 075 9306231 (pizzeria).

Pietralunga £ *Della Pace*.

Annual festival
Festa del Bosco an autumn fair held in the streets of **Montone** where local produce and homemade snacks are sold (31 Oct, 1–2 Nov).

Umbertide is in a district with numerous tobacco fields. Though heavily bombed in 1944, it is now a busy town (population 13,400) with industrial outskirts. An important trading centre on the Tiber for the Umbrians and Etruscans, it was later the Roman *Pitulum*. It is traditionally thought to have been reconstructed by the sons of Uberto, who was son of Ugo, Margrave of Tuscany, and called *Fratta*. From the 12C it was under the control of Perugia and then ruled by the Papal States. In 1863 it changed its name to Umbertide.

The conspicuous church of **Santa Maria della Reggia** has a fine octagonal exterior by Bino Sozi (16C), which was completed by Francesco Laparelli. The crenellated towers (1385) of the **Rocca** survive. It has been restored as a Centro per l'Arte Contemporanea and exhibitions are held here. Beyond is the piazza with **Palazzo Comunale** (which has a small collection of works of art) opposite the ex-Palazzo delle Poste with a clock, a neo-classical work by Giovanni Santini.

Via Cibo, at the far end of the piazza, leads down to the main road. On the other side of the railway (crossed by foot) is the quiet Piazza San Francesco where there are three churches in a row. Santa Croce, which has a 17C interior, and San Bernardino (usually open on Thur) stand on either side of the 14C church of **San Francesco** which has interesting 17C frescoes (very ruined) in the first north chapel. A museum was opened in 1999 in the church of **Santa Croce**. It houses a splendid *Deposition* by Luca Signorelli, commissioned in 1515 by the confraternity of Santa Croce (restored in 1999). Also here is a *Madonna and Child with angels* and Saints by Niccolò Pomarancio (1577).

BEYOND UMBERTIDE

A pretty road runs west from Umbertide through typical Umbrian countryside via Castel Rigone to Lago Trasimeno (see p. 110). It passes beneath Monte Acuto (926m), and close to **Preggio**, a medieval village in a beautiful position with an interesting church. A chestnut festival is held here in the autumn.

From Umbertide another beautiful road (N219) leads east to Gubbio past the fine 16C castle of **Civitella Ranieri** (sometimes open in the summer). In the wooded valley of the Assino is the **Abbazia di Campo Reggiano** (11C, with a fine crypt).

The Rocca

South of Umbertide, on the other side of the Tiber, is the **Badia di San Salvatore di Monte Corona** founded by St Romualdo c 1008. The Romanesque church (altered in subsequent centuries) has been restored. It has an unusual fortified bell-tower. It contains a lovely 8C ciborium and 15C choir stalls in the apse, remains of 14C frescoes on the triumphal arch and an ancient crypt. A road leads south to the **Eremo di Monte Corona** (693m), a hermitage built in 1530 and now abandoned.

On another byroad towards Corciano at **Antognola** there is a 9-hole golf course, which is being transformed into an 18-hole course by Robert Trent Jones, and a hotel is to be opened here.

Further south, on the opposite side of the Tiber a byroad for Gubbio leads up to **Civitella Benazzone** where there are two paintings by Benedetto Bonfigli and Domenico Alfani in its church. To the north-west are the remains of the medieval **Abbazia Celestina** (recently restored).

To the south is **Montelabate** (387m), which is dominated by the large church of Santa Maria, built in 1325. It contains a fresco of the *Crucifixion and saints* by Fiorenzo di Lorenzo and a *Madonna and Saints* by Bartolomeo Caporali. The fine cloister dates from the 13C and the crypt from the 11C.

Nearby, off the Gubbio road, are **Pieve Pagliaccia**, where the church has 13C frescoes, and **Colombella Bassa**, where the 12C church of San Giustino has an interesting crypt.

Montone

North-east of Umbertide is the charming little well-kept hill town of **Montone** in a splendid position (482m) with fine views. Cars are parked outside the walls. Probably founded in the 11C this was the birthplace of the famous condottiere Andrea Braccio Fortebraccio (1368–1424). It has imposing walls, and steps in one of the towers lead up to a terrace from which the remarkable view takes in: (to the west) the Sanctuary of Canoscio, Monte Santa Maria Tiberina and La Verna; to the north, on a hill-top, the Rocca d'Aries, and (behind) Monte Neroni, the valley of Carpina and the high Monte Catria; to the east is Monte Subasio.

Beside the terrace, beyond its pretty 16C cloister, is the **Museo Comunale** in the church and the convent of **San Francesco** (open May–Sept, Fri, Sat & Sun 10.30–13.00, 15.30–18.00; Oct–May as above but only on Sat & Sun; otherwise by request, ☎ 075 9306535). The church built in 1306 has remains of 14C–16C votive frescoes, including, in the the Gothic apse, scenes from the *life of St Francis* by Antonio Alberti of Ferrara (1422–23), unfortunately very ruined. Over the north altar is a damaged fresco of *St Anthony Abbot between two saints* signed by Bartolomeo Caporali (1491). The church retains its carved wooden doors (recently restored) by Antonio Bencivenni from Mercatello (signed and dated 1519).

On the first floor is a gallery of paintings. The beautiful standard of the *Madonna del Soccorso* is by Bartolomeo Caporali (1481), with a view of Montone below. The ruined *Annunciation* is by Vittorio Cirelli and Tommaso Papacello (1532), and the *Immaculate Conception with saints and sibyls* (with an extraordinary landscape and imaginary city) is also by Cirelli (a native of Montone). The 17C *Deposition* is a beautiful painting, despite its poor condition. The remarkable 13C life-size wooden group of the *Deposition* (or *Christ on the Cross*), with the *Madonna and St John the Evangelist* (another ruined figure, probably representing St Joseph of Arimathea or Nicodemus, which was part of the group, has recently been found) was restored in 1999. There is a wonderful view from the little terrace.

Another room contains 15C–20C fabrics and vestments, including a fragment of 15C Umbrian linen, and there is also a collection of church silver.

On the ground floor is the **Museo Etnografico 'Il Tamburo Parlante'**, which has a charming display of very interesting material from East Africa collected by a local resident, Enrico Castelli. It takes its name from the drums used for communication between African tribes of different languages.

In a higher part of the village is the **Collegiata** with a *Last Supper* by Calvaert. The church of **San Fedele** (usually closed; sometimes used for concerts) has an unusual relief above its portal of two flagellants. Below the village, in a group of farm buildings, is the **Pieve Vecchia**, a fine building of the 11C with very ruined frescoes (in urgent need of restoration). A rough road leads across the Carpina valley up to the **Rocca d'Aries**, an impressive Fortebracci castle, owned by the Regione and restored in 1998 (it has not yet been decided what to do with it).

The road continues up the valley from Montone to the pretty medieval village of **Pietralunga**.

Morra

On the other side of the Tiber Valley, where there are numerous tobacco plantations, a byroad passes close to the **Abbazia di Santa Maria di Petroia** with a crypt (11C–12C). The village of **Morra**, in a valley of chestnut woods, was the birthplace of Giuseppe Nicasi (1859–1915), a notable scholar of local history who discovered that the carbon signs made by the local millers on their sacks of flour derived from Archaic Roman numerals, a theory confirmed by modern mathematicians. These signs, handed down over the generations, enabled the illiterate millers to keep count of their merchandise. The bare stone church dates from the 12C.

Just beyond the village, on a little hill (signposted) is the **Oratorio di San Crescentino** (restored in 1974–76; the custodian lives in the modern house reached by a gravel road in front of the church; service on the first Sunday of the month at 11.00). A confraternity was founded here c 1264 and the church dates from 1420. After 1507 Luca Signorelli and assistants painted frescoes on the upper parts of the walls: those at the east end are the only ones well preserved, with the *Flagellation* and a crowded *Crucifixion* scene. In the niche behind the high altar (with a pretty carved stone arch) are frescoes of *Christ between two angels*, thought to be by the hand of Signorelli, and *Sts Mary Magdalene* and *Anthony Abbot*. The frescoes of the *Madonna of the Misericordia* and the *Madonna of Loreto* (a particularly delightful work) in the two niches on the side walls are by the school of Signorelli. The story goes that Signorelli first visited Morra on his way from Cortona to Città di Castello, and that he fell in love with a local girl here and decided to stay and paint the oratory. The former oratory (now the sacristy) preserves some interesting late Gothic frescoes including *San Crescentino on horseback*.

In the Tiber Valley at Fabbrecce is the **Santuario di Canoscio**, on a wooded hill, built by Emilio de Fabris in 1855–78, which has recently become an important pilgrimage shrine. At San Secondo, a byroad leads left for Monte Santa Maria Tiberina, which, together with Città di Castello and the district to the north on the Tuscan border, is described on p. 126.

GUBBIO

Gubbio, a town of 31,400 inhabitants in an isolated position on the lower slopes of Monte Ingino, is one of the most beautiful and best preserved medieval towns in Italy; its handsome old buildings are built of the polished light grey stone which is quarried locally. Its main streets, most of which preserve their lovely old paving and are extremely well-kept and clean, run parallel with each other following the contours of the steep hillside (529m) and between them towers the splendid Palazzo dei Consoli in Piazza Grande. The high green hillside which forms a background above the town, and the wide plain at its foot, are special features of Gubbio.

Practical information

Information office

IAT, 6 Piazza Oderisi (Corso Garibaldi), ☎ 075 9220693.

Getting there

By car Gubbio, 40km from Perugia, is reached by car along the Strada Eugubina (N298), a beautiful road which leaves Perugia near the hospital, and at a fork with the road for Ponte San Giovanni on the right, continues straight on to descend through Casaglia and crosses the Tiber at Ponte Valleceppi. It crosses under the superstrada to Bosco. The road becomes prettier as it begins to climb, and then it follows a ridge with wide views on both sides.

Car parking The centre of the town is closed to traffic. There are free car-parks off Viale del Teatro Romano (near the Roman Theatre); near San Domenico; and in Via del Cavarello (near the cable-car station) outside Porta Romana. There is a car-park with an hourly tariff in Piazza 40 Martiri (except on Tuesday).

By bus There are services run by *APM* (information office, Via della Repubblica) from Perugia (1hr 10mins), some with connections from Assisi, and from Città di Castello (1hr 30mins). On weekdays there is one bus a day from Florence (via Perugia, 3hrs 30mins) and from Rome (4hrs 30mins).

By rail The nearest railway station, on the line between Ancona and Rome, is at Fossato di Vico. There is a frequent bus service which takes 35mins, some buses connecting with trains.

Cable-car (10.00–13.15, 14.30–17.00; closed on Wed in winter; July and Aug 08.30–19.30) from outside Porta Romana to Sant'Ubaldo (827m) on Monte Ingino. It has open 'cages' for a maximum of two people, and takes six minutes to reach the top of the hill.

 Hotels

☆☆☆☆ *Relais Ducale*, Via Ducale, ☎ 075 9220157; fax 075 9220159. A very pleasant hotel, with a peaceful atmosphere, with 32 rooms in three adjoining edifices on different levels in the very centre of the town. It has two lovely gardens, including a hanging garden, and one of the rooms has its own terrace. A small restaurant is to be opened here, but the owners, the Mencarelli group, run a number of restaurants in the town (as well as some other hotels). It has rooms for meetings and lectures so it does also cater for groups.

☆☆☆ *Bosone*, 22 Via XX Settembre, ☎ 075 9220688; fax 075 9220552. 30 rooms in a lovely palace in the centre of the town, with a charming period dining room. It is owned by the Mencarelli group (see above) and has very friendly staff. Four of the rooms have views over the valley, two of which are suites which preserve splendidly decorated ceilings and period furniture.

✰✰✰ *Gattapone*, 6 Via Ansidei, ☎ 075 9272489; fax 075 9271269. In a lovely position in the centre of the town, also owned by the Mencarelli group (see above). It was restructured in 1997. Very friendly staff. It has 18 rooms, the smaller ones being the most characteristic with lovely views.

✰✰ *Grotta dell'Angelo*, 47 Via Gioia (off Via Carioli), ☎ 075 9271747; fax 075 9273438, with a good restaurant (**££**). *Residence di 'Pia Piccardi'*, 12 Via Piccardi, ☎ 075 9276108 was opened in 1996 in a small house in a quiet street with a little garden. It has six simple little rooms, with reasonable bed and breakfast terms (closed in Jan & Feb). Rooms to rent also through the Trattoria San Martino, at reasonable prices, ☎ 075 9273251; fax 075 9276088.

Monteluiano
✰✰✰ *Villa Montgranelli*, ☎ 075 9220185; fax 075 9273372. A good small hotel, with 21 rooms (no restaurant).

There are numerous *agriturismo* farms in the area, including the *Abbazia di Vallingegno* (on the Perugia road), ☎ 075 920158; fax 075 9221578.

Campsites
Open Easter – Sept at Ortoguidone: ✰✰✰✰ *Villa Ortoguidone*, ☎ 075 9272937, and ✰✰✰ *Città di Gubbio*, ☎ 075 9272037.

Restaurants
£££ *La Fornace di Mastro Giorgio*, Via Mastro Giorgio (off Via Savelli Della Porta), ☎ 075 9221836; *Taverna del Lupo*, Via Ansidei (off Via XX Settembre), ☎ 075 9274368.

££ *Grotta dell'Angelo* (see above), which has a garden, ☎ 075 9272747; *Fabiani*, Piazza 40 Martiri, ☎ 075 9274639; *Trattoria San Martino*, 6 Piazza Giordano Bruno, ☎ 075 9273251; *Dei Consoli*, Via dei Consoli, ☎ 075 9273335; *Federico da Montefeltro*, Via della Repubblica, ☎ 9075 9273949; *Funivia* on Monte Ingino, ☎ 075 9221259.

£ *Picchio Verde*, 65 Via Savelli Della Porta, ☎ 075 9276649; *Bargello Pizzeria*, Via dei Consoli, ☎ 075 9273724; *La Lanterna*, 23 Via Gioia (off Via Cairoli), ☎ 075 9276694.

Mengara: trattoria and snack bar *Il Panaro*, ☎ 075 920035. The *Caffè Ducale* in Piazza dei Consoli is a comfortable place to have a snack.

Pasticceria
Bar Garibaldi. There is a small snack bar with tables in the pretty little garden off Via Duomo.

Picnics
There are good places to picnic above the Duomo, near Sant'Ubaldo, or outside Porta Metauro.

Market day on Tuesdays in Piazza 40 Martiri.

Annual festivals
The *'Palio della Balestra'*, a crossbowmen's contest of medieval origin, against the citizens of Sansepolcro, is held on the last Sunday in May, preceded by a procession (at 16.30) up Via dei Consoli from San Domenico, through Palazzo dei Consoli and down the steps into the Piazza Grande. After a ceremony with flag-throwing and bands, four crossbowmen at a time aim at the targets set up in the piazza. In the evening of 14 August at the *'Torneo dei Quartieri'* the best marksmen in the town take place in another crossbow competition.

On **Good Friday** there is a traditional procession, and at **Christmas** the hillside is illuminated in the form of a gigantic Christmas tree.

Festa dei Ceri

The Festa dei Ceri is one of the most interesting annual festivals in Italy. This remarkably exciting event, which may have pagan origins, is held every year on 15 May, the vigil of the feast day of St Ubaldo (d. 1160), the town's patron saint and bishop. The whole town participates in the celebrations. At 08.00 a Mass is held in the little church of the Muratori, and the three statues of *St Ubaldo*, *St George* and *St Anthony* are taken in procession through the streets. At 10.30 another procession forms at Porta Castello which proceeds up to the Piazza Grande where at 11.30 the three extremely heavy wooden ceri (floats in the form of giant candlesticks), 4m high, crowned by the three statues of saints are erected by the three confraternities of the builders (*St Ubaldo*), peasants (*St Anthony*), and artisans (*St George*). They are then each carried through the streets to show the inhabitants. A splendid fish banquet is held in Palazzo dei Consoli for the participants and local dignatories while the ceri are left in Via Savelli della Porta.

At 16.30 there is another procession in which the clergy and Bishop participate (and the ceri are blessed in Via Dante); it traverses the entire town (Corso Garibaldi, Piazza 40 Martiri, Via Cavour and Via dei Consoli) before returning up to Piazza Grande at around 18.00. From here the mayor waves a white flag from the central window of Palazzo Pretorio to start the race which is the culmination of the day's festivities: the *ceri* are swiftly carried along Via XX Settembre, Via Colomboni, and Via Appennino to Porta del Monte where there is a halting place. The race then recommences and follows the steep path all the way up the hillside to the Basilica di Sant'Ubaldo. Each of the three confraternities have ten official bearers (who have to be replaced about every 10m without losing the pace). The race is a demonstration of strength and ability, and the first *cera* to arrive at Sant'Ubaldo attempts to shut the church door in the face of the following *cera*. The *ceri* are then left in the church while the three statues of the saints are brought down again in a triumphant candlelight procession to the church of the Muratori.

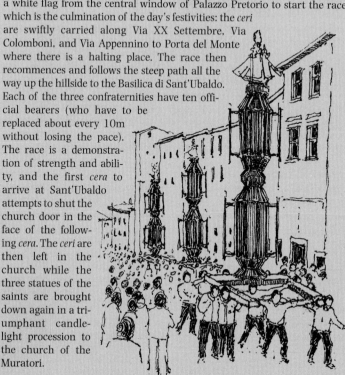

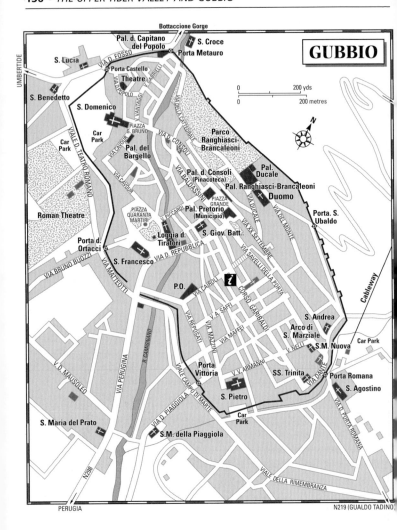

History

The town was founded by the Umbri in the 3C BC, and its political and religious importance is attested by the famous Iguvine or Eugubian Tables (preserved in Palazzo dei Consoli) which are fundamental documents for the study of the Umbrian language. The Roman city of *Iguvium*, at the foot of the hill, flourished in the Republican era when the theatre was built. It had a celebrated temple of Jupiter. *Eugubium*, as it later came to be called, was sacked by the Goths but became a free commune in the 11C. With the help of the bishop saint Ubaldo Baldassini, born here in 1100, the town was saved from

Barbarossa in 1155, when it was granted numerous privileges. Although often at war with Perugia, Gubbio retained its independence, and its civic pride is represented by Piazza Grande and Palazzo dei Consoli, constructed in 1322. From 1387 to 1508 it came under the peaceful rule of the Montefeltro, counts of Urbino. The buildings of the town were carefully restored after damage in an earthquake in 1982 which left 1500 inhabitants homeless.The more recent earthquakes in 1997–98 caused only very slight damage.

The art of Gubbio

The frescoes and altarpieces in the churches of Gubbio are mostly by native artists. The miniaturist Oderisio (who was born here, and died c 1299) is traditionally considered the founder of Gubbio's school of painting. In the 14C local artists included Guido Palmerucci and a certain Mello da Eugubio. Ottaviano Nelli (c 1375–1444/50) was the most celebrated painter of Gubbio, and his beautiful frescoes survive in a number of churches in the town. His father Martino and brother Tommaso also worked here. In the 16C Benedetto and Virgilio Nucci painted numerous altarpieces, and in the 17C Francesco Allegrini and Felice Damiani were active here. The Maffei family of woodcarvers also produced fine work in the 16C. The greatest architect of Gubbio was Matteo di Giovannelli, known as Gattapone, who died after 1376. The town has a number of churches with fine 17C and 18C interiors.

Giorgio Andreoli (Mastro Giorgio), born at Intra c 1465–70, spent most of his life in Gubbio where he died in 1552. He discovered a particular ruby and golden lustre which reflects the light on maiolica, but hardly any examples of his work survive in the city itself. The tradition of producing fine ceramics is carried on by a number of firms here, including Rampini and Aiò.

Many of the old houses in Gubbio (as in other Umbrian towns) have the curious Porta del Morto beside their principal doorway. This probably served to give access to the upper floors of the houses; it was formerly believed the small doorway was used when a coffin left the house.

The splendid **Piazza Grande** (or della Signoria) has a high balustrade overlooking the plain, and lovely herringbone paving. In 1322 the Consiglio del Popolo approved the construction of Palazzo dei Consoli and Palazzo del Podestà with the Piazza Grande between them at the centre of the town. In 1841 Francesco Ranghiasci obtained permission from the Comune to further embellish the piazza with the long neo-classical façade of **Palazzo Ranghiasci-Brancaleoni**, with its tall Ionic colummns. Above the palace the Duomo and Palazzo Ducale can be seen on the hillside.

Palazzo dei Consoli

The superb Palazzo dei Consoli is one of the most impressive medieval public buildings in Italy, begun in 1332. It towers over the city, and the south-west side, which rests on massive vaulting, is 92m high to the top of the bell-tower. It is usually attributed to the local architect Gattapone, although Angelo da Orvieto was also involved, but may only have designed the entrance door and the two Gothic windows on either side of it. It is approached by a delightful out-

Palazzo dei Consoli

side staircase. Above the Gothic portal is a lunette of the *Madonna and Child* with the patron saints of Gubbio, *John the Baptist* and *Ubaldo*, by Bernardino di Nanni.

In the interior is a **museum and picture gallery** (open daily, 10.00–13.00, 15.00–19.00; Oct–March 10.00–13.00, 14.00–17.00; ☎ 075 9274298), although there is a long-term project to transfer the contents to the convent of San Pietro. The collection was formed in 1860, and first exhibited here in 1909. The huge barrel-vaulted **Sala dell'Arengo**, where assemblies of the Comune were held, has a crowded old-fashioned arrangement of sculptural fragments, coats of arms, architectural fragments, Roman inscriptions and sarcophagi. Exhibitions are also sometimes held here.

A few steps lead up to a small room with a selection of **coins** from a large collection (which numbers 1619 examples) formed by Bishop Giacomo Ranghiasci-Brancaleoni in 1816–38, including Roman works and examples from the Gubbio mint. A case has an eclectic collection of weights, glass and keys. The room beyond, formerly the chapel, contains the seven celebrated **Iguvine** or **Eugubian Tables**. These are bronze tablets found by a local inhabitant in 1444 near the city and sold to the Comune by him in 1456. They bear inscriptions in the Umbrian language, five in Etruscan and two in Latin characters. They record the rules of a college of priests, and date probably from 250–150 BC. They are the most important epigraphs in the Umbrian language known, and the most notable ritual texts to have survived from antiquity. More coins minted in Gubbio are exhibited here, and two detached frescoes attributed to Guido Palmerucci, and the school of Ottaviano Nelli.

A very steep flight of stairs (constructed in 1488) leads up past a **loggia** in which **two plates by Mastro Giorgio Andreoli** are displayed showing the *Fall of Phaeton* (1527), and *Circe*, bought by the people of Gubbio at a Sotheby's sale in 1991 and 1996, the only two works by him left in the city. Other cases display pharmacy jars and **ceramics** produced in Gubbio from the 16C onwards (with particularly fine 19C works), and Deruta-ware. The display continues in the 'secret' corridor, with fine views of the town, from which a narrow staircase continues up to the **Picture Gallery**, which also contains some furniture. The rooms are not numbered and some of the paintings are in poor condition. In the main hall, which has a good brick vault, the symbolic 14C fountain and lavabo (now dry), are an unexpected sight. On a screen are two *Madonnas of the Misericordia*, one a 16C work and the other, the *Gonfalon of St Ubaldo* (1503) by Sinibaldo Ibi. The *Pentecost* (in an elaborate frame) is by Benedetto Nucci, and the *Deposition* was painted in the 16C. Near the fountain is the entrance to the **second room** which contains an early 14C painted *Crucifix* and *Madonna and Child with two angels* attributed to Palmerino di Guido, and 15C and 16C paintings. The third room (right) displays a German 15C terracotta *Pietà*. The **fourth room** (left), with a finely carved doorway, has a beautiful early 14C reliquary cupboard, decorated with miniatures; two 14C Crosses attributed to Puccio Capanna; a 13C metal Cross, and a painted *Crucifix* by the Maestro della Croce di Gubbio.

On the other side of the main hall is the **last room** with later paintings, including a *Madonna and Child* attributed to Sassoferrato, *San Crescentino* attributed to Simon Vouet, and a *Flight into Egypt* by Rutilio Manetti. The 19C portrait of a lady with a dog is by Augusto Stoppoloni. A door from the hall leads into a corridor which emerges onto the **loggia** where there is a splendid view: straight ahead is the church of San Francesco with the Loggia dei Tiratori, and below is the square campanile of San Giovanni. To the right is the Roman theatre in a green field, and further right the medieval district of the town with several towers. On the left is the Piazza, and the Duomo can be seen above on the hillside.

The **Archaeological section** (entrance with the same ticket) is displayed on the ground floor of the palace, at present entered by leaving the museum by the main door in the Sala dell'Arengo and following the palace round to Via dei Consoli, off which Via Gattapone descends to the side entrance. The lovely barrel-vaulted rooms here display finds from the area dating from the 6C–5C BC, as well as Roman and medieval fragments. The first room displays bronzes, and vases (including a graceful oinochoe with the figure of a woman, dating from the early 3C BC), and the second room has a Roman capital decorated with dolphins and terracotta friezes. Beyond a Roman head (1C AD) the last room has Roman statues, including an ephebus of 1C–2C AD, and a Byzantine sarcophagus complete with its lid (late 8C or early 9C). The old stairs which lead up to the Sala dell'Arengo are to be reopened.

In Piazza Grande opposite Palazzo dei Consoli is **Palazzo Pretorio** (or dei Priori; now the town hall), designed by Gattapone to pair with Palazzo dei Consoli, but left unfinished in 1350. Its interesting interior is constructed around a central pilaster which supports the Gothic vaulting on all floors. An L-shaped wing built in brick was added on the left in the 17C.

The lower part of town

From Piazza Grande Via dei Consoli (described below) descends to the stepped Via Gattapone which zig-zags down past the side entrance to Palazzo dei Consoli (see above) to Via Baldassini. Here the great height of Palazzo dei Consoli can be appreciated, and there is a view of the huge vaults which support Piazza Grande. The 14C **Casa di Sant'Ubaldo** (owned by the University of Perugia) contains a fresco of *St Anthony Abbot* by Guido Palmerucci.

An arched passageway leads on down to the characteristic **Via Piccardi**. On the left a street leads to the Romanesque church of **San Giovanni Battista** which has a fine campanile. On the first south altar is *St Charles Borromeo* by Claudio Ridolfi. In the baptistery (being restored) is a varnished majolica font. A *Baptism of Christ* by the school of Perugino has been removed. On the first north altar, there are two paintings of saints by Benedetto Nucci.

Via delle Conce leads back to Via Piccardi (from which there is a good view of Palazzo dei Consoli) which continues downhill across the Camignano torrent (its paved bed is dry for most of the year), to emerge on the busy **Piazza 40 Martiri**, planted as a public garden, from which there is a good view of all the main monuments of the town climbing the hillside. The **Loggia dei Tiratori** was built in 1603 and used for drying wool and hides. Beneath the 14C portico, where there is a fresco by Bernardino di Nanni, is a little fruit and vegetable market, and the church of **Santa Maria dei Laici** (dei Bianchi; closed except when in use by a choral society). It was built in the 14C but the interior was transformed in the 17C. It contains 24 small paintings of the *Life of the Virgin*, by Felice Damiani. At the east end is a fresco of *Paradise* by Francesco Allegrini and, on the left altar, the last work of Barocci (an *Annunciation*).

On the opposite side of the piazza is the large church of **San Francesco**, formerly attributed to Fra' Bevignate of Perugia (1259–92). It has a fine exterior, especially the Gothic east end, and octagonal campanile. The interior has lovely vaulting. South side. On the first altar is Antonio Gherardi's *Immaculate Conception*; on the second altar, *Crucifixion and saints* by the School of Virgilio Nucci. On the third altar is a copy of Daniele da Volterra's *Deposition* which is in the church of the Trinità del Monte in Rome, by his follower Virgilio Nucci. The chapel to the right of the apse, on two levels, has 14C frescoes of the life of St Francis in the upper chapel, and the *Redeemer* on the vault of the lower chapel and frescoes of saints on the walls. In the main chapel, high up, are very early frescoes of *Christ enthroned with saints* (13C). In the chapel to the left of the apse there is a complete fresco cycle of the *Life of the Virgin* by Ottaviano Nelli (very ruined).

North side. The third altarpiece of *St Anthony of Padua* (1673) is by Anna Allegrini; the second altarpiece of *St Charles Borromeo* is by Benedetto Bandiera; and the first altarpiece of *Madonna enthroned with Saints* was painted in the early 18C by Imperiali. The **sacristy** is in part of a 14C house which belonged to the Spadalonga, friends of St Francis. In the **cloister** are a 14C fresco of the Crucifixion and Roman polychrome mosaic pavement fragments (3C AD) found in Gubbio. In the **chapterhouse** is another ancient fresco (detached from the cloister) thought to represent the Santa Casa of Loreto.

The small **museum**, which has been closed since 1989, is being restored. It contains a seal (the *Sigillum Custodiae Eugubinae*) with St Francis and the tamed wolf (1350), Crosses and liturgical objects, and paintings by Spagnoletto and Domenico Morelli.

From Piazza Grande (see above), beneath a narrow archway at the right end of Palazzo Ranghiasci-Brancaleoni, steps lead up to the splendid medieval **Via Galeotti**, with its attractive brick paving. It continues right (past the garden of the Hotel Relais Ducale) and under an arch into **Via Ducale**, which climbs steeply uphill to the left past a huge 16C barrel in the cellars of the 14C **Palazzo dei Canonici**, which is being restored as the seat of the **Museo Diocesano**. The contents of the museum, which has been closed for many years, include a fresco of the *Crucifixion and Saints* and the *Madonna and Child* attributed to Guido Palmerucci (restored), and a celebrated Flemish **cope**, designed by a disciple of Justus of Ghent and presented by Marcello Cervini (Pope Marcellus II; 1555), part of which was stolen in 1990.

At a corner Via Ducale passes the **Voltone**, a huge vaulted gallery which supports part of the Lombard Corte and 12C Palazzo Comunale, near the former entrance to Palazzo Ducale. Above the arch a pretty carved window and balcony belonging to Palazzo Ducale can be seen. Beneath the Voltone is the entrance to a hanging garden (open to the public, with a little bar) from which there is a fine view of the town and Palazzo Ducale behind. The lovely old Via della Cattedrale, beyond the arch, follows the garden walls of the Parco Ranghiasci-Brancaleoni (described below).

The Duomo

In Via Ducale, a short distance uphill to the right, opposite the entrance to Palazzo Ducale, is the 13C Duomo (open all day). The **interior** has remarkable stone **vaulting** and fine works of art in its chapels, most of them by local painters. South side. In the first niche is Antonio Gherardi's, *Adoration of the Magi*; the second niche contains Virgilio Nucci's *Madonna of the Consolation*; and the fourth niche, Dono Doni's, *Pietà*. The chapel of the Holy Sacrament is a good Baroque work of 1644–72 decorated by Francesco Allegrini, with the *Birth of the Virgin* on the left wall by Antonio Gherardi. The sixth niche contains Benedetto Nucci's, *Christ with St Thomas*; the seventh niche, Dono Doni's *Way to Calvary*; and the eighth niche, Benedetto Nucci's *Madonna and saints*.

In the **presbytery** is a fine carved episcopal throne by Girolamo Maffei. The stained glass dates from 1913, and the frescoes are by the local painter Augusto Stoppoloni. A Roman sarcophagus serves as high altar. North side. In the tenth niche is Benedetto Nucci's, *St Ubaldo*, and, beneath the altar is a Roman sarcophagus; the eighth niche, Sinibaldo Ibi's *Madonna and Child with saints*, signed and dated 1507; the seventh niche, Timoteo Viti's *St Mary Magdalene*; the sixth niche a Nativity by the school of Pinturicchio in a handsome frame; the fifth niche, Virgilio Nucci's *Conversion of St Paul*; the fourth niche, Virgilio Nucci's *Resurrection*; the third niche Virgilio Nucci's *Christ in the Garden*; and the first niche, Antonio Gherardi's *Nativity* and, above, an early fresco.

A beautiful country lane climbs the hillside planted with orchards and olive groves, along the north flank of the Duomo, with its arches. It continues up through the 13C walls and passes through woods before reaching Sant'Ubaldo, high up above the town (this is the route followed by the ceri in the famous annual race on 15 May, see p. 135).

Palazzo Ducale

Opposite the Duomo is the entrance to the courtyard of Palazzo Ducale (open 09.00–13.30, 14.30–19.00 except first Mon of the month; ☎ 075 9275872). The palace was built for Federico da Montefeltro, Duke of Urbino, famous *condottiere* and man of learning, in imitation of his splendid residence in Urbino. Built on the site of the Lombard Corte and the 12C Palazzo Comunale, part of which still exists supported by the Voltone (see above), it was erected in 1476–80 by Francesco di Giorgio Martini (perhaps on a design by Francesco Laurana), and the carved decorations in the courtyard and above the doors and windows include the inscription 'F.D' (*Federico Duca*), and the Ducal emblems of the black eagle of the Montefeltro arms, pairs of dolphins entwined in a trident, and the Order of the Garter (which the Duke received from Edward IV of England). The palace was acquired by the state in 1957.

The beautiful peaceful Renaissance **courtyard** is built in pietra serena and red brick. A charming spiral staircase in pietra serena leads down to a barrel-vaulted storeroom. Beyond can be seen the **excavations** beneath the courtyard which revealed four different levels: rectangular dwellings of the 10C–12C, 13C–14C houses, a 14C cistern, and the 15C foundations of the Palazzo Ducale with its plumbing. Medieval and Renaissance ceramics found during excavations are displayed here.

On the ground floor (beyond the ticket office) is the entrance to the rooms of the palace, particularly interesting for their architecture, with beautifully carved doorways and windows in pietra serena, and good fireplaces. The fine terracotta floors with a simple flower motif also survive. In the first room is a painted cupboard signed and dated 1498 and a 17C cupboard. Off a room with a delightful vault is the studio of the Duke; the little room is now totally bare since the exquisite intarsia panelling carved by Giuliano da Maiano in 1478–82 was sold in 1874 to Massimo Lancellotti for his villa in Frascati, and in 1934 was acquired by the Metropolitan Museum of New York. In a room with a wooden ceiling, and charming views from the windows, are detached frescoes by Giacomo di Benedetto di Beda (15C) from the crypt of Santa Maria dei Laici. The huge **Salone** has a view of Palazzo dei Consoli and a particularly fine fireplace. On display here are paintings by Federico Zoi, Rutilio Manetti, and a processional standard by Pietro Paolo Baldinacci (early 16C). Two carved intarsia doors from other rooms of the palace by Mariotto di Paolo Sensi (known as Terzuolo) are also exhibited here. In two other rooms are a triptych attributed to Benedetto Nucci, two *Madonnas* by Mello da Gubbio (early 14C), as well as 15C painted window shutters and two pairs of 15C intarsia doors, all from other rooms in the palace.

From the courtyard a beautiful staircase leads up to the **loggia**, with a carved frieze in pietra serena and handsome doorways. Exhibitions are held here, and there is a permanent display (until at least 2004) of 50 works dating from the 1980s and 1990s from the Panza di Biume Collection.

Via dei Consoli and the western part of town

From Piazza Grande (see above) the wide **Via dei Consoli**, the main street of the town, leads downhill past a series of fine palaces and Via Gattapone, from which the back and side of Palazzo dei Consoli can be seen (with the entrance to the Museo Archeologico, see above).

Largo del Bargello has a pretty circular fountain. This is known as the **Fontana dei Pazzi** as anyone may obtain a *patente da matto* (a licence of madness) if he runs three times around the fountain while three native Eugubini drench him with water! The Gothic **Palazzo del Bargello**, built in 1302, was the first Palazzo Pubblico in Gubbio. Via San Giuliano on the left is an attractive road with a good view up of Palazzo dei Consoli. Via dei Consoli continues down past an ancient house with a tower to cross a bridge over the Camignano, lined with picturesque houses and orchards. The lovely view to the right takes in the houses on the river-front with the medieval tower of Palazzo Gabrielli on the left, and, above, the Eremo di Sant'Ambrogio on the hillside of Monte Calvo. At the end the charming little covered bridge across the river can be seen which leads into the Parco Ranghiasci-Brancaleoni (described below).

Via dei Priori ends in Piazza Giordano Bruno with the 14C church of **San Domenico** (closed since the earthquake). The interior dates from 1765 and has niches decorated with stuccoes around the side altars. South side. In the first two chapels there are 15C frescoes; the third chapel contains Francesco Allegrini's *Madonna and saints*. The choir has stalls dating from the 16C. The **lectern**, with intarsia, is attributed to Terzuolo. North side. In the seventh chapel, there is a seated 16C statue of *St Anthony* in varnished terracotta; the sixth chapel contains Giovanni Baglione's *Mary Magdalene*; fifth chapel, Tommaso Nelli's *St Vincent Ferrer*; the fourth chapel Raffaellino del Colle's (attrib.) *Madonna and Child*; and the second chapel Tommaso Nelli's *Scenes from the Life of Sts Vincent Ferrer and Peter Martyr*. The first chapel has 15C frescoes.

Just out of the piazza, at the beginning of Via Cavour, is the 15C Palazzo Beni. The medieval district can be explored by taking Via Cleofe Borromei on the right of San Domenico (with a view of the hillside) and then Via del Popolo left past the brick **Teatro Comunale**, built in 1727 by Bartolomeo Benveduti, to Porta Castello. Outside the gate, beyond Santa Lucia and on the corner of Viale del Teatro Romano, is the church of **San Benedetto**, with a fine 18C interior by Bartolomeo Benveduti. Beyond, in Via Tifernate, is the Gothic church of **San Secondo** which contains (second south altar) Stefano Tofanelli's (19C) *Martyrdom of St Secondo* and (second north altar) Bernardino di Nanni's *Madonna and Child with angels*. In the little cemetery, beyond the fine cloister, is a chapel with frescoes by Giacomo di Benedetto di Beda (1457).

Inside the gate, the pretty Via Capitano del Popolo, with 13C houses, leads towards the hillside, past the 13C **Palazzo del Capitano del Popolo** where there is a a private museum of instruments of torture and modern sculpture. At no. 25 Via Gabrielli, is **Palazzo Gabrielli**, next to its tower. Numerous alleys lead down to the pretty river-front. Outside **Porta Metauro**, in a picturesque corner of the town, a lane (right) leads over a bridge, with views, to the church of **Santa Croce** (being restored), which contains a gilded wooden decoration of the 17C, a 16C ceiling and paintings by Virgilio Nucci and Francesco Allegrini.

At no. 1 Via Gabrielli, just inside Porta Metauro, is the entrance gate to the **Parco Ranghiasci-Brancaleoni** (open daily). This large romantic park extends beneath the town walls as far as Palazzo Ducale. It was bought in 1988 by the Comune of Gubbio from the heirs of the Ranghiasci family and its restoration is nearly complete. It was created in the English style in 1841 by Francesco Ranghiasci, probably through the intervention of Matilde Hobhouse, who had married Francesco in 1827. Beyond the picturesque covered bridge a gravel carriage path zig-zags up the hillside below the town walls and fortifications (being restored) past various neo-classical garden houses (most of them recently carefully restored), with delightful views of the monuments of the town, including Palazzo dei Consoli. Near the top the path runs through an arch under the medieval tower of San Luca (the rest of the church was demolished when the garden was laid out). The fine trees include horse chestnuts, lime trees, maples and ilex. The stable block has been converted into a café.

From Piazza Migliorati, a second bridge leads over the Camignano (close to the covered bridge and a third bridge which carries the walls across the river) and the picturesque **Via della Cattedrale**, beautifully paved, follows the lower walls of the Parco Ranghiasci-Brancaleoni steeply uphill (passing close to the tower of San Luca), through the Voltone below Palazzo Ducale (see above) as far as Via XX Settembre.

The south-eastern part of town

Via XX Settembre leads out of Piazza Grande (see above) and steps descend to Via Savelli Della Porta (with a fine doorway at no. 16). At the end of this street is the former 13C church of **Santa Maria Nuova** (closed; for admission enquire at the offices of the Comune in Via della Repubblica or at Palazzo Ducale, ☎ 075 9275872) which has a fresco known as the *Madonna del Belvedere*, a very beautiful work by Ottaviano Nelli, perhaps his masterpiece. There are also other frescoes here by his pupils, 16C carved wooden altars and church vestments. Above Via Dante (left) is the 15C **Arco di San Marziale** on the site of the Porta Vehia of the Umbrian era. Beyond the arch is the simple church of **Sant'Andrea** with two naves, perhaps dating from the 11C.

Via Dante leads down to the 13C **Porta Romana**. A little private museum (open daily except Mon 08.30–13.00, 15.30–20.00; April–Sept 08.30–20.00) has been opened in the gatehouse and adjoining tollgate. Arranged on five floors, it gives a good idea of how a medieval gate was defended. Stairs lead up to a display of 19C and 20C ceramics from Gubbio, including some by the bottega of Mastro Giorgio Andreoli. On the floor, above a glass panel over the road shows how the mechanism of the drawbridge defences worked. Stairs continue up past a 15C trunk, a bell of 1584, and 18C and 19C keys. At the very top is a model of the gateway.

Outside Porta Romana is the church of **Sant'Agostino**, a 13C church with the triumphal arch and apse entirely frescoed with scenes from the *Life of St Augustine* by Ottaviano Nelli and his pupils (1420). On the third south altar is the *Baptism of St Augustine* by Felice Damiani, and on the fifth south altar there is a fresco of *St Ubaldo and two saints*, also by Nelli. At the end of the south side is a 14C–15C painted Crucifix. Near the church is the station for the cable-car (for opening times, see above) which climbs the hillside in six minutes to Sant'Ubaldo (see below). Via di Porta Romana leads out of the town into attractive countryside.

Inside Porta Romana, Via Dante (with a fountain and a fresco) leads down left. On the corner of Corso Garibaldi is an unexpected large tabernacle with a statue of St Ubaldo erected in 1761. Opposite is the church of **Santissima Trinità** (closed) next to its monastery with an interesting wall.

Corso Garibaldi, in which the 16C **Palazzo Accoromboni** is situated where Vittoria Accoromboni (the model for Webster's heroine in *The White Devil*) was born in 1557, continues downhill and Via Vincenzo Armanni bears left for the large church of **San Pietro**. It has four worn Corinthian columns on its façade, perhaps dating from the 11C. The 16C **interior** was decorated with stuccoes in the 18C. South side, on the first altar is Rutilio Manetti's *Martyrdom of St Bartholomew*; the fourth altar contains Giannicola di Paolo's *Visitation*; the fifth altarpiece and frescoes are by Raffaellino del Colle. The south transept contains

Agostino Tofanelli's (1770–1834) *Death of St Romualdo*. In the north transept is a venerated wooden 13C sculpture of *Christ deposed* (restored in the 15C). North side, on the third altar is Francesco Allegrini's *St Michael Archangel*; and on the second altar is Virgilio Nucci's *St Sebastian*. The fine Baroque organ was carved by Antonio and Giovanni Battista Maffei (1598).

Outside Porta Vittoria, Via della Piaggiola leads to the church of **Santa Maria della Piaggiola** (see plan) which has a beautiful Baroque interior (1613–25), with pretty stuccoes and statues (open for concerts). It contains a *Pietà* by Domenico di Cecco, and on the high altar a *Madonna and Child* by Ottaviano Nelli (repainted and restored), and paintings by Annibale Beni (1764–1845).

Across the Camignano, on the main road to Perugia, is the church of **Santa Maria del Prato** (see plan). It was built in 1662 on a plan taken from San Carlino alle Quattro Fontane by Borromini in Rome. The interior (reopened after restoration), with good stucco work, has an elliptical dome frescoed by Francesco Allegrini. The altarpieces are by Allegrini (*Martyrdom of St Stephen*) and Ciro Ferri (*St Ubaldo and Frederick Barbarossa*).

The outskirts of the town
Via della Piaggiola (see above) leads south-east across the Avarello to Via Frate Lupo (15-minute walk) and the little **Chiesa della Vittorina** (at present closed, awaiting restoration), a chapel in an isolated position surrounded by a park. Built in the 13C, it has a Gothic vault. It was transformed in the 16C when the frescoes were painted (attributed to Virgilio Nucci). In a wood near here, St Francis is traditionally thought to have tamed the wolf of Gubbio (commemorated in front of the church in 1973 by a bronze bas-relief by Francesco Vignola).

Via Reposati leads from San Pietro back down across the Camignano to Via Matteotti and Piazza 40 Martiri. Beyond Porta degli Ortacci is Viale di Teatro Romano, off which are the extensive remains of the exceptionally large **Roman theatre** (restored; open 09.00–13.00) of the 1C AD. It was ruined by the Lombards and used as a quarry in the Middle Ages. Classical plays are sometimes performed here in summer. There are remains of a **Roman mausoleum** further east (off Via Bruno Buozzi). It is 9m high and has a well-preserved burial-chamber but only the exterior can be seen.

BEYOND GUBBIO

Sant'Ubaldo
A cable-car (see above) rises (6mins) to the basilica of Sant'Ubaldo on Monte Ingino (827m), from outside Porta Romana, where there is a superb panorama. From the upper cable-car station a short walk (less than 5mins) leads steeply up to the church, which can also be reached by a steep serpentine path above the cathedral (followed by the annual race of the ceri), or by road from Porta Metauro via the Bottaccione gorge (see below) and the recreation area of Coppo. The church was rebuilt in 1514 and above the high altar St Ubaldo is buried. The three ceri are kept here (see above). On the hillside above (903m) are remains of the 12C **Rocca** where excavations are in progress.

Bottaccione

The **Gorge of Bottaccione** or Gola d'Iridio is reached outside Porta Metauro by the road for Scheggia. It ascends the lovely valley of the Camignano between Monte Ingino (right) and Monte Calvo (or Foce; left), on which the **Hermitage of Sant'Ambrogio** is situated (1331; being restored), near a prehistoric site. It passes several old water mills and on the right of the valley is a 14C aqueduct, still in use. At Bottaccione (585m) a dam was built in the 14C across the river to supply the watermills in the valley, and the basin is now filled with a lake. The valley is of great interest to geologists who have found in a thin layer of sedimentary rocks here a high concentration of minerals (including iridium) which may help to prove that the extinction of dinosaurs and most marine life 65 million years ago was caused by the impact of a huge meteorite on earth, which created an explosion of dust in the high atmosphere, big enough to have blocked out the sun's rays.

The road reaches a summit level of 777m at the **Passo di Gubbio** which has fine views of the Apennines, and descends to Scheggia on the Via Flaminia, described on p. 148.

On the Perugia road, south of Gubbio (where there are wonderful views of Gubbio backed by the Apennines), is the **Abbazia di Vallingegno**, a 13C Benedictine foundation, now privately owned (admission on request), partly used as an agriturismo hotel. The church has a Roman sarcophagus as its high altar in which the bones of the martyr St Verecondo are neatly preserved. The castle on a nearby hill is also privately owned.

GUALDO TADINO AND ENVIRONS

Gualdo Tadino is a small town noted for its ceramic production, with a fine castle, enlarged by Frederick II. The painter Matteo da Gualdo, active in the late 15C, was born in Gualdo and the Pinacoteca here displays many of his works. The town was one of the worst-hit places in the 1997–98 earthquake, its monuments were severely damaged and many of the inhabitants had to be temporarily housed in prefabricated villages on the outskirts.

Practical information

Information office
IAT di Gubbio, ☎ 075 9220693.

Getting there
By rail Gualdo Tadino and Fossato di Vico are on the railway line between Ancona and Rome.

Hotels
Gualdo Tadino
✩✩ **Gigiotto**, 5 Via del Morone, ☎ 075 912283; fax 075 910263.

Fossato di Vico
✩✩✩ **Del Ventura**, Osteria del Gatto, ☎ 075 9149470; ✩✩ **Camino Vecchio**, Osteria del Gatto, ☎ 075 9190121; fax 075 919983 and **Dal Cinese**, Via Filippo Venturi, ☎ 075 919131; fax 075 919759.

Sigillo
✩✩ **Monte Cucco**, Val di Ranco, ☎ 075 9177194 and ✩ **Capelloni**, Val di Ranco, ☎ & fax 075 9177131.

Youth hostels and campsites

A youth hostel is open in summer at Villa Scirca (Sigillo), and there is a refuge (**La Valletta**) on Monte Cucco. There are campsites at Valsorda ☆ **Valsorda** (open June–Sept), ☎ 075 913261, and at Costacciaro ☆☆ **Rio Verde** (open April–Sept), ☎ 075 9170138.

Restaurants
Gualdo Tadino
£ Da Clelia, Via Matteotti (in Valsorda in summer), ☎ 075 913261; **Dal Bottaio**, Via Casimiri, ☎ 075 913230; and **Gigiotto**, Via Morone, ☎ 075 910263.

History

The town stands near the site of the ancient Tadinum on the Via Flaminia where Narses routed the Goths and killed Totila in 552. In the 13C Gualdo became a free commune and its castle was strengthened by Frederick II. 'Tadino' was added to its name in 1833.

In the central **Piazza Martiri della Libertà** are the 18C **Palazzo Comunale** (cordoned off awaiting restoration) and the **Duomo** (**San Benedetto**), which has a lovely rose window, closed since 1997. The Gothic building of 1256 was transformed by Virginio Vespignani at the end of the 19C, when the pictorial decoration was carried out by Ulisse Ribustini. The cathedral owns a precious collection of works of art.

On the exterior of the wall of the Duomo (on Corso Italia) is a wall fountain attributed to Antonio da Sangallo the Elder. Opposite the Palazzo Comunale, a passageway leads out on to a terrace with a view. From here the fine apse of San Francesco can be seen (see below). On the right is the former **Palazzo del Podestà** with its 13C tower, lowered and surmounted by a Baroque lantern. A fine coat of arms from the Palazzo Comunale has been placed on the façade.

Beyond a pretty Art Nouveau chemist's shop is the church of **San Francesco**, now deconsecrated and not at present open. The exterior has a handsome north side with tall cylindrical towers. The beautiful light **interior** has a Gothic east end. Over the west door is the *story of St Julian*, a fresco by the school of Nelli (recently restored). Other frescoes in the church have been ruined by the infiltration of water. On the south side, high up, is a huge lunette of the *Dormition of the Virgin* (almost totally destroyed), an extremely interesting 14C work. In the chapel beneath is a lavabo and a 16C altarpiece in enamelled terracotta of local workmanship. In the apse are various frescoes including a *Crucifixion* by Matteo da Gualdo, and the 14C Gothic high altar. On the north side is a Roman sarcophagus front with two figures of winged Victories, and a large 14C pulpit on two columns. On the pilaster between the first and second arches, there is a *Madonna enthroned* with the colossal figure of St Anne behind, interesting for its iconography. A painted *Crucifix* by a follower of the Master of San Francesco (formerly in the Pinacoteca) has also been hung here.

In Piazza XX Settembre is the church of **Santa Maria**, with a 16C fresco outside (behind glass). Lower down the hill is the church of **Santa Chiara** (formerly Santa Maria di Tadino), thought to be the oldest church in the town, now deconsecrated.

Beyond the Duomo, Via della Rocca (partly stepped) leads up to the **Rocca Flea** which may date from before 1000. It was restored and enlarged by Frederick II who surrounded it with a wall. The interesting interior (☎ 075 9150248), with vaulted rooms, was restored just before the earthquake. It has an archaeological section, ceramics, and a good picture gallery with numerous works by Matteo da Gualdo, a polyptych by l'Alunno (1471), and a *Coronation of the Virgin* by Sano di Pietro.

BEYOND GUALDO TADINO

To the west of Gualdo a secondary road to Perugia runs through a pretty wooded valley and passes **Casa Castalda**, which has medieval walls and a triptych by Matteo da Gualdo in its church. Further on **Valfabbrica** preserves two towers of its medieval castle. Outside the village is a huge dam above the Chiascio river.

From Gualdo a byroad climbs north-east to **Valsorda**, where there is a magnificent view. This is wonderful walking country. Near here is the church of **Santissima Trinità** on Monte Serra Santa (1348m) dating from the 12C. The altarpiece is a copy by Giuseppe Pericoli (1928) of the glazed terracotta altarpiece now in San Francesco in Gualdo.

On the Gubbio road (N219) is **San Pellegrino**, an attractive little hill village. In the church, with frescoes by Matteo da Gualdo, is a triptych by Girolomo di Giovanni da Camerino (1465). At the festival of 'Maggio' here on the night of 30 April, a ceremony, which may have pagan origins, is held in the centre of the village to welcome the spring. Two poplars are cut down and stripped of their bark and branches and then 'married' to each other.

Further along the Gubbio road is the 11C **Castel d'Alfiolo**, in the middle of tobacco plantations, which has an attractive frieze on its façade dating from 1224.

The **Via Flaminia** leads north from Gualdo Tadino. At **Fossato di Vico**, in the upper medieval town, is the Cappella della Piaggiola with frescoes by Ottaviano Nelli and his school. The church of San Pietro has an interesting 11C interior.

In **Sigillo** is the church of St Anna which contains frescoes by Matteo da Gualdo, and a Palazzo Comunale with a neo-classical façade. Nearby is Ponte Spiano, the remains of a Roman bridge.

Costacciaro is an old village with the interesting church of San Francesco. It is now visited by cross-country skiers. A byroad climbs the slopes of **Monte Cucco** (1566m), an area of natural beauty now protected as a regional park (information office, Villa Anita, Sigillo, ☎ 075 9177326). It is a calcareous mass of carsic origin with beech-woods. It has interesting birdlife and wolves still live in the wild here. Beautiful walks can be taken here, and it is also popular with hang-gliders (information at the *Centro di Volo Libero*, Scirca, Sigillo) and cross-country skiers. It has numerous large caves and grottoes of great interest to speleologists (information from the *Centro Escursionistico Naturalistico Speleologico* in Costacciaro), including the Grotta di Monte Cucco, 922m deep. Remains of huge bears have been found here from centuries past.

Scheggia was a Roman station on the Via Flaminia. From here the N360 continues north-east around the base of **Monte Catria** (1700m). At **Isola di Fossara** a byroad leads left for the abbey of **Santa Maria di Sitria** founded by St Romualdo in the 11C, with a fine Romanesque church. This road winds on to the Eremo di Fonte Avellana in the Marche. The N360 continues along the Sentino valley through a protected area down to Sassoferrato in the Marche.

The beautiful road from Scheggia to Gubbio, 12km west, is described on p. 146. The Via Flaminia south of Gualdo Tadino, with Nocera Umbra, is described on p. 149.

Central Umbria, with Spoleto

NOCERA UMBRA AND ENVIRONS

Nocera Umbra was the worst-hit town in the 1997–98 earthquake. The entire old centre had to be abandoned and is still cordoned off awaiting the commencement of reconstruction. The population of some 6000 has had to be rehoused in prefabricated villages on the outskirts.

In a fine position, this was the *Nuceria Camellaria* of Pliny, and it was later a lordship of the Trinci family. The mineral water of Nocera Umbra, bottled at the Sorgente Angelica at Bagni (4km south-east of the town) is well known throughout Italy.

Information office

IAT del Folignate e Nocera Umbra, Foligno, ☎ 0742 354459.

An avenue with a war memorial leads up to the **Porta Vecchia** at the entrance to the Corso. On the right a portico leads to the church of **San Filippo**, built in 1886 by Luigi Poletti. The Corso continues up past **Santa Chiara** with three altarpieces by Carlo Maratta and a fine cantoria, and then winds left to Piazza Caprera.

Here, the church of **San Francesco** is the seat of the **Pinacoteca**, which was reopened in 1997 before the earthquake, but was then severely damaged and is at present closed. It contains frescoes and paintings by Matteo da Gualdo, a polyptych of the *Nativity and saints* by Nicolò Alunno, a large 13C Crucifix, and a *Madonna and Child* by Segna di Bonaventura. It also includes a collection of sculpture and some archaeological material from a Lombard necropolis excavated nearby. Opposite is a building with Gothic elements.

Beside an unusual church Via San Rinaldo continues up to the side door of the **Duomo** (also closed since 1997) which has an 18C interior with a barrel vault, neo-classical pilasters and four columns in each side chapel. The last chapel on the right side has good paintings of the *Life of the Virgin* by Giulio Cesare Angeli (1619) and stuccoes by Francesco Silva di Morbio. Opposite the façade of the Duomo the tall 11C tower of the **Rocca** was partially destroyed in the earthquake. From the terrace there is a fine view of the Topino valley. From Piazza Caprera a road descends to **San Giovanni** which has a carved door and an attractive interior with a 16C altarpiece of the *Birth of the Virgin*.

BEYOND NOCERA UMBRA

Between Nocera Umbra and Foligno is the **Valtopina**, an area which was also badly damaged in the earthquake, with some remains of medieval castles and a number of churches, including the **Villa di Postignano**, once a castle of the Trinci.

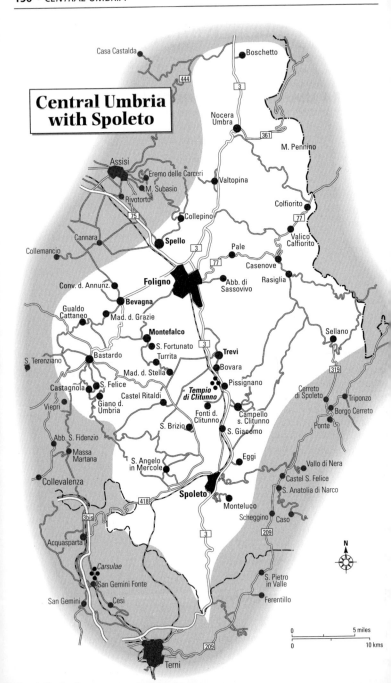

Central Umbria with Spoleto

A road runs east from Nocera Umbra to **Bagnara** at the foot of **Monte Pennino** (1571m; winter sports facilities).

In the wider valley north of Nocera are Costa, Colle and **Boschetto** (right) where the church, by a stream, has a chapel at the west end with frescoes by Matteo da Gualdo. Other works from the church have been removed for safety.

Gualdo Tadino is described on p. 146.

FOLIGNO

Foligno, on the River Topino, has numerous interesting palaces from the Renaissance to the neo-classical period, a fine Duomo, and some churches with good 18C interiors. Palazzo Trinci, beautifully restored, has remarkable frescoes of secular subjects. As the third largest town in Umbria (after Perugia and Terni), with 53,000 inhabitants, it has industrial suburbs, but is an excellent shopping centre. It was one of the worst-hit towns in the earthquake of 1997–98 and many inhabitants are still housed in prefabricated buildings on the outskirts. Most of the churches, including the Duomo, are still closed, but Palazzo Trinci is open daily.

Practical information

Information office
IAT del Folignate-Nocera Umbra, 126 Porta Romana, ☎ 0742 354459.

Getting there
By bus Run by *Spoletina*, ☎ 0742 357341, buses connect Perugia with Foligno, some of them via Assisi; other services from Rome, Spoleto, Spello, Trevi, Montefalco, Bevagna and Nocera Umbra.
By rail There is a station on the branch line from Terontola and Perugia, and on the main line from Ancona to Rome.
Car-parking There are car parks in Via Nazario Sauro, Via Chiavellati, and Via Oberdan; covered car-park with hourly tariff at Porta Romana; limited space (with hourly tariff) in Piazza San Domenico, Piazza San Francesco, Piazza Garibaldi, Piazzetta Beata Angela, and Porta Todi.

Hotels
☆☆☆ *Poledrini*, 12 Viale Mezzetti, ☎ & fax 0742 341041; *Italia*, 12 Piazza Matteotti, t 0742 350412; fax 0742 352258; *Le Mura*, 29 Via Bolletta, ☎ 0742 357344; fax 0742 353327.

☆☆ *Nunziatella*, 3 Via Pagliarini, ☎ 0742 341013; fax 0742 341014.
On the outskirts ☆☆☆ *Villa Roncalli*, 25 Viale Roma (1km from the centre), with restaurant, ☎ 0742 391091; fax 0742 391001.
Colfiorito ☆☆☆ *Villa Colfiorita*, ☎ 0742 681326; fax 0742 681327, and others.
Ponte Santa Lucia, ☆☆☆ *Guesia*, ☎ 0742 311515; fax 0742 660216.

Restaurants
££ *Villa Roncalli* (see above); *Da Remo*, 10 Via Fabio Filzi, ☎ 0742 340522; *La Spagnola*, 14 Via Rinaldi, ☎ 0742 352928; *Hostaria Sparafucile*, 30 Piazza Duomo, ☎ 0368 3827246. £ *Dei Franceschi*, Via dei Franceschi, ☎ 0742 357016; *Marechiaro*, 58 Via Piermarini, ☎ 0742 340551.

Wine bar
Il Bacco Felice, 73 Via Garibaldi, ☎ 0742 341019.
Scopoli £ *Sette Monti*, ☎ 0742 632356.

Market day on Saturdays and Tuesdays (in Via Nazario Sauro).

Annual festivals

The *Giostra della Quintana*, a joust dating from 1613, was reinstated in 1946 and is held in the stadium at Porta Romana in two heats on the second and third Sundays of September. The first joust is preceded by a procession in 17C costume on Saturday evening and on Sunday afternoon, and there is another procession before the second joust. There are celebrations in 17C costume in various districts of the town and in Piazza della Repubblica.

In September there is a Baroque music and theatre festival. Large **markets** are held in honour of San Manno (14 and 15 September) and San Feliciano (25 and 26 January), where typical local products can still be found.

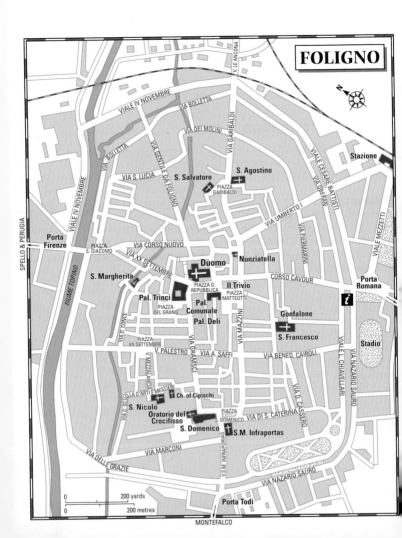

History

Foligno was the *Fulginia* of the Romans and absorbed the population of *Forum Flaminii*, another Roman town 3.5km west. Long a free commune, it came under the rule of the Trinci family in the 14C until it passed to the States of the Church in 1439. Angela of Foligno (1248–1309), who became a Franciscan tertiary, was born here, and became one of the most famous mystics of Europe. Its school of painting was largely indebted to Nicolò da Foligno, or Nicolò di Liberatore, called l'Alunno (c 1430–1502), who has a very unusual style. Printing was introduced to Foligno in 1470, only six years after the first book printed in Italy had appeared at Subiaco. The first edition of Dante's *La Divina Commedia* was published here in 1472. Vernon Lee took a 17C palace in Foligno as the setting for her story *The Doll* (1927). The town was badly bombed in 1943–44 and suffered extensive damage. Raphael's *Madonna di Foligno* is now in the Vatican.

The centre of the town is **Piazza della Repubblica**. **Palazzo Comunale**, with its neo-classical façade by Antonio Mollari and decorative bronze lamps, is situated here. A medieval tower of the earlier town hall protrudes above the façade, but its lantern toppled down during the earthquake. The municipal offices have been moved temporaraily to Palazzo Deli. The Renaissance **Palazzo Orfini** (with traces of external painted decoration) may have been the seat of the first printing-house in the town (see above). Next to it are remains of the **Palazzo del Podestà** with a large arch.

Palazzo Trinci

At the far end of the square is Palazzo Trinci which has a neo-classical façade (1841–47). This 14C Romanesque building was reconstructed and enlarged in the Gothic style in 1407–11 as the palace of Ugolino III Trinci, who ruled the city from 1386–1415. Part of the exterior, dating from 1389–1407, can be seen from Piazza del Grano. The restoration of the brick courtyard is almost complete.

Much of the **interior**, open daily 10.00–18.00, was beautifully restored in 1991–97 and survived the earthquake undamaged. It is remarkable for its Gothic architecture as well as its early 15C frescoed decoration of secular subjects, in late Gothic style, most of them commissioned by Ugolino Trinci.

A fine Gothic **staircase**, probably built 1390–1400, which preserves fragments of its original frescoed decoration with geometrical designs, leads up to the first floor where the Gothic vaulted halls (with some of their original wall decorations) are still being restored. A modern staircase and an old flight of stairs continue up to the second floor where the frescoes commissioned by the Trinci in the first three decades of the 15C are among the most interesting secular works to survive in Italy. The epigrams and inscriptions were devised by the Humanist Francesco da Fiano.

The **loggia** has very interesting frescoes illustrating the legend of the founding of Rome. A narrow staircase leads up to the **chapel** where there are well-preserved frescoes of the *Life of the Virgin* commissioned in 1424 from Ottaviano Nelli by Corrado, son of Ugolino Trinci. On the other side of the loggia is the **Sala delle Arti Liberali e dei Pianeti**. The Liberal Arts are represented by seated female figures in Gothic thrones: on the far wall (left of the chimney) are *Grammar*, *Dialectic* and *Music*; on the end (left) wall, *Geometry*, *Philosophy* (in the centre, but very ruined) and *Astronomy*. On the entrance wall, *Arithmetic* and *Rhetoric* are shown, both in the act of teaching pupils. The *Planets* are represented on the opposite wall, right of the fireplace: the *Moon* in a chariot drawn by grey chargers, and an allegory of *Decrepitude* in the tondo. Next to the standing figure of *Mars* in armour a tondo depicts *Infancy*. On the next wall, is *Mercury* and *Youth* (in the tondo), and *Jove* (very ruined, with *Adolescence* represented in the corner tondo). On the last wall there was the representation of *Venus* and *Saturn* (very damaged) with a chariot drawn by red horses.

A **corridor**, which connected the palace to the Duomo, has fine frescoes of 11 heroes of antiquity opposite the *Seven Ages of Man*. Two rooms display antique sculpture once owned by the Trinci family including a relief of *Amore and Psyche* (1C–2C AD), beneath which Ugolino Trinci added a long inscription in Gothic lettering recording the building of the palace; seven Roman heads (2C–3C AD), including Hadrian; and a 3C AD relief showing the games at the Circus Maximus in Rome.

On the other side of the staircase the **Sala di Sisto IV** has an original wooden ceiling, but damaged 16C frescoes attributed to Lattanzio Pagani and Dono Doni. The **Sala degli Imperatori** (temporarily closed) has a frescoed portico where there are gigantic figures of emperors with landscapes in the background dating from c 1415.

The **Pinacoteca** (not at present open) contains paintings by the native artist Pierantonio Mezzastris, detached frescoes by Bartolomeo di Tommaso, works by Lattanzio, son of Alunno, and Dono Doni, and a fresco of the *Annunciatory Angel* from the deconsecrated church of San Domenico, attributed to Benozzo Gozzoli.

On the last side of the square is the magnificent secondary (north) façade of the **Duomo** (1133–1201). The beautiful portal was carved by Rodolfo and Binello. Between the north façade and west entrance of the Duomo is the pink and white **Palazzo delle Canoniche** with Gothic two-light windows (reconstructed in 1926). The main façade (covered for restoration) of the Duomo, also pink and white, with a rose window, was restored in 1904.

The huge ornate **interior** (closed since the earthquake), reminiscent of St Peter's in Rome, was decorated by the native architect Giuseppe Piermarini in the 18C on a design by Luigi Vanvitelli. **South side**. On the first altar is Enrico Bartolomei's *Death of Messalina* (1860); on the second altar is Giovanni Andrea Lazzarini's *Holy Family* (18C). In the **sacristy** is a fine painting (in very good condition) of the *Madonna and St John* by Alunno, on either side of a 14C sculpted wooden Crucifix. Two busts here of *Bartolomeo* and *Diana Roscioli* have recently been identified as works by Gian Lorenzo Bernini. In a little room off the south transept is all that remains of a life-size 18C silver statue of *St Feliciano* by Giovanni Battista Maini, seated on a throne by Andrea Pozzo. Much of it was dismantled and stolen in 1982; some parts have been remade, but the scene of the saint's martyrdom on the back of the throne was recovered. When the statue leaves the Duomo in a procession on 24 January, it takes 16 men to carry it. There are also three 18C Crucifixes here. Between the first and second altars on the north side there is a detached 16C fresco.

Via Gramsci, with the finest *palazzi* in the town, leads out of Piazza della Repubblica past Palazzo Trinci (see above). It is adjoined by the graceful **Palazzo Deli** or **Nuti** (16C; beautifully restored in 1989), with a handsome portal and incorporating a medieval tower. The large **Palazzo Alleori Ubaldi** (restored in 1986) has a neo-classical façade and contains contemporary painted decorations by Marcello Leopardi. Via Gramsci continues past (right) Via della Scuola di Arti e Mestieri.

Beyond the tiny church of **San Tommaso dei Cipischi** (1190; closed) is **San Nicolò** (closed) which conserves two good paintings by Alunno: a polyptych of 1492 and a *Coronation of the Virgin* (c 1489). Via Mezzalancia leads from here to Piazza XX Settembre with the 17C Palazzo Barnabò which has an interesting staircase. Via San Giovanni dell'Acqua leads up to the picturesque **Via delle Conce** on a canal with the old porticoed tanneries (a district particularly animated during the *Quintana* celebrations in September). In this area, near remains of a Roman bridge, is the church of **Santa Margherita** (or San Giuseppe) with a Rococo interior (closed).

Via Gramsci ends by the huge 18C Palazzo Candiotti (now a school). Its chapel, called the **Oratorio del Crocifisso** has a 17C–18C interior (closed). In the adjoining piazza is the church of **San Domenico**, deconsecrated and now used as an auditorium. Important medieval frescoes have recently been discovered here. Also in the piazza is **Santa Maria Infraportas**, a Romanesque basilica with an interesting exterior and an ancient bell-tower. It contains 15C–16C frescoes, some by Pier Antonio Mezzastris.

Via Mazzini, with 16C palaces, leads back to the centre past (right) Via Cesare Agostini where there is a flying arch and **Palazzo Pandolfi Elmi**, still owned by the family and beautifully maintained until it was damaged in the earthquake. To the south is the church of **San Francesco** (closed) which contains early frescoes, next to the oratory of the **Gonfalone** (1735). In the medieval district here is the house of Beata Angela where interesting 13C–14C frescoes were discovered in 1989. Via Mazzini meets Corso Cavour, the main shopping street of the town, at a crossroads called Il Trivio.

Via Garibaldi continues past the **Nunziatella**, an oratory (closed) which contains a fresco by Perugino, and the deconsecrated church of the **Suffragio**, with a Greek-cross interior of 1728–35 (closed). In Piazza Garibaldi is the church of **Sant'Agostino** which has an 18C interior. An early 18C wooden statue of the *Madonna*, fully robed, is exhibited on 12 January and 31 May. Opposite is **San Salvatore** (closed), with a 14C façade. The restored 18C interior contains beautiful fragments of 16C Flemish tapestries illustrating the *Story of Joseph*.

BEYOND FOLIGNO

A road (N 77) leads east of Foligno towards Colfiorito, through an area severely damaged in the earthquake of 1997. Many of the little towns are totally abandoned and awaiting reconstruction, meanwhile the inhabitants are housed in prefabricated villages on the outskirts.

A byroad (signposted) leads through the village of **Uppello** (keep right) and under an archway and then left (signposted Casale); a rough road continues up to the **Abbazia di Sassovivo** in an isolated position on the beautiful wooded slopes of Monte Serrone. A Benedictine foundation of the 11C, the abbey is now occupied by a religious community. The church (rebuilt in 1851) and the delightful little **cloister** (1229–32, by Roman sculptors) were damaged in the earthquake. The main road continues through Colle San Lorenzo with fine views ahead.

Pale lies at the bottom of a valley, wedged in between two rock faces. It has been noted for its paper-mills since the 13C and one large old mill survives here. Beyond it (keep left) are remains of 14C walls. The little village is all but abandoned after it was severely damaged, and the church of San Biagio (whose pyramidal tower survived) is closed. It contained a lovely painted wooden statue of the *Madonna and Child enthroned*, by the 14C Umbrian school, and two paintings by Felice Damiani. The Hermitage of Santa Maria Giacobbe high up on the rock face (approached by a path on the other side of the valley) which contains 14C–15C frescoes was also damaged.

The main road continues along the floor of the valley. It passes **Scopoli** with a 15C castle. At **Casenove**, which was the epicentre of the 1997 earthquake, the road for Norcia (see below) forks right, while this route ascends, in places steeply, through the wooded river valley, with splendid views right, to the Valico Colfiorito (821m). To the north, Monte Pennino is seen beyond Monte Acuto, while to the right of the road rises Monte Profoglio (1322m). The cultivated and marshy upland plain, of great interest for its flora and fauna, on the borders of Umbria and the Marche around **Colfiorito** (also severely damaged in the earthquake), is known for its excellent produce (especially lentils, pulses, farro, potatoes and onions), all of which are sold by the local farmers on the side of the road. Many of the attractive villages, built of the light local stone, have been abandoned since the earthquake. Beyond the watershed where the river rises the road descends along the Chienti river in a deep enclosed valley towards Camerino in the Marche.

From Casenove (see above), the N319 bears right for Norcia. Just outside **Rasiglia**, the road passes beside the **Sanctuary of the Madonna delle Grazie** (right; well signposted), which dates from 1450 (altered at the beginning of the 20C). This has been closed since damage in the earthquake. In the interior, the walls have very interesting votive frescoes by the 15C Foligno school, including an unusual representation of an angel pacifying two warriors, *St Anthony Abbot enthroned* and a *Crucifixion*. In the apse, designed at the beginning of the 20C, are numerous ex votos. In the crypt (1947) is a recomposed and restored 15C sculptural group of the *Madonna in Adoration*.

The road now climbs gently up, winding through wooded hills to a summit level of 800m at the Valico del Soglio. It then descends through Villamagina to **Sellano**, founded by the Romans in 84 BC, in a lovely position with views of the wooded hills dotted with little hamlets, but severely damaged in 1997–98. The main road passes the elegant octagonal church of the Madonna della Croce (1538), closed since 1997. An avenue leads across a bridge into the old district, which has become a ghost town, totally abandoned since the earthquake. The church of Santa Maria (13C; enlarged in the 16C), with a coral and white façade, had an interesting interior. The road descends into another deserted wooded valley before reaching the Valnerina (described on p. 218).

SPELLO

●　●　●　●　●　●　●　●

Spello is a beautiful little medieval town (population 8000), well-preserved and charmingly situated on the southernmost slope of Monte Subasio (261m), over-looking the wide alluvial plain known as the Valle Umbra south-east of Perugia. The Roman **Hispellum**, it is particularly interesting for its Roman remains. The buildings are built of pink and white stone, quarried locally, and are well-kept and decorated with colourful flowerpots. The peaceful narrow streets retain their lovely old paving. The hillside is planted with olives.

Practical information

Information office

Pro Loco, 3 Piazza Matteotti, off Via Cavour (next to the church of Sant'Andrea), ☎ 0742 301009.

Getting there

By rail The railway station on the Terontola–Foligno line, c 1km from Porta Consolare, has services from Perugia (in 40mins).

By road Spello, 31km from Perugia, is just off the fast road (N75, N3) between Perugia and Spoleto.

Car parking There are two free car-parks outside the walls: at the top of the hill outside Porta Montanara, and at the southern entrance to the town near Porta Consolare. Within the walls cars can be parked but a parking card has to be purchased (numerous shops sell them) and displayed on the windscreen.

By bus Bus services, run by **Spoletina Trasporti**, from Foligno and Assisi (except on PH).

Hotels

☆☆☆☆ **Palazzo Bocci**, 17 Via Cavour, ☎ 0742 301021; fax 0742 301464. Opened in 1992 in a large 19C palace in a good position in the centre of the little town. There is a frescoed drawing-room and a very pleasant garden terrace (where breakfast is served in warm weather). It has, however, a rather gloomy atmosphere and the rooms are not very attractively fur-nished. It is sometimes taken over by groups. The hotel owns the good restaurant opposite (**Il Mulino**).

☆☆☆ **Albergo del Teatro**, 24 Via Giulia, ☎ 0742 301140; fax 0742 301612. Recently opened in an old building in the centre of the town, with 11 rooms and a terrace. **La Bastiglia**, 17 Via dei Molini (off Piazza Vallegloria), ☎ 0742 651277; fax 0742 301159. In an old house at the top of the town with a pretty terrrace. It has been filled with modern 'art'. There are 22 heavily decorated rooms, 14 of which have good views. Closed in January. It has a restaurant and half-board terms are available. It is sometimes occupied by groups, and there are plans to enlarge it.

☆☆ **Il Cacciatore**, 42 Via Giulia, ☎ 0742 651141; fax 0742 301603. Run by the same proprietors as the **Albergo del Teatro**, also in the centre of the town. It has a pleasant atmosphere and eight of the 17 rooms have wonderful views over the plain. There is also a lovely terrace overlooking the plain and a good restaurant. Friendly staff.

Restaurants

££ **Il Molino**, 6 Via Cavour, ☎ 0742 651305; **Il Cacciatore** (see above).

£ **Il Pinturicchio**, Largo Mazzini, ☎ 0742 301003.

Picnics

There are places to picnic outside Porta Montanara.

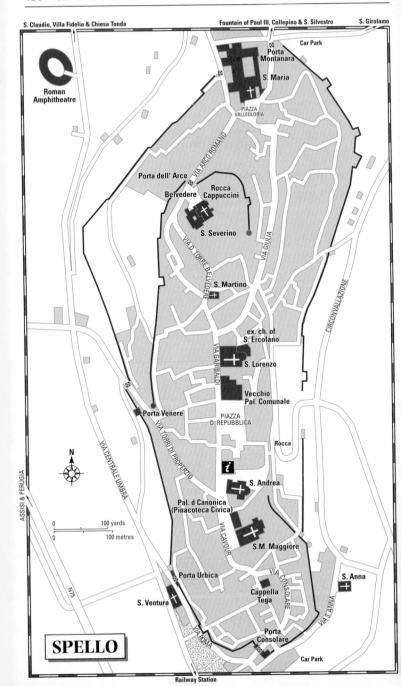

S. Claudio, Villa Fidelia & Chiesa Tonda

Fountain of Paul III, Collepino & S. Silvestro

S. Girolamo

Car Park

Roman Amphitheatre

Porta Montanara

S. Maria

PIAZZA VALLEGLORIA

VIA D. ARCO ROMANO

Porta dell' Arce

Belvedere

Rocca Cappuccini

S. Severino

VIA GIULIA

VIA D. TORRE BELVEDERE

S. Martino

CIRCONVALLAZIONE

ex. ch. of S. Ercolano

VIA GARIBALDI

S. Lorenzo

Vecchio Pal. Comunale

Porta Venere

VIA TORRI DI PROPERZIO

PIAZZA D. REPUBBLICA

Rocca

i

ASSISI & PERUGIA

VIA CENTRALE UMBRA

N

0   100 yards

0   100 metres

S. Andrea

Pal. d Canonica (Pinacoteca Civica)

VIA CAVOUR

S.M. Maggiore

VIA CONSOLARE

S. Anna

VIA S. ANNA

Porta Urbica

Cappella Tega

N75

S. Ventura

VIA ROMA

Porta Consolare

Car Park

SPELLO

Railway Station

Collepino
££ *Taverna di San Silvestro*, ☎ 0742 651203.

Annual festival
Infiorata on the Sunday after Corpus Domini (around late May – early June) when the streets are carpeted with fresh flowers in numerous different designs.

History

On the site of a settlement of the Umbri, it was a Roman Municipium and then the *Splendidissima colonia Iulia Hispellum* flourished here. Constantine named *Hispellum* the religious centre of Umbria. After destruction by the Lombards, it became part of the Duchy of Spoleto. In c 1238 it was destroyed by Frederick II and then came under the dominion of Perugia.

The main entrance to the town is through the 14C Portonaccio. Beyond is **Porta Consolare**, a fine Roman gateway with three arches. The ancient Roman road

The Romans in Umbria

The Tiber for centuries represented a boundary more or less in the centre of the region: to the west lay the Etruscan settlements of Perugia and Orvieto, while the district east of the river was inhabited by the Umbri (an Italic tribe of Indo-European origins) with centres round present-day Gualdo Tadino, Gubbio, Assisi, Spello, Todi, Terni and Narni. From the 4C BC onwards the presence of the Romans in the area is attested, and they established control of central Italy definitively after the battle of Sentinum in 295 BC in which the combined forces of the Umbri, Etruscans, Samnites and Gauls were beaten. The building in 220 BC of the Via Flaminia, which crosses Umbria, was of great strategic importance to the Romans since it gave them direct access to the Adriatic coast across the Apennines. From Ocriculum in the south (the remains of which can be seen) the road was carried over the valley of the Nar by an impressive bridge at Narni which also still survives in ruins. At Narni, where a colony had been founded in 299, and which still has important Roman remains, the consular road divided, one branch running though Terni and Spoleto (a Roman colony dating from 241 BC), and one (probably built later) through Carsulae and Bevagna. The two branches converged again beyond Foligno where the stretch across the Apennines began. Just three years after the opening of the road, the censor Gaius Flaminius who was responsible for its construction, met his death at the hands of Hannibal in the resounding victory over the Romans in the famous Battle of Trasimeno. It was largely due to the faithfulness of the Roman settlements in the region to the cause of Rome after their defeat here which meant that the Carthaginian victory was not to have lasting consequences.

Fine Roman remains are still to be found all over the region, including gateways, mosaics, temples, cisterns, amphitheatres, theatres and bridges, at Spoleto, Spello, Narni, Terni, Amelia, Todi, Bevagna, Spello, Assisi, Perugia and Gubbio. The Roman towns of Carsulae, Ocriculum and Urbinum Hortense have been excavated, and there are numerous archaeological collections in Umbria which preserve finds from local excavations.

has been revealed here. On the upper part of the façade, rebuilt in the Middle Ages, are three Republican statues found near the amphitheatre, and placed here at the end of the 17C. The gate is flanked by medieval buildings, including a tower on Roman foundations. On the left Via Roma follows a fine stretch of Augustan walls, built in pink and white stone from Monte Subasio, as far as **Porta Urbica** (or San Ventura), flush with the walls, also of the Augustan period. There is a small door through a tower in the walls here (from which steps lead up to Via del Tempio di Diana). The medieval church of San Ventura, outside the walls, has a 13C fresco fragment and an interesting high altar.

Porta Consolare

From Porta Consolare the steep and winding **Via Consolare** and **Via Cavour**, on the line of the ancient *cardo maximus*, climb to the centre of the town. At the beginning are a number of picturesque medieval streets. The 14C **Cappella Tega** has 15C frescoes by Niccolò Alunno and Pietro di Mazzaforte (attributed).

Santa Maria Maggiore

At the beginning of Via Cavour is the Collegiata of Santa Maria Maggiore (closed 12.30–14.30). Founded in the 12C it was reconsecrated in 1513. The **façade** was rebuilt in 1644 by Belardino da Como incorporating Romanesque carving traditionally attributed to Binello and Rodolfo (12C–13C). The carved wooden doors date from the 17C. At the foot of the Romanesque campanile are two Roman columns made from Luni marble.

The large **interior** was transformed in 1656–70 when it was decorated with fine stuccoes attributed to Agostino Silva. The funerary altar of Caio Titieno Flacco (60 AD), one of the best pieces of Roman carving found in the city, is now used as a stoup; an unfinished marble Corinthian capital serves as the other stoup. South side. The altarpieces date from the 17C. The font is by Antonio di Gasparino (1509–11). South transept. The altar of the Madonna di Loreto is perhaps the best work of Agostino Silva in the church. The Cappella del Crocifisso (which has been in restoration for a number of years) contains detached frescoes.

East end (being restored). The delightful baldacchino over the high altar was carved by Rocco da Vicenza (1512–15). It has eight terracotta heads of prophets by Gian Domenico da Carrara (1562). On the triumphal arch is a small stained-glass tondo attributed to Tommaso Porro (1538). On the two pilasters flanking the apse are two very late frescoes by Perugino (1521), a *Pietà* and a *Madonna and saints*. The choir stalls are by Pier Nicola da Spoleto (1512–20). North transept. In the **Cappella del Sacramento** is a tabernacle carved in 1562 by Gian Domenico da Carrara. Above a lavabo is a painting of an angel attributed to Pinturicchio. The intarsia bench dates from the 16C. In the little adjoining room a fresco of the *Madonna and Child* can be seen, also attributed to Pinturicchio (but largely repainted). The altar in the transept is decorated in stucco by the 17C Lombard school. Above the sacristy door, in a fine frame, is an altarpiece by the local painter Carlo Lamparelli (late 17C).

North side. The pulpit is a good work by Simone da Campione. The **frescoes** (restored in 1978) in the **Cappella Baglioni** (light; fee) were commissioned from **Pinturicchio** by Troilo Baglioni, prior of the church, in 1500. They are among his best works, and he may have been helped by Giovanni Battista Caporali and perhaps also by Eusebio da San Giorgio. The three large lunettes, which incorporate numerous classical details, represent the *Annunciation*, the *Adoration of the Shepherds*, and *Christ among the doctors*, and in the vault are four *sibyls*. In the Annunciation scene, beneath a shelf, hangs a self-portrait of the artist. In the scene of Christ among the doctors the figure in a black habit on the left is a portrait of Troilo Baglioni. The majolica floor dates from 1566 (perhaps manufactured in Deruta).

Palazzo dei Canonici, preceded by two Roman columns, houses the **Pinacoteca Civica** (open 10.00–13.00, 15.00 or 16.00–18.00 or 19.00, ☎ 0742 301497). It contains some beautiful works of art (recently restored) displayed chronologically. In room 1 is a fine wooden statue of the *Madonna and Child* dating from the end of the 12C or the beginning of the 13C. The detached frescoes date from the 14C. The 14C Crucifix (with moveable arms) belongs to Santa Maria Maggiore. The precious enamelled silver **Cross** is by Paolo Vanni of Perugia commissioned by the prior of Santa Maria Maggiore in 1398, and the little portable **diptych**, with the *Crucifixion* and *Coronation of the Madonna*, is signed by Cola Petruccioli (1391?). Room 2. Panels (including four saints and two predella scenes) from a 15C triptych attributed to the Maestro dell'Assunta di Amelia: these were recovered in France after their theft in 1970, but the central panel of the *Madonna and Saints*, attributed to Pinturicchio or l'Ingegno, and the last predella scene were never found. Also displayed here is a 15C Umbrian woven cloth. Room 3 contains a *Crucifixion* by l'Alunno, and a panel painted on both sides with the *Miracle of the Cross of Spello* and the *Madonna of the Misericordia* by the circle of l'Alunno. Also here is a 15C stone and terracotta *Pietà* (being restored). In a niche in room 1 is the bell from the campanile, signed and dated 1209 by Bencivenni da Pisa and, opposite, a wooden 15C statue. The five detached frescoes from Santa Maria in Paterno date from the 15C–16C.

On the other side of the entrance corridor is room 4 with 16C works, including a polychrome wooden statue of the *Madonna and Child*, and the *Gonfalon of Santa Barbara* dated 1576, and a fresco of the *Madonna and Child with two Saints* from the oratory of San Bernardino attributed to L'Ingegno. Room 5. Remains of the painted decoration from the 16C cantoria in Santa Maria Maggiore. Room 6 contains five works by Marcantonio Grecchi, who died in Spello in 1651. The four polychrome wooden candle-bearing angels date from the early 17C. Room 7 exhibits church vestments. The last room (8) contains a *Madonna of the Rosary* by Ascensidonio Spacca (il Fantino), two *Saints* attributed to Pier Francesco Mola, an elaborate reliquary of San Felice by Girolamo Salvini (1788), two *Saints* attributed to Andrea Camassei, and a small painting by Benvenuto Crispoldi (d. 1923).

Further up on the right is the church of **Sant'Andrea** (closed 13.00–14.30) built in 1258. In the **interior** there are lights for the frescoes. South side. First niche, Tommaso Corbo, *Madonna and Saints* (1532); second niche, Dono Doni,

Mary and Joseph (1565; unusual for its iconography). Beyond, in a smaller niche, there is a 13C fresco fragment of the *Madonna and Child*. In the right arm of the **crossing** there is a large altarpiece of the *Madonna and Child with saints* (light on the door to the right) by Pinturicchio and Eusebio da San Giorgio, and a tondo of the *Redeemer* (removed for restoration), also by them. The pretty **high altar** has 14C columns. The large Crucifix is attributed to an Umbrian master of the late 13C (a follower of Giotto, perhaps the Maestro di Farneto). In the apse are neo-Gothic frescoes and stained glass. In the left arm of the crossing are two detached frescoes found here during restoration of the altar of Sant'Andrea. North side. On the pulpit, there is a *Resurrection* (removed), attributed to Pinturicchio, a 14C Crucifix and (in the baptistery at the west end), 15C frescoes by a local master.

In front of the church, the picturesque **Via Torri di Properzio**, with charming little houses, descends to the **Porta Venere**, of the Augustan age, the best preserved of the Roman gateways. It is flanked by two handsome pink 12-sided towers.

A short way beyond Sant'Andrea is Piazza della Repubblica. In the atrium of the **Palazzo Comunale Vecchio** an archaeological collection is provisionally arranged including Roman fragments, sarcophagi and inscriptions. The upper floor (where some of the rooms are frescoed, and works by Emilio Greco are exhibited) has been closed since the earthquake.

Still higher is the Romanesque church of **San Lorenzo**, traditionally thought to have been founded in 1120. The interesting façade preserves Roman and medieval fragments. **Interior**. On the west wall there is a fresco of *St Bernardine of Siena* and the *Madonna and Child with St Catherine*. South side. On the first pilaster is a well-carved 15C tabernacle. The second chapel dates from 1793; the tabernacle is by Flaminio Vacca (1589). On the next altar is *St Catherine of Alexandria with Christ and the Virgin* by Fran van de Kasteele of Brussels (1599), and at the end of the south side, *Christ and the Virgin receiving Souls from Purgatory*, a very unusual painting also by Kasteele. The baldacchino over the high altar dates from 1631 and behind the **high altar** is a gilded silver Cross of 1820. The choir stalls were carved by Andrea Campano da Modena (1530–34) who also carved the fine intarsia furnishings in the **sacristy**. Also here is a 15C lavabo. The pulpit in the left aisle was carved by Francesco Costantini (1600).

Via di Torre Belvedere (keep left) leads up past the little Romanesque church of San Martino (usually closed) to the top of the hill. The **Belvedere** provides a fine view: to the left is Montefalco and the plain in front of the hills of Bettona and Perugia, and to the right Santa Maria degli Angeli, Assisi and Monte Subasio. Below the hill of Spello, the overgrown Roman amphitheatre is clearly seen beyond the main road next to the modern sports stadium. Nearby are the church of San Claudio and the Villa Fidelia with its garden. The Roman arch here (Porta dell'Arce) probably dates from the Republican era (part of it is underground).

Remains of the Rocca are incorporated in the convent of the Cappuccini, and the church of San Severino, one of the oldest in the town. Via Arco Romano descends to Piazza di Vallegloria with the church and monastery of Santa Maria founded c 1320. The road to the right leaves the town by the 18C **Porta Montanara** on the site of a medieval gate. Remains of the Roman aqueduct (re used in the Middle Ages) from Monte Subasio can be seen here. Viale Poeta, with fine views, leads into the country past the Fountain of Paul III, incorporating a medieval sarcophagus.

Via Giulia returns from Piazza di Vallegloria towards the centre of Spello. It passes the 18C theatre, a round tower of the Rocca, and (near the remains of a Roman gate) the characteristic Borgo dell'Arco d'Augusto. Just before rejoining Via Garibaldi an alley on the left leads to the former church of Sant'Ercolano of ancient foundation.

The road below the town on the west (parallel to the superstrada and railway) passes the ruined and overgrown **Roman amphitheatre** (no admission), dating from the 1C AD. It could hold some 15,000 spectators. On the other side of the road is the charming little 12C church of **San Claudio** (usually closed), with a bell-cote. Just beyond is the conspicuous **Villa Fidelia**, on the site of a Classical sanctuary dating from the Republican era. At the beginning of the 18C a villa was constructed here by Donna Teresa Pamphili Grillo, modelled on the Villa Madama in Rome, and the garden laid out. The present building dates from the late 18C or early 19C and is attributed to Giuseppe Piermarini. It is surrounded by a terraced garden with fine cypresses.

Since 1985 Villa Fidelia has housed the **Straka-Coppa Collection** (open daily July & Aug 10.30–13.00, 16.00–19.00; April, May, June & Sept Thur, Fri, Sat & Sun 10.30–13.00, 15.30–18.00; Oct–Mar weekends only 10.30–13.00, 15.00–17.30; ☎ 0742 301866) of Italian art (well labelled). On the ground floor is an interesting display of early 20C works and documents relating to the Futurists. The first floor has contemporary works. On the top floor are early paintings including (**room 1**) *Diana and a warrior* by Lodovico Carracci, and the *Portrait of a Gentleman* by Carlo Ceresa. **Room 6** has Venetian paintings including a *Madonna and Child* by Vincenzo Catena and the copy of a portrait by Titian of *Laura de' Dianti with a boy*. The collection also includes silver, ceramics, porcelain and furniture.

Nearby, right on the superstrada, is the Chiesa Tonda (1517–39), an attractive centrally planned Renaissance church. It is now deconsecrated and privately owned (closed).

From outside Porta Montanara (see above), a byroad leads up to **Collepino**, a medieval walled village (600m) with fine views. Above the village, on the slopes of Monte Subasio, is the Romanesque church of **San Silvestro**. The abbey was founded here by St Romualdo in 1025. It has a Roman sarcophagus as its altar and a fine crypt. This beautiful unsurfaced road continues across Monte Subasio towards Assisi (see p. 99).

Outside Porta Montanara (see above), another road leads to the church of **San Girolamo**, next to the cemetery. Founded in 1474, it is preceded by a portico beneath which are frescoes of the *Epiphany* by a follower of Pinturicchio and of *St Francis* by Mezzastris. Inside is a well carved Crucifix and another fresco by a follower of Pinturicchio.

The Circonvallazione (see plan) runs outside the walls on the east side of Spello and passes several gates. The church of **Sant'Anna** contains numerous frescoes by local 13C–16C artists. Via Sant'Anna returns to Porta Consolare.

BEVAGNA

Bevagna is an attractive ancient little town (population 2400) on low ground (225m) surrounded by a fertile plain watered by numerous rivers including the Topino, Clitunno and Teverone. It has considerable Roman remains and a beautiful medieval central piazza. Its walls are well preserved: the medieval circuit in places incorporates Roman fortifications of the 1C BC. An excellent red wine (including the strong *Sagrantino*) is produced in the district. The little town was badly shaken in the 1997–98 earthquake and the most important churches are closed for restoration, but the museum, opened in 1996, was undamaged and is open regularly. Bevagna has a particularly friendly atmosphere.

Practical information

Information offices
IAT del Folignate e Nocera Umbra, 126 Porta Romana, Foligno ☎ 0742 354459. Pro Loco in Bevagna, Piazza Silvestri, ☎ 0742 361667.

Getting there
By bus There are services from Foligno.
Car parking Outside the walls (Porta Todi).

Hotels
☆☆☆ *Palazzo Brunamonti*, 79 Corso Matteotti, ☎ & fax 0742 361932. Opened in 1998 in a delightful palace in the centre of the town, with 16 rooms furnished with great taste. Some of the rooms are frescoed, while others have old brick vaulting, and cool floors. Very good value and friendly staff. No restaurant.
'Historic residence' *L'Orto degli Angeli*, 1 Via Dante Alighieri, ☎ 0742 360130; fax 0742 361756. Nine rooms, with restaurant.

Simple but adequate accommodation is available at the monastery of *Santa Maria del Monte*, 15 Corso Matteotti, ☎ 0743 360135.

Campsite
☆☆☆ *Pian di Boccio*, at Gaglioli (open April–Sept), ☎ 0742 360164.

Restaurants
££ *Ottavius*, Via Gonfalone, off Piazza Silvestri, ☎ 0742 360555. **£** *Da Nina*, Piazza Garibaldi, ☎ 0742 360161.
Excellent pastry shop and bakery
Pasticceria Polticchia, 42 Corso Matteotti. There is another cake shop (*Alberto Trinari*) at Gualdo Cattaneo.

Picnics
There are good places to picnic outside the walls.

Annual fair
An annual fair called the *Mercato delle Gaite* (the *gaite* were the four districts of the town) is held here during the last eight or ten days of June. Artisans' workshops are reconstructed as they were in medieval times, and the inhabitants produce local handicrafts which are then sold in the streets. In the evening taverns serve traditional local specialities. For information, ☎ 0742 361847.

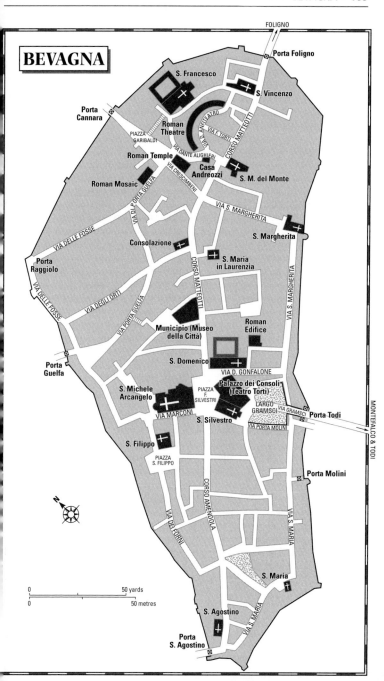

BEVAGNA

Porta Foligno

FOLIGNO

S. Francesco

S. Vincenzo

Porta
Cannara

Roman
Theatre

PIAZZA
GARIBALDI

VIA DELL'ANFITEATRO

VIA F. TORTI

CORSO MATTEOTTI

VIA DANTE ALIGHIERI

Roman Temple

VIA CRESCIMBENI

Casa
Andreozzi

S. M. del Monte

Roman Mosaic

VIA DI P. PORTA GUELFA

VIA S. MARGHERITA

Consolazione

S. Margherita

VIA DELLE FOSSE

S. Maria
in Laurenzia

Porta
Raggiolo

CORSO MATTEOTTI

VIA S. MARGHERITA

VIA DELLE FOSSE

VIA DEGLI ORTI

VIA PORTA GUELFA

Municipio (Museo
della Città)

Roman
Edifice

Porta
Guelfa

S. Domenico

VIA D. GONFALONE

Palazzo dei Consoli
(Teatro Torti)

S. Michele
Arcangelo

PIAZZA
F.
SILVESTRI

LARGO
GRAMSCI

VIA GRAMSCI

Porta Todi

MONTEFALCO & TODI

VIA MARCONI

S. Silvestro

VIA PORTA MOLINI

S. Filippo

PIAZZA
S. FILIPPO

Porta Molini

VIA DEI FORNI

CORSO AMENDOLA

VIA S. MARIA

0   50 yards

0   50 metres

S. Maria

S. Agostino

VIA S. MARIA

Porta
S. Agostino

History

Bevagna was the Roman Mevania on the Via Flaminia to Narni, opened here in 220 BC. It became a Roman Municipium by 90 BC, but had lost importance by the 3C AD when the new Via Flaminia was diverted through Spoleto and Terni. Later, part of the Duchy of Spoleto, Bevagna was ruled by the Trinci from 1371–1439. Hemp and flax were formerly cultivated in the surrounding countryside, and the craft of rope-making was still practised by a few inhabitants up until a few years ago.

Piazza Filippo Silvestri

The centre of the town is **Piazza Filippo Silvestri**, one of the most harmonious squares in Umbria. It is named after Filippo Silvestri (1873–1949) an eminent entomologist born in Bevagna. The Roman column has a Corinthian capital and the pretty fountain dates from 1896. The handsome 13C **Palazzo dei Consoli** has Gothic two-light windows and a wide external staircase. This was the seat of the government of the town until 1832 when it was severely damaged by earthquake. In 1872–86 the charming **Teatro Torti** was built inside the Gothic shell, with painted decoration by Domenico Bruschi and Mariano Piervittori. The theatre was beautifully restored in 1994 (for admission enquire at the Pro Loco) when a new backcloth was painted by the local painter Luigi Frappi. The stage extends above three Gothic arches towards the restored two-light windows on Largo Gramsci next to the apse of San Silvestro. The ballroom, gaming room and *ridotto* (foyer) also preserve their delightful decorations.

An arch (built in 1560) connects the palace to the church of **San Silvestro** (closed since the earthquake), with an unfinished façade and no campanile. As recorded in the inscription on the right of the portal it was constructed by Maestro Binello in 1195. It is built partly of travertine and partly of pink and grey stone from Subasio. The arch of the handsome portal is carved with a frieze with symbols of the Church and the devil in the form of a dragon. On either side is a comfortable stone bench. The three windows have pretty columns, and above is a cornice decorated with animal heads. The exterior of the fine apse can be seen from Largo Gramsci.

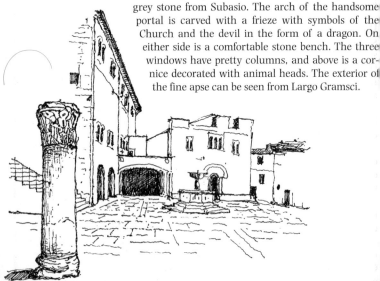

Piazza Filippo Silvestri

The beautiful **interior** has a barrel vault in the nave, unusual flying buttresses in the aisles and a raised chancel. The handsome columns, with a slight convex curve (entasis), are crowned with double Corinthian capitals.

Opposite is **San Michele Arcangelo**, the parish church and the most important in the town, built in the late 12C or early 13C. The façade incorporates a fine 14C campanile and a central **portal** signed by Rodolfo and Binello beneath the relief of the dragon beside the bust of *St Michael* on the left impost. Opposite, on the right impost, is a flying angel. The door posts are made up of reworked Roman friezes. The wooden doors, with classical decoration and a relief of *St Michael* date from the 16C. The outer arch has Cosmatesque and marble decoration. Above is a frieze of human and animal heads and a large tondo, once filled with a rose window. The exterior of the beautiful apse, and the interesting flank, can be seen from Via Marconi.

The lovely **interior** (closed since the earthquake) is similar to that of San Silvestro, with a raised chancel. South side. The first chapel is a neo-classical work by Vincenzo Vitali, decorated by Traversari. Between the first and second chapels is a processional painted wooden statue of *St Vincent enthroned* (1638). The second chapel has very ruined frescoes by the native artist Andrea Camassei (early 17C). In the sanctuary, beyond a glass door, a silver processional statue of *St Vincent* by Perter Ramoser (1785) can be seen. On the north side is a 15C Crucifix between paintings of the *Madonna, St John the Evangelist* and *Mary Magdalene*. The **crypt** has ancient columns with Romanesque capitals and Roman bases (one of them an upturned Doric capital).

In a piazza near the east end of San Michele Arcangelo is the church of **San Filippo** (for admission enquire at the Pro-loco), built in 1725. It has a Baroque interior with elaborate white stucco decoration around the organ and cantorie and a vault fresco attributed to Domenico Valeri (1757).

In Piazza Silvestri, beyond Palazzo dei Consoli, is the church of **Santi Domenico e Giacomo** (closed since the earthquake). In the **interior** the 18C side altars have been eliminated in recent restoration work. On the south side are scagliola altar frontals. The paintings include works by Giovanni Battista Pacetti (*St James*, 1642), Andrea Camassei (*Madonna and saints*, surrounding a *St Dominic* by Pacetti), and the native artist Fantino (c 1557–1646; *Madonna of the Rosary*). The tomb of Vincenzo Antici (d. 1552) bears his bust. Above the 17C **high altar** is a bronze urn containing the body of the Blessed Giacomo Bianconi (1220–1301) who founded churches and convents in the town after its destruction by Frederick II in 1249.

In the **choir** are remains of interesting early 14C frescoes including the figure of the Madonna (from an Annunciation scene). In the chapel to the right of the choir is a 13C wooden Crucifix, and in the chapel to the left of the choir is a 13C wooden statue of the *Madonna and Child*. On the north side are more 18C scagliola altar frontals, a *Madonna in Glory* by Fantino, and the tomb of the doctor Properzio Antici with his bust (d. 1596). The church also owns a Roman sarcophagus which was used as the first tomb of the Blessed Giacomo Bianconi.

Via del Gonfalone leads down past the side door of the church (with a tabernacle above and traces of a 14C fresco) to the church and oratory of the **Gonfalone**, once the most important confraternity in Bevagna. The church has an 18C façade. On the left, Vicolo del Gonfalone leads beneath four arches to remains of a **Roman edifice** (sometimes unlocked on request at the Pro Loco), probably dating from the 2C AD, beneath the Dominican convent. Formerly identified as baths, it is now thought this may have been part of a port built on the River Clitunno. The walls are decorated with opus reticulatum.

Corso Matteotti, on the line of the old Via Flaminia, leads out of Piazza Silvestri. At no. 107 is the entrance to the **cloister of San Domenico** (1629–32; ring for admission at the convent) with very worn frescoed lunettes by Giovanni Battista Pacetti painted in 1641. The chapterhouse has 14C frescoes.

On the left (no. 72) is the **Municipio** in Palazzo Lepri, designed by Andrea Vici, with a neo-classical façade (1787). The upper floors were severely damaged in 1997, and the municipal offices have had to be moved to temporary accommodation outside Porta Cannara, but the **Museo della Città** (open Apr–Sept daily except Mon 10.30–13.00, 14.30–17.00; Oct–March weekends only 10.30–13.00, 14.30–16.30; ☎ 0742 360031) arranged in 1996 on the ground floor was unharmed. It is a beautifully arranged small local collection with some interesting paintings.

In the first section is **archaeological material** from a collection formed in 1787 by the local historian Fabio Alberti, and first arranged in this palace in the 19C. The interesting Roman material, all of it found in Bevagna or its vicinity, includes architectural fragments from the Roman theatre, inscriptions, sepulcral stelae, cinerary urns of Etruscan type, fragments of reliefs and statues, and two fine portrait heads of the Republican era. Two statues from the Imperial era have been removed for restoration. The **medieval** section includes a bull of 1249 signed by Innocent IV. The **wooden model of the sanctuary of the Madonna delle Grazie** was made by Valentino Martelli in the 16C. The **Ciccoli altarpiece** shows the *Madonna and Child* with a boy of the Ciccoli family, who died at the age of ten. The work was commissioned in his memory by his uncle from Dono Doni c 1565. Works by the local artist **Il Fantino** include an *Annunciation*, a very damaged *Crucifixion*, the painted casket of the *Beato Giacomo* (1589), and the *Madonna of Constantinople with saints*. Paintings by **Andrea Camassei** include *St Charles Borromeo* and *Filippo Neri*, and a fragment with the head of a female saint. *The Adoration of the Magi* by **Corrado Giacinto** is one of the best works in the collection. The painting of St Sebastian is by Giovanni Battista Michelini (c 1640) and the last rooms have 17C and 18C works, including a silk altar frontal.

The upper floors of Palazzo Lepri have been closed since damage in the earthquake. Here the **sala consiliare** is decorated with wall-paintings (1867) of famous natives of the town by Mariano Piervittori, and the **biblioteca comunale** has interesting archives.

On the other side of the Corso is a **pharmacy**, with an attractive interior (including some Roman masonry) and 18C cupboards. It adjoins Palazzo Brunamonti, now a hotel. Further on in the Corso is a little piazza with the pretty 13C façade of the former church of **Santa Maria in Laurenzia** (now a shop) with a relief of the *Madonna nursing the Child*. On the left is the church of **Santa Maria della Consolazione**, with an 18C interior decorated with stuccoes. The high altarpiece of the *Holy Family* is by Etienne Parrocel (1738). A statue of the

Risen Christ (late 16C) is exhibited at Easter. A road on the right leads down from the Corso to the church of **Santa Margherita** (closed since the earthquake), rebuilt in 1640. The high altarpiece of the *Martyrdom of St Margaret* is by Andrea Camassei. In a niche behind the altar (seen through a grille) is a good fresco of the *Madonna and Saints* by Fantino (1592). In the atrium of the adjoining Agostinian convent (closed order; ring on the left), founded in 1271 there is a *'Scala Santa'* (recently restored) decorated c 1665 by Francesco Providoni with a 15C Crucifix.

Further along the Corso is the church of **Santa Maria del Monte** (ring for admission at the monastery at no. 15). The façade has two handsome 18C portals on either side of a 14C travertine arch. It contains (right altar) a fine bronze altar frontal. Near the end of the Corso (left) is the interesting façade of the former church of **San Vincenzo**, partly faced in travertine, with four Roman fluted pilasters on either side of the portal.

Porta Foligno (restored in 1797) leads out through the Roman and medieval walls to a park with ilexes, a war memorial by Vincenzo Jerace, and fragments of Roman buildings (1C AD). Inside the gate, Via Francesco Torti leads up under a passageway to Via dell'Anfiteatro, with pretty houses which follow the curve of the **Roman theatre** built on this site in the 1C AD (the scena faced Via Flaminia, now the Corso). A yellow sign marks the entrance to part of the barrel-vaulted corridor which supported the cavea of the theatre (later used as a wine-cellar). On the left the road emerges beneath an arch in Via Dante Alighieri. Here a fine Roman frieze of bucrania has been set into the wall of the Casa Andreozzi (now Angeli Nieri Mongalli). The road continues right beneath an arch supporting a terrace and emerges above Piazza Garibaldi and a Roman temple (described below).

The church of **San Francesco** (closed since 1998) is at the highest point of the town. The interior dates from 1756. On the south side is a chapel attributed to Galeazzo Alessi, with terracotta decoration in the cupola attributed to Sante Buglioni, and a 15C carved tabernacle in the last chapel. The church also contains works by the local painter Fantino.

Steps, lined with rose bushes, descend to Piazza Garibaldi. On the right is the 13C **Porta Cannara**, the best preserved gate in the walls (outside of which a path leads left along a fine stretch of walls). At the opposite end of the square, standing on a high basement, is a **Roman temple**, later converted into a church. The exterior preserves some semi-columns and pilasters (with fragments of stucco fluting). It is thought to date from the 2C AD. In Via Porta Guelfa is the entrance to a building which protects a large **Roman mosaic** (if closed, the custodian lives at no. 2), depicting beautiful marine creatures, including octopus, lobsters and dolphins, in a symmetrical design. It was made of black and white tesserae at the beginning of the 2C AD. Discovered before the 17C, it decorated part of a thermal building, more of which can be seen beneath the modern grid.

From Piazza Garibaldi, Via Crescimbeni returns to the Corso.

From Piazza Silvestri (see above) the Corso Amendola is a continuation of Corso Matteotti in the opposite direction. It passes a number of interesting palaces before reaching the church of **Sant'Agostino**, just inside the walls, with a 15C fresco of the *Madonna* over the door. It contains numerous ruined 15C–16C frescoes. The pretty Via Santa Maria leads round to the left past the former church of

Santa Maria. Beyond the house at no. 1 a road leads out to **Porta Molini**, an impressive 15C gate flanked by a tower with a semicircular wall, in a fine stretch of Roman walls. Beyond a mill here is a public wash-house on the Clitunno, in use since c 1900. Via Porta Molini leads back up to Largo Gramsci with the apse of San Silvestro and the back of Palazzo dei Consoli adjoining Piazza Silvestri.

BEYOND BEVAGNA

Just outside the town, off the straight road to Foligno (the old Roman Via Flaminia) behind the little octagonal church of the **Madonna della Rosa** (1691) the elliptical form of the Roman **Amphitheatre of Mevania** can be seen in a field. Further along the road is the massive square medieval **Torre di Montefalco**. A pretty little hamlet here, with an old mill, lies at the confluence of two rivers (the Clitunno and the Timia) and two canals. Nearer to Foligno are the conspicuous remains of two Roman tombs.

Two kilometres north of the town, on the road for Cannara and Bettona, is the **Convento dell'Annunziata**. In the interior, the first south altar, a fine 16C work in wood, contains a painting of the *Incredulity of St Thomas* by Fantino. The first north altar, also dating from the 16C, has a sculpted Crucifix with painted mourners by Fantino. The beautiful terracotta high altarpiece of the *Annunciation* is attributed to Sante Buglioni. Below the convent (reached from the right of the main road) is a picturesque little lake (25m in diameter) surrounded by poplars known as the '**Aiso**' (from '*abisso*'), some 13m deep and fed by an abundant spring. A local legend relates how a rich and miserly peasant was drowned in his house on this spot for attempting to thresh his grain on a feast day. His pious wife who tried to escape saving her child was submerged by another spring now called '*Aisillo*'.

Another road from Bevagna, to the south-west, leads up to the **Santuario della Madonna delle Grazie** from which there is a fine view. It was begun in 1583 by Valentino Martelli, with an octagonal drum surmounted by a lantern. In the interior (north transept) is a 15C sculpted Crucifix. The high altar of 1641 protects a venerated image of the *Madonna*. In the south transept is a 15C fresco of the *Madonna and Child*. The altarpieces in the nave are by Fantino, including the Byzantine *Madonna of Constantinople* (1603).

Gualdo Cattaneo, a tiny well-preserved medieval town, lies in a beautiful position in wooded hills west of Bevagna. Of ancient foundation, its name derives from the Saxon '*Wald*' from the forests which were once here. In the attractive piazza is a fine circular tower (recently restored) dating from 1494 and a war memorial. Just out of the square is the **parish church** (usually open in the afternoon). Inside, on the left wall, there is a *Madonna* by a certain Bastiano, dated 1350. The two scagliola altars date from 1732. In the apse is a fine *Last Supper* by Fantino. The chapel to the left of the apse was decorated in 1608 with stuccoes and paintings by Ferraù Ferroni da Faenza. The crypt (1220) has pretty vaulting and columns.

To the left a passageway and steps lead down to Piazza Mazzini from which a long flight of steps continues down to **Sant'Agostino** (closed for restoration) which contains (in a niche on the left) a fresco of the *Crucifix and four saints* (1482) by the school of Alunno.

MONTEFALCO
• • • • • • • • • • • • • •

Montefalco is a delightful little hill town with wonderful views. It is known as 'the Balcony of Umbria' because of its panoramic position (427m). It has picturesque streets and numerous interesting frescoes in its churches. It is surrounded by extensive olive groves and its water-tower is visible for miles. The area is known for its excellent wines including *Sagrantino* and *Rosso di Montefalco* which, together with other local specialities, are sold in a number of shops here.

Practical information

Information office
At the Museo Civico di San Francesco, ☎ 0742 379598.

Getting there
Montefalco is situated just over 6 km south of Bevagna.
Car parking outside Porta Sant'Agostino.
By bus There are services from Foligno.

 Hotels
☆☆☆☆ *Villa Pambuffetti*, 20 Viale della Vittoria, ☎ 0742 378823; fax 0742 379245, in a lovely villa outside the walls.
☆☆ *Ringhiera Umbra*, 20 Via Mameli, ☎ & fax 0742 379166. In a pretty old house in the centre of the town, a simple but very friendly family-run hotel, with good restaurant.

There are also some good *agriturist hotels* in the vicinity, including

Camiano Piccolo, in a 16C villa (with a swimming pool), at Camiano Piccolo, ☎ & fax 0742 379492.

 Restaurants
££ *Coccorone*, Largo Tempestivi, ☎ 0742 379535 and *Ringhiera Umbra* (see above).
£ Pizzeria next door to the Ringhiera Umbra (run by the same family) and *Il Fallisco*, 14 Via XX Settembre, ☎ 0742 379185. *Enoteca Metelli* in Piazza del Comune. *Pasticceria Ponziani*, beneath the water-tower.

Locally woven linens and furnishing fabrics are sold by Emanuela Valecchi at *Tessuto Artistico Umbro* in Piazza del Comune (and a new shop is to be opened opposite San Francesco).

History
Called *Coccorone* in the Middle Ages, the town was a free commune by the 12C. In 1249 Montefalco adopted its new name, probably from the eagle (*falco*) of the arms of Frederick II who visited the town in 1240. From 1383–1439 it came under the rule of the Trinci family. Apart from Benozzo Gozzoli (see below) other artists who worked here include Pier Antonio Mezzastris and the native artist Francesco Melanzio.

Several roads lead up to the charming circular **Piazza del Comune**, unfortunately used as a car-park, with a medley of buildings, at the highest point of the town. The **Palazzo Comunale** has a 15C portico. Its older tower (closed for restoration) has a **panoramic view** which takes in Perugia, Assisi, Spello, Trevi and Spoleto (and on a very clear day the sea can be seen beyond the Monti Martani). On the left (no. 18) is the former church of **San Filippo Neri** converted into a theatre in 1895 (closed since the earthquake). The Oratory of **Santa Maria di Piazza** (also closed) has a terracotta door. The 15C Palazzo Senili (no. 12) is next to the 16C Palazzo Camilli (no. 9). On the last side of the piazza is a small neo-classical palace (no. 6) next to a portico.

Museo Civico di San Francesco

Via Ringhiera Umbra leads downhill from the piazza past a neo-Gothic covered passageway to the Museo Civico di San Francesco which consists of a frescoed church, a pinacoteca and a lapidary collection (open daily 10.30–13.00, 14.00–18.00; June–Aug 10.30–13.00, 15.00–19.30; Nov–Feb closed Mon, otherwise 10.30–13.00, 14.00–17.00; ☎ 0742 379598). The church has been the property of the comune since 1863, and since 1895 the seat of the Pinacoteca Civica.

The **church** was built in 1335–38 and contains **frescoes** of the greatest interest (most of them restored before 1997; only the apse was damaged in the earthquake and is undergoing further restoration). In the 15C chapels on the south side: first chapel, frescoes of the Evangelists in the vault, and a frescoed triptych with the *Madonna and saints*, and of *saints*, *angels* and the *Crucifix* all by Benozzo Gozzoli (1452); second chapel, frescoes by the 15C Umbrian school; third chapel, painted *Crucifix*, an Umbrian work dating from the late 13C or early 14C; fourth, fifth and sixth chapels, frescoes by Giovanni di Corraduccio of Foligno. In the sixth chapel is a fine painting of the *Madonna del Soccorso* by Tiberio d'Assisi (1510). It depicts the unusual story of the *Madonna saving a child from the devil* (who has appeared after the mother's chastisement, threatening the child with the devil if he didn't behave!). The seventh chapel has frescoes of *Christ and the Evangelists* in the vault, and imitation wall-hangings on the walls, by Giovanni di Corraduccio and his bottega. In the chapel to the right of the main apse are some very ruined 15C Umbrian frescoes.

The **main apse** has a beautiful fresco cycle of the *Life of St Francis* by **Benozzo Gozzoli**, one of his best works. It was damaged in the earthquake and is at present being restored.

In the chapel to the left of the main apse are more frescoes by Giovanni di Corraduccio.

Benozzo Gozzoli

Gozzoli was a collaborator of Fra Angelico, and worked with him in 1447 on the vault frescoes in the Cappella di San Brizio in the Duomo of Orvieto. The frescoes he carried out in Montefalco here and at San Fortunato in 1450–52 had a wide influence on the Umbrian school of painters, including Benedetto Bonfigli and Alunno. The charming scenes here illustrating the life of St Francis show the influence of the *St Francis* cycle in the upper church of Assisi. Altarpieces by Gozzoli which can be seen in Umbria include those in the Galleria Nazionale in Perugia, and the galleries of Terni and Narni. His most famous works are, however, in Tuscany, notably in Palazzo Medici Riccardi in Florence and the Duomo of San Gimignano.

On the north wall is a niche with a lunette fresco of the *Madonna between St Louis of Toulouse and an angel* by the school of Perugino. The square domed **Cappella Bontadosi** dates from 1589 with stuccoes and paintings by Il Fantino. Beyond are two niches, one with frescoes of *the miracles of St Anthony of Padua* by Jacopo Vincioli, and the other with a fresco of the *Madonna enthroned between two saints* by Tiberio d'Assisi. On the west wall is a semicircular fresco of the *Nativity* (with Lake Trasimeno in the background) by Perugino (1503). Beneath the cantoria (1644) is a detached fresco of c 1471 attributed to Cristoforo di Jacopo of Foligno.

Stairs lead up to the **Pinacoteca**. In the first room there is a municipal collection founded in 1870, with 18C costumes, an 18C wooden statue of the '*Quintana*' saracen. In the second room there is a terracotta relief of the *Coronation of the Virgin* by the bottega of Andrea Della Robbia (from a country shrine at Cerrete); fragments of Umbrian woven cloth; and a wooden ciborium of 1569. In the third room there are paintings and frescoes by Francesco Melanzio including the *Madonna del Soccorso*, and the *Madonna enthroned between six Saints* (1498), the town standard. The fourth room displays a 14C *Pietà* (recently donated to the museum); a lovely *Madonna and Child* by the bottega of Melozzo da Forlì; small panels with *Stories of the life of Christ* by a painter from Foligno (c 1450–60); a sculpted *Crucifix, between Mourners and St Francis of Assisi* painted by the circle of Alunno (from the church of San Fortunato); *three saints* by Antoniazzo Romano, a very fine but damaged painting; and 17C and 18C paintings.

The **Museo Lapidario** is arranged in well-vaulted rooms downstairs. The sculptural fragments dating from the 9C–15C include a stone lion (1270) and a beautiful marble 16C statuette of a river god, a statue of Hercules (1C AD, probably restored in the 17C), Roman funerary altars (1C AD) and a Corinthian capital. A slab decorated with acanthus leaves in the 1C AD was re-used as an altar in the Middle Ages.

At the bottom of Via Ringhiera Umbra there is a splendid viewpoint.

Corso Mameli, the main street of the town, leads down from Piazza del Comune to a gate in the walls. On the right it passes the picturesque Vicolo delle Conserve and (no. 51) **Palazzo Pambuffetti**, with a 15C façade. On the left is the 16C Palazzo Tempestivi. Further down is the church of **Sant'Agostino** (1279–85; enlarged in 1327; closed since the earthquake) which contains numerous interesting frescoes (14C–16C), many of them showing the influence of Benozzo Gozzoli. Roman fragments decorate the façade of **Casa Angeli**, the last house on the left, just before the 14C castellated **Porta Sant'Agostino**, outside of which a well-preserved stretch of the 13C–14C **walls** can be seen, which still encircle the town.

From Piazza del Comune (see above) the steep Vicolo degli Operai descends to another gate, **Porta Federico II** (right; 1244) which bears a relief of the Imperial eagle. The apse of the 12C church of **San Bartolomeo** (closed since the earthquake) is situated here. It contains 17C paintings including the high altarpiece of the *Madonna and Child with saints* by Giacinto Gimignani. The ancient church of **Santa Maria Maddalena**, with 15C frescoes in its 18C interior is also closed. The medieval district nearby, with the church of Santa Lucia, the 13C Porta Camiano decorated with the arms of the town and Vicolo del Monte, is worth exploring.

Outside the walls, on the corner of Via Verdi, is the church and convent of **Santa Chiara**. This is the greatly venerated shrine of St Clare of Montefalco (1268–1308), who became a nun at a very early age and was abbess here from 1291. She was a Franciscan tertiary, but later followed the rule of St Augustine, and was famous for her devotion to the Passion of Christ. When she died the symbols of the Passion were found on her heart and her embalmed body is preserved here. She was cannonised in 1881. The **church** has a fine 17C interior. The east end of the earlier church is now the **Cappella di Santa Croce** (ring at the convent door at the end of the left aisle, 09.30–11.30, 15.30–17.00 or 18.00). It has interesting Umbrian frescoes of 1333, including a crowded *Calvary* scene, the *Evangelists* (depicted with the heads of their symbols) in the vault, and *scenes from the life of St Clare* (as a child asking to be admitted to the convent; in her nun's habit, having a vision of Christ carrying the Cross; and her death, surrounded by nuns and friars). The **convent** has a 14C cloister, a collection of 16C marriage chests, a 14C Crucifix, the painted wooden chest (1430) where St Clare was interred, and a fresco of her by Benozzo Gozzoli.

Via Verdi continues to **Sant'Illuminata** where there is a very worn fresco of the *Madonna of the Misericordia* by Francesco Melanzio over the door. The interior has three large semicircular chapels on either side of the nave decorated with more early 16C frescoes (in poor condition) by the native artist Francesco Melanzio and by Bernardino Mezzastris.

Opposite, with two Renaissance portals, is the church of **San Leonardo** next to the convent (entrance at no. 1) of a closed order of Clarisse nuns, 27 of whom still live here and worship in a chapel adjoining the church. The church, which was redecorated in 1789, contains a *Madonna enthroned* by Francesco Melanzio (in poor condition) over the high altar, and a delightful well-preserved detached 15C fresco of the *Madonna and Child* (as Saviour of the world), attributed to Jacopo Vincioli.

San Fortunato

From Porta Spoleto the road continues to a byroad (left; c 1km from the gate) for the church of San Fortunato (open all day; if closed ring at the monastery where three Franciscan monks live), in a beautiful position surrounded by ancient ilex trees. A church was built here in the 5C dedicated to St Fortunatus (d. c 400), the parish priest of the church of Turrita (see below) who was known for his charity to the poor. The convent was founded in 1442.

Off the 15C **cloister**, which incorporates four antique columns, is a **chapel** (left) with frescoes (not in very good condition) of the *Life of St Francis* (1512) by Tiberio d'Assisi with a charming vault frescoed with *God the Father*. In the lunette over the door into the **church**, there is a *Madonna with saints and angels*, frescoed by Benozzo Gozzoli. On the right of the door is *St Sebastian*, a fresco by Tiberio d'Assisi. In the church, on the south altar is a beautiful fresco fragment of *St Fortunatus*, in his priest's robes, enthroned, a very striking work, also by Gozzoli, and on the right an *Adoration of the Child*, a fragment by Gozzoli. On the north side there is an 18C painting of *St Michael Archangel*, and in a little chapel off this side, is a sarcophagus supposed to be that of St Severus with three very worn frescoed tondi by Gozzoli.

To the south of Montefalco a byroad runs via **Turrita** where the parish church has interesting votive frescoes (14C–16C) to the sanctuary of the **Madonna della Stella**, an elaborate work by Giovanni Santini (1862–81) with painted decoration by Cesare Mariani. On the south side the first altar has a *Holy Family* by Enrico Pollastrini, and the third altar, a *Santa Chiara* by Giuseppe Mancinelli. The church was built in honour of the miraculous 16C fresco fragment on the high altar. On the north side the third altar has a *Madonna and Saints* by Giuseppe Sereni, and the first altar a *Visitation* by Friedrich Overbeck.

TREVI
• • • • • •

Trevi is a pretty, well-preserved little town (population 6500) in an attractive position on a hill covered with olive groves. It has peaceful brick and cobbled lanes (mostly inaccessible to cars) and many of its old houses are decorated with pots of flowers. Many of the churches were badly damaged in the 1997 earthquake, and some of the inhabitants had to be temporarily housed on the plain below.

Practical information

Information office
Pro Loco, 6 Piazza Mazzini, ☎ 0742/781150.

Getting there
There are splendid views of the little town from the roads from Foligno and from Spoleto (via Bovara).
Car parking in Piazza Garibaldi.
By bus There are services (run by *Società Spoletina*, ☎ 0742 670746) from Foligno.

Hotels
✶✶✶ *Trevi Hotel*, 2 Via Fantosati, ☎ 0742 780922; fax 0742 780772. A delightful hotel opened in 1997 in an old house inside the walls. Just 12 rooms, some of them with their old brick vaults, and all beautifully furnished. There is an attractive little terrace. Very peaceful and with very friendly management. It could easily be given a higher grading. *Casa San Martino*, 4 Viale Ciuffelli, offers simple hospitality along the lines of a youth hostel at the Capuchin convent outside

the town on the approach road from Foligno. *Casa Giulia*, 1 Via Corciano, Bovara, ☎ 0742 78257; fax 0742 381632. Classified as a 'country house', with just six rooms in a lovely old building below the town on the Bovara road.

Rooms to let in the *Residenza Cochetto*, 6 Via Natalucci, ☎ 0742 780566, an old-fashioned former hotel in a large palace in the centre of the town.

Restaurants
££ *Maggiolini*, Via San Francesco, ☎ 0742 381534; *La Vecchia Posta*, Piazza Mazzini, ☎ 0742 381690, with tables outside in the piazza in summer.

On the Via Flaminia below the town (near the Tempietto del Clitunno): *Taverna del Pescatore*, ☎ 0742 780920.

Picnics
There are pleasant places to picnic outside the walls in the gardens near Piazza Garibaldi.

Annual festivals

In early October the *Palio dei Terzieri* takes place here. Later in the month a fair is held when the **celery** of Trevi, called *sedano nero*, well known for its distinctive strong flavour, is sold. A market is held every Thursday morning in October. The **olive oil**, for which Trevi is also famous, can be tasted and bought after the harvest in early December. The festival of *St Emiliano* has been celebrated since the Middle Ages on 27 Jan with the procession of the *Illuminata*.

History

Trevi became an important Roman town when the Via Flaminia was diverted through Spoleto and Terni. In the Middle Ages it was part of the Duchy of Spoleto and seat of a bishopric. It later came under the rule of Perugia and of the Trinci of Foligno. After 1439, when it was incorporated in the Papal States, it became a commercial centre and in 1470 the fourth printing press in Italy was set up here.

From Piazza Garibaldi the short Via Roma leads past a little piazza (left) with the orange-coloured **Teatro Clitunno** built by Domenico Mollaioli in 1874 (restored in 1991) with a back-cloth painted by Domenico Bruschi in 1877. Beyond the church of San Giovanni (open only for services at weekends) is **Piazza Mazzini** with **Palazzo Comunale** with a 15C portico, beneath which is a huge terracotta vase dating from the 2C AD, found in the vicinity in 1979. The tall 13C **Torre Civica**, lowered in the 14C, is the emblem of the city.

In front of the town hall the stepped Via Placido Riccardi leads up to the **Duomo**, hemmed in among the old buildings of the town. It is dedicated to the city's patron saint Emiliano, a bishop martyred here in the 4C AD. Founded in the 12C, it preserves Romanesque elements on the exterior. The 15C portal has a charming relief of *St Emiliano between two lions* and is flanked by two very worn Roman capitals. The three original apses survive, as does another door with a statue of St Emiliano. The centrally planned interior (closed since the earthquake) was reconstructed in 1775 and again in 1893 by Luca Carimini. The **altar of the Sacrament** was beautifully carved by Rocco da Vicenza (1522). The two statues are by Mattia di Gaspare da Como. On the opposite side of the nave is a statue of the *Redeemer* by Cesare Aureli and a seated wooden processional statue of *St Emiliano*. At the west end of the church is a large cupboard which protects another wooden statue of *St Emiliano* by a German sculptor (1751).

Beside the Duomo is the fine old **Palazzo Lucarini**, seat of the **Flash Art Museum** (open 10.00–13.00, 15.00–18.30 except Mon and Tues), a private museum of contemporary art. Steps lead down beside the palace to Via Dogali, a pretty old street, which leads left to the medieval **Portico del Mostaccio**, once the main gate of the town. It continues up to the left and back to Piazza Mazzini.

Via San Francesco (on the opposite side of the square) leads past the fine 16C Palazzo Valenti to the Gothic church of **San Francesco**, the west end of which has been concealed. In the former convent (entrance on the left) is the **Raccolta d'arte di San Francesco** (open Aug 10.30–13.00, 15.00–19.30; June & July 10.30–13.00. 15.30–19.00 except Mon; Apr, May and Sept 10.30–13.00, 14.30–18.00 except Mon; Oct–Mar open Fri, Sat & Sun 10.30–13.00,

Olive oil

Trevi is one of the most important centres in Umbria for the production of olive oil (and a museum dedicated to the olive was opened here in 1999). Olive trees were first introduced to Italy from Greece in the 6C BC, and the Etruscans were particularly skilled in their cultivation. The Roman farms in this area based their wealth on the production of large quantities of olive oil and wine. The Romans recognised the commercial importance of olive oil which was transported by sea in specially designed amphorae. In ancient times the olive tree was also considered sacred and its leaves and oil used for medicinal purposes. Athletes were massaged with olive oil, and the winners in athletic competitions were sometimes crowned with a wreath of olive branches. In the Middle Ages the Benedictines and Cistercians planted olive groves and vineyards on their monastic lands throughout Italy.

Nowadays the olives, which are at first green and then turn black as they ripen, are still usually harvested by hand so as not to damage the trees; ladders are propped up against the trees from which the olives are picked and put into baskets, and sheets spread out on the ground beneath to collect the olives as they fall. The harvest, in November and December, usually takes many weeks or even months. The olives are taken to an olive-press, once a stone-mill worked by mules, but now mechanically operated. To facilitate the pressing the olives are usually slightly heated, but purists make sure the temperature of the olives is not altered. The oil straight from the first pressing is the best and can be labelled *olio extra vergine di oliva* if its acidity is less than one per cent. When newly pressed it has a bright green colour and particularly aromatic flavour. Its qualities are especially appreciated on garlic toast (*bruschetta or fettunta*) or as a dip for raw vegetables (*pinzimonio*). Umbrian oil can usually be preserved for up to two years if it is stored at a stable temperature in a dry (preferably dark) room.

In February the land around the trees is usually tilled to a depth of no more than 25–30cm (in order not to damage the trees' sturdy roots) and the trees given fertilizer. The pruning of the trees in March is also a very long and laborious process done with a hand-saw and secateurs. The trunks are also sometimes 'cleaned' of rot or mould at this time. Copper sulphite is then sprayed on the trees to protect them from disease. The olive oil of Umbria, bright green in colour, is considered one of the best in Italy, with a good delicate taste. The trees, if carefully tended, usually flourish and bear fruit for hundreds of years. South-facing low hills exposed to light breezes, and a dry stony soil, are the ideal terrain for olive trees.

Olive oil, which is expensive even in Italy, is recognised for its exceptional nutritional value and is considered the most healthy vegetable oil, both in its raw state and when heated for cooking or frying. It is the only type of oil which retains its qualities even when heated to a high temperature. It is the basis of the Italian cuisine, and replaces butter in the Mediterranean diet. It is free of cholesterol. Italians have a habit of adding a little raw olive oil (*un filo d'olio*) to soups, beans and lentils after they have been cooked. Local recipes provide numerous different ways of preserving or pickling the olives, both when green and when black, to be eaten as hors-d'oeuvre or added to many meat, fish, vegetable or pasta dishes.

14.30–17.00; ☎ 0742 381628), with a particularly fine collection of 14C–15C paintings.

On the ground floor, in the ticket office, is a detached fresco attributed to the Maestro di Fossa. Another room has Roman finds, including the head of Janus. On the first floor, beyond a room with 16C paintings, is a large *Coronation of the Virgin*, and two paintings of *Sts Catherine and Cecilia* all by Lo Spagna. From the cloister there is access to the **church of San Francesco** which contains various fresco fragments and two pretty scagliola altars. At the west end, beside a semicircular niche with a fresco of the *Madonna and saints and Christ carrying the Cross* (1577) is the sarcophagus (3C or 4C), used as the tomb of St Ventura (d. 1310). In the nave is an interesting organ of 1509 (removed for restoration) by Pietro di Paolo of Montefalco with a wooden gallery decorated with paintings in the 17C. Over the high altar is a fine 14C Crucifix. In the chapel to the right of the apse are 15C votive frescoes and an 18C wooden altar with a statue of the *Madonna*. In the chapel to the left of the apse is the tomb of Ottavia Attavanti and her son Alessandro Valenti (1576–77) with two fine busts, and the pavement tomb (set into the wall) of Valente Valenti (1357) and an 18C wooden altar with a statue of *St Anthony*.

On the top floor, on a balcony overlooking the room with the Spagna altarpiece, are the earliest works in the collection, of great interest. The delightful small scenes from the *Life of Christ* (part of a polyptych) are attributed to Giovanni di Coraduccio of Foligno (c 1430). The very worn painted Crucifix dates from c 1310 (the head of Christ is particularly beautiful). The *Adoration of the Magi* by a Flemish master dates from the late 15C, and the processional frame decorated with *Christ and two angels*, and the *Madonna of the Misericordia* are both attributed to the bottega of Alunno. The *Pietà* from the Madonna delle Lacrime is a good work of c 1520–30. Another work attributed to Giovanni di Corraduccio is the tabernacle with charming little scenes from the *Life of Christ*.

The **Museo della Civiltà dell'Ulivo**, a museum dedicated to the production of olive oil was opened in the same building in 1999.

From the 13C walls nearby there is a good view.

BEYOND TREVI

The church and monastery of **San Martino** (admission usually on request in the mornings at the Capuchin monastery) are built on a rock and surrounded by cypresses. In the lunette over the door is a fresco by Tiberio d'Assisi. In the two tabernacles either side of the presbytery are frescoes by Mezzastris (*Madonna and Child*) and Tiberio d'Assisi (*St Martin and the Beggar*). To the left of the church is a little chapel (1512; unlocked on request at the monastery) with an *Assumption and Saints* by Lo Spagna and *St Emiliano* by Tiberio d'Assisi. There is a fine view of the plain from the belvedere.

One kilometre below the town, on the hillside, is the church of the **Madonna delle Lacrime** (closed since damage in the earthquake), a Renaissance church by Antonio Marchisi (1487). The lovely portal (1495) is by Giovanni Giampietri da Vicenza. In the interior on the south side, the first altar has 16C frescoes and the second altar an *Epiphany* by Perugino with a delightful background. In the south transept, in an altar of 1621, is a lovely fresco of the *Madonna and Child*

(1483). Behind the high altar is a worn detached fresco of the *Crucifixion with the Marys at the foot of the Cross*, between a *Madonna and Child* and an *Annunciation*. In the left transept chapel are **frescoes** by Lo Spagna. The church also has particularly fine 16C–17C funerary monuments, many with busts, of the Valenti family.

On the plain below the town, next to the main road, is the tall medieval **Torre Matigge** (covered with scaffolding since the earthquake).

Three kilometres south of Trevi is **Bovara** where the church of **San Pietro** has a conspicuous campanile, heightened in 1582. The interesting façade dates from the 12C. The Romanesque interior (only open for services) preserves a 14C wooden Crucifix. Nearby is an ancient olive tree, known as the *Olivo di Sant'Emiliano*, hundreds of years old with a trunk some 9m in circumference.

Five kilometres north of Trevi, the 14C church of **Santa Maria di Pietrarossa**, which has numerous 15C votive frescoes, was severely damaged in 1997.

SPOLETO

Spoleto is a beautiful old town (population 36,000) with Roman and medieval monuments of the highest interest. It has a somewhat austere atmosphere. Many of the old streets are still cobbled, and in some of them charming details such as the old street lanterns and shop fronts have been retained. It is built on a hill (317m) surrounded by a lovely landscape of high and thickly wooded hills, but the plain to the north has been spoilt by sprawling suburbs. A famous music and drama festival is held here in June and July, and the town is particularly well equipped with good hotels (most of them ✰✰ or ✰✰✰✰).

Practical information

Information office
IAT, 7 Piazza della Libertà, ☎ 0743 220311.

Getting there
By rail The station is on Viale Trento e Trieste and reached from Piazza della Vittoria. There are services on the Ancona–Rome line from Terni (25mins) and Foligno (25mins). From Perugia it takes 1hr 15mins. Buses run from the station every 15mins to Piazza della Libertà.

By bus Buses run by the *Società*

Spoletina (*SIT*, ☎ 0743 47807) go to Piazza Stazione from Foligno and Terni. There are services to Norcia, Cascia, Montefalco, Campello sul Clitunno, and Monteluco in summer.

Town buses run from the station (Circolare A, B, C, & D) every 10mins through the town to Piazza Carducci.

Car parking Parking is extremely difficult in the old town. Most car-parks charge an hourly tariff. There is long-term (free) car parking off Viale Cappuccini and in Via Don Bonilli near the stadium.

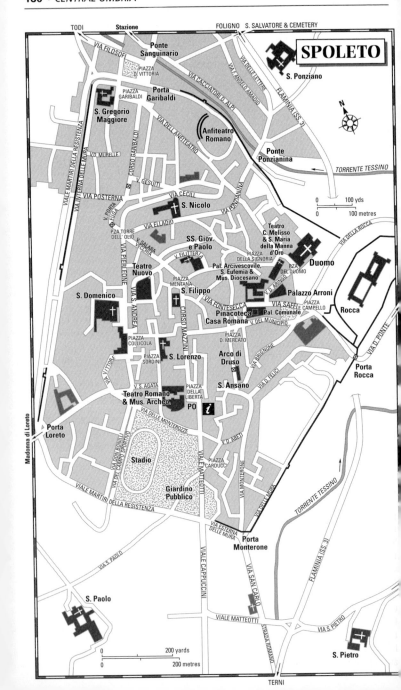

Hotels

★★★★ *Gattapone*, 6 Via del Ponte, ☎ 0743 223447; fax 0743 223448. A particularly charming little hotel in one of the most remarkable positions in Italy. In an extremely peaceful spot, it has panoramic views of the Ponte delle Torri and its wooded valley. It was opened in 1964 and a wing added in 1987. It has just 15 rooms so it cannot accommodate large groups. All rooms have large windows overlooking the beautiful valley towards Monteluco. Although some rooms are larger (but more expensive) than others, they are all delightful with fine wooden floors (those in the earlier wing are the best). There is a little terrace and a lovely simple garden on the hillside. Although five minutes' walk from the Duomo, country walks can be taken directly from the hotel. No restaurant.

Palazzo Dragoni, 13 Via del Duomo; ☎ 0743 222220; fax 0743 222225. Opened in 1993 and classified as an 'historic residence', but the equivalent of a good ★★★★ hotel. In a splendid spacious 16C palace in a very quiet position below Piazza del Duomo, beautifully furnished, with great taste. Many of the frescoed rooms have views over the valley and breakfast is served in a handsome well-lit corner room. No restaurant.

★★★★ *San Luca*, 21 Via interna delle Mura, ☎ 0743 223399; fax 0743 223800. A pleasant hotel opened in 1995 in a restored 19C building, in a peaceful but slightly less central position than the other hotels in the old town. Thirty-five comfortable rooms, and a patio and rather stark garden. It has conference rooms, so it also takes groups.

★★★ *Charleston*, 10 Piazza Collicola, ☎ 0743 220052; fax 0743 222010. In a fairly peaceful piazza in the lower part of the centre, close to the church of San Domenico. It has a somewhat eccentric atmosphere with a sauna in the basement. The rooms are small and rather unimaginatively furnished, but the management and staff are very pleasant. Garage next door. No restaurant.

★★ *Aurora*, 3 Via Apollinare, ☎ 0743 220315; fax 0743 221885. In a lovely quiet position just off Corso Mazzini next to the Roman Theatre, in a little cul-de-sac. The 15 rooms are simply furnished, but comfortable, and some of them look out over the hills. Nice atmosphere. There is a restaurant, so half-board or full-board terms are available.

★★ *Dell'Angelo*, 25 Via Arco di Druso, ☎ 0743 222385; fax 0743 221695. In a palace built in 1476, this historic little 'locanda', one of the first to be opened in the town, where Rossini and Goethe stayed, has just seven rooms, all of them with charm and all very quiet. The old-fashioned slightly decadent atmosphere has been retained. Although there is a restaurant on the ground floor of the same building, it is now run by different owners.

★★ *Il Panciolle*, 3 Via Duomo, ☎ 0743 45677. Seven spotless rooms, the best two looking over the valley. In a quiet road below the Cathedral, with a very pleasant atmosphere. No restaurant.

In the environs

On the road to **Monteluco** *Eremo delle Grazie*, ☎ 0743 49624; fax 0743 49650. Classified as an 'historical residence', of at least ★★★★ standard. In a beautiful position with 11 charming rooms and a restaurant.

Monteluco ★★ *Ferretti* (with restaurant), ☎ 0743 49849; fax 0743 222344.

On the road to **Aquasparta** (7km from Spoleto) ★★★ *San Sebastiano in Spoleto*, ☎ 0743 539805; fax 0743 539961. Thirteen lovely rooms in a well-run hotel.

Camping

★★ *Monteluco*, ☎ 0743 220358, beside the church of San Pietro, open in summer.

Restaurants

£££ *Il Tartufo*, 24 Piazza Garibaldi, ☎ 0743 40236; *Tric Trac*, Piazza Duomo, 0743 44592. **££ *Sabatini*,** 56 Corso Mazzini, ☎ 0743 221831; *Il Pentagramma*, 4 Via Martani, ☎ 0743 223141; *Del Mercato*, Piazza del Mercato, ☎ 0743 45325; *Del Quarto*, 1 Via Cattaneo, ☎ 0743 221107 (run by a Neapolitan, specialising in fish); *Il Panciolle*, 3 Via del Duomo, ☎ 0743 45677; *La Lanterna*, 6 Via Trattoria, ☎ 0743 49815.

£ *Del Festival*, 8 Via Brignone, ☎ 0743 220993; *Da Sportellino*, 2 Via Cerquiglia, ☎ 0743 45230; *Tre Fontane*, 15 Via Egio, ☎ 0743 221544; *La Barcaccia*, Piazza Fratelli Bandiera, ☎ 0743 221171; *Pecchiarda*, Vicolo San Giovanni, ☎ 0743 221009.

In the environs

££ *Antica Posta di Fabria*, Località Fabbreria 15, ☎ 0743 49035. **Monteluco** on the approach road (next to the church of San Giuliano) *San Giuliano*, ☎ 0743 47797 and in Monteluco Ferretti, ☎ 0743 49849. **Pasticcerie** *Bar Vincenzo*, Corso Mazzini; *Forno Bonucci* bakery, Piazza dellea Vittoria; *Pasticceria Vincenzo*, Viale Marconi; *Zampolini*, Viale Trento e Trieste.

Picnics

There are good places to picnic in Via del Ponte, near the Ponte delle Torri, in the little public gardens in Piazza della Signoria (below the Duomo), and in the public gardens off Via Giacomo Matteotti. Also at Monteluco.

Market day on Friday in Via Cacciatori delle Alpi.

Theatres and festivals

Teatro Nuovo, Via Vaita; **Sant'Andrea**; **Teatro Caio Melisso**, Piazza Duomo; **Teatrino delle 6**, Piazza della Signoria, **Teatro Romano**, Piazza Libertà. Puppet performances are given in the church of Santa Maria della Piaggia during the festival.

The renowned *Festival dei Due Mondi* has been held annually in the town since 1958 (at the end of June and beginning of July). Theatre, ballet and opera performances are given in the Teatro Nuovo, Teatro Caio Melisso, the Roman theatre, the Sala Frau, the Teatrino delle Sei, Santa Maria della Piaggia and the former church and cloister of San Nicolò. An open-air concert is given on the last day in Piazza Duomo.

History

Numerous Bronze Age finds have been made in the town and surrounding territory. The Umbrian *Spoletium* was colonised by the Romans in 241 BC, and survived an attack by Hannibal in 217. It suffered severely in the conflict between Marius and Sulla. The town was particularly important since it was on the Via Flaminia. In 1354 the Duchy of Spoleto (see below) was incorporated in the States of the Church by the papal viceroy Cardinal Albornoz who built the castle to dominate the town. It was the birthplace of the painter Lo Spagna (d. 1528).

The stepped **Via dell'Arringo** (opened in the 13C) provides a remarkable view down to the cathedral and the green hillside behind it. Its worn brick steps were replaced in 1998, using 'modern' terracotta bricks which have no character and are of a different colour. They descend past the pretty apse of Sant'Eufemia (see below) and a sculpture by Lynn Chadwick (1962). On the right the 16C Palazzo Arroni has very worn graffiti decoration in great need of restoration.

The Duchy of Spoleto

The Lombard Duchy of Spoleto was established here in 570–76. The Lombards were a western Germanic people who settled near the River Elbe in northern Europe during the Roman Imperial era. At the end of the 5C AD they moved south to the Danube and their historian Paul the Deacon relates that they invaded Italy in 568 under Duke Alboin. It seems that they established themselves with ease in the north, with Pavia as their capital, before descending into central Italy. By 603 they were in control of a large part of the peninsular. They chose the strongly defended site of Spoleto, with its strategic position, as the centre of a Duchy which ruled over a large area of Umbria and the Marche. Further south they created the Duchy of Benevento. However, the exarchate of Ravenna maintained power on the Adriatic coast and a narrow corridor through Umbria was retained by the Byzantine power as a link with Rome (through Gubbio, Perugia, Todi and Amelia). In 742 Liutprand expelled the Duke of Spoleto after he had allied himself with the papacy. In 774 the Franks took Pavia and conquered Spoleto and Benevento. From 789 the duchy of Spoleto was absorbed into the Carolinigian empire, although it remained largely independent for nearly a century under a series of counts or dukes.

It was at this time that the temporal power of the papacy was established through the papal states, and centuries later Spoleto was again to be important for its strategic position in central Italy when in 1353 Innocent VI made Gil Alvàrez Albornoz, Archbishop of Toledo, a cardinal and sent him to Italy in an attempt to dominate the papal states. Albornoz (see p. 188) built the castle above Spoleto, as well as several others in Umbria, in an attempt to re-establish the power of the Papacy in this region.

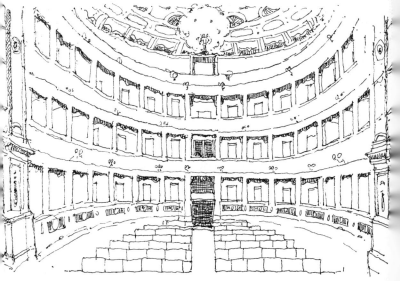

Teatro Caio Melisso

The brick paving in a herringbone pattern of **Piazza del Duomo** (where the final concert of the Festival is held) was also unfortunately renewed in 1998. On the old wall here, above which there is a view of the Rocca at the top of the wooded hillside, a Roman sarcophagus (3C AD) serves as a wall fountain. Opposite is the pink and white building of the Opera del Duomo, the **Teatro Caio Melisso**, a little chamber theatre (at No. 3–5) built by Giovanni Montiroli (1877; restored for the festival) and decorated by Domenico Bruschi, and the church of Santa Maria della Manna d'Oro, with an octagonal top (described below).

The Duomo

The Duomo (open 07.30–12.30, 15.00–18 .00) was consecrated by Innocent III in 1198 and later much altered. It was severely damaged in the earthquake of 1997 and restoration work is in progress (although the building is fully open). The very beautiful **façade** is preceded by an elegant Renaissance portico (1491) by Ambrogio da Milano and Pippo di Antonio da Firenze, incorporating two charming little pulpits. Above are eight rose windows, of varying design and a splendid mosaic signed by Solsternus (1207). The **campanile** (12C, with additions from 1416 and 1518) incorporates Roman fragments. On the right of the façade is the elegant little exterior of the Cappella dell'Assunta. The main portal is a fine 12C Romanesque work (in need of restoration).

Interior The interior was transformed in 1634–44 for Urban VIII whose bust, by Bernini, surmounts the central door. The polychrome marble pavement dates in part from the 12C. South side. The first chapel, the **Cappella Eroli** (light; fee), dating from 1497, has an attractive pavement and a carved frieze with animals. The frescoed altar niche is by Pinturicchio (*Madonna and Child with two saints* and the *Eternal Father*). In the adjoining

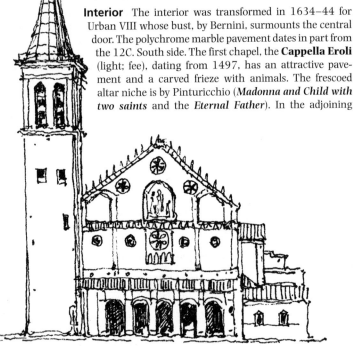

The Duomo

Cappella dell'Assunta are early 16C frescoes attributed to Jacopo Siculo. The first two 18C altarpieces are by Domenico Corvi (*Deposition*) and Antonio Concioli (*Death of St Andrea Avellino*). The third altarpiece of the *Visitation* is by Giovanni Alberti (16C).

South transept. On the right wall, recomposed funerary monument of Giovanni Francesco Orsini by Ambrogio da Milano (1499). The altarpiece of the *Madonna and Child with saints* is by Annibale Carracci. On the left wall is the tomb of Fra Filippo Lippi (see below) erected by Florentine artists at the order of Lorenzo il Magnifico, with a fine bust, and an inscription by Politian. Beneath the organ is the **Cappella della Santissima Icone** rebuilt in 1626 by Giovanni Battista Mola. On the elaborate marble altar is a highly venerated icon of the Madonna painted in Constantinople in the 11C or 12C, traditionally thought to have been given to the church by Frederick Barbarossa in 1185. It is surrounded by ex votos and flanked by two statues of Prophets attributed to Alessandro Algardi. On the walls of the chapel are two paintings by Cavalier d'Arpino.

In the 12C **apse** are **frescoes** of the *Life of the Virgin* by **Fra Filippo Lippi** (light; fee), perhaps his best work, and one of the masterpieces of the Renaissance (beautifully restored in 1987–90). He worked on them from 1467 until his death in 1469 (when he was buried in the neighbouring chapel, see above). The scenes, with monumental figures (larger than life-size), which cover the vast space of the semicircular walls are divided by painted columns and friezes, the classical motifs of which are copied from buildings in Spoleto (including San Salvatore). In the central scene of the *Transition of the Virgin*, the group on the right includes Fra Filippo's self-portrait (in a white monk's habit over a black tunic and with a black hat), a portrait of his son Filippino, then ten or twelve years old (the angel in front), and portraits of Fra Diamante and Pier Matteo d'Amelia, who were his assistants and who painted the *Nativity* scene. In the half-dome is the wonderful *Coronation of the Virgin*, the best preserved fresco in the cycle, rich in blue and gold. The numerous figures include the sibyls, Eve and other female personalities from the Old Testament, and angels with a great variety of musical instruments. Above, God the Father takes the place of Christ. No evidence of cartoons was found during restoration work on the figurative scenes. Many of the details (some of which have been lost) were added in tempera and highlighted with gilded wax roundels.

The fine **Cappella del Sacramento** was built in the early 17C: the 17C–18C paintings are by Francesco Refini, Pietro Labruzzi and Liborio Coccetti. In the north transept is a good 16C painting of the *Madonna and Child with two saints*, and on the altar, *St Ponziano among lions* by Cristoforo Unterberger.

North aisle. The **Cappella delle Reliquie** (light; fee) was built as a sacristy, and decorated in 1546–60. The cupboards (1546–54), with pretty intarsia panels, were carved by the local carpenters Giovanni Andrea di Ser Moscato and Damiano di Mariotto. The two panels with architectural perspectives on the end wall were made by Fra Giovanni da Verona for the choir of the Duomo. The painted panels with figures from the Old Testament are by Francesco Nardini, a painter from Sant'Angelo in Vado, who also executed the fine vault, with stuccoes and paintings. On display here are a 14C *Madonna and Child* in polychrome wood and an autograph letter of St Francis to Fra Leone (one of only two letters written by St Francis which have survived).

On the third altar is Antonio Cavallucci's (18C) *Presentation in the Temple*; on the second altar, Etienne Parrocel's (attrib.), *Madonna and Child with saints*; and the first altar contains a brightly coloured *Crucifix*, signed and dated 1187 by Alberto So(tio), the earliest known Umbrian painter. It was in the church of Santi Giovanni e Paolo until 1877, and was restored in 1991.

In the piazza is the church of **Santa Maria della Manna d'Oro** (usually closed), built as an ex voto after the Sack of Rome in 1527. The octagonal drum was probably added later. In the 17C interior are a 16C font and paintings by Sebastiano Conca (*Rest on the Flight* and *Birth of the Virgin*) and his pupil Nicola Costantini. Above the door are the remains of a funerary monument of Bishop Bernardino Lauri (d. c 1516).

Steps beside the campanile lead down to Piazza della Signoria where the 14C arcade of Palazzo della Signoria can be seen. The palace, which was never completed, adjoins the Teatro Caio Melisso (see above).

In Via Saffi, at the top of Via dell'Arringo (right) is Palazzo Arcivescovile. In the courtyard is the 12C church of **Sant'Eufemia**. The beautiful plain Romanesque interior (temporarily closed) has a matroneum, interesting capitals, some 15C frescoes on the columns and a 13C Cosmatesque altar.

At the end of the courtyard a double flight of steps leads up to the **Museo Diocesano** (closed since damage in the earthquake; ☎ 0743 231021) arranged in pleasant 18C rooms. The Sala del Trono contains 18C portraits of bishops and an 18C sedan chair.

Room 1 contains a 13C *Madonna and Child* from Manciano di Trevi, and a *Madonna and Child with two angels and two prophets*, dated 1315. The dossal from Cerreto di Spoleto is by the circle of the Maestro di Cesi (early 14C). The 15C triptych from the church of Sant'Eufemia (see above) is attributed to Bartolomeo da Miranda. In room 2 is an *Adoration of the Child* by Domenico Beccafumi.

Room 3 contains the following sculptures: a 13C *Madonna and Child* from Santa Maria di Ferentillo; a 15C Paduan statue of *St Sebastian*; a 13C *Madonna and Child* from Sant'Anatolia di Narco; a 14C statue of *St Cristina*; a 13C *Madonna and Child* (called the *Madonna Rosa*); a 14C *Madonna and Child* (*Madonna del Colera*); a 14C *Madonna* from Colle di Avendita; a 14C *Crucifix* and a 14C statue of *St Andrew*. Room 4. On display here is a polyptych by Giovanni Sparapane (15C); a *Madonna and Child* by the Maestro della Madonna Straus; a 16C polyptych of the *Madonna and Child with Saints* and a 15C painted Cross.

Room 5 (from the windows are delightful views of the city and surrounding countryside). This room contains a *Madonna and Child with Sts Montano and Bartolomeo* by Filippino Lippi and his bottega (from Todiano in the Valle Oblita), and a *Madonna 'della Neve' with Sts Sebastian and Nicholas* by Neri di Bicci (from Abeto in the Valle Oblita) and five cases of church silver, including 18C works by Pietro Ramoser. On the walls are ex votos. Off room 2 is the Anticamera del Cardinale (room 7) with an exhibition illustrating the local craft of weaving, including 18C looms. The chapel, decorated c 1660, has interesting frescoes by the Roman school.

The Pinacoteca Comunale and the Roman House

Off Via Saffi, opposite Palazzo Arcivescovile (see above) a narrow road leads to Piazza del Comune. Facing a pretty row of old houses is **Palazzo Comunale**, begun in the 13C, which retains a tall tower. The rest of the building was transformed in the 18C (and the left wing added in 1913).

The **Pinacoteca Comunale** here is open 10.00–13.00, 15.00–18.00, except Mon, ☎ 0743 43722; cumulative ticket with the Roman House and Galleria Comunale d'Arte Moderna). The Museo Civico, with a collection of paintings founded by Pietro Fontana in the late 18C, was first opened in this palace in 1910 and the interesting museum retains its arrangement from that time (but with the addition of numerous other works). A list is given to visitors since the works are not numbered and have no labels.

Room 1 was decorated in 1906 and contains some fine 16C furniture. The paintings here include (entrance wall) a *Madonna and Child enthroned* by Antonello da Saliba, in a beautiful frame; (right wall) the *Madonna delle Grazie*, a triptych by l'Alunno; (window wall) a 14C polychrome wooden statue of the *Madonna*, and a 14C fresco of the *Crucifixion* detached from the basilica of San Salvatore. On the left wall is a painting of the *Madonna and Child with St Catherine*, attributed to Giacomo Francia. On the entrance wall is a very interesting detached frescoed lunette dating from the late 12C with scenes of the *Martyrdom of Sts John and Paul*, attributed to Alberto Sotio (it was detached from the former church of Santi Giovanni e Paolo). A 15C processional Cross and the 16C reliquary of Sant'Eutizio are on display in the case.

Room 2 (with a view of the Duomo) has a painted Crucifix by the Maestro di Cesi (late 13C or early 14C). Another Crucifix of the same period, and one dating from the 12C, have been removed for restoration. The 14C polychrome wooden effigy comes from the crypt of San Ponziano. The frescoes of *Justice*, *Charity* and *Clemency* by Lo Spagna were detached in 1824 from the Rocca Albornoz and inserted into a monument (with a bust) installed here in honour of Pope Leo XII, a native of Spoleto. Another fresco of the *Madonna and Child with Saints* detached from the Rocca is by Lo Spagna. In the case an exquisite reliquary Cross painted on both sides and two small reliquary paintings of saints by the Maestro di Sant'Alò (late 13C or early 14C) are displayed. Also preserved here is a beautiful little 13C icon of the *Redeemer*, showing Byzantine influence and encrusted with jewels. In the wall case are coins, seals and choirbooks, as well as a drawing of the *Pietà* attributed to Alunno.

Room 3 contains mostly 16C and 17C paintings and a walnut cupboard dating from the early 17C. On the left wall is a *Holy Family* by Bartolomeo Spranger, and *St Helena* attributed to Livio Agresti. On the wall opposite the window is a *Madonna and Child with the young St John* by Sebastiano Conca, in an elaborate frame, and a painting by Paolo Antonio Barbieri depicting a pharmacist in his shop. On the right wall is a *Mary Magdalene* by Guercino. Church silver is displayed in three cases.

Beneath the left wing of Palazzo Comunale (entrance beneath the piazza in Via Visiale) are remains of a **Roman house** (admission as for the Pinacoteca Comunale and with the same ticket), supposed to have belonged to Vespasia Polla (1C AD), mother of Vespasian, found and excavated in 1885–1912 by

Giuseppe Sordini. It has very fine black and white geometric mosaic pavements (being restored in situ, using a special technique of reintegration using a mortar of quicklime: the places where this has been done can be identified by their slightly opaque appearance). In the large atrium is a beautiful well-head (the sides apparently worn away by the iron chain used to draw up the water) and marble impluvium. On the right is a case of finds supported on two handsome Roman marble pedestals. The tablinum, triclinium and peristyle have been identified and a fragment of red wall painting survives. The walls and vaults are medieval or modern.

The pedestrian Via del Municipio leads uphill out of the piazza to the busy **Piazza Campello**, where several roads converge (now used as a car-park). It has a few cedars of Lebanon and a monument dedicated to those who fell in the struggle to liberate Spoleto from the Papal States by Cesare Bazzani (1910). Palazzo Campello was transformed in the 18C, and the former church of Santi Simone e Giuda (13C) is being restored. The splendid colossal mask serving as a wall fountain (1642; restored in 1736) marks the end of the Roman (and medieval) aqueduct.

Rocca Albornoz

Here is the entrance gate to the huge Rocca Albornoz erected in 1359–64 by Gattapone for Cardinal Albornoz, which still dominates the town. It was used as a prison up until 1982, and since then has been undergoing a complicated restoration, but is now finally expected to reopen in the year 2000.

The Spanish priest Gil Alvarez **Albornoz**, archibishop of Toledo, was appointed cardinal by Innocent III and in 1353 sent as Papal legate to administer the Papal States in central Italy. He devised a code of government using apostolic vicariates to reassert Papal authority outside Rome. He brought Spoleto under Papal control and used this castle as his headquarters, although he built other fortresses (some of them also designed by Gattapone) in Assisi, Narni and Piediluco. When he died in 1367 he was temporarily buried in the lower church of San Francesco in Assisi (in a chapel designed by Gattapone), before his body was escorted back to Toledo.

There are plans to provide escalators and lifts to replace the long climb uphill to the main buildings around the **Cortile d'Onore**, with a beautiful well by Bernardo Rossellino, added when Nicholas V enlarged the castle. Here the **Museo Nazionale del Ducato di Spoleto** is to be opened, with material relating to the medieval Duchy of Spoleto. Next to the **Salone d'Onore**, to be used for exhibitions and conferences, is the **Sala Pinta** with interesting early 15C frescoes. The **Cortile delle Armi** will be adapted as a huge open-air **theatre**, and in the buildings here a European book restoration school will be installed as well as a technical restoration laboratory for works of art. The hillside, where interesting remains of the 7C church of **Sant'Elia** have been found, is to be opened as a **public park**. Roman and medieval finds from excavations on the hillside are displayed in the Archaeological Museum (see below). The delightful view to the south takes in the Ponte delle Torri, the unspoilt valley of the Flaminia, and the walls which descend the hillside. To the north, the view extends over new buildings on the plain towards Assisi.

Ponte delle Torri

From the top of Piazza Campello the peaceful **Via del Ponte** leads past the old wall of the Rocca (a plaque records 94 political prisoners who escaped from the Fascist prison here in 1943 to join partisans in the surrounding hills). Beyond a stretch of cyclopic walls and a row of ilex trees, there is a view to the right of the line of the city walls descending into the valley, enclosing old houses with their orchards, and of San Pietro in trees beyond the busy road. The road continues to the wooded ravine crossed by the magnificent **Ponte delle Torri**, a bridge and aqueduct, also probably built by Gattapone, but possibly on Roman foundations. It spans a deep ravine amidst ilex groves, and is 230m long and 80m high; it is one of the most remarkable sights in Italy (and was greatly admired by Goethe in 1786: his description of it is given here). This is an incredibly peaceful spot where the view is still unspoilt. The bridge can be crossed on foot and a path on the far side leads to the Monteluco road (see below).

Via del Ponte (closed to cars) continues round the castle hill, and steps lead down to the pretty hillside below it. There are a few picturesque old farmhouses on the opposite side of the valley, and then the busy plain comes into view with the superstrada (and the church of San Ponziano conspicuous beside it and, behind, San Salvatore, with its dome, in a group of dark trees). Beyond, the ugly suburbs can be seen and then, in a stretch of the road open as a car-park (here called Via Matteo Gattapone), there is a fine view of the roof, dome and campanile of the Duomo, and the tower of Palazzo Comunale. The road ends in Piazza Campello (see above).

Piazza del Mercato

Just below Piazza del Municipio (see above) is the central Piazza del Mercato, on the site of the Roman Forum. A small daily market is held here, with local farmers' produce. The monumental wall fountain by Costantino Fiaschetti (1746) incorporates a monument to Urban VII by Carlo Maderno (1626; restored).

On the left of the fountain is Via dei Duchi, a very attractive street with lovely old shop fronts (many of them owned by antique dealers). It runs into Via di Fontesecca, another pretty street where the old street lanterns and shop signs have been preserved. Via del Mercato, which leads downhill out of Piazza del Mercato to Corso Mazzini (see below) is also picturesque, with fine paving.

From the piazza Via Arco di Druso leads past the huge 17C Palazzo Leti next to a 15C palace housing the Albergo dell'Angelo where Gioacchino Rossini used to stay. It passes beneath the Roman **Arco di Druso**, dedicated in AD 23 to Drusus and Germanicus (the lower part of the arch is buried). Beside the arch the foundations of the cella of a Roman temple and Roman shops can be seen. These are now part of the wall of the church of **Sant'Ansano**, which was built above it in the Middle Ages. The church was redesigned in the 18C by Antonio Dotti, and contains a fresco fragment of the *Madonna and Child* by Lo Spagna. Remains of the Roman temple (1C AD) have been exposed around the altar. Steps lead down (light on left) to the 11C **Cripta di Sant'Isacco** which has ancient columns with 8C–9C capitals, and very interesting primitive (11C–12C) frescoes (detached and restored).

The Roman Theatre and Museo Archeologico

The steep Via Brignone leads downhill from here through Piazza Fontana where there is an elegant little fountain and Palazzo Mauri (16C–17C), to **Piazza della Libertà**, which has a fine view, beyond railings, of the Roman theatre. This is entered down the passageway to the right: steps lead down past the ancient portico of the former church of **Sant'Agata** (now a restoration centre) to the entrance. The **Roman theatre** and **Museo Archeologico** are open 09.00–19.00; PH 09.00–13.00 (☎ 0743 223277). The **theatre** dates from the Imperial era; it was damaged by landslides and built over in the Middle Ages. The ruins were drawn in the 16C by Baldassare Peruzzi, and were rediscovered by Giuseppe Sordini in 1891. Since 1954 they have been uncovered and heavily restored. A remarkable barrel-vaulted passageway survives beneath the cavea. The scena retains part of its lovely polychrome marble pavement (covered in winter), and behind it is the Romanesque apse of Sant'Agata.

In the conventual buildings is the **Museo Archeologico**. On the **ground floor** are two rooms with well-labelled finds from the town and surrounding territory. These date from the Bronze Age to the Middle Ages and include material from the tomb of a warrior found in Piazza d'Armi, and jewellery and pottery (7C–4C BC) found, part of it by Giuseppe Bellucci, at the end of the last century. More recent excavations in various parts of the city have yielded Bronze Age material. In the former **refectory** is a fine display of Roman busts and portrait heads (2C–3C AD), the torso of a boy found in the theatre, and portraits of Augustus and Julius Casesar (1C AD). Beyond is a section with beautifully carved epigraphs (1C AD) and, at the end, two remarkable **inscriptions** of the 3C BC forbidding the cutting of timber in a sacred grove. On the **floor above**, diagrams and plans explain the history of the occupation of the Colle Sant'Elia following excavations during the restoration of the Rocca Albornoz in 1983–86, which yielded Roman and medieval finds. Another room on the upper floor may one day be opened.

Corso Mazzini, the main shopping street of the town, particularly crowded with people taking their *passeggiata* on Sundays, leads north out of Piazza della Libertà. It passes Via delle Terme in which Palazzo Rosari-Spada is situated, which houses the **Galleria Comunale d'Arte Moderna** (open 10.00–13.00, 15.00–18.00 except Mon).

San Domenico and the northern part of town

From Corso Mazzini (see above) Via Plinio il Giovane leads down past the tiny 12C church of **San Lorenzo** to a piazza with the grand **Palazzo Collicola** (1737, by Sebastiano Cipriani, being restored). Close by is the 13C church of **San Domenico** with its pleasant pink and white banded exterior.

In the **interior**, the first south altar has a charming early 15C fresco of the *Triumph of St Thomas Aquinas* (detached and restored). In the south transept is a *Madonna and four saints* by Giovanni Lanfranco (removed), and off the transept is a barrel-vaulted chapel entirely covered with frescoes by a 15C artist. On the east wall of the church (below Gothic windows with 20C stained glass) are more frescoes. Above the altar hangs a 14C painted Crucifix. In the chapel to the left of the presbytery, with a dome decorated by Liborio Coccetti, is a *Christ in the Garden* by Cesare Nebbia. On the north wall of the nave is a touching fresco of the *Pietà*, and on the west wall, a 14C painting of *St Peter Martyr*. In the centre of the nave is a striking polychrome wooden Crucifix. The crypt has further remains of frescoes.

The stepped Via Filippo Marignoli leads uphill to the **Teatro Nuovo** (being restored) built by Ireneo Aleandri (1854–64). It is decorated inside by Giuseppe Masella and Vincenzo Gaiassi, with a back-cloth by Francesco Coghetti. Beside it is a hall decorated by Cesare Bazzani (1910).

Further uphill is the church of **San Filippo**. The impressive façade dates from 1640 (by the local architect Loreto Scelli). Inside (closed since the earthquake), on the south side, is a *Presentation of the Virgin in the temple* and a *Crucifixion* by Gaetano Lapis da Cagli. The altar in the north transept has columns in verde antico and a *Holy Family* by Sebastiano Conca. On the first north altar is a *Descent of the Holy Spirit* by Lazzaro Baldi. In the elegant panelled 18C Sacristy is a marble bust of *St Filippo* Neri by Alessandro Algardi.

In the piazza is the little medieval church of **Sant'Angelo** (now used as a parish office) with 16C frescoes.

Via Tobagi leads from San Filippo to the former church of **Santi Giovanni e Paolo** (left), consecrated in 1174. For admission ask at the Galleria Comunale d'Arte Moderna. The frescoes inside are particularly interesting, and include a contemporary scene of the *Martyrdom of St Thomas Becket* (d. 1170) and a figure of *St Nicolò*, both attributed to Alberto Sotio (late 12C or early 13C). The other votive frescoes date from the 14C and 15C.

From San Domenico (see above) Via Pierleone Leoni leads down to Piazza Torre dell'Olio which takes its name from the tall thin tower beyond Porta Fuga (12C?) or di Annibale, beneath which Via Porta Fuga descends to join Corso Garibaldi. The busy Via Cecili follows the best section of **walls**. The polygonal masonry dates from the end of the 4C BC; the walls were consolidated by the Romans and in subsequent centuries up to the 15C. They are interrupted by the 14C apse of **San Nicolò**. The church is used as a theatre and the cloister may sometimes be visited (enquire at the comune). Excavations here, during restoration work, brought to light Bronze Age material. The ruins of the **amphitheatre**, further on, are within the former conventual barracks (no admission).

Corso Garibaldi, the main street of the lower town and the scene of the crowded *passeggiata* on weekdays, and Via dell'Anfiteatro meet at the unattractive **Piazza Garibaldi** where the church of **San Gregorio** was well restored in 1949. In the fine Romanesque interior there is a tabernacle attributed to Benedetto da Rovezzano (chapel to the left). Outside **Porta Garibaldi** (rebuilt since the Second World War) are the remains (below ground level) of the **Ponte Sanguinario** (recently restored), a Roman bridge which crossed the Via Flaminia in the 1C BC. It was abandoned when the river was diverted in the 14C and rediscovered in 1817 when the existing bridge was built.

From **Piazza della Vittoria**, a busy road junction, Viale Trento e Trieste leads to the **railway station**, outside which is a huge iron sculpture by Alexander Calder (1962).

Via Flaminia Vecchia leads straight out of Piazza della Vittoria and about 800 metres further on passes the gardens of **Villa Redenta**, which are open to the public and sometimes used for exhibitions. The villa was renovated in the 18C and bought by Pope Leo XII c 1825. Since 1973 it has been owned by the Province of Perugia. A garden building has rococo decorations, and the neo-classical park has fine trees including a huge cedar of Lebanon which is over 200 years old.

San Ponziano and San Salvatore

These two important churches on the outskirts of the town, on the far side of the Flaminia superstrada, are very unpleasant to approach on foot. By car they are at present very poorly signposted and difficult to find. They can only be reached from Piazza della Vittoria (see above) along an inconspicuous road (signposted once to the cemetery) which leads beneath the Flaminia superstrada to (c 1km) the cemetery.

The first turning on the right, after the superstrada bridge, leads to the 12C church of **San Ponziano** (shown by a custodian, 09.00–12.00, 15.00–18.00), dedicated to the patron saint of Spoleto. It has a fine façade, with symbols of the Evangelists around the oculus, and a lovely Cosmati portal with delicate carving.

The **interior** was remodelled by Giuseppe Valadier in 1788. Some huge old Corinthian columns embedded into the later wall of the church can be seen in the corridor on the way to the crypt which leads past a sarcophagus from the Lombard period and a 15C terracotta sarcophagus. The **crypt** has two rare con-ical pillars, thought to be metae from a Roman circus, serving as columns, and another column is an up-turned Roman column (the capital serves as its base, and its base serves as capital). The 14C and 15C fresco fragments include a fine *Trinity* beneath a little vault painted with four charming angels. The three old sarcophagi still keep their lids.

The convent next door is being restored to offer hospitality to visitors in Holy Year 2000.

Via San Salvatore continues to the cemetery and the remarkable church of **San Salvatore** (or Il Crocifisso), an early Christian church of the late 4C or early 5C of the greatest interest for its numerous classical elements. The damaged **façade** (covered for restoration since 1996) has fine portals and three unusual windows showing Oriental influence. The venerable **interior** (open 07.00–17.00; 07.00–19.00 in summer) has numerous classical columns and Roman architraves. In the beautiful domed presbytery are 16 huge columns, mostly with Corinthian columns (but some with Ionic and Doric ones). Splendid acanthus leaf capitals at the four corners of the presbytery stand out above the classical cornice. The walls are completely bare and there are more Roman columns in the nave.

San Pietro and San Paolo Intervineas

Outside the town to the south (c 1km from the centre) is the ancient church of **San Pietro** (reached on foot from Piazza del Mercato by the steep old Via Monterone, Via San Carlo and then left across the Flaminia superstrada; or by a pretty walk across Ponte delle Torri by the di Monteluco road). The church, reconstructed in the 13C, has a Lombard **façade** with a magnificent variety of large 12C reliefs, among the most important Romanesque sculptures in Umbria. On the upper part are statues of *Sts Peter and Andrea above two bulls* looking down. Around the central oculus are symbols of the *Evangelists*. The central door is surmounted by an Oriental lunette with Cosmatesque decoration and flanked by two eagles. On either side of the classical decoration around the door, in between panels of blind arcading, are paired reliefs representing allegories of *Work* and *Eternal Life* (a farmer with two bullocks and a dog, a deer feeding its offspring and eating a serpent, and two peacocks pecking at grapes). The ten larger reliefs flanking the door represent (right) *Christ washing St Peter's feet*, the *Calling of Sts Peter and Andrew*, and three symbolic scenes relating to animal fables. On the left side: *Death and Judgement of the Just*, *Death and Judgement of Sinners* and three scenes showing struggles between lions and men.

The **interior** (opened by the custodian who lives next door 15.30–19.00; PH 10.00–13.00) was remodelled in 1699. On the west wall are 16C votive frescoes. The stoups date from the 15C. On the third south altar is an *Adoration of the Magi* by a 16C Umbrian painter. The font dates from 1487. The Canonica outside has antique fragments in its façade. A path leads to the little church of San Silvestro, behind San Pietro, with a 14C fresco of the Calvary.

The church of **San Paolo Intervineas**, c 1km south-west of the town (reached from Piazza della Libertà by Viale Matteotti and Viale Martiri della Resistenza) was mentioned by St Gregory the Great. It was rebuilt in the 10C and again in the 13C. It has a fine façade with a rose window. In the interior (for admission ring at the old people's home next door, 09.00–14.00) there are early 13C frescoes of prophets and the Creation, and an old altar.

Also on the west side of the town, beyond Porta Loreto, a straight road lined with a long portico leads to the church of the **Madonna di Loreto**, begun in 1572 by Annibale Lippi on a Greek-cross plan with three paintings by Giovanni Baglione (1609).

BEYOND SPOLETO

A winding road ascends from San Pietro to Monteluco through ilex woods. It passes the end of the Ponte delle Torri (described above) and negotiates hairpin bends. It passes the isolated 12C church of **San Giuliano**, in a group of pine trees. The church (opened on request at the restaurant next door, except on Wedneday) incorporates fragments of its 6C predecessor. The frescoes in the apse are by the Maestro di Eggi (1442). The road climbs up to **Monteluco** (804m), a little old-fashioned summer resort with a number of hotels and a grassy field between them. The hill was occupied from the 7C by anchorites, and there is a convent of San Francesco here (belvedere).

A pretty road (N395) from Spoleto climbs across the hills to Piedipaterno in the Valnerina, described on p. 216.

The main road (N3) which leads north to Foligno passes close to **Eggi** where there are frescoes by the Maestro di Eggi in the church of San Michele Archangelo. San Giacomo, Campello sul Clitunno, and the famous spring and temple of Clitunno are all described on pp. 194–97

Another road leads north-west towards Montefalco via **San Brizio** with its 13C walls and an interesting Romanesque church with a crypt (closed since 1997), and **Bruna**, which has a sanctuary of 1510. Castel Ritaldi is described on p. 197.

The road (N 418) which leads across the hills from Spoleto to Acquasparta (see p. 270) passes close to the pretty village of Sant'Angelo in Mercole.

CLITUNNO AND ENVIRONS

This area near Spoleto is interesting for the Clitunno spring, near which is an ancient little temple, remarkably well preserved. On the hillside above Campello sul Clitunno lovely countryside can be explored.

Practical information

Information offices
IAT di Spoleto, ☎ 0743 220311; Pro Campello office beside San Cipriano e Giustina on the Via Flaminia near Clitunno.

Getting there
The scattered district of Campello sul Clitunno is south of Trevi, on the main road between Spoleto and Foligno.

Hotels
Clitunno *Vecchio Molino*, Via del Tempio, Località Pissignano, ☎ 0743 521122; fax 0743 275097. Just below the Tempietto del Clitunno, close to the Fonti del Clitunno, this carefully restored old water-mill is classified as an 'historic residence' (it has 13 rooms). It is unfortunately rather close to the busy Via Flaminia, but is below it and the sound of water from the Clitunno river effectively competes with the sound of traffic.

Near **Campello sul Clitunno** ✶✶✶ *Benedetti*, Località Settecamini, ☎ 0743 520078; fax 0743 520080. A very pleasant hotel with 22 rooms and an excellent restaurant. ✶✶ *Ravale*, Località Ravale, ☎ 0743 521320. There are plans to open a small hotel at the **Castello di Poreta**, a fine castle

restored in 1997 in a beautiful position above Campello sul Clitunno. At present only a restaurant is open here (see below).

On the road between Campello sul Clitunno and Campello Alto, ✶✶ *Le Casaline*, ☎ 0743 521113. A delightful little hotel on a farm, with a restaurant.

Above **Campello Alto**, in a little hill resort, is the secluded little ✶✶ *Le Fontanelle*, ☎ 0743 521091, with a good restaurant.

Camping
Giano nell'Umbria ✶✶ *Pineta di Giano* (open April–mid Sept), ☎ 0742 930040.

Restaurants
Near **Campello sul Clitunno** £ *Pettino* at Pettino Colle, ☎ 0743 276021.

There are good restaurants (££) in the hotels of *Benedetti*, *Le Casaline* and *Le Fontanelle* (see above). A restaurant has also recently been opened in the *Castello di Poreta*, ☎ 0743 275810 (see above).

A small **antiques fair** is held at Campello sul Clitunno on the first Sunday of each month.

Tempietto del Clitunno
The little Tempietto del Clitunno (open 09.00–20.00; winter 09.00–14.00; closed Mon) is on the left of the Via Flaminia, the main road between Spoleto and Foligno, behind railings in a group of pine trees above the Clitunno river. Although adjacent to the road, it is easy to miss: it has to be approached from the

Tempietto del Clitunno

old road which runs parallel to the fast road (signposted inconspicuously together with the Hotel Vecchio Mulino, 1km towards Trevi from the Fonti del Clitunno).

It is now very well kept and surrounded by a little garden. The temple is thought to have been erected in the 4C or 5C using antique fragments from the pagan edifices which once lined the river here (see below; the old mill below it is now a hotel). It has a beautiful exterior with handsome classical columns (two of them decorated to imitate the trunks of palm trees) and carved early Christian friezes in the pediments. The charming little **interior** also has lovely carved decoration around the apse and a tiny tabernacle. The very faded frescoes of *Sts Peter and Paul* and *God the Father* are of the greatest interest since they are thought to date from the 7C–8C.

About 1 km south of the Tempietto del Clitunno (well signposted; also on the left of the Via Flaminia between Spoleto and Foligno) is the entrance to the Fonti del Clitunno, a green oasis at the spring of the River Clitunno, the classical *Clitumnus*. The river flows from here to Bevagna where it joins the Teverone and then becomes an affluent of the Tiber. The park (now disturbed by the main road), laid out in 1852 by Paolo Campello with weeping willows and poplars surrounding a lake inhabited by swans, is open every day (the custodian lives here) from 09.00 to dusk; a small entrance fee is charged from Easter to October. There is a snack bar at the entrance.

Fonti del Clitunno

These cool crystal clear waters were well known in antiquity and the abundant spring was dedicated to the god Clitumnus, a famous oracle whose temple was erected here. Ovid tells of the white sacrificial oxen which were bred on its banks. The beauty of this sacred spot was celebrated by Propertius Virgil, and Pliny the Younger, but soon after the Roman era the waters diminished considerably.

In later centuries the little temple was sketched by Antonio da Sangallo the Younger, Piranesi, and Palladio. Richard Wilson painted the spring and it captured the imagination of the Romantic poets. Byron visited the site in 1817 and includes a description of it in *Childe Harold's Pilgrimage* (Canto IV), when he recognises the 'Genius of the place' and calls the spring 'the purest god of gentle waters'. He contrasts the serenity of this spot with Lago Trasimeno, which he describes in the preceding verses recalling scenes of violent slaughter at the famous battle in which Hannibal was victorious over the Romans. He goes on to describe the lovely little temple here, and then in the following verses sings the grandeur of the mighty Marmore falls which he must have visited in the same period. Giosuè Carducci composed a famous ode to the Clitunno in 1876.

A byroad (poorly signposted off the other side of the Via Flaminia) leads up to the medieval village of **Pissignano** where there is a fine castle built c 1000, visible on the hillside.

About 500m from the lake, on the other side of the main road towards Spoleto, is the tiny chapel of **San Sebastiano** (being restored) which is surrounded by poplars. Inside are lovely frescoes by Lo Spagna and votive figures of *St Sebastian*. Close by, also right on the main road, and surrounded by a fence, is the little 12C church of **San Cipriano e Giustina** which was ruined in the 19C, except for its pretty apse. Next door, in a well-restored old stone house, is a local tourist office.

A byroad leads up to the pleasant spaciously laid out village of **Campello sul Clitunno**, with numerous trees. The church of the Madonna della Bianca (open only for services) was built in 1514 and has a fine classical portal by Cione di Taddeo. The interior with an elaborate high altar was designed by Valadier. The fresco in the apse is by Fabio Angelucci (1574). In the sacristy are two frescoes by the school of Lo Spagna.

A road continues uphill through lovely open countryside with extensive fields of olive trees. A byroad (right) leads past a villa with a beautiful garden towards the picturesque **Castello di Poreta**, visible on the hillside above, in a lovely isolated position (reached by an extremely steep road). The church and castle were restored in 1997 and a restaurant has recently been opened here (there are plans to open a small hotel here as well).

The main road from Campello continues up through fields and woods (where truffles are often found, and wild boar hunts take place) to **Lenano** where the church of San Lorenzo (usually closed) has 15C frescoes. A byroad leads left to **Campello Alto**, a well-preserved picturesque little hamlet, founded in the 10C, on a mound in a beautiful position, with its walls intact. Beyond the gate, in the tiny circular piazza is the church of San Donato (approached by curving steps) with an 18C organ and a font of 1610. Just outside the walls is a convent with a fresco of the *Crucifixion and Saints* by the 15C Umbrian school.

Further uphill is a little resort in the woods.

On low ground just off the main Spoleto—Foligno road, is **San Giacomo di Spoleto**. The **church** of San Giacomo has interesting 16C frescoes (in poor condition): those in the apse with the *Coronation of the Virgin* and below *St James* and two scenes from his life and the left niche of the presbytery are all by Lo Spagna; the *Deposition* is by Fabio Angelucci, and the *Madonna* in a niche on the north wall, is by Dono Doni and Bernardino d'Assisi. Opposite the church is a very ruined rectangular **castle** with four angle towers built by Cardinal Albornoz, interesting for the double street of little houses inside its walls, some of which are still inhabited.

To the west is **Castel Ritaldi** which has a 13C castle, an old gate and a church (Santa Marina) with an attractive side portico. It has been closed since 1997. In the presbytery (behind a curtain) in a niche on the right is a *Madonna with angels and saints*, an extremely worn fresco by Tiberio d'Assisi. Outside the village is the Pieve (being restored) dedicated to San Gregorio, built in the 12C with a decorated portal.

Giano dell'Umbria is a peaceful medieval walled village in a lovely position, well known for its olive oil. At the top of the hill is the piazza with the town hall (being restored after earthquake damage). The centrally-planned church here has an 18C interior, and a greatly revered 14C fresco fragment of the *Madonna and Child* over the high altar. The side altarpiece of the *Madonna and child with saints* is a fine work by Andrea Polinori, signed and dated 1620. It is a well-composed painting, and the pretty muted colours have recently been restored. In the same piazza is the Romanesque apse of San Michele, which has an attractive exterior.

Near **Castagnola**, with a 13C–14C castle, there is a good view of the handsome 19C sanctuary of the **Madonna del Fosco**, in the valley below. A road leads along a pretty wooded ridge to **San Felice**, a 12C Benedictine abbey built of pale red stone, in a lovely peaceful position. The **church** has a fine façade, and an impressive interior with a raised presbytery, and columns constructed out of red stones. Light is provided by the three-light window on the façade, and there is a two-light window at the entrance to the sanctuary. The **crypt**, has good columns and a medley of capitals, two Corinthian, and others with primitive animal carvings. An ancient sarcophagus, complete with its lid, rests on five miniature columns and the lovely old paving remains. The pink **cloister**, with delightful frescoes, has been restored. The abbey buildings have been occupied by a missionary congregation since 1815 (visitors are welcome).

Cascia, Norcia and the Valnerina

CASCIA

• • • • • • • •

Cascia (population 4000), is famous for its sanctuary of St Rita: after her canonisation in 1900 her popularity was such that a huge new basilica dedicated to her was built at the top of the town in 1937–47, still visited by thousands of pilgrims every year. The hillside below the old centre was disfigured in the 1950s and 1960s by ugly high-rise buildings. The little town has all the usual characteristics of important pilgrimage shrines.

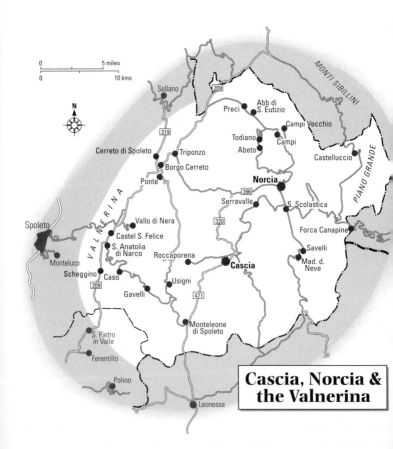

Cascia, Norcia & the Valnerina

Practical information

Information office

IAT della Valnerina-Cascia, Piazza Garibaldi, ☎ 0743 71147.

Getting there

Car parking There are several small car-parks clearly signposted just below Piazza Garibaldi. A large car-park on the side of the hill (mostly used by coaches) is soon to be connected to the church of Santa Maria by a series of escalators and a lift.

By bus There are services (run by *Società Spoletino*, ☎ 0743 221991) from Norcia and Spoleto, and (less frequently) from Perugia (via Foligno), and from Rome (via Terni and the Valnerina or via Rieti). There is a bus twice a day between Cascia and Roccaporena.

 ### Hotels

☆☆ *La Tavernetta*, Via Gaetano Palombi, ☎ & fax 0743 71387. A tiny simple hotel in a pleasant position in the old centre with just eight rooms and a good restaurant. Another small hotel in the old centre is the ☆☆ *Centrale*, 36 Piazza Garibaldi, ☎ 0743 76736.

The ☆☆☆ hotels are in more modern buildings with little character outside the old centre.

A youth hostel is to be opened in the former convent of Sant'Antonio Abate. **Monteleone di Spoleto** (in the environs) a hotel (*Brufa*) has just been opened in a modern building just below the piazza (with a restaurant).

 ### Restaurants

££ *La Tavernetta* (see above); £ *Il Caminetto*, ☎ 0743 71525 and *Il Grottino da Orlando*, ☎ 0743 76420.

Market day is on Wednesday.

Annual festival *Festa di Santa Rita* on 22 May. Good Friday procession.

History

The Roman municipium of *Cursula* was destroyed by earthquake and a new city founded on the side of the hill. By 553 it was known as Cascia. The town has had a tumultuous history and has also been frequently devastated by earthquakes (especially in 1599, 1703 and 1979). Giovanni da Cascia, the musician, was born here in the 14C. Santa Rita, the Agostinian nun born nearby at Roccaporena, died here in 1457.

The centre of the town is **Piazza Garibaldi**. The church of **San Francesco**, built in 1424, is situated here and has a fine portal and rose window. The **interior**, redesigned in the 17C and in 1925, has white stucco decoration. In a niche on the west wall, there is a fresco of the *Madonna and Child with two saints* and three saints by the Umbrian school (1443). South side, on the first altar, there is the pavement tomb of Bishop Antonio Elemosina, who ordered the building of the church. On the third altar is a *Madonna and Child enthroned with two saints*. In the nave are Roman fragments. Near the finely carved 17C wood pulpit are more frescoes including a *Trinity*, attributed to Bartolomeo di Tommaso da Foligno (c 1440).

In the **apse** are 14C stalls and worn 15C frescoes. In the north transept is a beautiful large gilded wooden altar by Fiorenzo di Giuliano incorporating an *Ascension* by Nicolò Pomarancio (signed and dated 1596), and on either side,

Local saints

Umbria is known for its numerous **saints and mystics**. Its two most famous saints are St Francis of Assisi (1181–1226), canonised two years after his death, whose Order was founded on the rule of poverty, chastity and obedience, and St Benedict of Norcia (480–550), whose Benedictine Order was based on work and prayer. His abbey at Montecassino in Lazio was to be of fundamental importance to the civilised world throughout the Middle Ages. However, Umbria is particularly interesting for the number of women saints and mystics who were born here and lived exemplary lives. Benedict's twin sister Scolastica is usually considered the first nun of the Benedictine order (their story is illustrated in a fresco cycle discovered in 1978 in the church of Santa Scolastica in the cemetery of Norcia, traditionally supposed to be on the site of their mother's house). Chiara of Assisi, follower of St Francis, was dedicated to relieving the suffering of the poor, and had a great influence on the spread of the Franciscan movement. She was born around 1193 and her order was approved by Innocent IV in 1253 two days before she died. She was canonised in 1255.

Perhaps the most famous woman saint in Umbria today, whose shrine has been visited by thousands of pilgrims every year since her canonisation in 1900, is Rita (or Margherita) of Cascia, born here in 1381. The story is told that after her marriage to a violent man who was killed by his enemies, she persuaded their two children not to take vengeance on his murderers, but they both soon died in an epidemic. Rita then became an Augustinian nun for the last 40 years of her life but suffered terrible pain after receiving the Stigmata. She is considered the protectress of all those who are dogged by inordinate misfortune.

St Chiara di Montefalco, born in 1268, who spent her life as a nun following the rule of Augustine, is particularly revered by the local inhabitants. On her death aged 40 it is said that the symbols of the Passion of Christ were found engraved on her heart. She was canonised in 1881. Her convent in Montefalco is still occupied by nuns who show her embalmed body and relics. Angela of Foligno (1248–1309), who, after having married and borne children, became a Franciscan tertiary aged 37, was famous for her mystical apparitions, and her cult was validated by Clement XI in 1701.

In Perugia Dominican nuns preserve relics of the Blessed Colomba of Rieti (1467–1501) who lived in their convent. In Città di Castello there are still no fewer than three convents of the Clarisse, all closed orders. St Veronica Giuliani (1660–1727) lived in one of them for 50 years (she was canonised in 1839): her possessions are all carefully preserved in a little museum shown by the nuns. There is also a convent of the Clarisse next to the church of San Leonardo in Montefalco, where the nuns can be seen at worship in their adjoining church. Three Franciscan monks still live at the convent of San Fortunato just outside Montefalco: since the 1997 earthquake they have given hospitality to a community of Clarisse whose convent in Assisi was badly damaged.

Noli me Tangere and *Christ appearing to the Apostles*, attributed to Pierino Cesarei. The church also owns a 15C wooden statue of *St Bernardine*.

Just out of the other end of the piazza is the collegiata of **Santa Maria**, the oldest church in Cascia, founded in 856, beside a little piazza where a Romanesque lion is used as a charming little fountain. The façade has two door-ways (1535 and 1620) and the other Romanesque lion rather uncomfortably inserted into a niche above. In the interior, at the west end, are interesting fresco fragments, including (on the south wall) a *Deposition* by Nicola da Siena. On the first south altar is Gaspare and Camillo Angelucci's, *'Pala della Pace'* (1547). At the east end of the north aisle is a 16C font and an altarpiece by Niccolò Frangipane of the *Mysteries of the Rosary*, surrounding a 15C carved Crucifix. Here, on an old flight of steps, some Romanesque sculptural fragments have been placed.

Near the church is the Oratorio della Confraternità del Sacramento with a 16C *Madonna and Child with saints*.

From Piazza Garibaldi steps lead down through an old gate to a road which leads to the church of **Sant'Antonio Abate** (open Oct–Dec on weekends 10.30–13.00, 15.00–17.00; in June, July & Sept: Fri, Sat & Sun 10.30–13.00, 16.00–18.30; in Aug every day 10.30–13.00, 16.00–19.00; ☎ 0743 751010). The interior, restored after earthquake damage in 1599 and 1703, has 17C altars with wooden statues and a carved 16C tabernacle over the altar. The organ dates from 1630. Two chapels survive from the earlier church at the east end.

In the **presbytery** is a well-preserved late 14C or early 15C fresco cycle with stories from the *life of St Anthony Abbot* attributed to an Umbrian master known as the Maestro dello Dormitio di Terni. The charming scenes include numerous details of wild flowers which still grow in the district. The frescoes on the east wall show the *Annunciation* and a lovely little *Madonna and Child with two angels*. Behind is the **monks' choir** entirely decorated with more fine frescoes of the *Passion* by Nicola da Siena, dated 1442. A splendid wooden statue of the *archangel Raphael with Tobias* is exhibited here, attributed to Antonio Rizzo or his bottega. It is a very rare work and extremely beautiful.

Above Piazza Garibaldi (see above) is the town hall in the recently restored **Palazzo Frenfanelli**. Close by is the **Museo di Palazzo Santi** (open as for Sant'Antonio Abate, see above). This 17C palace has been restored and contains a small local archaeological collection on the ground floor. On the upper floor the collection of 13C–16C wooden sculptures in the first room include a beautiful early 13C seated *Madonna and Child*, a statuette of an angel, a 15C *Christ deposed* (with moveable arms), and a statue of *St Sebastian* attributed to the bottega of Antonio Rizzo. Also on this floor is a terracotta head of the *Virgin* and a German *Pietà*. Other rooms contain paintings by Giacinto Boccanera and Lazzaro Baldi, vestments (17C and 15C) and some furniture.

Another fine palace in the old town, **Palazzo Carli**, with 18C decorations, is now the seat of the town library and precious and extensive archives which document local history from the 13C onwards.

At the top of the town is the ugly white **Basilica di Santa Rita**, built in 1937–47 on the site of an earlier church which dominates the town. The interior, in an unsuccessful combination of styles, is lavishly decorated.

Beyond Cascia

Above the town is the church and convent of **Sant'Agostino** (signposted off the Monteleone road), built in 1380. It contains 15C frescoes and a *Madonna and Sts Augustine and Rita* by Virgilio Nucci (1590). Above are the remains of the **Rocca**, built in 1465 and destroyed by papal troops in 1517.

The village of **Roccaporena**, 6km west of Cascia, in another beautiful valley, was the birthplace of St Rita (see p. 200). Above it towers a fantastic isolated rock (827m), now called the **Scoglio della Preghiera**. A path (signposted from the village) leads up to the summit where the chapel of the saint was reconstructed in 1981. In the village below, her house was transformed into a chapel in 1630 by Cardinal Fausto Poli, who was responsible for promoting the beatification of Rita in 1628. It was restored in 1946 and the painting of the saint is attributed to Luca Giordano. On the left of the road is the parish church of **San Montano** which dates from the 14C, beside the large sanctuary and pilgrim centre of Santa Rita, erected in 1948 (the statue of the saint in the cryptoporticus is by Venanzo Crocetti).

Monteleone di Spoleto

A hilly road (N471; signposted Leonessa) leads south from Cascia crossing beautiful farming country with very few houses. In the river valley N471 continues south towards Leonessa in Lazio while another road bears right to climb up to the remote little village of **Monteleone di Spoleto** (990m).

At the beginning of this century, late Bronze Age tombs were found in the vicinity and a remarkable wooden chariot decorated with bronze reliefs, thought to be an Etruscan work (which was sold to the Metropolitan Museum of New York). The castle of Brufa, erected here in 880, came under the control of Spoleto from 1265 until 1559. After that date the little town prospered until it was severely damaged by earthquake in 1703 (and again hit in 1979).

A garden with old stone medieval measurements and sculptural fragments including columns, slopes up past the impressive south wall of the church of San Francesco (see below) to the 14C **Torre dell'Orologio** with an archway beneath. Beside it is a picturesque portico, and the former **Palazzo dei Priori** which has been partially restored. Inside is a theatre (in need of total reconstruction). From Piazza del Mercato, with a few trees, there is a fine view of the valley. The houses and churches (including San Nicola) further up the hill, were badly shaken in 1979.

The huge church and convent of **San Francesco** were founded in the 1280s. The Gothic portal has fine carving. The interesting **interior** (if closed, entrance on the left of the façade) has been restored. Off the south side is a second nave with Gothic arches and vaulting. The **central nave** has an unusual painted wooden ceiling with *symbols of the Madonna* signed by an artist from Norcia and dated 1760. Along the nave are 13 paintings of *Christ and the apostles* dating from 1666. At the west end are a fine font and stoup, and, near the 16C organ, is a fine seated wooden statue of *St Anthony Abbot*, complete with his little pig, dating from the 15C–16C.

On the north wall, near the side door, are remains of frescoes including the *Madonna at the foot of the Cross*, and a 15C *St Giuliano* on horseback next to the *Madonna enthroned with St Catherine*. The graceful painting of the *Annunciation* is by Agostino Masucci (1723).

The handsome **high altar** has pretty carvings and marble intarsia. Behind it is a small Crucifix, thought to date from the 14C. On the right is a carved stone tabernacle with two angels, a Renaissance work attributed to Benedetto da Rovezzano. In the **south nave**, on the altar, is a late 15C Crucifix. The fresco fragments include a remarkable 15C *Christ as King*, fully robed, which recalls the Volto Santo at Lucca, and (at the west end) the charming little figure of a stonemason in his overalls.

Other treasures belonging to the church, including a 13C wooden statue of the seated *Madonna with the Child*, a 17C polychrome *Madonna and Child*, church silver, vestments and antiphonals are kept in the **sacristy**.

In the **cloister**, also recently restored, are sculptural fragments, including a very ruined Roman female statue. From here there is access to the **lower church**, with well-preserved 14C–15C frescoes in the presbytery, including *St Antony Abbot* near a frieze of animals, *St Anthony of Padua*, *Saints* and a *Madonna of the Misericordia*.

At the bottom of the garden is the short Corso which leads straight down to the 14C Porta Spoletina through the pretty district of San Giacomo, laid out on a grid plan, with arches off the left side. On the right is Porta San Giorgio and at the beginning of the Corso is **Palazzo Bernabò** with a fine façade. Beyond a house built in 1517, is the 17C Palazzo Rotondi, now the town hall, and another Palazzo Bernabò dating from the 17C with balconies. Beside the gate is the church of San Giovanni.

From Monteleone a beautiful road leads across the hills towards the Valnerina. It passes a signpost (right) for the area where the Etruscan finds were made (see above). At first it descends into another deserted valley and then passes a turning for **Usigni** (1000m), a remote little picturesque hamlet, with fine views and attractive paving. The Baroque church of **San Salvatore** (well signposted) is attributed to Bernini. It was commissioned by Cardinal Fausto Poli who was born here and was a member of the court of Urban VIII. It is open only on Sunday (the key is kept by the priest in Poggiodomo).

The mountainous Valnerina road continues through woods where truffles are found above the tiny lonely village of **Gavelli** (mostly restored after severe damage in the 1979 earthquake) on a precipitous cliff. The coral-coloured church of San Michele has been restored but is kept locked (key at the house by the bell-tower). It has an interesting interior with early 16C frescoes, some by Lo Spagna. Next to the church is a public fountain and a little stable under an arch where wooden beams survive, used by the local inhabitants when 'shoeing' the cattle to protect their hooves on the mountainous slopes.

The road continues steeply down towards the Valnerina past a byroad (signposted right) for the charming little Romanesque church of **Santa Cristina**, surrounded by woods. Standing on an old brick pavement, and with a quaint apse and bell-cote, it contains 14C–16C frescoes, but is kept locked. Below it is the little hamlet of **Caso** (728m), with picturesque old roofs and archways, and an old public fountain near the church which has been repaired since 1979 (ask locally for the key). This is typical of the little mountain villages in this area which are slowly becoming depopulated: one of the 15 or so inhabitants who still live here remembers that she was one of some 250 residents when she was born in Caso (nine of her ten children now live in Rome).

The Valnerina is described on p. 215.

NORCIA AND ENVIRONS

Norcia is a delightful little town (population 5400), situated in a fertile basin surrounded by a wide amphitheatre of hills. Over the centuries local architects have carefully reconstructed the principal monuments of the town damaged by a series of destructive earthquakes, the last of which was in 1979. It has particularly attractive buildings, the height of which was limited to two storeys in 1859, and the lower walls of its palaces and churches are often buttressed for added solidity. Norcia has a notably cheerful atmosphere with numerous excellent food shops and restaurants, specialising in local delicacies (including black truffles and cured hams and salami). The town has a great many churches and a number of pretty fountains within its 14C walls which survive intact.

Practical information

Information office

IAT di Cascia, ☎ 0743 71147.
Information office of the Parco Nazionale dei Monti Sibillini in Norcia at the Casa del Parco, 22 Via Solferino (just out of Piazza San Benedetto), ☎ 0743 817090.

Getting there

By bus Services are run by *Società Spoletino* ☎ 0743 221991, from Cascia, Spoleto, Foligno, Perugia, Ascoli Piceno, Terni and Rome.
Car-parking outside Porta Romana.

Hotels

✱✱✱✱ *Salicone*, ☎ 0743 828081; fax 0743 828076, just outside the walls off the main road about a hundred metres below Porta Romana. Part of the Best Western hotel group it is a large hotel built in 1994 with an athletics centre used by international sports teams. There are plans to build a swimming-pool also. Extremely friendly and efficient staff, the spacious comfortable rooms have balconies overlooking the hills and all modern facilities. Full-pension and half-pension terms with the *Granaro del Monte* restaurant (see below).

The same proprietors (the Bianconi family, who have been hoteliers in Norcia since 1850) also own the ✱✱✱

Grotta Azzurra,12 Via Alfieri, ☎ 0743 816513; fax 0743 817342. Inside the walls in an old palace close to Piazza San Benedetto, it has great charm and an excellent restaurant now called *Granaro del Monte*. There are two ✱ annexes attached.
A few metres outside the walls beside Porta Romana is the ✱✱✱ *Garden*, 12 Viale XX Settembre, ☎ & fax 0743 816687.
The monastery of **Sant'Antonio**, ☎ 0743-828208 in the old town also takes guests.
In the environs
A few kilometres above Norcia on the road to Preci, at **Fontevena** is *Il Casale del Parco*, ☎ & fax 0743 816481, opened in 1998 in a restored farmhouse, which offers agriturismo accommodation.

Serravalle di Norcia

✱✱ *Italia*, ☎ 0743 822320, with a good restaurant (£), but on the main road.
Val Castoriana at the **abbey of Sant'Eutizio**, *Bianco Fiore*, ☎ 0743 939319 rents five simple rooms in a fine position at the door of the abbey, family-run above a good trattoria (£).

Preci

✱✱ *Agli Scacchi*, ☎ 0743 99221, at the top of the little old town, with a small swimming-pool right on the byroad and a restaurant.

NORCIA

Medieval Public Fountain

Porta Palatina

Chiesa del Crocifisso

VIA FOROSETTE

Oratorio di S. Agostinuccio

VIA DELLE VERGINI

VIA AMICA

VIA TRIESTE

VIA PALATINA

VIA FORO SETTE

S. Antonio Abate (Monastery)

Madonna degli Angeli

Ex. Monastero della Pace

PIAZZA PALATINA

VIA GALILEO

VALLE CASTORIANA & PRECI

VIA UFENTE

VIA GOVONE

V. DELLE VERGINI

V. ANICIA

Palazzo Colizzi

VIA VESPASIA POLLA

Porta S. Giovanni

P. CARLO ALBERTO

VIA UMBERTO

V. MANZONI

PIANO GRANDE, CEASTELLUCCIO & THE MARCHE

Tempietto

S. Agostino

S. Giovanni

VIA CAPPELLINI

PIAZZA ELENA

Palazeo Bucchi-Corazzini

V. DISTILLERIA

S. Caterina

V. LO FARDELLO

PIAZZA MARGHERITA

V. FUGA

VIA CIOMPI

VIA MUGNIA

VIA CAIROLI

Monastery of the Clarisse

V. DM. AMADIO

V. GIGANTI

Roman Cryptoporticus

V. GIOBERTI

V. SFORUCCIO

V. CACCIATORI

VIA CAIROLI

V. CELLIERA

V. COLOMBO

S. Filippo

V. DM. AMADIO

Porta Massari

Porta Romana

V. CAPPELLO

V. CAPPELLO

OLLETTIVI

VIA PRIORI

BANDIERA

V. COLOMBO

V. REGUARDATI

V. ANICIA

VIA ROMA

Car Park

CORSO SERTORIO

V. TORRENTE PUBBLICO

Palazzo Cav di Malta

VIA LEGNANO

CASCIA & SPOLETO

Teatro Civico

PIAZZA V. VENETO

VIA FIUME

S. Benedetto

P.V. FORTI

V. FOSCOLO

VIA DANTE

VIA ALFIERI

Palazzo Comunale

V. MAZZINI

VIA ANICIA

V. PULZELLE

V. CASCI

Chiesa della Misericordia

V. MARCONI

Monte di Pietà

PIAZZA S. BENEDETTO

S. Lorenzo

V. TORRE

V. MATTIOLI

P. GARIBALDI

VIA C. BATTISTI

S. BENEDETTO

P.ZA VERDI

P. C. CARIGNANO

Palazzo Accica

VIA CAVOUR

V. ORTI

V. BENGA

V. RENZI

S. Francesco

V. STAMPERIA

Duomo

VIA ANICIA

V. LEGNANO

La Castellina (Museo Civico Diocesano)

VIA SOLFERINO

V. S. MARTINO

VIA S. MARTINO

VIA S. MARTINO

0 — 100 yds
0 — 100 metres

Forca Canapine

✩✩ *Canapine*, ☎ 0743 823005; fax 0743 823006, a typical mountain hotel, with restaurant. Mountain refuge: *Rifugio delle Guide*, ☎ 0368 646189, in a pleasant little chalet a little way off the road.

On the road between Norcia and Castelluccio, just below the summit, *Rifugio Perugia*, ☎ 0743 823015, in another pleasant modernised building.

Castelluccio *Guerrin Meschino*, ☎ 0743 821125, *agriturismo* accommoda-

tion open all year. Opened in 1997 it has five very simple but pleasant rooms (most of them only with skylights), on the outskirts of the village, with a good little restaurant run by the same family who live on the first floor. ✩ *Sibilla*, on the road at the entrance to the village, with a restaurant.

Campsite

✩✩ *Il Collaccio*, ☎ 0743 939084, in the Val Castoriana near Preci at Castelvecchio.

Restaurants

There are numerous good restaurants in Norcia, including ££ *Granaro del Monte* (formerly *Grotta Azzurra*, see above), and *Dal Francese*, 16 Via Riguardati. For restaurants in the environs, see the hotels above.

Picnics

There are good places to picnic outside the walls, and beautiful countryside on the roads to Preci, Castelluccio and Cascia.

Pasticceria at 13 Corso Sertorio.

Local honey is sold at *Il Massaro*, 26 Via Roma.

Market day is on Thursday.

Annual festival

Good Friday procession. Since 1975 an exhibition has been held of modern graphic art in the summer, in aid of a local restoration project.

History

On a site occupied in prehistoric times, Norcia came under Roman influence from 290 BC and was called *frigida Nursia* by Virgil. It was the birthplace of St Benedict (480–550) and his twin sister St Scolastica. It was a powerful free commune in the 13C–15C. The first public service of steam carriages in Italy was inaugurated from Spoleto to Norcia in 1926. The town has suffered from terrible earthquakes throughout its history, particularly in 1703, 1730, 1859, and most recently, in 1979.

Major construction work is in progress (using special funds allocated to the town in preparation for the Millennium) outside Porta Romana (to provide a huge new local museum building and reception centre, mostly underground), and a new road and car-park are being built outside the walls on the south-eastern side of the town. It is not clear why this is necessary and it is to be hoped that this will not damage the peace and appearance of this lovely little town.

The main entrance to the town is through the impressive 19C **Porta Romana** which leads into Corso Sertorio, opened at the end of the 19C. It leads to the charming **Piazza San Benedetto**, centre of the town, surrounded by handsome buildings. It has an attractive circular pavement with a monument to St Benedict (1880). The **Basilica of San Benedetto** (closed for major restoration work being carried out through special funding for the Millennium) has a fine 14C **façade** with statues of Sts Benedict and Scholastica in two tabernacles, and in the lunette above the portal a good relief of the *Madonna and Child with two angels.* On the right side is a portico, added c 1570, beneath which are interesting old stone measures for corn. Beyond the campanile of 1388 (restored in 1635) is a little tabernacle with a 15C fresco of the *Madonna and Child*.

The **interior** was remodelled in the 18C. On the left of the entrance is a 16C fresco of the *Madonna with Sts Barbara and Michael Archangel*. On the second north altar is the *Resurrection of Lazarus*, by the local painter Michelangelo Carducci (1560). In the north transept is Filippo Napoletano's *St Benedict and Totila* (1621). In the apse is a 16C wooden Crucifix and choir stalls by local craftsmen (1515). In the south transept is Vincenzo Manenti's *Madonna and St Scolastica and other saints*. Off the south side, stairs descend to the crypt where there are remains of a late Roman house.

Norcini and the curing of pork

Pork is the basis of the local cuisine, and in the Middle Ages herds of pigs fed off the acorns in the oak woods which used to cover the surrounding hills. The inhabitants of Norcia have been known for centuries for their traditional skill in the butchering and curing of pork. It is said that before the surgeons of Preci became famous in the 14C they first practised their skills on swine. In Perugia on the Romanesque Fontana Maggiore the butchering of a pig is shown as the *Labour of the Month* of December.

Up until the last war the *Norcini* used to emigrate for the winter months to other parts of Italy, particularly Tuscany and Lazio, where they were employed on pig farms. Some of them (notably those from the village of Todiano) settled in Rome and towns in Tuscany and started up successful food businesses. In Florence the Spedale di San Giovanni Decollato in Via San Gallo was founded in 1317 to provide medical assistance and care for the *Norcini* staying in the city (it was suppressed only in 1751). Numerous Florentine works of art were brought back to Todiano and Abeto by their inhabitants who had emigrated temporarily to Florence as pork butchers. In the early 17C the *Norcini* of Rome had their own church in Via Torre Argentina. Pork butchers all over Italy came to be known as 'Norcini' and grocery shops selling ham and salami are still called 'Norcineria' in some Italian towns. The cured pork of Norcia retains its fame for its high quality. Excellent salami and hams are sold at *Fratelli Ansuini*, 105 Via Anicia (corner of Via Roma) and numerous other shops all over the town.

The delightful **Palazzo Comunale** has a portico (1492) on the ground floor and a handsome enclosed loggia above (rebuilt in 1876 by Domenico Mollaioli). Steps (flanked by two lions, also by Mollaioli) lead up to the main portal (late 16C) at the base of the bell-tower (1703). In the 18C **Cappella dei Priori** (closed for restoration) is a reliquary of St Benedict in gilded silver by the local goldsmith Giovanni di Giovanni di Antonio (1450).

Opposite is the handsome fortified palace, with four angle towers, called **La Castellina**, commissioned from Vignola by Julius III in 1554. Outside are two lions (from San Benedetto). In the courtyard are Roman fragments of statues and inscriptions.

On the upper floor (reconstructed in 1779) the **Museo Civico Diocesano** (open 10.00–12.30, 15.30–18.30 except Mon; ☎ 0743 817209) was reopened in a temporary arrangement in 1996 with restored works (others will be housed here after their restoration). The rooms, some with pretty windows, have good views over the piazza.

In room 1 is a gilded ciborium (16C–17C) and a 15C ballot box decorated with a painting of *Sts Benedict and Scholastica*. Room 2 displays a very fine painted Cross dating from the late 12C or early 13C. Although in very poor condition it has an unusual *Ascension* in the cimasa at the top and two *Marys* on either side of *Christ* (there were originally four). The ropes have been installed to help the survival of the Cross in case of an earthquake. In room 3 is a very beautiful *Deposition* group of five life-size wooden statues dating from the late 13C, and a very ruined *Madonna and Child* in stone. Room 4 displays four more high reliefs of the *Madonna enthroned with the Child*, three dating from the 13C and one, in polychrome wood, from Serravalle, dating from the 14C. Also here is a beautiful painted Cross signed by 'Petrus pictor' and thought to be dated 1241. The **Salone**, with a panelled wood ceiling displays paintings of the *Madonna* by the Sparapane, and Antonio da Faenza (in a lovely frame); a good 15C wooden statue of *St Giuliana*; a 15C Sienese painting of *St Francis in glory* (also attributed to Francesco Botticini); a *Risen Christ* by Nicola da Siena (c 1460); and a 16C polychrome wood statue of *St Sebastian*.

In room 6 are two large altarpieces by Durante Alberti and Feliciano Trapassi, and a 16C cassone. Room 7 displays stone sculptures (1469; restored in 1986) by Giovanni Dalmata from the altar known as the *Madonna della Palla* in the church of San Giovanni, including a relief of the *Madonna and Child* and two statues of *St John the Evangelist* and *St John the Baptist*. Also here is a 16C stone German *Pietà*. The last room displays two terracotta statues (partly enamelled and glazed) of the *Annunciation* by Luca Della Robbia the Younger (1475–1548).

In the **loggia** detached frescoes are displayed, and more rooms on this floor are used for temporary exhibitions of interesting material from the important historic city archives.

Beside the Castellina, just off the piazza, is the **Duomo** (Santa Maria Argentea), built in 1560 by Lombard artists working with Vignola. The two statues in niches date from 1935, and the campanile was rebuilt in 1869. The **interior** was designed c 1755 by Cesare Maggi. **South side**. The first altar contains Giuseppe Paladini's *St Vincent Ferrer* (1756); the second altar Pomarancio's *Madonna and saints*. On the third pilaster is a bust of Pius VII (1825), opposite one of the present Pope (1980). At the end of the north aisle is the **Cappella della Madonna della Misericordia**. Surrounded by a beautiful altar in coloured marbles and intarsia attributed to Francesco Duquesnoy (1640–41) is a charming early 16C fresco fragment detached from a miraculous shrine. It shows the *Madonna between St Scholastica and St Benedict* (who is holding a representation of the town of Norcia). On the first altar in the north aisle there is a wooden *Crucifix* of 1494 by Giovanni Tedesco. The organ dates from the 18C.

A road on the left side of the Duomo leads to **San Lorenzo**, an early Christian church rebuilt in the Middle Ages. It has interesting Roman fragments, with inscriptions, low down on its outer wall at the east end. The interior, with a wooden ceiling and stalls, has been restored by the local inhabitants, but is usually locked. From Piazza San Benedetto, Via Battisti leads past **San Francesco** (covered for restoration) a fine 14C Gothic church with a portal and rose window. It contains early 16C frescoes, and the large painting of the *Coronation of the Virgin* by Jacopo Siculo (1541) from the Sala del Consiglio in Palazzo Comunale is also to be kept here after its restoration.

Also in Via Battista is a building (now a restaurant) which, from the 16C onwards, housed the **Monte di Pietà** (public pawn shop), one of the earliest institutions of its kind in Umbria (founded in 1466). The portal, with the date 1585, records the Monte Frumentario, a similar institution founded in 1490, which lent grain on security to those in need, and also served as a reserve grain store in times of famine.

Across Piazza Garibaldi, with a round fountain, is the **Chiesa della Misericordia** with an 18C façade. At no. 12 Via Cavour is Palazzo Accica with another 18C façade.

From Piazza Garibaldi Via Marconi leads across Corso Sertorio, the main street of the town, to Piazza Vittorio Veneto. Here the **Teatro Civico**, on the site of an 18C theatre, was rebuilt by Domenico Mollaioli in 1876. Destroyed by fire in 1952 it has been reconstructed.

Via Colombo leads out of Piazza Vittorio Veneto past the **Monastery of the Clarisse** (Santa Maria della Pace) which comprises two fine palaces, one of which is being restored. Via Anicia continues up left to the church of **Sant'Agostino** with a 14C portal and fresco in the lunette. It contains good early 16C frescoes and the wooden altars, organ and cantoria date from the 17C. The 17C altarpieces include a *Pietà with saints* by Gaspare Celio in the apse, and a *Madonna and Child with Saints* by Anastagio Fontebuoni (in very poor condition). In a little niche in the apse is a charming fresco fragment.

Palazzo Bucchi-Corazzini dates from the 17C. Nearby Via Amadio leads under an arch to the church of **San Filippo** (or the **Addolorata**) which has a 19C façade (with statues from 1935). The charming white and gold oval interior decorated with stuccoes has been restored. Next door is the **Palazzo Cavalieri di Malta** with a private local ethnographical museum (open at weekends). Nearby a passageway incorporates Roman masonry, and near **Porta Massari** are the remains of a **Roman cryptoporticus** (for admission enquire at the comune).

In Via Manzoni is **Santa Caterina** (closed) with its campanile set into the walls. It has a 16C fresco of the *Coronation of the Virgin*. Beyond Sant'Agostino, is **Palazzo Colizzi** (or Mannocchi) with a fine portal and windows of 1755, on the corner of Via Umberto, once the main street of the town. It leads left past the restored Palazzo Cipriani with a rose coloured intonaco (18C–19C) to the **'Tempietto'**, on a street corner, a very unusual edifice built by a local stonemason in 1354 (and restored in 1975). It is a large tabernacle with classical elements and is thought to have been erected in connection with a Holy Week procession. It has delicate little reliefs in dark stone depicting animals and birds.

Beyond is Piazza Carlo Alberto with a pretty fountain, just outside of which is the church of **San Giovanni** (closed since the 1960s), with its square campanile built into the walls. It has a fine wooden ceiling (1713), and a fresco of the

Madonna and Child with Sts Benedict and Scholastica (1520). The altar of the *Madonna della Palla* was erected in 1469 by Giovanni Dalmata (restored in 1986). He carved the frame, with the roundels of the *Annunciation* (other carvings by him from the altar are now in the Museo Civico Diocesano), which encloses a venerated 15C painting of the *Madonna and Child* attributed to Giovanni Sparapane, around which were added stucco decoration in the late 16C and small paintings in the 17C.

Via delle Vergine leads up to the huge **Monastero della Pace** built behind a high wall in 1507, and abandoned after the earthquake of 1859 (and further ruined in 1979, although a small part of it has recently been restored). Nearby, in Via delle Vergine, against the walls, is the monastery and church of **Sant' Antonio Abate** with a conspicuous 18C campanile, where 14 Benedictine nuns live (and run a guesthouse). They also sell honey. Beyond a walled garden is the closed church of the **Crocifisso** with a façade of 1747.

In front of the façade Via Anicia leads back down towards the centre past the **Oratorio di Sant'Agostinuccio** (key at no. 18 Via Anicia), the oratory of a local confraternity which has an early 17C interior with very fine woodwork by local craftsmen, including the delightful panelled ceiling (restored in 1981), with five painted and gilded statues of saints *Scholastica*, *Benedict*, *Augustine* and *Chiara of Montefalco*, on either side of the *Madonna Assunta*, and the stalls which line the entire oratory. The high altar and the sacristy are also interesting. Near Piazza Palatina, with a fountain and trees, is the church of the **Madonna degli Angeli** (also closed) with more good stalls.

The 14C **walls** preserve numerous gateways, and are well worth exploring. Outside Porta Palatina is a medieval public fountain.

BEYOND NORCIA

In the lovely valley at the foot of the walls south-west of the town is an area of great interest and natural beauty known as the **Marcite**, which extends for some 100ha nearly as far as Serravalle. The River Sordo, and numerous springs and streams here were for centuries regulated by a complicated series of dams and locks to provide abundant irrigation to the meadows which were used exclusively to provide a maximum yield of fodder. Because of the optimum conditions and abundance of water the crop in the marshes could be harvested up to seven or eight times a year (but due to the marshy terraine this could only be done by hand). It is thought this system of agriculture was introduced by Benedictine monks. Seven water-mills also operated here, three of which have recently been bought by the local branch of the Comunità Montana, and one of them has been carefully restored. The mill is again in working order, next to the simple house where the miller lived. There are plans to reclaim this area and open a small museum here and protect the flora and fauna (the streams abound in trout).

Further up the valley, beyond the hamlet of **Serravalle** in the narrow gorge of the River Corno (where the ugly cement basins of a trout farm are conspicuous), is the ruined village of **Biselli** abandoned after the earthquake of 1979. The church of San Leonardo here has been vandalised but the early 16C frescoes, some of them attributed to Francesco Sparapane, are to be restored. Above, the tall tower of the castle survives.

The main road between Cascia and Norcia follows a beautiful uninhabited and wooded valley. In the peaceful little village of **Logna**, reached by a byroad, the exterior of the 15C–17C parish church of San Giovenale is being restored after damage in 1997. The pretty loggia has remains of frescoes, and the interior (enquire locally for the key) has more 16C votive frescoes and a very well-preserved polychrome wooden statue of the *Madonna and Child* (16C or earlier). The painting of the *Madonna of Loreto with Sts Paul and Francis* is by Francesco Vanni. The church also has a charming high altar, a number of devotional statues, a wall tabernacle preserving its original door, and an old font.

South of Norcia, the road passes some small factories before reaching the cemetery surrounded by trees, 3km from the town, next to which is the church of **Santa Scolastica**. After damage in 1997 it is officially closed, but the custodian of the cemetery has the key. On the site of a very early church the present building dates from the 17C–18C. The ceiling is in urgent need of restoration. During restoration work in 1978 an interesting fresco cycle with scenes from the *life of St Benedict* was discovered beneath the whitewash. This dates from the late 14C and early 15C.

The straight road continues across the beautiful plain called the **Piano di Santa Scolastica** to the village of **Savelli**. The road then begins to climb through woods and a byroad is signposted (left) to the ugly little modern hamlet of **Castel Santa Maria**, built after the 1979 earthquake (the ruins of the former village were razed to the ground by bulldozers in 1994). Below it, by an abandoned house, is the site of the **Madonna della Neve**. This beautiful Renaissance octagonal church (1565–71), built by Lombard masters strongly influenced by Bramante, was ruined in 1979 (the most important building to be destroyed in that earthquake). A concrete band inserted into the drum during restoration work shortly before 1979 may have caused its destruction. Although only two walls remained standing, it has been partly 'restored' in questionable taste, enclosing the mediocre 16C frescoes behind glass.

The Valle Castoriana

The Valle Castoriana is a lovely solitary valley north of Norcia with interesting churches and small villages, nearly all of which were damaged in the earthquake of 1979, and there were bad tremors again here in 1997. The approach road leads uphill to the **Forca d'Ancarano** (1008m) in pine forests, before descending into the valley.

On the right of the road (signposted) is the church of **Santa Maria Bianca** (restored in 1994; for the key ask at the house in front). It has a charming 15C loggia, with primitive capitals, along the south side, and a 16C portico at the west end, and an unusual campanile. On the left of the portal are very worn frescoes (now almost invisible) in an edicola by a follower of Lo Spagna. The **interior** has a row of fine columns and numerous 15C votive frescoes on the south wall. A pretty altar surrounds the *Madonna Bianca*, a high relief attributed to the Florentine artist Francesco di Simone Ferrucci (1511), with two angels painted on the doors. Over the high altar is a wooden Crucifix, and on another attractive side altar are devotional stucco statues of *Sts Roch and Sebastian* dating from the 16C. The church also has a lovely old pavement, font and stoup.

A short distance away is the parish church of San Benedetto (closed since damage in 1997) with a *Madonna of the Rosary* by Vincenzo Manenti.

At **Ancarano** a road is signposted (right) for **Capo del Colle** (850m) with the 15C church of Sant'Antonio Abate, and high above, remains of the 14C Castelfranco.

Another road right (signposted Sant'Andrea) leads up to the picturesque hamlet of **Campi Alto** or **Campi Vecchio**, much of which has been carefully restored since 1979. It has 15 inhabitants. Conspicuous from the plain below is the delightful portico, with its well proportioned columns and arches, of the church of **Sant'Andrea**. On the façade, asymmetrically placed, is a Gothic portal with two delightful lions. The square campanile has been rebuilt. The charming interior (key at no. 15 Via Entedia) is filled with a medley of works, and numerous small devotional paintings and ex votoes around the 16C gilded wooden altars. It has an attractive floor and a particularly graceful 16C font. Below the church, by the old arched entrance gate, is a public wall fountain beside a circular pavement. Higher up the hill is another church (closed indefinitely) with a bell-cote, and 15C frescoes in the nave by the Sparapane. Still higher the tower of an old ruined castle can be seen.

The main road continues through the lower hamlet of Campi and beyond it, on the right of the road beside the cemetery, is the church of **San Salvatore** with a delightful primitive low **façade**. Above two portals are two rose windows on slightly different levels, and the porch is supported by one column. The interesting interior (ask for the key in Campi Basso) contains frescoes by Giovanni and Antonio Sparapane and Nicola da Siena and a font for total immersion.

The picturesque villages of **Todiano** and **Abeto** in the lovely **Valle Oblita** to the west, have had close connections with Tuscany (particularly Livorno, Pisa and Florence) over the centuries since many of the inhabitants worked in Tuscany during the winter months as *norcini* (butchers skilled in the preparation of pork), some of whom settled there permanently and opened butchers' shops (see p. 207). The Florentine works of art in their churches have mostly, however, been removed for safekeeping (see p. 186). Nowadays these two villages only come to life in the summer months when the owners of many of the houses, who live most of the time in Tuscany or Rome, come here for their holidays. Other houses are awaiting internal restoration after the 1997 earthquake.

Outside **Todiano** which now has only seven permanent residents, is an old public font. The village is preceded by a gate with a Gothic arch, just inside which is the parish church which owns a *Crucifix between two angels*, and *St Bartholomew, John the Baptist and Mary Magdalene*, signed and dated 1623 by Francesco Furini, and a collection of 15C Crosses, 17C copes and chasubles and 18C silver, all of which show Florentine influence. At the top of the village is the clock-tower and a pretty wall fountain.

Abeto, now with only 18 residents, has an attractive fountain dating from 1884, and some handsome palazzi, beside the steps (decorated with a Roman altar) which lead up to the impressive church of San Martino, rebuilt in the 18C (locked). It owns an *Annunciation* signed and dated 1603 by Pompeo Caccini, and a *Madonna of the Rosary* signed and dated 1641 by Matteo Rosselli. The paved byroad continues through the village to descend through beautiful country-side and rejoin the main road between Norcia and Preci below the Forca d'Ancarano (see above).

The main road continues towards Preci through the sparsely populated green valley. It winds through **Piedivalle** on the river, just beyond which (right; signposted) is the former **Abbey of Sant'Eutizio** (being restored in 1998), in a little side valley, just off the road, opposite its village. St Gregory the Great refers to the hermits St Spes and St Eutizio who lived in grottoes here in the 5C when they were visited by St Benedict. The Benedictine monastery was particularly important in the 12C–14C. Giacomo Crescenzi, friend of St Philip Neri, took a special interest in the monastery in the late 16C, but the decorations of that date in the church were eliminated in 1956.

Beside the entrance is the pentagonal east end of the **church** which was added in the 14C. The façade has a rose window (1236) with symbols of the Evangelists, and beside it, built on the top of an outcrop of rock is the 17C campanile.

The beautiful **interior** (1190) has a single nave with a raised and vaulted apse. On the high altar is a painted Crucifix by Nicola da Siena (c 1460). Behind the altar is an unusual funerary monument to St Eutizio, a finely carved work of 1514 attributed to Rocco da Vicenza. The stalls are by Antonio Seneca (1516). A little room off the south side, used as a sacristy, has interesting furniture, paintings and a German *Pietà*. The ancient **crypt** has two huge sandstone columns. An archway leads into the former **abbey** with good two-light windows, and a fountain in the courtyard from which steps lead up to the grottoes in the rock face. The abbey is being restored as a hospice for pilgrims in preparation for Holy Year 2000.

Numerous poplar trees grow along the river valley near **Preci**, the old hamlet of which is high up above the left of the road. It was badly damaged in 1979 and again in 1998, and most of the buildings are inaccessible. It was famous from the 14C to the 17C for its school of surgeons, who attended patients as illustrious as Sixtus V, Elizabeth I of England, the Sultan Mehjemed and the empress Eleonora Gonzaga. Two roads continue from here to join N209 in the Valnerina (see p. 215), on the border with the Marche close to Visso.

The Piano Grande and Castelluccio

This area lies within the south-eastern part of the **Parco Nazionale dei Monti Sibillini** constituted in 1988–93, most of which lies in the provinces of Ascoli Piceno and Macerata in the Marche. It has an extension of some 70,000ha, and is a protected mountainous area in the heart of the central Apennines of great natural beauty and interest for its flora and fauna. Its highest mountain is Monte Vettore (2476m). There are signs that steps are being taken to make it more accessible for hikers and visitors. The main park office is at Visso in the province of Macerata in the Marche, ☎ 0737 972711. The information offices are called *Case del Parco*, and there is one at Norcia, 22 Via Solferino, ☎ 0743 817090 and another at Preci, Via Santa Caterina, ☎ 0743 99145. The best map available is the one published by the Club Alpino Italiano.

From Norcia a well-engineered road, with magnificent views back down to the plain of Norcia all the way up, leads up through woods towards Forca Canapine, Castelluccio and the Monti Sibillini reaching a height of 1500m. Just below the summit a road bears right for **Forca Canapine** (1541m), a small group of holiday villas, near skiing facilities, with a refuge and hotel. It is on the border with the Marche, and there is a wonderful panoramic view from the pass (there is now a road tunnel under the mountains).

Castelluccuio

A short way after the Forca Canapine turn the Castelluccio road reaches the pass at 1521m from which there is an extraordinary view of the great **Piano Grande**, or **Piani di Castelluccio**, a remarkable deserted upland plain beneath Monte Vettore (2478m), a huge carsic basin which occupies the site of a glacial lake, one of the most beautiful spots in central Italy. The scenery is quite remarkable: surrounded on all sides by bare hills, the basin is filled with well-watered pastureland. In late May and June the basin is covered with wild flowers, of great botanic interest. Livestock are grazed here. The migratory birds which can sometimes be seen include a plover called a dotterel which nests in the Arctic tundra. At the opposite end of the valley the hill village of Castelluccio is visible, the only sign of habitation for miles around.

The road descends to the floor of the valley and leads straight across it for **Castelluccio** (1452m), a very untidy village, with a hotel and agriturist accommodation. It is visited by hikers, hang-gliders, and by cross-country skiiers in winter. It has a centrally planned parish church (recalling the Madonna della Neve, see above) which contains a wooden statue of the *Madonna* (c 1530).

The Visso road continues beyond Castelluccio to the Pian Perduto, another upland basin on the border with the Marche.

Lentils

Fields on the plain at the foot of the hills are cultivated with lentils, for which the area is famous throughout Italy. The crop is planted as soon as the snow melts, usually in March, and has bright yellow flowers in June. It is harvested at the end of July or early August. The characteristic lentils of this area are very small and each bean differs slightly in colour. They are grown without the help of chemical fertilizers, and the success of the crop depends entirely on the weather conditions. The plants, which grow to a height of about 30cm, were picked by hand up until the 1950s (when women would walk here from neighbouring villages for the harvest). Lentils are recognised as a very nutritious healthy food (rich in iron), and are usually cooked with celery.

THE VALNERINA

This chapter covers a beautiful remote part of Umbria at its south-east corner. The little village of Vallo di Nera is particularly attractive, and the lovely Romanesque church of San Felice di Narco has recently been restored. There is another fine church at Ponte. Numerous earthquakes over the centuries have shaken the towns and villages in this valley, but they have always been carefully reconstructed and well restored. Work is still in progress in numerous localities to repair the damage wrought in 1979 and 1997. Nearly all the monuments of interest are well signposted, but many churches in the more remote villages are kept locked for safety (the key can sometimes be found by asking locally; otherwise they are open only for services).

Practical information

Information office
IAT di Cascia, ☎ 0743 71401.

Getting there
By road
From the north and Perugia, the Valnerina (traversed by N209) is best reached by the Norcia road from Foligno (described on p. 156), but it can also be approached from Terni (see p. 268). There is also a fine road across the hills from Spoleto which reaches the Valnerina near Vallo di Nera (a tunnel under the hills opened in 1998 which shortens this route by many kilometres).

Hotel
Scheggino
☆☆ *Del Ponte*, ☎ 0743 61253, fax 0743 61131, with a good restaurant.

Campsite
☆☆ *Valnerina* at Valcasana, ☎ 0743 61115.

Restaurant
Sant'Anatolia di Narco
£ *Da Franchina Ripanti*, ☎ 0743 61136.

This is excellent walking country: information with printed guide and map from the IAT office in Cascia.

Sant'Anatolia di Narco is in the centre of the Valnerina. Tucked in amongst the narrow streets is the church of **Sant'Anatolia**, recently restored and usually kept open (or ask for the key at the house opposite Palazzo Angeli Bufalini). It has a pretty altar in pietre dure, worn frescoes, a 16C wooden Crucfix and a charming rococo gilded frame with cherubims in the south transept. A narrow street leads down from the church through a 13C archway of the former Palazzo Comunale (with a little relief of a knight on horseback on its outer face) and out through the Porta Castello beside the clock tower. Here is the church of **Santa Maria delle Grazie**, which has a pretty exterior (1572–75). In the interior (closed after structural damage in 1997; but the key is kept in the house near Sant'Anatolia, see above) is a charming 15C fresco of the *Madonna with the standing Child blessing and Saints* by the Maestro di Eggi on the east wall, surrounded by later frescoes by Pier Matteo Piergili who also frescoed the vault.

On the floor of the valley (signposted along a white road off the main road) is the delightful 12C church of **San Felice di Narco**. A legend relates that Mauro, a holy man given to prayer, emigrated to Italy from Palestine at the time of Theodoric. When he settled with his son Felice in this valley, the inhabitants asked him to liberate them from a dangerous dragon. With the help of God, Felice was able to kill the dragon, and he went on to perform other miracles in the district and died here in 535. Mauro built an oratory over Felice's grave and named the nearby castle after him, and founded a Benedictine monastery here.

The lovely **façade** (recently restored) has a beautiful rose window surrounded by symbols of the Evangelists, beneath which is a frieze depicting the *Legend of Mauro and his son Felice*. It shows the fearsome dragon beside his cave, with an angel helping Felice to chop off his head. To the right is Mauro in prayer beside an angel protecting his son. The last scene shows Felice beneath a canopy bringing back to life the son of a widow. In the tympanum is the *Lamb of God*.

The beautiful **interior** (key at 34 Via Orichelle in the village above) has massive red and white paving stones. The raised sanctuary is flanked by two transennae, with damaged Cosmati work. On the left wall of the nave is an interesting 15C fresco of the *Adoration of the Magi* (among the elongated figures is that of a falconer). In the apse is an early 15C fresco of the *Redeemer*. The crypt preserves an ancient little sarcophagus, complete with its lid, supposed to contain the remains of Sts Mauro and Felice. The former abbey buildings next door are being restored for the Millennium. Nearby is a medieval fountain and a small chapel (the former pieve di Santa Maria di Narco), near a bridge over the Nera.

The picturesque little medieval village of **Castel San Felice** (or San Felice di Narco) is on a small hill in the middle of the valley. It has stepped streets and has been restored since 1979.

North of Castel San Felice, also on a little hill, is **Vallo di Nera**, a carefully restored village, particularly picturesque, with attractive roofs. The lower church of **Santa Maria** (if closed ring at no. 9) contains well-preserved frescoes in the sanctuary by Cola di Pietro da Camerino and Francesco di Antonio (1383). The scenes include *St Francis preaching to the birds*, the *Flagellation of Christ*, the *Crucifixion* flanked by five saints, the *Nativity*, *Adoration of the Magi* and *Annunciation*, and the *Dormition* and *Assumption of the Virgin*, the *Madonna enthroned with saints*, and the *Flight into Egypt*. On the walls of the nave are numerous other votive frescoes, including a charming frieze of pigs (the symbol of St Anthony Abbot) and an elegant female figure.

Lovely old red and white marble steps lead up past the impressive side of the church (keep left) and the arches of Palazzo Comunale to the 14C church of **San Giovanni Battista** at the top of the town (closed after damage in 1997; but the key is kept at the house next door), with apse frescoes by Jacopo Siculo (1536). Outside is a well, and behind the apse a barrel-vaulted chapel.

From Piedipaterno a winding road (N395) leads across hills to Spoleto (see p. 193), replaced in 1998 by a new road and tunnel.

Further north at a road junction where several valleys meet is **Borgo Cerreto**, which has a shop selling good salami and cheese produced locally. A road (signposted) leads across the river to the church of **San Lorenzo** with a 14C portal. The rose window has been removed since the earthquake and the interior, with

Truffles

This is an area where numerous black truffles are found, particularly around Sant'Anatolia di Narco and Scheggino. These rare tubers grow wild and can be found between 20 and 50cm beneath the ground around the roots of trees, usually oak or beech. They are famous for their penetrating scent and very unusual taste. Despite their unappetising appearance, truffles have been considered an exotic delicacy since Greek and Roman times.

The white truffle (*tuber magnatum Pico*) which grows in Italy, is found mostly in Piedmont, but also sometimes in Umbria in October–December, and can cost up to 3,000,000 lire a kilo. The only black truffle of high quality (*tuber melanosporum Vittadini*) is the kind found in the Valnerina and near Norcia and Spoleto, and at Périgord in France. It matures from late November to early March and usually costs around 1,400,000 lire a kilo (all the other types of black truffle are much less highly prized and cost from 100,000–300,000 lire a kilo).

A truffle usually weighs between 30 and 100 grammes, but the largest can weigh up to one kilo. For centuries their origins were a mystery: Aristotle's pupil Theophrastus mentions their excellent taste but, observing their lack of roots, he came to the conclusion that they were formed by a combination of rain and thunder. The first scientific study of them was made in 1831 by Carlo Vittadini, and although they are a type of fungi, they are still not precisely understood by botanists. They are known to have a high protein content.

Nowadays there are plans to protect the rare black truffle exclusive to this area, and, although truffles cannot be cultivated, experimental reafforestation is taking place and reserves established in an attempt to augment the number of truffles growing in the wild. Unfortunately, in the past few years it has become easier to produce false synthetic truffle aromas, and the fame of the exceptional quality of this black truffle has been damaged by the sale in the region of inferior quality black truffles imported from North Africa and southern China.

Truffle-hunters usually work on their own with the help only of a trowel, and sometimes a dog (usually a pointer or a setter) trained to detect their odour below the surface of the earth. Up until a short time ago truffles were often sold house to house. In the past pigs were used to help search for them, but are now rarely used as they also find them delicious and tend to gobble them up as soon as they find them!

Truffles have a particularly strong scent only when they are fully mature, and once extracted from the ground they lose their taste and perfume after a few days. They can be preserved in oil, but the fresh black truffle is now an essential part of the cuisine of Umbria and is used in countless different ways: as a spread on *crostini* as an hors-d'oeuvre, as a sauce for pasta, or in risotto, as well as a flavouring for meat, game, fish and egg dishes. An annual international gastronomic festival has been held in Norcia in February since 1951 in honour of the black truffle of Norcia and the Valnerina, and there is also a truffle festival at Città di Castello on the second weekend in November.

15C votive frescoes, has been damaged and is closed. This byroad continues up to **Ponte**, in a fine position between the valleys of the Nera and Tissino, beneath its ruined castle. There is a view of Cerreto di Spoleto (see below) across the Nera valley. It escaped much damage in the 1997 earthquake and the church of Santa Maria Assunta (1201) is open. It has an unusually tall rectangular façade with a splendid rose window above a telamone surrounded by symbols of the Evangelists. The exterior of the apse is also decorated. The beautiful **interior** (the custodian lives at the house surrounded by an iron fence in Via Nortosce, beyond the arch on the left), which was carefully restored in 1940, has a fine dome and crossing. Roman fragments include a beautiful small green granite font. The lovely old pavement was also restored in 1940 using the pretty red sandstone quarried locally. The 14C and 15C Umbrian frescoes (in poor condition) include a detached *Crucifixion*, and a fragment of the *Trinity*, unusual for its iconography. In a charming little wooden cupboard is a statue of the *Madonna and Child*, fully dressed (which has replaced a 13C polychrome wood statue stolen some years ago from the church). The fine painting of the *Deposition* dates from the 17C.

The main road continues north towards Triponzo. Just before a tunnel a byroad leads left to **Cerreto di Spoleto**, high up (558m) on a rock face above Borgo Cerreto. The piazza has a pretty fountain and lamp-posts. Next to the 15C former Palazzo Comunale, with coats of arms on its façade, is a 17C palace. Just outside the square is the church of the **Annunziata**, closed after damage in 1997. In the interior, at the west end, is an unusual octagonal font carved in local stone by Lombard sculptors in 1546. On the third right altar there is a *Madonna of the Rosary*, signed and dated 1583 by Felice Damiani. Beyond the church is the tall 15C **Torre Civica** which survived the earthquake intact.

At the other end of the piazza a road descends left past a public garden and, above (right), the church of **Santa Maria Delibera** (closed) with 16C altarpieces, beside a gate in the walls. Beyond, reached by steps right on the edge of the hill (with a view, framed by an arch, of the valley), is the 14C church of **San Giacomo** (also closed after damage in the earthquake). The interior contains important 15C frescoes (some attributed to the Maestro di Eggi). The high altarpiece of the *Visitation* is signed and dated 1573 by Camillo Angelucci.

The main road to Triponzo traverses a tunnel, outside which is a Roman inscription (signposted) recording work carried out here by the Romans. **Triponzo** has been all but abandoned since the earthquake of 1979. This road continues up the Nera valley to cross the border into the Marche and continues to Visso, a lovely little town.

Norcia (see p. 204) is reached from Triponzo, and Sellano north of Cerreto di Spoleto is described on p. 156.

South of Sant'Anatolia di Narco (see above) the Terni road descends the valley past the pretty village of **Scheggino**, below its castle. On the left bank of the Nera is the church of San Nicolò with frescoes by Lo Spagna and a *Madonna of the Rosary* signed and dated 1595 by Pierino Cesarei. The road continues through **Ceselli** which has two interesting churches and a rough road (right) leads up to the hamlet of **San Valentino** with a 13C church. Sambucheto is near the splendid abbey of San Pietro in Valle. This, together with the road from here to Terni, is described on p. 268.

Todi and Orvieto

TODI

· · · · ·

Todi is a beautiful old town (population 16,000) in a delightful position on an isolated triangular hill (410m). It retains many interesting medieval buildings and steep old streets. The surrounding countryside is particularly lovely and unspoilt. The terrain is subject to landslips and work is being carried out to shore up the hill.

Practical information

Information offices

IAT del Tuderte, 6 Piazza Umberto I, ☎ 075 8943395; Pro Loco information office, 38 Piazza del Popolo, ☎ 075 8942526.

Getting there

By rail at Ponte Rio, 2km north of Porta Perugina on the Ferrovia Centrale Umbra line from Perugia to Terni (bus in connection with trains).

By bus To Piazzale della Consolazione from Perugia (six times a day) and from Terni (six times a day). Once a day to Piazza Jacopone from Rome via Massa Martana (except Sunday) and from Orvieto.

By car Todi is about 40km south of Perugia, reached by a fast *superstrada*. The prettiest approach road (unsign-posted) from the exit north of the town is by the country road which leads right up to the **Porta Perugina**, where there is a small free **car-park**. The centre has not yet been closed to traffic (except sometimes on weekends), but it is best to park outside the walls. Other free car-parks outside **Porta Romana**, and (larger) in **Piazzale G. Fabrizio Atti** (with a minibus service to the centre). In the centre (limited space) there is a car-park with an hourly tariff in **Foro Tempio di Marte** (or Piazza del Mercato Vecchio). There are long-term plans to build a car park off Viale della Consolazione with an escalator to the Rocca.

Hotels
San Lorenzo Tre, 3 Via San Lorenzo (☎ 075 894455) is a delightful small guesthouse (classified as an 'historic residence') in the centre of the town, in an old palace which retains its elegant furnishings. Good value.

Also in the centre of the town is the much more pretentious and over-restored ✫✫✫✫ *Fonte Cesia*, 3 Via Lorenzo Leoni, off Piazza Jacopone, ☎ 075 8943737; fax 075 8944677.

On the outskirts of the town
✫✫✫✫ *Bramante*, Circonvallazione Orvietana, in a lovely old building near Santa Maria della Consolazione (☎ 075 8948381) and ✫✫✫ *Villa Luisa*, Viale A. Cortesi (outside Porta Romana), ☎ 075 8948571.

For hotels in the **environs**, see p. 227.

Restaurants
££ *Umbria*, 13 Via San Bonaventura, ☎ 075 8942390; £ *Jacopone*, 3 Piazza Jacopone, ☎ 075 8942366 and *Cavour*, 23 Corso Cavour, ☎ 075 8943730.
Pasticcerie *del Papa* and *Mazzuoli*, both off Via Mazzini.

There are pleasant places to **picnic** on the Rocca hill or outside Porta Perugina.

Market day is on Saturday below the old centre near the sports fields.

An **antiques fair** is held here around Easter.

History

Todi was founded by the Umbri, and later absorbed Etruscan influence. By 42 BC it had become the Roman colony of *Tuder*. One of the first free communes in the Middle Ages, by the early 13C when the Palazzo del Popolo was built, it was at the height of its power (with Terni and Amelia under its rule). Todi was the birthplace of Jacopo de' Benedetti (c 1230–1306), called Jacopone da Todi, poet and mystic, the reputed author of the *Stabat Mater*. In 1523 more than half the population died of the plague. In the 19C numerous unsystematic excavations took place in Todi and its surroundings; nearly all the remarkable Etruscan and Roman finds made then now belong to the Museo Archeologico in Florence or to the Villa Giulia in Rome. The famous bronze statue of Mars, dating from the beginning of the 4C BC and found here in 1835, is now in the Vatican.

The central **Piazza del Popolo**, one of the finest in Italy, is bordered by well-proportioned Gothic buildings. It is built above a series of Roman cisterns and is on

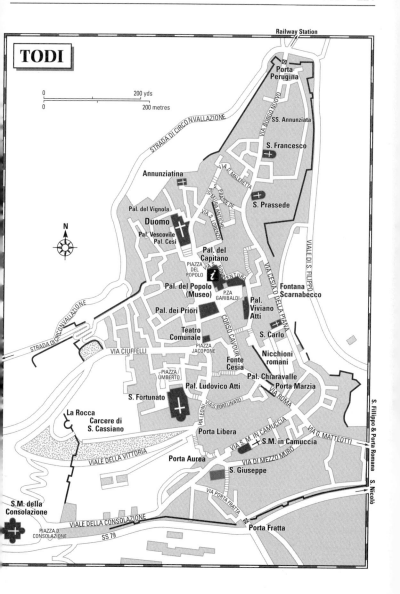

TODI

0 — 200 yds
0 — 200 metres

Railway Station

Porta
Perugia

SS. Annunziata

STRADA DI CIRCONVALLAZIONE

VIA BURGO NUOVO

S. Francesco

Annunziatina

VIA D. MALERETTA

VIA P. PRASEDE

S. Prassede

Pal. del Vignola

VIA M. DRACONTTRA

VIA S. LORENZO

Duomo

Pal. Vescovile
Pal. Cesi

N

Pal. del
Capitano

PIAZZA
DEL
POPOLO

VIALE DI S. FILIPPO

VIA S. BONAVENTURA

Pal. del Popolo
(Museo)

PZA
GARIBALDI

Fontana
Scarnabecco

VIA CESIA DELLA PIANA

Pal.
Viviano
Atti

Pal. dei Priori

CORSO CAVOUR

S. Carlo

Teatro
Comunale

PIAZZA
JACOPONE

Nicchioni
romani

STRADA DI CIRCONVALLAZIONE

VIA CIUFFELLI

PIAZZA
UMBERTO

Fonte
Cesia

Pal. Chiaravalle

Pal. Ludovico Atti

Porta Marzia

VIA ROMA

S. Fortunato

VIA LEONI

VIA S. FORTUNATO

La Rocca
Carcere di
S. Cassiano

Porta Libera

VIA S. M. IN CAMUCCIA

S.M. in Camuccia

VIA G. MATTEOTTI

S. Filippo & Porta Romana

Porta Aurea

VIA DI MEZZO MURO

S. Giuseppe

S. Nicolò

VIALE DELLA VITTORIA

VIA PORTA FRATTA

S.M. della
Consolazione

PIAZZA D
CONSOLAZIONE

VIALE DELLA CONSOLAZIONE

SS 79

Porta Fratta

the site of the Roman forum. Opposite the cathedral stands the battlemented **Palazzo dei Priori** (now used as civic offices) which dates from 1293–1337. The bronze eagle, coat of arms of the town, was put up here in 1339. Additions were made to the façade in the 16C, and the 14C tower had to be lowered for reasons of stability.

The Duomo

The Duomo (open 08.30–12.30, 14.00–17.30 or 18.30; weekdays in winter open 08.30–16.30) is reached by an imposing flight of steps (1740). The **façade** was altered in the early 16C when the three rose windows and the portal were decorated. The carved door is by Carlo Lorenti (1639; the four highest panels survive from the earlier door of 1513 by Maestro Antonio). In Via del Seminario and Via del Vescovado the fine exterior of the apse can be seen.

The lovely **interior** has superb Corinthian **capitals**, a raised presbytery and a semi-dome in the apse. On the west wall is a fresco of the *Last Judgement* (c 1596), inspired by Michelangelo's famous work, by Ferraù Fenzoni.

On the south side a pretty Gothic arcade with graceful little columns was added in the 14C as a fourth aisle. The stained glass is by 19C local craftsmen. Beneath the arcade is a detached fresco of *Mary Magdalene between two angels*, and a fragment of the *Trinity* by Lo Spagna (1525). The beautiful font dates from 1507. At the end of this aisle is an altarpiece by Giannicola di Paolo. At the end of the two main aisles are gilded wooden organs (the one on the right dates from 1765 and the one on the left from 1852).

The **high altar** has little Gothic columns (14C–15C). In the **presbytery** are carved and inlaid **stalls** by Antonio Bencivenni da Mercatello and his son Sebastiano (1521–30). A Crucifix (late 13C) hangs in the apse. On either side of the presbytery are small paintings by Lo Spagna of *Sts Peter and Paul*, and to the left is the **Cappella Cesi** built in 1605. The tombs of Angelo and Giovanni Andrea Cesi have portraits attributed to Annibale Carracci.

At the end of the north aisle steps lead down to the **Lapidary Museum and crypt** (entrance fee). Off a long corridor in little cells (which were used as tombs up until the 19C) is a charming collection of lanterns, bells and plaster reliefs, as well as a cast of the famous statuette of *Mars* now in the Vatican museums. Stairs continue down to the crypt with fine vaulting where three mutilated statue groups are exhibited. They may have belonged to a funerary monument and are attributed to the school of Giovanni Pisano.

On the left of the cathedral façade is **Palazzo Rolli** (formerly Cesi), attributed to Antonio da Sangallo the Younger (1547). Paolo Rolli (1687–1765), the translator of Milton, was born in Todi. Beyond is a portal by Vignola, at the entrance to the courtyard of Palazzo Vescovile (1593). The medieval district to the south is well worth exploring.

Museo della Città and the Pinacoteca

In Piazza del Popolo a monumental flight of steps (1267) provides an entrance to the Palazzo Comunale which occupies the Gothic **Palazzo del Popolo** (1213), one of the oldest town halls in Italy (the battlements were added in 1901), and the adjoining **Palazzo del Capitano** (c 1290) which has two orders of elegant three-light windows (those on the first floor beneath pretty foliated triangular frames).

The Museo della Città and Museo and Pinacoteca in these two palaces has recently been reopened after being closed for many years (open 10.30–13.00, 14.00–16.30, 17.00 or 18.00; closed Mon except in April, ☎ 075 8944148).

The **Museo della Città** illustrates the history of the city. Section I is dedicated to the eagle, symbol of the city since 1267. Section II has pre-Roman finds from

Palazzo del Popolo

the city and Section III Roman inscriptions. Section IV is devoted to representations of the patron saints of the city, including Fortunatus, shown in a 10C–11C marble relief found in 1993 near the church of San Fortunato, and on 14C gilded glass plaquettes. Section V illustrates the medieval city including fresco fragments and two sculpted angels from the church of San Nicolò de Criptis, a 14C processional Cross, and a 14C Umbrian linen cloth. Section VI has a small collection of 15C–17C domestic objects belonging to noble families of the town and a wooden model of Santa Maria della Consolazione thought to date from 1571. Section VII has ecclesiastical objects including a wooden and bronze Crucifix attributed to the circle of Ippolito Scalza. The last section dedicated to the Risorgimento includes the comfortable saddle made in Todi for Anita Garibaldi, when she passed through the town, heavily pregnant, in 1849.

The **Museo** has an archaeological section exhibited in two rooms with finds from tombs in the district of Todi (5C–3C BC) including red-figure Attic vases, architectural terracotta fragments, terracotta antefixes and two doves, and Roman fragments including a charming bronze weight in the shape of a pig. In the second room are votive small bronzes and bronze domestic objects. The well-labelled numismatic section has some 1475 coins dating from pre-Roman to modern times, with a particularly important collection of Republican and Imperial Roman coins. The textile section has church vestments (15C–17C). The ceramic section, with domestic pottery found in the town dating from the 8C to the 18C, is exhibited in the **Sala del Consiglio dei Priori**, frescoed from the 17C to early 20C, with portraits of illustrious citizens of Todi and a map of the territory of Todi by Pietro Paolo Sensini (1612). There is a view of San Fortunato from the windows.

The **Pinacoteca** is exhibited in a fine large hall with a wooden roof. The paintings include works by Pseudo Ambrosio di Baldese (four Saints), Lo Spagna (a fine large altarpiece of the *Coronation of the Virgin*, and Bernardino of Feltre), and a *Madonna and Child* of 1524. The 16C paintings include works by Felice Damiani and Pietro Paolo Sensini. There are also six works by Ferraù Fenzoni (including *Christ and the Virgin and souls of Purgatory*). Beyond a 15C Crucifix are works by the local artist Andrea Polinori (including a *Presentation in the Temple*) and the last section exhibits local 18C works.

San Fortunato

Via Mazzini leads out of the opposite end of the piazza past the handsome façade of the **Teatro Comunale**, a fine theatre enlarged in 1872 by Carlo Gatteschi. Beyond is **San Fortunato** (open 09.30–12.30, 15.00–17.00) in a raised position with steps above a garden laid out with box hedges at the beginning of this century (but recently altered). The unfinished **façade** (covered for restoration) was begun c 1415–58, and the campanile with its cusped top dates from 1460. The **portal** has exquisite carving with saints beneath baldacchini and curious figures entwined with leaves. On either side are statues of the *Annunciation*; the angel, with her robes flowing over her wings, is particularly fine and is attributed by some scholars to Jacopo della Quercia.

The exceptionally light **interior** is typical of German late Gothic hall churches, with all three naves of equal height, clustered pilasters and a polygonal apse. It was begun in 1291 at the east end but not completed until 1459. The attractive tiled brick floor dates from 1463. The grey stone brackets have been installed to counteract the outward lean of the pilasters. The two stoups may have belonged to an earlier church on this site. Many of the chapels have 14C–15C fresco fragments.

South aisle. In the fourth chapel is a lovely *Madonna and Child* with two angels by Masolino (restored in 1987). The late 14C frescoes in the sixth chapel include damaged fragments with scenes from the *life of St Francis*. The seventh chapel (being restored) is a fine domed Baroque work, decorated with stuccoes.

At the end of the south aisle is the **Chapel of the Sacrament**. High up on the outside is a 14C stone pulpit. The chapel has a large wooden altar (1758) and fresco fragments by Niccolò Vannucci da Todi. The 14C **high altar** has little Gothic columns (in between which figures of saints were painted in 1860). Above it is a statue of *St Fortunato* (1643). The choir stalls were carved in 1590 by Antonio Maffei.

In the **crypt** the remains of Fra Jacopone are preserved (see above) with a monument erected by Bishop Angelo Cesi (1580). North aisle. The fifth chapel contains 14C–15C fresco fragments of the *Banquet of Herod*. The third chapel (being restored), with a dome, was well decorated by the local painter Andrea Polinori (1586–1648).

Beside the church is the 16C **Palazzo Ludovico Atti**, attributed to Galeazzo Alessi, and, at the bottom of the steps, a monument to Jacopone del Todi, made of antique fragments and with a bronze statue (1930). To the right of the church is **Piazza Pignattaria** which is laid out as a garden. The entrance to the former convent of San Fortunato (now a school), with a large 15C cloister is situated here. A lane leads up from here to the top of the hill, where the large round tower of the ruined **Rocca** is surrounded by a delightful public garden with lovely views above Santa Maria della Consolazione. The so-called **Carcere di San Cassiano** is a ruined Roman cistern, later converted into a chapel.

On the left of the church of San Fortunato, **Via San Fortunato** leads down to an archway (right) on Via Lorenzo Leoni which bears right to the edge of the hill-side, just above the ruined **Porta Libera**, a gate in the inner Etruscan walls. The dome of Santa Maria della Consolazione can just be seen from here, as well as crumbling steps descending through orchards to the old borgo di Porta Fratta. The view extends to another gate, the **Porta Aurea**, in the Roman walls, near the church of Santa Maria in Camuccia (described below), and farther downhill, the **Porta Fratta**, in the third circle of walls (c 1244).

The charming old stepped Via San Fortunato continues down through an interesting medieval district to **Corso Cavour**. Here is the **Porta Marzia**, a medieval archway constructed with Roman material in the first circle of walls. It is surmounted by an elegant balcony. From here Via Roma continues down-hill and the first road on the right leads to the 13C church of **Santa Maria in Camuccia**. On either side of the door are two handsome Roman columns. Inside the precious 12C wooden statue of the seated *Madonna and Child* (the *Sedes Sapientiae*) has been restored since its theft in 1988. In the first north chapel is the font and a 15C fresco of the *Madonna and Child*. Roman remains have been found beneath the church. Just inside Porta Aurea is the church of **San Giuseppe** which contains a *Holy Family* considered to be one of the best works of Andrea Polinori (1623). Outside the gate (from which there is a fine view) Via di Mezzo Muro (left) has notable traces of the Roman walls.

Via Matteotti is a continuation of Via Roma (see above) down to the 16C **Porta Romana** (c 500m from Porta Marzia). Just inside the gate (left) is the church of **San Filippo** which contains a marble statue of *St Filippo Benizi* attributed to Paolo Naldini, or the school of Lorenzo Bernini. Opposite is the Gothic church of **San Nicolò**. Via del Anfiteatro Antico on the left passes scant remains of the **Roman amphitheatre** of Todi.

From Porta Marzia (see above) Corso Cavour leads back up to the centre. On the left (no. 58) is the 13C **Palazzo Chiaravalle**. Higher up, in front of a group of palm trees, is the **Fonte Cesia**, erected in 1606 by Bishop Angelo Cesi. On the right the stepped Via del Mercato Vecchio leads under a passageway down to **Piazza Mercato Vecchio** (or Foro Tempio di Marte) where there are four remarkable tall **Roman niches**, with semi-domes, from a Roman building. Below the piazza is the Romanesque church of **Sant'Ilario** (or San Carlo) with a charming façade and bell-cote. In the interior (usually closed) is a fresco of the *Madonna of the Misericordia* by Lo Spagna. Nearby (left) is the **Fontana Scarnabecco** (1241) which has a pretty portico.

The Corso ends in **Piazza Garibaldi** with a monument to the hero by Giuseppe Frenguelli (1890). The handsome **Palazzo Viviano Atti** (1552) is here. There is a superb view of the countryside beyond a flourishing tall cypress (supposed to have been planted in 1849 to commemorate Garibaldi's visit to Todi) and a small garden; below the centrally planned church of the Crocifisso (described below) is visible.

The northern part of the town

At the upper end of Piazza del Popolo, Via del Duomo runs alongside the flank of the Duomo past the campanile and an external flight of steps. In Via del Seminario is the 16C **Palazzo del Vignola** or Palazzo delle Arti (heavily restored after a tragic fire in 1982), named after its architect, which ingeniously fits its corner site. Beyond is the church of the **Annunziatina** (or Nunziatina), built in 1609, which contains two frescoes by Andrea Polinori. Via del Vescovado skirts the beautiful apse of the cathedral.

From Via del Duomo (see above) Via San Prassede descends past an old arch and fragments of the earliest walls built into the houses (right; plaque). Via delle Mura Antiche, a lane beneath a low arch, leads right to emerge beside the walls. Via Santa Prassede, a peaceful old street, continues right (at the end of Via della Maleretta a stretch of medieval walls may be seen) and descends steeply to the 14C church of **Santa Prassede** (if closed, ring for the priest). It contains two late 16C wooden statues, and two 17C paintings: *Mourning over the dead Christ* by Hendrick de Clerck, and *St Teresa of Avila* by Andrea Polinori.

Beyond Porta Santa Prassede is the monastery of **San Francesco**, with its arch over the street. The interior of the church was decorated in 1860 by the Agretti brothers. The 16C high altarpiece is by Livio Agresti. On the left of the altar is an interesting large 14C fresco representing an allegory of *Salvation*.

Via Borgo Nuovo continues out of the town through the double **Porta Perugina**, with its round tower in the medieval circle of walls (begun c 1244), beyond which is beautiful countryside.

Outside the walls to the south-west best reached on foot from San Fortunato along Via Ciuffelli (or from a path which descends from the Rocca), on a busy road (and beside a bus park) is the church of **Santa Maria della Consolazione** (closed 13.00–15.00), a masterpiece of the Renaissance. A domed church on a Greek-cross plan, it clearly shows the influence of Bramante. Begun in 1508 and finished in 1607, it is thought to have been built by Cola da Caprarola, and perhaps completed by Ambrogio Barocci and Francesco da Vita. In the interior the vault decoration dates from 1579–82.

Beyond Santa Maria della Consolazione, on the Orvieto road, is the church and convent of **Monte Santo** on a little

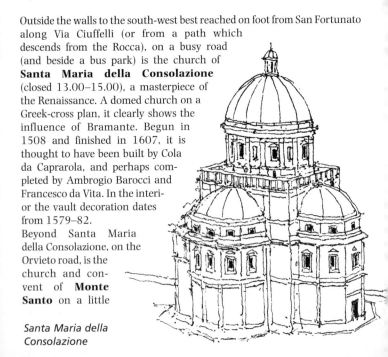

Santa Maria della Consolazione

hill and approached by an avenue. In front of the church is an ancient lime tree. Inside is a 16C fresco of the *Nativity* and a *Crucifixion* attributed to Alunno.

Outside Porta Romana (see above), reached by Viale Cortesi and (left) Viale del Crocifisso, is the Greek-cross church of **Santissimo Crocifisso** in brick and marble. It is attributed to Valentino Martelli (1591).

BEYOND TODI

There are small little-known villages in the environs of Todi, one of the most attractive of which is Collazzone. East of Todi are the pretty hills known as the Monti Martani which separate the Valle Umbra from the Tiber valley. They are particularly beautiful in autumn when the leaves of the oak trees turn red. The highest peak is Monte Martano (1094m).

Practical information

Information office
IAT del Tuderte, ☎ 075 8943395.

Hotels
Collazzone
✩✩✩ *Abbazia dei Collemedio*, at Collepepe, ☎ 075 8789352; ✩✩✩ *Relais il Canalicchio*, ☎ 075 8707325.
Montecastello di Vibio
✩✩✩ *Il Castello*, 5 Piazza Marconi, ☎ 075 8780560.
Massa Martana
✩✩✩ *Delle Terme San Faustino*, ☎ 075 8856421.

Collevalenza
Relais Todini, ☎ 075 887521, a guest-house in a lovely old building, with a swimming-pool.
Agriturist accommodation at Marsciano, Massa Martana, and near Todi, including *La Palazzetta*, with restaurant, at Izzalini-Asproli (10km outside Todi).

Restaurants
Near **San Terenziano** at Grutti: £ *Le Noci*.
Izzalini-Asproli, *La Palazzetta* (see above).

In the hills to the north of Todi is **Collazzone**, a pretty little medieval village surrounded by walls, in a splendid position amidst olive groves and oak and pine woods. The houses are well kept and the streets retain their old lamps. The buildings of interest are discreetly labelled. In the large piazza (where there is a comfortable bar) is the parish church of San Lorenzo with terracotta decoration on its neo-Gothic façade. The interior (which has been closed since the earthquake) has a wooden tabernacle with a 14C polychrome seated statue of the *Madonna and Child*.

The Corso leads through Piazza Jacopone with a portal attributed to Vignola of the former monastery of San Lorenzo (now the town hall). The coat of arms of Angelo Cesi, Bishop of Todi, was set up here in the 16C when he enlarged and restored the monastery where Jacopone da Todi had died in 1306. Further downhill is the 16C church of San Michele Archangelo (with a palace façade) and a fine 16C defensive tower in the corner of the walls, first built in the 13C, but restored in the 16C.

To the south is **San Terenziano**, a picturesque village with an old gate and the handsome Palazzo Cesi. Outside the village, beyond the playing fields, is a fine Romanesque church built of pink stone. It has been closed since the earthquake, but the crypt (entered by stairs from the outside) is open. It has interesting primitive columns, two of them made of marble, with a miscellany of capitals, and the altar is made up of Roman fragments.

Monti Martani

Massa Martana, in the wooded hilly country of the Monti Martani, east of Todi, has remains of its walls with a round tower and a fine 10C gate.

Just outside Massa Martana a secondary road winds down to the 12C church of **Sant'Illuminata** (usually locked) with frescoes of 1430. Beyond, on the opposite side of the road (unsignposted) is the abbey of **Santi Fidenzio e Terenzio**, dating from the 11C, with an interesting interior (also closed).

South of Massa Martana is **Santa Maria in Pantano**, next to the road on the site of the Roman Vicus Martis on the old Flaminia. It has a rose window in its façade and a fine apse, and beside it stands a medieval tower to which a belfry has been added. Of ancient foundation, it has interesting architectural features in the interior (key at the house on the right). A column in the sanctuary is partly made out of a huge Corinthian capital. A Roman altar serves as high altar. It has remains of primitive frescoes and Roman fragments.

Further south is the attractive walled village of **Villa San Faustino**, outside which is the 12C **Abbazia di San Faustino** (key at the house next door), with pieces of a Roman frieze on its façade. It is surrounded by interesting old buildings. The **catacombs** here were first excavated in 1940 and restored in 1997. Excavations of a small funerary basilica are in progress nearby. The catacombs, near the old Flaminia, were in use as a cemetery from the 4C to the 5C AD. They are open on Tues, Thur, Sat, and PH 09.00–13.00. Below, the factory which bottles the mineral water from the spring of San Faustino is visible.

On the road from Massa Martana to Todi is **Collevalenza** with the large Santuario dell'Amore Misericordioso by Julio Lafuente (1955, enlarged in 1965).

North of Massa Martana are **Viepri**, a lovely old group of buildings around a church in the valley, and **Montecchio** with remains of its walls.

Other villages in the eastern part of the Monti Martani are described on pp 170 and 197.

North-west of Todi is **Marsciano**, a busy little town with some remains of a feudal castle. The church has a campanile by Giovanni Santini. From here a scenic road (N317) follows a ridge of hills towards Perugia through lovely countryside. At **Cerqueto** the parish church (unsignposted) contains a fresco fragment with a very beautiful figure of *St Sebastian*, the earliest dated work of Perugino (1478).

Nearer Perugia is **San Martino in Colle**, with another church by Giovanni Santini. In a country chapel near San Martino is a *Madonna and Child* restored in 1981 and recently attributed to Pinturicchio.

Between Marsciano and Todi is **Fratta Todina** which was important in the Middle Ages when its castle was contested between Todi and Perugia; remains of its walls survive. The 16C Palazzo Vescovile was enlarged by Cardinal Giovanni

Battista Altieri in the following century (with an interesting courtyard and garden). The 19C parish church was built by Giovanni Santini.

Nearby is **Montecastello di Vibio** a medieval hill town (423m) dominating the Tiber valley. Of ancient foundation, its name is derived from the Roman family gens Vibia. In the Middle Ages it came under the dominion of Todi. Remains of its walls can be seen. In 1808 the Teatro della Concordia was built in honour of the French Revolution. This remarkable little theatre, which can seat just 99 spectators, was restored in 1993. It is open at weekends 09.30–12.00, 15.00 or 16.00–18.30 or 19.30; or by appointment, ☎ 075 8780307.

From Todi a very pretty road (N79bis) climbs over the hills to the north of Lago di Corbara with superb views across to Orvieto. Beyond **Pontecuti**, an old walled village which was almost totally destroyed in the Second World War, it climbs to a height of 637m. It then descends steeply to the Paglia bridge by Orvieto station. The Lago di Corbara and the main road between Todi and Orvieto, south of the Lago di Corbara is described on p. 244.

ORVIETO
· · · · · · · · · ·

Orvieto (population 23,600), built on a precipitous tufa crag (315m) dominating the valley, is famous for its magnificent position (it is especially well seen from the Bolsena road to the south-west). It is a city of great antiquity, with notable Etruscan remains, preserving its medieval atmosphere through its numerous narrow streets with many arches. The oldest buildings are built in a rich golden-coloured tufa. It is renowned for the beauty of its cathedral which, at the highest point of the town, stands out on the skyline.

New building has taken place around the station (Orvieto Scalo) leaving the old town and the cultivated fields beneath its rock remarkably unchanged. However, in the past few years landslips have been caused by the infiltration of water in the tufa strata which is 40–70m thick. Work has been in progress since 1980 to consolidate the rock and reconstruct the hydraulic and sewerage systems of the town, an incredibly complicated task which is nearing completion.

Because of its position close to the A1 motorway and main railway line between Florence and Rome, and its proximity to the capital, it is one of the most visited towns in Umbria and can be very crowded, especially at weekends between March and June and from September to November. It is in the centre of a famous wine-growing area and local crafts include lace-making and pottery. The hilly environs are particularly attractive with many handsome old farmhouses and very few ugly buildings.

Practical information

Information office
IAT dell'Orvietano, 24 Piazza Duomo, ☎ 0763 341772, or 0763 341991 (open every day).

Getting there
By rail At Orvieto Scalo at the bottom of the hill, on the main line from Florence to Rome (although only a few

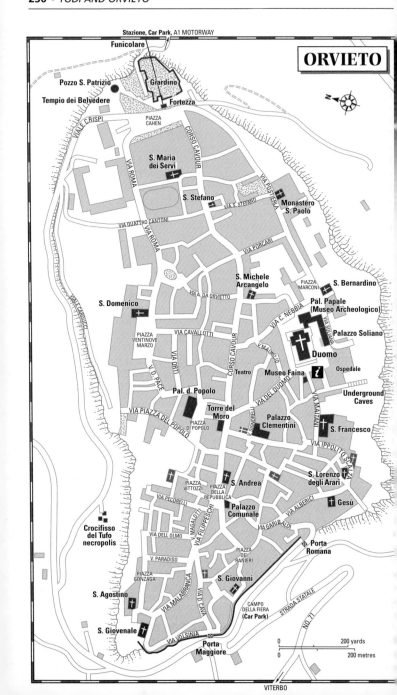

Stazione, Car Park, A1 MOTORWAY

ORVIETO

Funicolare

Pozzo S. Patrizio

Giardino

Tempio dei Belvedere

Fortezza

PIAZZA CAHEN

VIALE CRISPI

CORSO CAVOUR

VIA ROMA

S. Maria dei Servi

S. Stefano

VIA S. STEFANO

VIA POSTIERLA

Monastero S. Paolo

VIA QUATTRO CANTONI

VIA ROMA

VIA PORCARI

VALLE CARBONE

S. Michele Arcangelo

VIA A. DA ORVIETO

PIAZZA MARCONI

S. Bernardino

S. Domenico

VIA CAVALLOTTI

PIAZZA VENTINOVE MARZO

CORSO CAVOUR

VIA C. NEBBIA

Pal. Papale (Museo Archeologico)

Palazzo Soliano

VIA SOLIANA

Duomo

V. MADONNA

V. D. ORTI

VIA D. PACE

Teatro

Museo Faina

VIA DEL DUOMO

i

Ospedale

Underground Caves

Pal. d. Popolo

Torre del Moro

PIAZZA D. POPOLO

VIA PIAZZA DEL POPOLO

VIA FIORDELLI

Palazzo Clementini

VIA MALTANI

S. Francesco

VIA IPPOLITO SCALZA

S. Andrea

PIAZZA VITTOZZI

PIAZZA DELLA REPUBBLICA

VIA PECORELLI

S. Lorenzo degli Arari

VIA ALBERICI

Gesù

Palazzo Comunale

VIA MAGALOTTI

VIA FILIPPESCHI

VIA GARIBALDI

Crocifisso del Tufo necropolis

VIA DELL'OLMO

V. PARADISO

PIAZZA DEI RANIERI

Porta Romana

PIAZZA GONZAGA

S. Giovanni

VIA MALABRANCA

VIA D. CAVA

S. Agostino

CAMPO DELLA FIERA (Car Park)

STRADA STATALE

NO. 71

S. Giovenale

VIA VOLSINIA

Porta Maggiore

0   200 yards

0   200 metres

VITERBO

of the fastest trains stop here). *ATC* buses run to the railway station (except on Sundays) from Bolsena, Narni, Terni, Amelia and Todi.

By bus Services are run by *ATC*, ☎ 0763 301224, on weekdays from Todi, Narni and Terni. Services also to Civitella del Lago.

Town buses Minibus **A** (every 15 mins) from Piazza Cahen via Via Postierla to Piazza Duomo. Minibus **B** (every 20 mins) from Piazza Cahen via Piazza XXIX Marzo, Piazza della Repubblica, Via Alberici and Via Maitani to Piazza Duomo.

Funicular railway From the railway station to Piazza Cahen (in just over 2 mins) every 15 mins. Built in 1888 when it was operated by water, it was reopened (powered by electricity) in 1990. It ascends through an avenue of trees and then tunnels beneath the Fortezza (see below). You can buy a ticket to include the minibus service from Piazza Cahen direct to Piazza Duomo (line A) or via Piazza della Repubblica (line B; see below).

Car parking By far the best way of visiting Orvieto by car is to park at the bottom of the hill in the large **free car-park beside the railway station** and take the underpass to Piazza Stazione for the funicular (see above). There is another car-park (with a small hourly tariff) below the town at **Campo della Fiera** connected by a lift to the piazza in front of the church of San Giovanni, or by a frequent minibus service to the centre, or by underground escalators and a moving walkway up to Piazza de' Ranieri. There are free car-parks in the centre of the town at **Piazza Cahen**, or off **Via Roma**. Other areas of the city called *stanze* are reserved for residents' cars.

The **Carta Orvieto Unica** (which can be purchased at the car-parks or at the tourist office) allows five hours' free car-parking at Campo della Fiera or a free round-trip ticket for the funicular railway and minibus service from the car-park by the station. It also allows free entrance to the Cappella di San Brizio in the cathedral, the Museo Claudio Faina, the 'Orvieto Underground' tour and the Torre del Moro.

 Hotels
☆☆☆☆ *Palazzo Piccolomini*, 36 Piazza Ranieri, ☎ 0763 341743; fax 0763 391046. Opened in 1997 in a beautiful 16C palace in the centre of the old town. Carefully restored and simply furnished with great taste, with cool stone floors. There are 32 charming bedrooms. Breakfast is served in the cellars.

☆☆☆ *Gran Hotel Reale*, 27 Piazza del Popolo, ☎ & fax 0763 341247. A beautiful old palazzo in a lovely piazza facing Palazzo del Popolo. A very old-fashioned hotel which has never been renovated but retains its decadent charm, the rooms have high frescoed ceilings and wonderful views. *Grand Hotel Italia*, 13 Via di Piazza del Popolo, ☎ & fax 0763 342065. In a handsome old palace between Piazza del Popolo and Corso Cavour. Spacious public rooms, a small terrace overlooking the valley, and old-fashioned bedrooms and bathrooms, simply furnished. Garage on the ground floor at extra cost. Friendly staff.

☆☆ *Duomo*, 7 Vicolo di Maurizio, ☎ 0763 341887. A small house just out of the cathedral square with a tiny garden, this was one of the first hotels to be opened in the town. Extremely simply furnished with an old-fashioned rather run-down atmosphere, it could do with renovation. Breakfast is an optional extra. *Posta*, 18 Via Luca Signorelli, ☎ 0763 341909. Also in a fine house in the centre of the town, but also very old-fashioned and extremely simple, in need of restoration. Breakfast is an optional extra.

The *Istituto Santissimo Salvatore* run

by Dominican nuns (1 Via del Popolo, ☎ and fax 0763 342910; Suor Tarcisia) accepts guests for a minimum stay of two nights. It is in a good position with a lovely garden and is very reasonably priced.

On the outskirts (car necessary) below the town: ☆☆☆☆ *La Badia*, 8 Località La Badia, ☎ 0763 301959; fax 0763 305455 in a beautiful peaceful position, with swimming-pool. Favoured by Americans it is, however, not cheap and could be better run.

The ☆☆☆☆ *Villa Ciconia*, 69 Via dei Tigli, ☎ 0763 305582, fax 0763 302077, in a beautiful 16C villa, is now sadly engulfed by new buildings in an anonymous suburb.

In the environs ☆☆ and ☆ hotels at **San Venanzo**. At **Fabro** ☆☆☆ *La Bettola del Buttero*, ☎ 0763 82063; fax 0763 82016, with restaurant.

There are numerous *agriturist* farmhouses which offer all kinds of accommodation in the vicinity (information from the tourist office), including *Titignano* near the Lago di Corbara, ☎ 0763 308022.

Campsites
Lago di Corbara

☆☆☆ *Orvieto*, ☎ 0744 950240, and **Falcone** (open April–Sept), ☎ 0744 950249; and ☆ *Scacco Matto*, ☎ 0744 950163.

Restaurants
£££ *Il Giglio d'Oro*, 8 Piazza Duomo, ☎ 0763 341903.

££ *Etrusca*, 10 Via Lorenzo Maitani, ☎ 0763 344016; *Maurizio*, 78 Via del Duomo, ☎ 0763 341114; *I Sette Consoli*, 1 Piazza Sant'Angelo, ☎ 0763 343911; *Dell'Ancora*, 7/9 Via di Piazza del Popolo, ☎ 0763 342766; *Dell'Orso*, 18 Via della Misericordia, ☎ 0763 341642; *La Grotta*, 5 Via Luca Signorelli, ☎ 0763 341348; *Le Grotte del Funaro*, 41 Via Ripa Serancia (also pizzeria), ☎ 0763 343276; *Antico Bucchero*, 4 Via de' Cartari, ☎ 0763 341725.

£ *Osteria dell'angelo*, 166 Corso Cavour, ☎ 0763 341805; *La Bottega del Buon Vino*, 26 Via della Cava, ☎ 0763 342373; *La Palomba*, 16 Via Cipriano Manente, ☎ 0763 343395; *La Pergola*, 9 Via dei Magoni, ☎ 0763 343065; *Mezza Luna*, 3 Via Ripa Serancia, ☎ 0763 341234; *La Volpe e l'Uva*, 1 Via Ripa Corsica, ☎ 0763 341612.

In summer the very small *Asino d'oro* is open in the evenings at 1 Vicolo del Popolo, ☎ 0763 344406. A good pizzeria, frequented by the young in the evenings is *Charlie*, 194 Corso Cavour, ☎ 0763 344766.

Al San Francesco 10 Via Cerretti, ☎ 0763 343302 is a large self-service restaurant.

Civitella del Lago
£££, a famous luxury-class restaurant *Il Padrino* (or Vissani), ☎ 0744 950206. Also £££ *Trippini*, ☎ 0744 950316.

Orvieto Scalo
£ *Trattoria La Graticola*, Località La Svolta, ☎ 0763 90202.

Café *Pasticceria Montanucci*, 21 Corso Cavour.

The Fortezza public gardens and the Parco delle Grotte (below Piazza Duomo) are pleasant places to **picnic**. Excellent traditional savoury buns and cakes can be purchased (mornings only) at the two shops called *Il Dolce Forno di Fausto Scimmi*, 6 Piazza della Scalza and just out of Piazza della Repubblica in Via Cozza. Another traditional local pasticceria and bakery is *Moscatelli* at 11 and 282 Corso Cavour.

Local **wines** can be tasted and purchased at the *Enoteca Regionale San Giovanni* cellars. Information on winetasting and visits to the wine-cellars in the locality from Consorzio Tutela Vino Orvieto Classico, 36 Corso Cavour, ☎ 0763 343790.

The **Teatro Mancinelli** has an important theatre season and is also used frequently for concerts etc.

Market days are on Thursday and Saturday in Piazza del Popolo.

 Annual festivals
In Orvieto in 1264 Pope Urban IV instituted the festival of *Corpus Domini* (see below) and a procession in honour of the Holy Corporal (see p. 235) has been held in the town since 1337. It now takes places in period costume on the Sunday after Corpus Domini (early June), starting in Piazza del Duomo.

Various festivities are held in the town in the preceding two weeks including the 'Palio dell'Oca' and the 'Palombella' at midday on Whit Sunday in front of the Duomo which celebrates Pentecost with a 'dove' and fireworks. An Eastertide concert is held in the Duomo. A winter *jazz festival* is also held here.

History

The rock of Orvieto was already occupied in the Iron Age, and an important Etruscan city grew up here in the 9C BC, usually identified as *Volsinii Veteres*, one of the chief cities of the Etruscan Confederation. The town was destroyed in 264 BC by the Romans, and the inhabitants resettled at a spot on the northeast side of Lago di Bolsena which developed into the town of Bolsena (*Volsinii Novi*). In the Middle Ages the commune of *Urbs Vetus* (from which the modern name is derived) was important, and it became especially powerful in the 13C. Pope Gregory X received Edward I of England here on his return from the Crusades. The rivalries between the Guelf Monaldeschi and the Ghibelline Filippeschi dominated events in the town during the 14C, and later Alexander VI and Clement VII were to take refuge here from revolts in Rome. The architects Angelo da Orvieto (14C), Ascanio Vittozzi (d. 1615) and Ippolito Scalza (c 1532–1617) were born here. There are now several military barracks in the town.

Piazza del Duomo is dominated by the magnificent exterior of the cathedral. On the north side of the piazza beside a simple row of low houses is a clock-tower called the **Torre del Maurizio**, surmounted by a bronze figure known as Maurizio (1348) which strikes the hours.

The Duomo

The Duomo is one of the most striking buildings of its period in the country. It dominates the view of the city for miles around. Apart from its superb architecture and splendid façade with beautiful 14C carvings, it contains a chapel (recently restored) frescoed by Luca Signorelli, and another chapel preserves the exquisite reliquary of the *Holy Corporal*, and a very beautiful painting of the *Madonna* by Lippo Memmi, both dating from the 14C.

The festival of Corpus Domini was instituted in Orvieto by Urban IV in 1264 to commemorate the miracle which took place in Bolsena the previous year when a Bohemian priest who had doubts about the doctrine of Transubstantiation was convinced when he saw blood drop from the Host on to the altar cloth during Mass. The Duomo was built to preserve the stained corporal, and the first stone

The Duomo

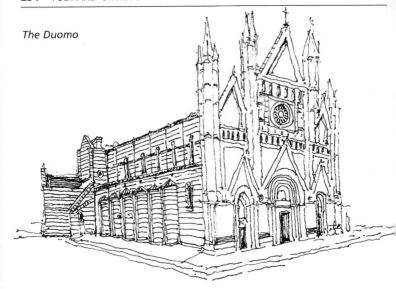

was laid on 3 November 1290, when it was blessed by Nicholas IV. The church was begun to a Romanesque plan, perhaps by Arnolfo di Cambio, but continued in the new Gothic style by Lorenzo Maitani, who took over in 1310. He was followed by his son Vitale; Nicolò and Meo Nuti (1331–47); Andrea Pisano (1347–48); Nino Pisano (1349); Andrea di Cecco da Siena (1356–59) and Andrea Orcagna (1359). Michele Sanmicheli became master in 1509–25 and the façade was not completed until the early years of the 17C.

Exterior The church stands on a plinth of seven steps, alternately red and white, surrounded by a lawn on the south side. The two beautiful sides built in horizontal bands of white travertine and grey basalt are decorated with the exteriors of the tall semicircular side chapels and handsome Gothic windows. On the north side are the **Porta di Canonica**, with a very worn fresco by Andrea di Giovanni, and the **Porta del Corporale** (three statues by Andrea Pisano have been removed from the lunette for restoration). On the south side is the **Porta di Postierla**, probably the oldest doorway. The two statues of *Sibyls* at the foot of the façade (on the corners) are by Fabiano Toti (1588) and Antonio Federighi.

The huge **façade**, designed and begun by Lorenzo Maitani, which covers the west end, is one of the finest Italian Gothic works and has been compared in design to a painted triptych in an elaborate frame. It has remarkable sculptural details. The harsh polychrome mosaics were mostly remade in the 17C–19C. Four elegant spires with high crocketed turrets divide the façade vertically. On the pilasters at their bases are superb marble **bas-reliefs** (c 1320–30) ascribed to Maitani, his son Vitale and Nicolò and Meo Nuti. They are very well preserved and the numerous scenes are divided by delicately carved vine tendrils or acanthus branches. On the right pilaster, above crowded dramatic scenes of *Paradise* and *Hell* is the *Last Judgement*. The next pilaster illustrates the *Life of Mary and of Christ*. At the bottom are prophets and above numerous scenes which read chronologically: start with the *Annunciation* and end with the *Marys at the* *tomb* in the top-most register. The third pilaster has stories of **Abraham and David**, and on the last pilaster (on the extreme left) the story of the **Creation** is depicted from Adam and Eve below to the time of Tubal Cain above. The large bronze symbols of the **Evangelists** are also by Maitani.

The **Madonna** by Andrea Pisano and bronze angels by Maitani, formerly in the lunette above the main door, were removed for restoration many years ago. The bronze doors are by Emilio Greco (1964–70). The great rose window, surrounded by statues in niches, is Orcagna's work.

Interior In the uncluttered interior (open 07.30–13.00, 14.30 or 15.00–dusk) the fine architectural lines can be appreciated to the full above the lovely pavement in dark red local stone. The walls are lined with horizontal bands of white and grey. The columns of the nave, with fine capitals, carry round arches, over which a graceful triforium, with a clerestory above it, runs all round the church, except in the transepts. The semicircular side chapels are particularly well designed (and many of them have interesting fresco fragments of the 14C–15C). The lower panels of the stained-glass windows are made of alabaster.

In the **nave** are a stoup by Antonio Federighi (1485) and a beautiful font of 1390–1407. At the beginning of the north side the fresco of the **Madonna and Child** is by Gentile da Fabriano (1425; well restored in 1987). The three stoups against the wall are attractive works of the 16C.

In the north transept is a *Pietà* by Ippolito Scalza (1579) and a carved altar and altarpiece by Simone Mosca and Raffaello da Montelupo. Here is the **Cappella del Corporale**. On the walls are restored frescoes illustrating *Miracles of the Eucharist* by Ugolino di Prete Ilario (1357–64). On the right wall is the story of the *miracle of Bolsena*; on the altar wall, the *Crucifixion*; and on the left wall are more scenes of miracles involving the **Holy Sacrament**. In the vault are *symbols of the Eucharist* and *saints*. In the Gothic recess the huge panel of the **Madonna dei Raccomandati** by Lippo Memmi (1320) is one of the loveliest paintings in Italy.

On either side of the altar are statues of angels by Agostino Cornacchini (1729). Over the altar, incorporated in a large tabernacle, designed by Nicolò da Siena (1358) and continued by Orcagna, is the corporal (linen cloth) of the miracle of Bolsena, displayed only on religious festivals. It is taken in procession on Corpus Domini. Displayed in a showcase near the left wall of the chapel is the original **Reliquary of the Corporal**, a superb work in silver-gilt with translucent enamels, by the Sienese Ugolino di Vieri (1337).

Above the entrance to the chapel is the huge colourful organ (1584, by Ippolito Scalza). The **choir**, uncovered in 1999 after many years' restoration, is decorated with frescoes by Ugolino di Prete and other Sienese artists (1331–41). The beautiful stained-glass of the great east window is by Giovanni di Bonino (1325–34). On either side of the sanctuary are statues of **Christ: Ecce Homo** by Ippolito Scalza (1608) and **Christ at the Column** by Gabriele Mercanti (1627).

The south transept contains the carved *Altare dei Magi* (begun 1514), a good early work of Sanmicheli, with bas-reliefs by Raffaello and Francesco da Montelupo. In neo-classical niches here are statues of Adam and Eve by Fabiano Toti.

Cappella della Madonna di San Brizio

The Cappella della Madonna di San Brizio, or Cappella Nuova, contains famous **frescoes by Signorelli**, one of the most remarkable fresco cycles of the Italian Renaissance. They have recently been restored as they were suffering from the effects of humidity. The chapel is open 10.00–12.45, 14.30–17.15 (or 19.15 in summer); on PH 14.30–17.45 or 18.45 (☎ 0763 342477). The ticket has to be purchased outside the Duomo at the tourist office or in a shop in the piazza (admission also with the Carta Orvieto, see above).

The chapel was built in 1409–19, financed by the Monaldeschi, a wealthy local family. In 1447 Fra Angelico, with the help of Benozzo Gozzoli, began the decoration of the chapel: he had completed just two sections of the vault over the altar before he was recalled to Rome.

At the end of the century Luca Signorelli was commissioned to complete the frescoes (1499–1504). They represent the *Day of Judgement* and *Life after death*, celebrating the importance of salvation through the Eucharist based on Dominican texts, *De Civitate Dei* by St Augustine and *La Divina Commedia* of Dante. They are particularly interesting for their iconography since there are very few other pictorial representations in Italy of these subjects. The beautiful nude figure studies are among the most important works of the Renaissance, and the chapel is Signorelli's masterpiece.

On the left wall (in the lunette nearest to the entrance) is the *Sermon of Antichrist*. Around the central figure of Antichrist (a false prophet) standing on a pedestal and being prompted by the devil, is a crowd showing scenes of corruption and violence. The two solemn bystanders (dressed in black) are thought to represent Signorelli himself, and, behind, Fra Angelico. To the right can be seen the figure of Dante (in profile with his characteristic red hat). In the background is the splendid Temple of Solomon (which shows the influence of the architecture of Bramante), and the three groups of figures in front of it represent the execution of two penitents, a false miracle, and monks reasserting the authority of the Bible. In the sky St Michael is shown preventing the ascension into Heaven of Antichrist and causing a storm of fire to fall on the corrupt below.

On the entrance wall, above the arch on which a group of putti display the monogram of the Opera del Duomo, and a cartouche with the signature of Signorelli, is the *Day of Judgement*. On the right is a group of figures around a man in a turban, presumably a prophet, and above various scenes which foreshadow the end of the world, including unnatural events such as the sea in flood, the red moon, and the black sun, and the stars falling out of the heavens, scenes of torture and buildings crashing to the ground. On the left is the *Day of Judgement*, where winged devils are emitting a rain of fire which destroys the world.

On the right wall the first lunette shows the *Resurrection of the Body*, heralded by two splendid angels in the sky above and on the altar wall, *Angels guide the elect to Paradise, and drive the damned into Hell*. Here the influence of Dante can be seen. Fragments of frescoes showing devils and a figure thought to represent Cain were discovered behind the altar during restoration work. In the second lunette on the right wall, the *Casting out of the Wicked*, has three archangels in armour repudiating the fallen angels above an extraordinary crowded scene of Hell. The nude studies here are particularly famous, showing the influence of Antonio Pollaiolo and the atmosphere of terror and suffering in this apocalyptic scene is quite remarkable.

Luca Signorelli

Born in Cortona, just across the Umbrian border in Tuscany, around 1450, Signorelli was influenced by Piero della Francesca, with whom he worked as a young man, as well as by Florentine painters, notably Antonio Pollaiolo, from whom he learned how to convey movement and energy in his figure studies. Before carrying out this, his most important commission, he was called to Rome, with other leading artists of the day, to paint a fresco in the Sistine chapel, and he also worked in Città di Castello (where he was proclaimed citizen of the town in 1488) and Cortona. But the frescoes in Orvieto were immediately recognised as his masterpiece and established his fame. They were to have a profound influence on Michelangelo and Raphael when they were at work in the Vatican in Rome. Signorelli was also an extremely accomplished draughtsman, and his male nude figure studies are superb. He carried out other fresco cycles at Loreto in the Marche and in the cloister of Monteoliveto Maggiore in Tuscany, and produced numerous panel paintings, including a number of charming tondi with the Holy Family. 19C British collectors became particularly interested in his work, and the first important exhibition of his paintings was held in London in 1893.

In Umbria other works by him can be seen in the Duomo of Perugia, the oratory of San Crescentino near Morra, and in the gallery at Città di Castello. In 1515 a very fine *Deposition* was commissioned from Signorelli by a confraternity in Umbertide and since 1999 this is again on view in the church of Santa Croce after fifteen years' careful restoration.

The second lunette on the left wall shows the *Blessed entering Heaven* and the crowning of the elect by a beautiful group of angel musicians.

The exquisite decoration on the lower part of the walls, framed with grisaille friezes and grotteschi, includes medallion portraits of Dante and classical authors. This was the last part of the chapel to be decorated by Signorelli. On the right of the entrance, with his back to us, is *Empedocles*, and on the left wall, *Cicero*, *Dante* and *Statius* (formerly believed to be Homer). On the right wall are *Ovid*, *Virgil* and *Lucan*. The tondi have scenes from classical myth and from Dante's *La Divina Commedia*. In the recess on the right wall, the *Mourning over the Dead Christ*, also by Signorelli, includes the figures of Pietro Parenzo who, when podestà of the town at the end of the 13C was killed by a group of heretics, and San Faustino, both of whom were buried here.

In the two ceiling vaults the **celestial host** is depicted in a series of triangular compositions on a gold ground. Signorelli received the commission to complete the vault before he started the frescoes on the walls. In the first bay of the vault (nearest to the altar), the two cells by Fra Angelico show the *Saviour in Glory* and (right) *Prophets*. The other two cells by Signorelli show the *Apostles*, and the *Signs of the Passion of Christ displayed by angels* (on either side of the *Column of the Flagellation*). In the second bay (nearest to the entrance) are *martyred Saints and Virgins* (nearest to the entrance), and the two last cells show *Doctors of the Church and Patriarchs*.

The chapel received its present name when the charming altarpiece of the *Madonna di San Brizio*, by a local 14C painter, was moved here. The altar was designed by Bernardino Cametti in 1712.

The **crypt**, with traces of frescoes and part of the substructure of the Duomo, can be seen outside the east end (reached along the north side).

Piazza Duomo

Opposite the façade of the cathedral is the **Palazzo dell'Opera del Duomo**, a medieval building with a façade completed in 1850 by Virginio Vespignani. Next door is **Palazzo Faina**, seat of the **Museo Claudio Faina** and **Museo Civico Archeologico**, reopened in 1997 after restoration (open 10.00–13.00, 14.00 or 14.30–17.00 or 18.00; closed Mon from Oct–March; ☎ 0763 341511).

On the ground floor the **Museo Civico Archeologico** is arranged in three rooms. The finds from Cannicella include the so-called *Venus of Cannicella*, a statue probably representing a female goddess of fertility made from Naxos marble and thought to be an Archaic Greek original of the 6C BC. In the rooms to the left are a colossal stone head of a warrior from the Crocifisso del Tufo (6C BC) and a tomb with bas-reliefs (4C BC). In the room to the right are polychrome terracotta decorations from the Belvedere Temple (4C BC), including fragments of sculptures from the pediment.

The **Museo Claudio Faina**, founded in 1864 by Mauro Faina, enlarged after 1868 by his nephew Eugenio with finds from excavations in the necropoli of Orvieto, and donated to the city by the family in 1954, is arranged on the two upper floors. Some of the rooms have charming 19C painted decorations. On the first floor are exhibited Etruscan gold jewellery; an important numismatic collection (rooms II and IV); Etruscan urns from Chiusi; black-figure amphorae and craters; red- and black-figure vases from the Crocifisso del Tufo necropolis; and (room VIII) three large black-figure amphorae attributed to Exekias (550–525 BC). The second floor has prehistoric finds; Bucchero ware; fine black- and red-figure Attic vases; Etruscan bronzes and ceramics; a crater (in room XVIII) by the Vanth group (320–300 BC); amphorae by the Vanth group (room XX); and the torso of a Greek marble statuette dating from the 4C BC.

Near the Duomo is the battlemented **Palazzo Soliano** (or dei Papi), begun in 1297 for Boniface VIII, built in yellow tufa, typical of Orvieto, with arches and an external staircase. In 1991 the **Museo di Emilio Greco** (open 10.30–13.00, 14.00 or 15.00–18.00 or 19.00; closed Mon) was arranged with sculptures on the ground floor, which were left to the city in 1980 by Emilio Greco (1913–95).

The **Museo dell'Opera del Duomo**, formerly exhibited in this building, has been closed indefinitely for many years. There are plans to rearrange it on the upper floor.

The contents include: **statues** of the *Madonna* in marble by Andrea Pisano and his school, by Nino Pisano (1349), and (in wood), by Giovanni Pisano. The *Madonna and angels* by Pisano and Maitani from the central door of the Duomo may be exhibited here after their restoration. Among unfinished works by Arnolfo di Cambio are two damaged angels. A wooden statue of *Christ blessing* is attributed to an assistant of Maitani (1330). The paintings include parts of a fine polyptych by Simone Martini, a self-portrait and other works by Signorelli, and a *Madonna* by Coppo di Marcovaldo (1268). Outstanding among the metal work is the *Reliquary of the Head of San Savino*, by Ugolino di Vieri; and the collection of vestments is notable. There are two sketches for the façade of the cathedral; as built with three gables (by Maitani), and with only one gable, now thought to be by Arnolfo di Cambio. The colossal figures of the *Apostles* (16C–18C) which formerly lined the nave of the cathedral, and two statues of the *Annunciation* by Francesco Mocchi, formerly on either side of the high altar, may be returned to the Duomo.

Palazzo Papale, by the east end of the cathedral, is also built in yellow tufa, with three large Gothic arches and fine windows. This impressive 13C building has recently been restored. It houses the **Museo Archeologico Nazionale** (open 09.00–13.30, 14.30 or 15.00–18.00 or 19.00; PH 09.00–13.00; ☎ 0763 341039). So far four huge rooms with fine barrel vaults on the ground floor have been opened, and the museum has a somewhat abandoned atmosphere. The most notable exhibits include: Etruscan material from the Cannicella necropolis at the foot of the rock of Orvieto (see below; from excavations in 1900, 1936 and 1971) dating from the late 7C to the early 6C BC. Finds (1982–83) from the Crocifisso del Tufo necropolis and material (including armour) from the tomb of a warrior (4C BC) at Settecamini, the Etruscan burial ground south-west of the town near La Badia. Two painted tombs (lit on request, as they have to be protected from light for long periods for conservation reasons) discovered in the 19C at Settecamini have been reconstructed and their original paintings displayed (detached in 1951). There is also a fine collection of Greek red- and black-figure vases (4C BC), bucchero ware and bronze mirrors.

On the south side of Piazza Duomo is the neo-classical façade (1835; in very poor repair) of the church of **San Giacomo Maggiore**, and the fine **Palazzo Buzi**, on the corner of Via Soliana, by Ippolito Scalza. Beside the hospital is a small park of pine trees from which there is an excellent view of the valley with the Badia of Santi Severo e Martirio.

Here is the entrance gate to a path (2mins walk) which leads downhill with wonderful views over the valley to visit the **Underground Caves** or **Parco delle Grotte** (guided tours to 'Orvieto Underground' start from the IAT office in Piazza Duomo every day at 11.00 and 16.00). A labyrinth of some 1200 man-made caves has been identified in the tufa rock on which the town is built; about 30 per cent of the terrain below ground level has been excavated at one period or another (from Etruscan to medieval times) for wells, aqueducts, cisterns, wine cellars, tunnels, quarries, etc. In this area a 16C olive-press is shown in an Etruscan edifice (with a typical carved ceiling imitating a wood roof). The two Etruscan shafts (40 other similar shafts have been found beneath the town), one of which has been excavated to a depth of 42 metres, were presumably used as wells (since they pierce the tufa rock as far as the clay level). Beyond is a medieval pozzolana quarry.

The town centre

Via del Duomo, with numerous touristy ceramic shops, leads out of Piazza Duomo. In a little piazza is the Baroque octagonal church of **San Giuseppe** and **Palazzo Gualterio** attributed to Simone Mosca with a doorway by Ippolito Scalza. In Piazza Scalza, off the other side of Via del Duomo is **Palazzo Clementini**, also by Ippolito Scalza.

Via del Duomo ends in **Corso Cavour**, the main street of the town. To the right it descends gently all the way to Piazza Cahen (see below) passing the **Teatro Mancinelli** (1844–55) and **Palazzo Urbani (Petrucci)** by Michele Sanmicheli.

Near the junction with Via del Duomo is the tall **Torre del Moro** (12C) which can now be climbed (by lift to the second floor and then by a long modern wooden flight of stairs (open 10.00–19.00; Nov–Feb 10.30–13.00, 15.30–17.00; an easy climb and well worth it). From beside the bell (which strikes every quarter of an hour!) there is a remarkable **view** of the town and the lovely countryside beyond. It is one of the best views in Umbria. To the south, beyond the garden of the school in Palazzo Clementini the large church of San Francesco can be seen near a group of cypresses. To the right is the yellow façade of San Lorenzo de' Arari and the dome and campanile of the church of the Apostoli further right. Between them, in the woods on the hillside beyond, is the Badia. To the east the view is dominated by the huge cathedral, and Corso Cavour can be seen running straight to Piazza Cahen. To the north there is a splendid view of Palazzo del Popolo and its piazza. To the west Corso Cavour can be seen ending in Piazza della Repubblica with the octagonal bell-tower of Sant'Andrea. Beyond is a tall medieval tower, to the left of which the campanile of San Giovanni can be seen and to the right of which, on the edge of the hill, is the little bell-tower of San Giovanale near the large church and former convent of Sant'Agostino.

From Corso Cavour, Via di Piazza del Popolo leads to the large peaceful **Piazza del Popolo** dominated by the unusual **Palazzo del Popolo**, which was restored in 1990 as a conference centre. The impressive exterior, built in tufa with decorated arches and windows, was probably begun in 1157, and later altered. Excavations beneath the building have revealed Etruscan remains and a medieval well filled with ceramics (13C–16C). A market is held in the surrounding piazze on Thursdays and Saturdays.

Corso Cavour ends in **Piazza della Repubblica**, the central square of Orvieto.

The 12C church of **Sant'Andrea** is situated here. Its fine 12-sided campanile was over-restored in 1928. Under the portico on the north side flowers are sold. The beautiful interior has a lovely nave with Composite Ionic capitals and fine vaulting at the east end. The pulpit is made up of Cosmati fragments, and there are remains of 14C and 15C frescoes. In 1281 Martin IV was crowned here in the presence of Charles of Anjou. Excavations beneath the church (entered via the steps at the west end, but not at present open) have revealed a 6C pavement from the primitive basilica which overlies Etruscan and Roman remains. Here, also, are pieces of relief sculpture (8C–9C?) from a choir screen, embedded on the reverse side with Cosmatesque mosaic work.

In the piazza is **Palazzo Comunale**, first built in 1216, with a façade (c 1580) by Ippolito Scalza, opposite a neo-classical palace by Virginio Vespignani.

The western part of town

From Piazza della Repubblica Via Loggia dei Mercanti, characteristic of the old city, with several towers, leads past the former 14C church of the **Carmine**, recently restored as a theatre workshop, to Piazza de' Ranieri. The raised Via Ripa Serancia continues under a lovely old arch to an attractive piazza with two churches. **San Giovanni Evangelista** was founded in 916, and rebuilt in 1687 on an octagonal plan. In the apse is a framed fresco fragment of the *Madonna and Child* of 1356. The pretty cloister (restored and used for exhibitions) dates from 1513 with fine dark columns and a well-head of 1526. The terrace in the piazza is built on the top of the sheer rock face which drops abruptly here to the car-park at Campo della Fiera. There is a view of part of the old town and the countryside beyond.

From here a splendid old road (pedestrians only) can be followed downhill to a picturesque part of the town, well worth exploring. It crosses above the **Porta Maggiore**, one of the oldest city gates (which can be reached by taking the road on the right which descends to Via della Cava, see below) and then ascends along the walls to the church of **San Giovenale** with a square bell-tower, which stands in a beautiful position on the edge of the rock, with orchards below. The church, of ancient foundation, has a charming old interior with an unusual east end and little columns and lecterns in the sanctuary made up of old sculptural fragments. An early Christian carved panel serves as the altar frontal. There are numerous other sculptural fragments in the church including a little transenna decorated with peacocks, as well as 13C–16C frescoes.

Behind San Giovenale is the former church of **Sant'Agostino** with a Gothic façade, and an 18C interior, which is being restored and may be used for exhibitions. Beside it a huge Gothic arch is now incorporated in a modern restaurant.

Via Malabranca leads back past Palazzo Caravajal and the 15C **Palazzo Filippeschi**, with a lovely old courtyard and a view of the medieval town, and down to Via della Cava which leads downhill (right) to a restaurant at no. 28, which has an interesting **Etruscan well** used by Clement VII in 1527 (see the Pozzo di San Patrizio, p. 242). It can be seen from 08.00–20.00 or 21.00 except on Tues. Excavated in the tufa rock (now some 25m deep), it has the remains of a pottery next to it, thought to have been active from the 13C to the 15C. At no. 8 Via della Cava, another underground medieval pottery may be visited on request at the antique shop.

Via Filippeschi continues back up to Piazza della Repubblica (see above).

The southern part of town

Via Maitani leads out of Piazza Duomo to the large church of **San Francesco** in Piazza dei Febei, with a 13C façade and a white interior (altered in 1773). The wooden Crucifix is attributed to Lorenzo Maitani. Here, in the presence of Edward I of England, the funeral of Prince Henry of Cornwall took place, who was murdered at Viterbo in March 1271; here also, Boniface VIII canonised St Louis of France. In 1998 interesting late 14C frescoes were discovered in the sacristy and attributed to Pietro di Puccio.

Via Ippolito Scalza leads south to the Romanesque church of **San Lorenzo de Arari** (or dell'Ara) over-restored at the beginning of this century. It takes its name from an Etruscan altar beneath the altar-table. Above it is a pretty little 12C ciborium. The apse fresco of *Christ enthroned with four saints* in the Byzantine style and the frescoes illustrating four episodes in the life of *St Lawrence* (1330) in the nave were all poorly restored in 1919. On the columns are 14C–15C fresco fragments. In Via Alberici nearby is the church of the **Gesù** (1618), with Baroque stucco work inside.

The Pozzo di San Patrizio and the Rocca

At the easternmost part of the town is **Piazza Cahen**, with the funicular terminus and where the main approach road enters the town. The grounds of the **Fortezza** (1364) here are now a pleasant public garden with fine views of the valley. An avenue to the left of the funicular station descends to the **Pozzo di San Patrizio** (open daily 10.00–18.00; April–Oct 10.00–18.45), built by Antonio da Sangallo the Younger (1527–37) to provide an emergency water supply in the event of a siege, by order of Clement VII, who fled to Orvieto after the sack of Rome. The well, surmounted by a low tower, is 63m deep, and is encircled by two spiral staircases each with 248 wide steps and lit by 72 windows. It is called St Patrick's Well because it is supposed to be similar to St Patrick's cavern in Ireland. In the public gardens above the well are conspicuous remains of an Etruscan Temple, known as the **Tempio del Belvedere**.

From the piazza Corso Cavour ascends gently towards the centre of the town passing the side of the Romanesque church of **Santo Stefano** in yellow tufa, with a vaulted interior and a fragment of a 14C fresco of the *Madonna and Child*, and further on, in a small square, the church of **San Michele Arcangelo**, with a relief of a classical temple on its façade (1832). The western part of Corso Cavour is described above.

From Piazza Cahen Via Roma also leads towards the centre of the town through a less attractive part of the town near the church of **San Domenico**, thought to be the first church dedicated to St Dominic, built in 1233–64. In its former convent St Thomas Aquinas taught theology. The church, of which only the transept remains, has a pretty exterior. In the interior the **tomb** of Cardinal de Braye (d. 1281), by Arnolfo di Cambio, has been dismantled and cannot at present be seen. The Cappella Petrucci (below the main church, entered from a door in the south wall) is an interesting architectural work by Sanmicheli. It also has various mementoes to St Thomas Aquinas.

BEYOND ORVIETO

The countryside around Orvieto is particularly pretty and unspoilt and has a varied landscape with woods and small orchards and olive groves, and some lovely old farmhouses. The little villages are mostly well preserved and some fine castles survive.

At the foot of the rock to the north, and just off the road to the station is the Etruscan necropolis of **Crocifisso del Tufo** (open daily 09.00–dusk) of the 4C BC, with small chamber tombs many of which survive intact. It can be reached on foot from outside Porta Maggiore, or by the main road from Piazza Cahen (keeping right at every crossroads). Bus no. 1 (infrequent service) can be taken back uphill from the necropolis via the railway station to Piazza XXIX Marzo.

At the foot of the rock to the south-west of the town, next to a hotel and restaurant, is the Premonstratensian abbey of **Santi Severo e Martirio**, also known as **La Badia**, dating from the 12C. It can be reached by road (2.5km) followed by bus no. 3 from Piazza della Repubblica, or in 30mins by footpath from the Porta Romana. Parts of the ruined abbey may be visited on request at the hotel: these include the abbot's house, the former refectory (now the Chiesa del Crocifisso), and the original church with its 12-sided campanile.

Another road runs south to **Porano** a picturesque little village with an interesting church. At **Castel Rubello** nearby is a painted Etruscan tomb called the Tomba degli Hescanas (admission on request to the custodian).

Castel Viscardo, 13km west of Orvieto, in a lovely position surrounded by woods, has a 15C castle still privately owned (no admission). The picturesque entrance, with crumbling statues, and the well-designed farm buildings can be seen by its garden with some ancient cypresses, but it appears to be in very poor condition. It was owned by the Monaldeschi and Spada families. In the church close by there is a good 17C copy of a *Madonna enthroned* by Perugino. Preserved in a cupboard left of the high altar is a very fine 17C ivory *Crucifix* presented to Cardinal Spada by Louis XIV. Part of the spacious little town is paved in local bricks which are still hand-made in eight or nine kilns on the outskirts (most of them on the Orvieto road). The bricks for the pavement of the Campo in Siena came from here.

Monte Rubiaglio is another pleasant little place with a 13C castle very well restored in 1978 and divided up into homes for local people. It was occupied by the Germans in the Second World War, and the fountain outside dates from the Fascist period. A bronze eagle decorates the war memorial. Just outside the little piazza is the church with a brick façade and a neo-Gothic and Art Nouveau interior, complete with its furnishings, stained-glass and frescoes.

The impressive **Castello della Sala**, on the edge of the hillside, is very well preserved. It has been owned by the Antinori family since 1940 who produce white wine here on their large estate.

Ficulle, north of Orvieto, founded in the 8C–9C, is still surrounded by its medieval walls, and was for centuries famous for its potteries. The 17C Collegiata was designed by Ippolito Scalza. There are lovely views. Opposite the Romanesque church just outside the village, is one of the two terracotta potteries still in operation. It is run by Fabio Fattorini and you can buy lovely traditional hand-made pots, jugs and bowls. There is a good bakery and confectioner in the town at Piaggia Cola di Rienzo (off Corso della Rinascita).

Further north is **Monteleone d'Orvieto**, an attractive little hill town. To the east, in lovely wooded country, is **Montegabbione** which preserves a tall tower and has a centrally planned Art Nouveau church with a terracotta façade.

About 1km beyond the village of **Montegiove** is a right turn (with a small inconspicuous signpost for 'Santa Maria della Scarzuola'). A white road continues for 2km through thick woods to the entrance to **La Scarzuola**, with an extraordinarily odd garden, one of the few in Italy created since the Second World War. Admission only by appointment, ☎ 0763 837463, 20,000 lire. The entrance leads into an enclosed lawn with 18C stations of the Cross and a church with a 17C portico (an early fresco of St Francis, c 1250, has recently been discovered inside). The Franciscan convent here was bought in 1956 by the architect Tomaso Buzzi (1900–81) and on the hillside he created an eccentric folly with a landscape of tufa ruins, pastiches of vaguely classical and medieval buildings, as well as a masonic temple, all of them designed as stage sets, to be seen following a precise itinerary. Some of the stranger elements include a musical staircase constructed in iron, a transparent pyramid, a sun dial in a rotonda around a dead cypress, and an organ with cypresses serving as the pipes. Occupying a deceptively small area, the contrived views of this fantasy city take their inspiration from an illustrated book entitled *Hypnerotomachia Poliphili* (or *The Strife of Love in a Dream*) thought to have been written by a Venetian Dominican and published by Aldo Manuzio in Venice in 1499, which was famous in the Renaissance as an allegorical celebration of love and beauty, and in which canons of architecture and garden design were discussed.

Buzzi left the garden unfinished at his death and the work of its completion (apparently following the original designs) has been taken on by his nephew who lives here. Buzzi was a well known architect before the advent of Fascism when he withdrew from public life and from then on only worked for private clients. The convent garden (not usually shown) is being replanted in a sequence of coloured flower beds, between pergolas of roses and vines. From this garden, beyond a 'boat' surrounded by water symbolising the beginning of the 'voyage' into the main garden, a 'tunnel' leads downhill to a dramatic view of the first theatre in the main garden, where the landscape serves as backdrop.

The fastest route between Orvieto and Todi is the N448, a lovely road through beautiful unspoilt countryside which runs alongside the Tiber and the artificial **Lago di Corbara**, created in 1958–63 to regulate the flow of the Tiber and to supply a hydroelectric station. The lake, 13 square kilometres, is the largest in Umbria after Lago Trasimeno, and is a favourite place for fishermen and canoeists. A good white wine is produced in this area. The road passes close to the village of **Civitella del Lago**, with the famous *Vissani* restaurant (see p. 232). Beside the lake is a Franciscan convent, founded by St Francis in 1218 on land given to him by the Baschi family. It was rebuilt in 1703, and is now occupied by the Comunità Incontro di Don Gelmini, a comunity which helps those in need. The hermitage of the Pasquarella was founded by monks from Camaldoli in the 11C. Nearby is the hill town of **Baschi**, visible from the Florence – Rome motorway. It is near the confluence of the Rivers Paglia and Tiber, where remains of the Roman port of Palianum can be seen (the Tiber used to be navigable all the way from Rome to this point). The town takes its name from the powerful Baschi family who owned many castles in the area. The church of San Niccolò, built by Ippolito Scalza in 1584, contains a triptych by Giovanni di Paolo.

The other very beautiful road (N79bis) between Orvieto and Todi is described on p. 229. Off this road is the borgo of **Titignano**, now owned by the Corsini family. At **Colonnetta** another fine road heads north (N317) towards Marsciano. It crosses lovely deserted countryside around **Monte Peglia** (837m) where there is a nature reserve. There are hotels at **San Venanzo**.

Amelia, Narni and Terni

AMELIA
• • • • • • • • •

Amelia is a beautifully situated hill-top town (406m) above the Tiber surrounded by spectacular countryside. Its fine polygonal walls are a remarkable survival from around the 5C BC. The peaceful old town has interesting buildings of several different periods, and there are numerous small orchards within the walls.

Practical information

Information office
IAT dell'Amerino, 1 Via Orvieto (outside Porta Romana); ☎ 0744 981453.

Getting there
By rail The nearest stations are Narni (on the Ancona–Rome line), 11km east and Orte (on the Florence–Rome line),

15km south (there are bus services from both stations).
By bus (*ATC*) From Terni, Orte and Orvieto. Services from the towns in the environs including Alviano, Avigliano Umbro, Attigliano and Lugnano in Teverina.
Car parking Traffic is officially exclud-

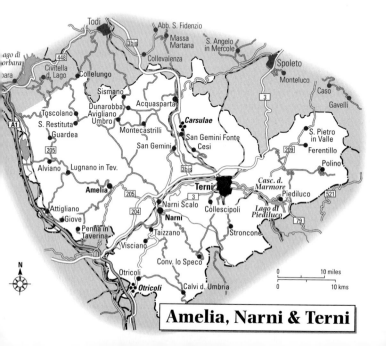

Amelia, Narni & Terni

ed from inside the walls on weekdays 09.00–13.00, 17.30–19.30. Visitors should park outside the walls (and use the frequent circular minibus service which traverses the old town). Free car-parks are on the right of Porta Romana beside the walls (with a lift up to Via Pomponia or a minibus service through the town); and outside Porta Leone. The car-park beside Porta Romana has an hourly tariff (inclusive of a ticket for the minibus service up to the centre).

 ### Hotels
Il Piccolo Hotel de' Carleni, 21 Via Pellegrino Carleni, ☎ 0744 983925, fax 0744 978143. A charming old house with a lovely little garden orchard across a bridge over the road, in the quiet old centre of the town reached on foot from Piazza Marconi, with an excellent restaurant (££). The seven bedrooms are beautifully furnished, and have ultra-modern bathrooms. The hotel is run by the propri-

etors who live here. This is one of the most delightful places to stay in Umbria.

 ### Restaurants
££ Carleni (see above), and *£ Trattoria Montenero*, outside on the road to Giove.

Picnics
There are good places to picnic outside the walls in the public gardens near Porta Romana; outside Porta della Valle and Porta Posterola; and in the little garden by the Duomo.

The district south of the town used to be well known for its **figs** (delicious dried candied figs are still produced by the Ditta A. Girotti and sold in numerous shops and cafés in the town).

 ### Festivals
The annual festival of *Santa Fermina* (martyred in AD 304) takes place here on 24 November, with a candlelit procession.

History

This was the ancient *Ameria*, said by Pliny to have been founded three centuries before Rome. It became a Roman municipium in 90 BC on the Via Amerina from Nepi to Chiusi. Virgil and Cicero mention the fertile countryside surrounding the town, noted especially for its vineyards. A remarkable bronze statue of *Germanicus*, father of Caligula, was found here in 1963; since its restoration it has been exhibited in the Museo Nazionale Archeologico in Perugia. The native painter Pier Matteo d'Amelia (Manfredi; 1440–1509) has recently been identified with the anonymous painter, up to now known as the Maestro dell'Annunciazione Gardner. Alessandro Geraldini (1455–1525) was born here: he helped obtain the approval at the court of Spain for Columbus' expedition, and later travelled as bishop to Santo Domingo.

The main entrance to the town is through the 16C **Porta Romana**, outside which to the right the best stretches of the polygonal (Pelasgic) **walls** can be seen, thought to date from the 5C BC. They are now c 8m high and 3.5m thick. They can also be seen from a garden and path to the left of the gate.

Via della Repubblica leads up towards the centre of the old town. It has recently been repaved, and the old Roman road beneath with its large paving stones is revealed in places. On the right is a pretty piazza with a war memorial (1923, by Angelo Guazzaroni) and the church of **San Francesco** (or Santi

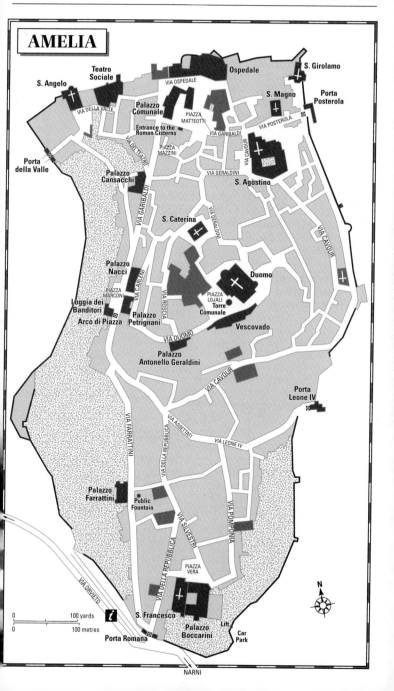

AMELIA

S. Angelo

Teatro
Sociale

VIA DELLA VALLE

Porta
della Valle

Palazzo
Comunale

Entrance to the
Roman Cisterns

VIA OSPEDALE

Ospedale

S. Girolamo

S. Magno

Porta
Posterola

PIAZZA
MATTEOTTI

VIA GARIBALDI

VIA POSTEROLA

VIA DEL TEATRO

PIAZZA
MAZZINI

VIA CAVOUR

Palazzo
Cansacchi

VIA GERALDINI

S. Agostino

VIA GARIBALDI

S. Caterina

VIA GERALDINI

VIA CAVOUR

Palazzo
Nacci

VIA CARLENI

PIAZZA
MARCONI

Duomo

Loggia dei
Banditori

VIA ROSCIA

PIAZZA
LOJALI

Arco di Piazza

Palazzo
Petrignani

Torre
Comunale

VIA DUOMO

Vescovado

Palazzo
Antonello Geraldini

VIA CAVOUR

Porta
Leone IV

VIA ASSETTATI

VIA FARRATTINI

VIA DELLA REPUBBLICA

VIA LEONE IV

VIA POMPONIA

Palazzo
Farrattini

Public
Fountain

VIA SILVESTRI

VIA DELLA REPUBBLICA

PIAZZA
VERA

VIA ORVIETO

N

0   100 yards
0   100 metres

i

S. Francesco

Lift

Palazzo
Boccarini

Car
Park

Porta Romana

NARNI

Filippo e Giacomo), with a rose window in its façade of 1401. In the chapel of Sant'Antonio off the right side are six beautifully carved **funerary monuments of the Geraldini family**. The one on the right above is by the school of Agostino di Duccio (1477). Palazzo Boccarini nearby is destined to become an archaeological museum.

Via della Repubblica continues uphill and, beyond a fork with Via Silvestri a narrow stepped street leads under an arch down to the handsome **Palazzo Farrattini** with a long inscription dividing the first and second floors. Modelled on Palazzo Farnese in Rome, it was built in 1520 by Antonio da Sangallo the Younger. Privately owned, the exterior has been covered with scaffolding for many years (the interior contains a restored Roman mosaic). In front of the palace, beneath a high arch, is a public fountain still in use on the site of Roman baths (part of the Roman wall in opus reticulatum can be seen here).

Via della Repubblica next reaches the fork with Via Assettati which descends right past a fine palace at no. 3. Its continuation Via Leone IV leads down past simpler houses, some with medieval arches or doorways (nos 85–91, 63, and 2) to **Porta Leone** in the walls.

Via della Repubblica continues up past another palace in a piazza named after an old chain (*catena*) here (with a view of the countryside beyond Via Farrattini which has a picturesque old arch) and, with its beautiful old paving now well preserved, climbs up beneath several flying arches. It then tunnels under the splendid **Arco di Piazza**, an impressive medieval gate made from Roman masonry. It emerges in the delightful old **Piazza Marconi**, once the centre of the city, with attractive old paving. There is a little medieval pulpit for public proclamations here, as well as the 16C **Palazzo Petrignani** (which contains the frescoed Sala dello Zodiaco) and the 15C **Palazzo Nacci**.

Piazza Marconi

The stepped Via del Duomo leads steeply up out of the square past the picturesque Via Carleni (left) and the rear façade of Palazzo Petrignani. Further up on the right is the handsome Palazzo Antonello Geraldini and the **Vescovado** with Roman altars set into its façade. Here, at the top of the hill, in a very peaceful position is the **Duomo**, rebuilt in 1640–80. The fine 12-sided campanile, which incorporates Roman fragments, was built as the Torre Civica in 1050. The **interior** (open 10.00–12.00, 16.00–18.30) was decorated with frescoes and stuccoes in the 19C by Luigi Fontana. There is a little Romanesque column by the door. On either side of the entrance to the second south chapel are two Turkish flags, thought to have been captured at the battle of Lepanto. The octagonal chapel (attributed to Antonio da Sangallo the Younger) contains two Farrattini funerary monuments by Ippolito Scalza, and an altarpiece attributed to Taddeo Zuccari.

In the **south transept**, in a pretty frame, is a *Last Supper* by the local painter Gian Francesco Perini (1538; restored in 1989). In the Oratorio del Sacramento (unlocked on request) are two paintings by Nicolò Pomarancio, restored in 1998. In the **north transept** is a beautiful painting of the *Assunta* attributed to Duccio di Buoninsegna which is only shown in May and 15–20 August, when it is displayed on the high altar. Off the north transept is a chapel with a 15C–16C wooden Crucifix. In the first chapel in the **north aisle** is the recomposed tomb of Bishop Giovanni Geraldini (1476) by Agostino di Duccio and assistants.

Outside the Duomo there is a fine view from the peaceful little garden.

A road continues around the Duomo and Via Alessandro Geraldini descends past the church of Santa Caterina, which has a red façade, to Via Cavour. The church of **Sant'Agostino** is situated here. In the façade (1477) is a good portal with a very worn fresco and a lovely rose window. The interior (open 09.30–12.00), which retains its old terracotta pavement, was decorated in 1747 by Francesco Appiani. The *Vision of St John at Patmos* on the first south altar is by Pomarancio. The fine Morettini organ was made in 1841. In the sacristy, interesting sinopie have been uncovered, thought to date from c 1000 (left unfinished and never frescoed): in the vault there is a red star decoration and standing figures of saints, and unusual floral motifs on the walls. There are also remains of primitive frescoes here. The walnut choir stalls are also notable.

On the left of the façade, beyond a house with pretty terracotta decoration, Via Garibaldi continues past Via Posterola. This descends steeply between Sant'Agostino and a large Benedictine convent founded in the 13C (seven nuns still live here) and the unusual little tower of the church of **San Magno**. The church is entered through the courtyard of the convent (at no. 6) and contains a precious organ of 1680 (the pipes may be even earlier), which is played on two keyboards. It was carefully restored in 1996 and it is used for concerts, usually in May and August. The high altarpiece (in very poor condition) of the *Death of St Benedict* is by Antonio Viviani.

The road continues down past a locked gate beyond which a path leads to the pretty 18C octagonal church of **San Girolamo**, owned by a confraternity and surrounded by woods. Outside the 13C **Porta Posterola** there is a path below the walls and a view of a wooded landscape.

Via Garibaldi (see above) emerges in **Piazza Matteotti**, a pleasant square with a medley of buildings and an attractive clipped ilex tree surrounded by a circular hedge below the curving façade of the hospital. **Palazzo Comunale**, with its clock, is a quaint building. In the courtyard are numerous Roman sculptural fragments, including several carved altars. In the **Sala Consigliare** (admission on request) is a *Madonna with Saints* by Pier Matteo d'Amelia and a *Crucifix with two Saints* by Livio Agresti.

Opposite Palazzo Comunale is the entrance to the **Roman cisterns** beneath the piazza (for admission ask at the tourist office; usually open Sat 16.30–18.00; PH 10.30–12.30, 16.30–19.30). A very steep staircase, installed in 1996, leads down to ten remarkable vaulted reservoirs probably built between the 1C BC and 1C AD. These provided a huge collecting place for the rainwater channelled from the piazza above (sited in a declivity between two hills on which the Duomo and the hospital now stand), capable of holding some 4400 cubic metres of water, which provided the Roman town with an emergency drinking-water supply. The water, which filled the halls to a height of about 3 metres, was used by means of wells constructed through openings in the vaults. The room to the left of the stairs retains its original proportions and three large terracotta Roman floor tiles with their original stamps (it appears that there were plans to floor the whole room in this way). The vaults survive intact in six of these rooms with their waterproof walls and original floors. The four rooms in the centre have been divided by retaining walls for the later palaces built above and have lost their original vaults (rebuilt in 1820). The entire floor slopes gradually down all the way to the tenth room where the entrance to the underground channel can be seen; this ran for some 300 metres to emerge near Porta Posterula, and was used for flushing out the cisterns periodically so that the water would not remain stagnant.

Via Garibaldi (here beautifully paved) leads out of Piazza Matteotti. The first narrow lane on the right leads under a passageway down to the charming and well-preserved **Teatro Sociale**. Usually shown by the custodian on Saturdays and Sundays in summer; at other times enquire at the tourist office. It has been beautifully restored and its season runs from November to May. It was built in wood in 1783 to a design by the local architect Stefano Cansacchi (it bears a strong resemblance to the former Fenice theatre in Venice, built ten years later). It can seat 92 in the stalls, 208 in the boxes, and 100 (seated and standing) in the 'gods'. It was restored in 1880 when Domenico Bruschi frescoed the foyer and the backcloth. In the entrance is a fire extinguisher made by the firm of Bale and Edwards in Milan in 1816. The boxes are all preserved (some with their wooden cupboards for picnics during the performances) and the 'gods' (with a lovely view from a window), the stage apparatus, the artists' changing-rooms and their kitchen, and an old projector used for silent movies in 1913 when the theatre was used as a cinema.

Via Studiosi, with lots of flying arches, is a picturesque street nearby. Below the theatre Via della Valle leads downhill past the large church of **Sant'Angelo** (being restored) and an impressive wall of ancient polygonal blocks to the **Porta della Valle**, outside of which are paths through orchards and olive groves.

Via del Teatro leads back up to Via Garibaldi which continues past the grand **Palazzo Cansacchi** which has a fine portal and ground floor windows. Via Piacenti on the left leads back down towards Porta della Valle. Via Garibaldi ends at Piazza Marconi (see above).

BEYOND AMELIA

Amelia is in the centre of a beautiful district in the south-west corner of Umbria between the Tiber and the Nera rivers. Here, little medieval villages and castles are dotted among low wooded hills (noted for their chestnuts) with vineyards and olive groves. This area is ideal walking country, especially around Monte Cimamonte, Monte Castellari and Monte Croce di Serra. Lugnano in Teverina, with its beautiful church and Alviano with a fine castle, are among the most interesting villages to visit.

Practical information

Information office
IAT dell' Amerina, ☎ 0744 981453.

Getting there
By bus Buses run from Amelia to most of the places of interest in the environs.

Hotel
Lugnano in Teverina
☆☆ *La Rocca*, ☎ 0744 900064. A very simple family-run hotel with ten rooms (some with views over the valley) and a restaurant, in the old centre. Half- and full-board rates.

Penna in Teverina and Giove
From Amelia a road runs south-west downhill towards Attigliano in the Tiber valley. **Penna in Teverina** is a little medieval borgo overlooking the Tiber. The view from the fields to the south of the houses built into the walls is remarkable. From the quaint little central piazza the street leads down to an archway, beyond which is a charming circular terrace with a wide view from which curving steps lead down into the fields.

At the other end of the street the grand palace (privately owned; no admission), which formerly belonged to the Orsini, is approached by an elaborate gateway in a group of old cypresses with 18C busts of the *Four Seasons* above benches. It has a 19C garden on the hillside. On the Amelia road is a gateway to the estate with monumental carved herms known as the *Mammalocchi*.

Giove has medieval walls. The huge **Palazzo Ducale** (still owned by the Dukes of Acquarone), which dominates the town and is visible for miles around, is an interesting building begun in the 16C by Duke Ciriaco Mattei, incorporating a pre-existing castle. It is built in a mixture of styles and part of it is in very poor condition. In the interior (which is not open to the public) a spiral staircase leads up to the piano nobile, and rooms decorated by the school of Domenichino. Beside it is the **parish church** with a painting of the *Assumption* by the school of Alunno. In the chapel of San Rocco is a fresco of the *Crucifixion* by the Foligno school.

Attigliano, now virtually abandoned, is on an Etruscan site. The few inhabitants have moved to houses below near station. Four kilometres away, on the other side of the Tiber and across the motorway, is the famous park of Bomarzo in Lazio.

Lugnano in Teverina and Alviano
N205 leads west from Amelia across the high **Ponte sul Rio Grande**, a pretty bridge, with a view of **Porchiano** on its thickly wooded hill.

Lugnano in Teverina is an interesting old hill town with picturesque well-paved streets and fine views. In the main street is the huge **Palazzo Pennone**, which towers above the little town, with numerous windows and a tunnelled passageway beneath it. It was built by Cardinal Ridolfi and finished by Cardinal Farnese in the 16C as a residence for clerics, and was then owned by the Vannicelli family. It was restored in 1979 as the seat of the town hall. On the first floor a small **antiquarium** has been arranged in one room to display finds from a Roman villa excavated nearby at Poggio Gramignano, in 1988. These include fragments of mosaics and wall-paintings.

Close by is the splendid **Collegiata di Santa Maria Assunta**, a remarkable 12C church with important sculptural decoration. The delightful façade, with interesting carving, is preceded by a pronaos of 1230, with an unusual roof. The beautifully proportioned **interior**, with a Cosmatesque pavement, has a miscellany of carved capitals, including one with allegories of the Eucharist with a scene of the celebration of Mass according to Byzantine rites. The *'schola cantorum'* has been recomposed and includes two interesting bas-reliefs showing two robed men greeting each other, and St Michael archangel overcoming the devil in the form of a dragon, and a ciborium restored in 1937 (with a rare stone hanging tabernacle in the form of a lantern for the Host). In the apse is a charming portable triptych with the *Assumption of the Virgin and two Saints* by Alunno. The crypt has graceful columns. At the top of the left flight of steps is a painting of *St Jerome* by Leandro da Bassano, and at the top of the right flight of steps, a Crucifix from the 13C (a fresco transferred to canvas), and, in the chapel on the right, Livio Agresti's *Beheading of the Baptist* (1571).

Behind the campanile is a pretty raised well. There is a good bakery in Via Cavour.

The road goes on, with superb views, to a turning which leads down to **Alviano**. Its impressive square **castle** can be seen on a spur with the village behind it. The first castle on this site dated from 933; the present building was begun in 1495 by the *condottiere* Bartolomeo d'Alviano, and incorporates a cylindrical tower of the earlier castle (the three others were added at this time). The castle was bought by Donna Olimpia Pamphili in 1651 and the Doria Pamphili left it to the comune in 1920. It has been restored and on the upper floor is the town hall. The piano nobile has handsome windows. Beside the bridge at the entrance is a lion with an iron collar, and on the round tower to the left a Medusa's head can be seen.

Inside is a Renaissance **courtyard** with a well, off which is a **chapel** with frescoes illustrating a miracle of St Francis, who in 1212 silenced the song of the swallows who were disturbing his preaching outside the castle. The old herringbone paving of the staircases has been preserved. In underground vaulted rooms a charming little local **ethnographical museum** has been arranged (open 09.00–13.00 on request), with exhibits illustrating the traditional agriculture of the area.

In front of the castle, Via Umberto I leads past an alley with a view of the campanile and then steps descend left to the **parish church** built in 1506 with a pleasant interior with old columns and capitals and a wooden roof. Here is a fresco by Pordenone of the *Madonna and Saints* with a striking portrait of Pentesilea Baglione, the elderly widow of Bartolomeo d'Alviano (on the right, protected by St Anthony), who commissioned the fresco. At the end of the right aisle is a lovely painting of the *Madonna in Glory* by Alunno (c 1484), similar to the central panel of the triptych in the Collegiata of Lugnano. There is a pretty view from the little terrace of the countryside below the town.

The road continues from Alviano above the Tiber, and the **Oasi di Alviano**, a lake created in 1963, which since 1978 has been an area protected by the Worldwide Fund for Nature, interesting for its birdlife in early spring, autumn and winter (red herons, bitterns, reed warblers, cormorants, wild geese, etc). Seven bird-watching stations have been built here and it can be visited on guided tours from September–April at weekends, 10.00–12.30, 14.00–17.00 or by appointment. For information, ☎ 0744 903715 or ask at the Municipio of Alviano (however, it is best visited from Lazio).

The road passes the ruins (right) of **Guardea Vecchia** (Guardege), once an important stronghold acquired in 1158 by Pope Hadrian IV, before reaching **Guardea**. Above the town on a lovely wooded hill and surrounded by a park (signposted) is the 15C **Castello del Poggio** (open on the second Sat and third Mon of the month; or sometimes by request) purchased in 1981 and being slowly and carefully restored. It has Byzantine origins and was later a Norman castle. In the 16C it was restored by Antonio Sangallo the Younger and was subsequently owned by the Doria Pamphil family. Within the walls is a little borgo with well-restored houses and the castle has a fine 16C staircase in the courtyard. It is used as a cultural centre and residence, and a guesthouse may be opened here. It is also the seat of the international Club Budapest. It has spectacular views of the lake of Alviano and the Tiber.

Avigliano Umbro, Dunarobba, Montecastrilli and Toscolano

N205 leads east out of Amelia and beside the huge monumental gateway of Villa **L'Aspreta** (privately owned), seen at the end of a long cypress avenue, with a theatrical external staircase, is a turning (left) signposted for Montecastrilli and Avigliano Umbro. This road leads north through thick ilex woods and open farming country and then branches left towards Avigliano past **Sambucetole**, with a bright coral-coloured church. Nearby on a tiny wooded knoll, naturally defended, is the ruined borgo of Sambucetole, abandoned when the present town was built. It is high above Lagoscello, a lovely little lake with a waterfall. Nearby is a single-arched Roman bridge across the Rio Grande (close to the Collicello turning). The Roman Via Falisca Amerina, between Amelia and Todi, can still be traced in this area. **Castel dell'Aquila** has a very tall tower. Nearby, conspicuous on a ridge above woods the abandoned hamlet of Forte Cesare can be seen, built from the 16C to 18C and inhabited up until 1920 when it was left to the comune of Amelia. The splendid old buildings have been vandalised.

Avigliano Umbro became a municipality in 1975. It has an original castellated water-tower. Its little theatre dates from 1928. **Dunarobba**, north of Avigliano, has a massive 15C–16C castle.

Just outside the village, on the Montecastrilli road, is the **fossil forest of Dunarobba**, one of the most important palaeontological sites in central Italy. Here in 1983–87, during work in a clay quarry, a group of some 40 fossilised tree trunks were found, particularly remarkable since they were still in an upright position. They grew on the south-western shores of the huge Lago Tiberino, which in the Pleistocene era occupied a large part of Umbria. Some of them are 1.5m in diameter and 8m high: they date from the Villafranchian or Pliocene era and are similar to the present-day Sequoia. For admission ☎ 0744 933531 or ask at the municipio of Avigliano Umbro: in the school next door is a research centre with documents and exhibitions relating to the fossils.

On the Todi road north of Dunarobba is **Sismano**, a tiny village in beautiful country at the foot of a medieval castle owned by the Florentine Corsini family since 1607. The parish church contains a painting of *St Andrea Corsini* by Andrea Polinori. In the Arnata valley, in an isolated locality known as **Molinella**, are three 18C water-mills, one of which is perfectly preserved by its owners (the same family have lived here for generations). The road continues down to Todi (see p. 219).

Montecastrilli is east of Avigliano in lovely country, well seen from below. Of Roman origin, it was important from 962 onwards as part of the Terre Arnolfe. The old district of the town has lost its character, but the large 17C convent of the Clarisse (still inhabited by 14 nuns of a closed order) is an interesting building with prison-like windows next to the church of Santa Chiara, which has a section reserved for the nuns. At the other end of the street the parish church, with a tall brick campanile rebuilt in 1952, contains a 15C wooden Crucifix.

The Romanesque churches in the district include the tiny **San Lorenzo in Nifili**, dating from the 11C, next to a huge old oak tree.

A road leads west from Avigliano to the tiny village of **Santa Restituta** surrounded by chestnut woods, near which, on Monte l'Aiola, is the Grotta Bella where excavations in the early 1970s yielded finds from the Neolithic to the Roman era including small bronzes of the 5C BC.

Beyond is **Toscolano**, a small village built on a circular plan, in beautiful countryside amidst chestnut woods. It is entered by a gate, above which is the eagle of Todi and the campanile of **Sant'Apollinare** (key at the bar to the right of the gate) which contains a *Crucifix and Saints* by Andrea Polinori, and an interesting church treasury, including a precious Cross. Its fine organ has recently been restored. The *Madonna and Saints* on the left altar dates from 1633. Outside, at the beginning of an avenue (left) is the peach-coloured chapel of **Santissimo Annunziata** (ask for the key in the village), with frescoes (restored in 1987) attributed to Pier Matteo d'Amelia. Below the town is a picturesque group of houses used as a European music centre (Centro Europeo di Toscolana).

Melezzole, nearby, is particularly attractive when seen from a distance, and above it a beautiful unsurfaced road leads over Monte Croce through splendid woods to **Montecchio** where there is a panoramic view of the Tiber valley. Near Montecchio **Tenaglie** has a grand villa, with a local ethnographical museum.

Further north is **Collelungo**, a pretty little village surrounded by its walls. The castle was held from 1394 onwards by the Monaldeschi. The church of San Mattia, with an unusual font and late 13C frescoes, has recently been restored. An altar of the 7C–8C has been found here.

NARNI

● ● ● ● ● ● ● ●

Narni is a pleasant old town (population 20,600), 12km west of Terni, which has many interesting medieval buildings along its attractively paved streets. It has extremely fine palaces, some of which have been restored, while others preserve a dark and somewhat grim appearance. It is built on a hill (244m), and has fine views over the plain of Terni and the deep wooded gorge of the Nera river.

Practical information

Information office
Pro-Loco, Palazzo Comunale, ☎ 0744 715362.

Getting there
By rail There is a station at Narni Scalo at the foot of the hill, on the Ancona—Rome line (slow trains only). Bus to Piazza Garibaldi.

By bus Services are run by *ATC*, ☎ 0744 715207. There are frequent services from Terni and Amelia, also to Otricoli and San Gemini.

Car-park There is parking at del Suffragio is situated off Via Roma, partly underground and partly open-air, with lifts up to Via Roma and near Piazza Cavour.

Hotel
✶✶✶✶ *Dei Priori* (with *La Loggia* restaurant), 4 Vicolo del Comune, ☎ 0744 726843; fax 0744 722744. The hotel is in a splendid position in the old centre just out of Piazza dei Priori, in a very quiet narrow alleyway. The bedrooms were modernised some years ago (with poor sound-proofing) but they are comfortable and some on the third floor have pretty balconies. A handsome room survives on the first floor with fine portals where a rather frugal breakfast is served. There is a very good restaurant (*La Loggia*) on the ground floor in three vaulted rooms, which has an interesting menu with local specialities. Friendly, efficient management.

Campsite
✶✶ *Monte del Sole*, ☎ 0744 796336, 4km outside the town at Borgaria di Narni (open in summer).

Restaurants
££ *La Loggia* (see above); also £ *Il Grifo*, 3 Via Roma, ☎ 0744 726625 (also pizzeria) and £ *Il Gatto e La Volpe*, Vicolo Belvedere, ☎ 0744 726294.

£ *Il Cavallino*, 2km outside on the Via Flaminia, località Testaccio, ☎ 0744 761020.

Picnics
There are good places to picnic in the garden behind San Domenico, or around the Rocca.

Annual festival
On the second Sunday in May a medieval tournament, the *Corsa all'Anello* is held, preceded by two weeks of festivities in honour of the patron saint Giovenale. A torch-light procession takes place on the eve of the race, and the competition is held in Via Maggiore, where a ring is suspended across the street and the contestants from the three districts of the town attempt to thrust a lance through it. The town is illuminated by candle-light during the festivities (iron candelabra have survived on all the palaces).

History

Originally called Nequinum, it changed its name to *Narnia* (after the river) when it became a Roman colony in 299 BC. It was the birthplace of the emperor Nerva (AD 32), of John XIII (pope, 965–972) and of Erasmo da Narni, known as Gattamelata, the Venetian *condottiere* (d. 1443). Virgil, followed by Macaulay ('the pale waves of Nar'), refers to the whitish turbidity (due to its content of sulphur and lime) of the stream washing the foot of the hill.

The main road from Perugia and Terni runs through the modern industrial suburb of **Narni Scalo** and then begins to climb before crossing the Nera river. From the bridge there is a brief glimpse of the remains of the so-called **Ponte d'Augusto**, which was probably built in 27 BC for the Via Flaminia which crosses the river gorge here. The monumental bridge had a span of 160m, supported by three or four arches of different heights, and was built of concrete faced with blocks of white travertine. It was already famous in Roman times because of its height (it is mentioned by both Martial and Procopius). It was ruined in the Middle Ages and a third pier fell in 1855. One arch survives, 30m high, but it is extremely difficult to see as there is nowhere to stop on the road bridge, and from the road beyond it is lost to view. The only way it can be seen at closer range is by taking the rough road (signposted 'Molino Feroli') by the Co-op supermarket at Tre Ponti: the road descends and passes beneath the Roman arch, now in very unromantic surroundings. There is a good view of the ruins from the iron footbridge over the Nera here.

The Narni road climbs up round the hill and passes through the **Porta Ternana**, commissioned by Pope Sixtus IV. Via Roma continues past a war memorial (1927, by Pietro Lombardi) in the form of a lighthouse, to the right of which is the entrance to the large car-park (with a lift to the centre). Beyond, Via Roma runs through the middle of **Piazza Garibaldi**, always busy with traffic. This is the unusual main square of the town, with a quaint neo-classical palace, a clock-tower and the side door of the Duomo. The fountain (restored in 1998), which has a bronze centrepiece with fantastic animal heads, dates from the 14C (remade in the 17C). Beside it steps lead down to the **Lacus**, an early medieval cistern on the site of a Roman piscina. The vaulted hall, dating from the 13C and later, with part of its herringbone paving intact, can be seen through an iron door (and illuminated by the light switch).

On the right of the square is the most interesting part of the town, regularly laid out on the site of the Roman *Narnia*; on the left some medieval streets survive and the hill-top is crowned by the Rocca (see below).

A road leads up under an archway to the main entrance of the **Duomo** preceded by a fine **portico**, a Lombard work of 1490. The main 12C portal has classical carvings. The **interior** (closed 12.30–15.30), consecrated in 1145, has a very unusual nave with Corinthian columns supporting a wall with low arches. The outer south aisle was added in the 15C. The two pretty pulpits on either side of the nave date from 1490. On the west wall, in a niche, is a fresco of the *Madonna and Child* by a local painter. South aisle. The third chapel has a fine carved Renaissance entrance arch (1490), a decorated barrel vault and a lovely tabernacle for the Host. In the nave remains of the Cosmatesque pavement can be seen.

Beyond is the remarkable old **Sacello di San Cassio** where in 376 St Giovenale was buried. It is preceded by an old marble screen with Cosmatesque decoration and a relief above the door with two Lambs adoring the Cross. In the two niches are a 13C terracotta *Pietà* and a 13C statue of *St Giovenale*. The two portals are also decorated with Cosmati work. High up on an inner wall (very difficult to see; the sacristan turns on a light on request) is a ruined 10C mosaic of the *Redeemer* and remains of Roman masonry. Inside the oratory, with its old pavement made out of Cosmatesque fragments, there is an interesting bas-relief and, in the inner cell, the open sarcophagus (6C) of St Giovenale. On the last south pilaster of the nave is a beautiful painting of *St Giovenale* attributed to Vecchietta.

In the **south transept** the Cappella della Beata Lucia was built in 1710 and decorated with paintings by Francesco Trevisani. The **high altar** and **presbytery**, elaborately decorated in coloured marbles, dates from 1669–1714. In the apse, which retains its French Gothic form, are choir stalls of 1474. **North aisle**. At the east end is a colossal wooden statue of *St Anthony Abbot enthroned*, signed and dated 1475 by Vecchietta. Beyond a chapel (with glass doors) which

---

The lure of the Antique in 18C and 19C Italy

The Ponte d'Augusto at Narni provided one of the famous 'views' of classical ruins in Italy, sketched and painted numerous times by travellers on their way to Rome in the 18C and 19C. Its romantic ruined state surrounded by a wild landscape meant that it was much admired by visitors on the Grand Tour. The famous Marmore waterfalls outside Terni nearby were also a great attraction to painters as well as the Romantic poets. The waterfalls are described in verse by Byron in *Childe Harold's Pilgrimage*, written in 1818, and in a note he claims they are 'worth all the cascades and torrents of Switzerland put together' and advises his readers to view them both from above and below, and then go on to visit the Lago di Piediluco. The bridge at Narni was often included in the cultured traveller's itinerary south to Rome which led through Perugia, Assisi and Spoleto, and then proceeded to the Marmore waterfalls, the Lago di Piediluco and Narni. In the 1760s, Richard Wilson, on his way south from Venice to Rome, crossed the Apennines near Foligno to sketch the Marmore waterfalls and the bridge at Narni. He executed two paintings of the bridge (inserting a classical temple into the landscape). Turner also sketched the falls, lake and bridge around 1818.

Corot made three trips to Italy between 1825 and 1843, and the outdoor paintings he made at this time are amongst his most important works. His paintings had a great influence on subsequent landscape painters, and were important in developing the idea of outdoor painting in Italy. He was one of numerous artists who, while staying in Rome, made frequent sketching trips out of the city and this area near Terni was the place he favoured, along with the Roman Campagna, Tivoli, and the Alban hills. In 1826 he travelled up from Rome to stay at Papigno above the River Nera near Terni. At this time, apart from views of Papigno, he also painted the Lago di Piediluco, the Marmore waterfalls and the bridge at Narni. He added a pastoral scene, in the manner of Claude and Poussin, to an exhibition picture of the bridge he produced in the following year (now in the Louvre).

contains a 15C *Madonna and Child* and a funerary monument of Bishop Pietro Gormaz (1515), is the wall monument of Pietro Cesi, attributed to Bernardo da Settignano (1470).

Outside the Duomo, in the little **Piazza Cavour**, is a house partly built with Roman blocks of stone, which once formed part of the town walls. The former **Palazzo Vescovile** situated here is to become the seat of the town museum and pinacoteca (see below). Just out of the piazza, off Vicolo Belvedere, is Via Arco Romano (right) with the **Porta Superior**, a Roman arch restored in the Middle Ages.

The straight **Via Garibaldi**, with fine paving, on the line of the Roman Cardo Maximus, leads towards Piazza dei Priori. It passes (left) the pretty arched Via del Campanile which leads up beneath three arches, two of them decorated with windows, to the **campanile** of the Duomo, constructed on a Roman base. It was completed in the 15C and is decorated with majolica plaques.

Via Garibaldi continues and beyond the 19C **Teatro Comunale** the road widens to form **Piazza dei Priori** with its interesting medieval buildings. On the right is **Palazzo Sacripante** with fine medieval bas-reliefs on its façade next to the tall Torre Civico with an 18C clock restored in 1992, and little pulpit used for reading public proclamations. The **Loggia dei Priori** is attributed to Gattapone, with two very tall arches and a Roman inscription.

Via del Campanile

Opposite is **Palazzo dei Podestà** (now **Palazzo Comunale**) with more interesting Romanesque reliefs, especially above the door into the Pro-Loco tourist office (which has a fresco by Torresani inside). In the untidy and ill-kept courtyard are numerous Roman and medieval architectural fragments including columns, sarcophagi and a lion from a funerary monument. Upstairs (admission on request) some restored works of art are temporarily displayed in a small room (they belong to the **Pinacoteca**, formerly exhibited in San Domenico and eventually to be rehoused in the former Palazzo Vescovile, see above). There is an *Annunciation* by Benozzo Gozzoli, and a Standard of 1409 with the *Dormition and Coronation of the Virgin* (and, on the back, the *Madonna enthroned*), by the Maestro di Narni. The Egyptian mummy, dating from the 1C BC (in a re-used sarcophagus of the 5C–4C BC), was brought to Narni at the beginning of the century by the local collector Edoardo Martinori.

Among sculptures at present not on view are a bust in terracotta of *St Bernardine* by Lorenzo Vecchietta and a wooden Romanesque statue of the *Madonna and Child*. The **Sala del Consiglio** is also shown: it is dominated by the *Coronation of the Virgin*, a beautiful altarpiece by Domenico Ghirlandaio.

Beyond the lovely circular 14C fountain (covered for restoration), with a bronze basin (1303), Via Mazzini continues gently downhill past the church of **Santa Maria in Pensole** (1175). The unusual name is derived from the fact that the church was constructed on the vaults of a previous church (hence *pensile* or *pensole*, meaning 'hanging'). It is preceded by a Romanesque portico and three doors surrounded by fine (if worn) carving. The arches in the interior are similar to those in the Duomo, and the high altar is interesting. On the walls are remains of 14C–15C frescoes. An earlier church on this site, probably dating from the 8C, and two Roman wells can be seen beneath the church by appointment with the Associazione Culturale Subterranea, ☎ 0744 722292. Opposite the church is the 17C **Palazzo Bocciarelli** next to the 16C **Palazzo Scotti**, with a loggia in the courtyard.

Further downhill is the former church of **San Domenico** beside its tall campanile dating from the 12C, now the seat of the Public Library and Archives (admission on weekdays during office hours). The **façade** has a portal with interesting, if worn, decorations including medallions with busts of the 12 Apostles and, higher up, a cornice with animal and human heads as brackets. The **interior** contains numerous 13C–16C fresco fragments, and remains of Cosmati paving in the south aisle. Beside the steps at the east end, opposite a marble tabernacle by the school of Agostino di Duccio, is the fine wall monument of Gabriele Massei (1494). In a chapel off the left side (where exhibitions are held) are very worn frescoes by the Zuccari. Also displayed here is the tusk of an elephant dating from the Pleistocene era, found in 1988 near Taizzano above the Nera river.

I Sotterranei della Chiesa di San Domenico, the rooms beneath the church and former monastery, can be visited on PH 10.00–13.00, 15.00–18.00; winter 11.00–13.00, 15.00–17.00; or by appointment with the Associazione Culturale Subterranea, ☎ 0744 722292. The entrance is from the public gardens to the left of the church and there is a lovely view of the ravine from a pretty courtyard. Stairs lead down past a little garden to an earlier church with interesting frescoes, a Roman well and a prison used during the Inquisition with 18C graffiti. Excavations and restoration work are in progress with the help of local volunteers.

Behind the church (left), in the public garden, are remains of two sides of a very tall tower. There is a remarkable view over the deep Nera gorge to the wooded cliffs beyond, with the picturesque Abbey of San Cassiano (see below). The road and railway to Rome run on either side of the river.

Via Mazzini ends in Piazza Galeotto Marzio with the palaces (in poor repair) of various educational institutions. Vicolo degli Orti (with steps) leads steeply down past orchards and a tall medieval tower to **Porta della Fiera** (or Porta Nuova), in a picturesque spot in the walls. The gate is attributed to Vignola. Via Gattamelata, with some old houses, leads uphill from the gate past no. 113 (plaque), traditionally supposed to be the birthplace in 1370 of Gattamelata, the *condottiere* (his father was a baker here).

The road continues up past the fine Palazzo Capocacci (now a school) to **Sant'Agostino** (closed for restoration) with an unusual massive plain portal and a worn fresco attributed to Antoniazzo Romano on the façade. The **interior** has an exceptionally high nave with a 16C painting in the carved ceiling by the local artist Carlo Federico Benincasa. The first south altar has four saints and a predella by a follower of Antoniazzo Romano. In the apse is a massive 14C stone altar. Off the west end of the north aisle is a chapel with 16C frescoes by Lorenzo Torresani. On the right of the main door is a fresco attributed to Pier Matteo d'Amelia. The convent and cloister next door are being restored.

Via Ferrucci, nicely paved, leads uphill past several palaces, some of them still awaiting restoration, and a tower on the picturesque old Via San Giuseppe and emerges on Via Garibaldi.

Above the other side of Via Garibaldi is the church of **San Francesco** (burnt down in 1998) which had a very worn carved portal. It contained interesting 14C–15C frescoes on the columns and in the Cappella Eroli. In the sacristy were 16C frescoes by Alessandro Torresani.

From the south side of Piazza Garibaldi (see above) Via del Monte leads up through another district of the town which has a number of stepped medieval streets. Beside the little Fontanella di Bucci, which was once fed by the Formina aqueduct (see below) a street leads left to the 17C church of **Santa Margherita**, which has a charming façade with twin doors. It contains frescoes of the life of St Margaret by the Zuccari. In Via del Monte, just above the fountain, is an arch pierced with windows and decorated in terracotta.

At the very top of the hill (best reached by car) is the **Rocca**, a huge square-towered castle, very conspicuous above Narni from the plain of Terni. It was built for Cardinal Albornoz in the mid-14C and is attributed to Gattapone. It has been undergoing restoration for many years but is due to reopen soon (and will be used for exhibitions).

Outside the town, on the Amelia road which leads west, beyond the Nera bridge, is the Madonna del Ponte (rebuilt, after having been blown up along with the medieval road bridge in 1944).

BEYOND NARNI

The most interesting place in the environs of Narni is the village of Otricoli, with its fine church, and the ruins of the Roman town of Ocriculum nearby.

Practical information

Information office
Pro-Loco di Narni, ☎ 0744 715362.

Getting there
By bus *ATC*, ☎ 0744 715207, run from Narni to Otricoli.

Restaurants
Moricone on the road between Narni and Calvi dell'Umbria: trattoria £ *Da Sara*, ☎ 0744 796138.

Otricoli ££ *Locanda Carole*, in a fine building in the centre of the old town, open for lunch only at the weekends (on weekdays only in the evening).

Just outside Narni (reached by a road near the bridge over the Nera, from which it is clearly seen) is the 12C Benedictine abbey of **San Cassiano**. Recently restored, it is open for a short period on Sunday afternoons (☎ 0744 722080).

On the other side of the town to the east, off the Via Flaminia by the Strada di Santo Urbano, about 3km below the town, is the single-arched **Ponte Cardona**. It is approached by a path from near the **Montagnone** restaurant through woods. It is part of the Roman aqueduct 15km long, known as *Formina*, built in the 1C AD, which was in use up until the middle of the 20C. The interior can sometimes be visited by appointment (☎ 0744 722292, or enquire at the Narni tourist office). A narrow low tunnel, some 700 metres long, can be followed (boots and rainwear necessary; a helmet with a light is provided), but the visit is not advisable if you suffer from claustrophobia. The bridge is recognised as being positioned at the geographical centre of Italy.

A road winds south-east of Narni to the **Speco di San Francesco** (568m; admission on request), a picturesque Franciscan convent isolated in woods, founded by St Francis in 1213. St Bernardine built the present building in the 14C.

Another road winds due south from Narni to **Calvi dell'Umbria**, where the church of Sant'Antonio (usually closed) has a *presepio* of more than 30 large terracotta figures (1546). The church of San Paolo was designed in 1744 by Ferdinando Fuga (who also built the façade of Sant'Antonio).

Otricoli is approached from Narni by the Rome road which ascends the Nera valley. At **Taizzano** is the abbey of Sant'Angelo in Massa (10C; now privately owned), and the ruined church of San Martino.

A byroad leads to the hamlet of **Visciano**, where some houses have recently been carefully restored. A very steep rough road continues downhill for roughly 1km to the charming little church of **Santa Pudenziana**, isolated in a group of trees. Probably dating from the 11C, it has a very tall campanile, and is preceded by a primitive portico with four Roman columns (restored in 1929).

Otricoli
Further south, near the border with Lazio, is Otricoli an old walled village, with numerous Roman fragments, on the site of the first settlement of Ocriculum (which later moved down to the banks of the Tiber). In the Middle Ages the inhabitants returned to this hill-top site to avoid the floods of the river. The street below the walls has attractive wide porticoes, and the main street leads up through a gate past interesting buildings, many with Roman carvings inserted in their masonry, to the church of **Santa Maria** (entered by the side door) founded in the 6C or 7C with a neo-classical peach-coloured **façade** by Ireneo Aleandri (1840) and 19C campanile (which bears a very worn Roman carving of the head of Medusa). The interesting **interior** has brickwork in the nave in opus reticulatum, an ancient crypt, and numerous sculptural fragments, some Roman, some early Christian, and others medieval. Two Roman columns sup-

port the organ (1530; restored in the 17C–18C and again in 1980). The choir stalls date from the late 15C. Above the 12C altar is an elegant early 16C tabernacle with re-used Roman columns. The pretty side chapels were decorated in the 17C–18C.

A house in the piazza is decorated with more interesting Roman and medieval carvings.

About 1.5km below the town, signposted off the Rome road, is the (unenclosed) site of the Roman **Ocriculum** on the Tiber, now semi-abandoned and in need of protection (it is dangerous to get too close to the ruins because of falling masonry). It is surrounded by lovely fields and the abandoned vineyard is full of birds. Excavations were carried out here in 1776–84 by order of Pius VI and they resulted in numerous finds, now in the Vatican Museum (including a beautiful mosaic and the colossal head of Jupiter, both displayed in the Sala Rotonda).

A single-track approach road leads downhill (keep left) for about 1km to a parking place beside a wooden fence by the impressive ruins of the **baths** (partly covered in scaffolding), which include the remains of a circular hall. It is necessary to return on foot up the approach road for a few metres and take the track on the left to see the romantic overgrown ruins of a vaulted substructure and the **theatre** beyond. On the other side of the approach road a solitary tower in a field can be seen, which was part of the **entrance gate** to the city and (surrounded by a wooden fence) a stretch of the old **Via Flaminia** and two **funerary monuments** (the circular one still keeps part of its marble facing). Nearby are remains of the **amphitheatre**. The road continues back to a second entrance on the main road where there are signs that the site may one day receive the attention it deserves.

TERNI

• • • • • •

Terni (130m) is the second largest town in Umbria and capital of its second province. It faces the broad plain of the Nera river, and the presence of abundant water here has led to its expansion as a thriving industrial centre, particularly important for its steelworks, and the production of plastics and machinery. Its population (106,000) has trebled since the beginning of this century. Badly damaged in the Second World War, it was reconstructed with pleasant residential suburbs, particularly spacious and planted with trees, under the guidance of the architect Mario Ridolfi (1904–84), who lived here at the end of his life.

Practical information

Information office
IAT del Ternano, 5 Viale Cesare Battisti, ☎ 0744 423047.

Getting there
By rail The station is on Piazza Dante Alighieri. Services on the Rome–Ancona line, and the Rieti–Aquila line. The Ferrovia Centrale Umbra has services from Perugia, Umbertide, and Sansepolcro.

By bus *ATC*, ☎ 0744 409457, to Piazza Dante Alighieri from Narni, Perugia and Orvieto. Services to the environs, including Acquasparta, the Cascata delle Marmore, Piediluco, Sangemini and Otricoli (see p. 266).

Hotels

Although the town is well supplied with hotels of all categories they are mainly for people on business, and Narni, close by, is a much more pleasant place to stay. There are also some good simple hotels in the environs, see p. 266. Hotels in Terni include ✩✩✩✩ *Valentino*, 5 Via Plinio il Giovane, ☎ 0744 402550 and ✩✩✩ *De Paris*, 52 Viale della Stazione, ☎ 0744 58047.

Outside the historic centre
✩✩✩✩ *Garden*, 4 Via Bramante, ☎ 0744 300041, in a quieter position, with restaurant, and ✩✩✩ *Allegretti*, 76 Strada del Staino, ☎ 0477 426747. There is pleasant agriturist accommodation at *Casale Maratta*, 25 Via Maratta Bassa, ☎ 0744 300248, and rooms to rent at *Due Pini*, 17 Via Grabher, ☎

744 304565.

Restaurants

£££ *Alfio*, Via Galilei, ☎ 0744 420120; *La Fontanella*, 3 Via Plinio il Giovane, ☎ 0744 402550; *Il Gatto Mammone*, 15 Vico Catina, ☎ 0744 400863; *Il Melograno*, 4 Via Bramante, ☎ 0744 300375; *Lu Somaru*, 106 Via Cesare Battisti, ☎ 0744 300486.

££ *Da Carlino*, 1 Via Piemonte, ☎ 0744 420163; *Da Graziano*, 186 Via XX Settembre, ☎ 0744 800090; *La Piazzetta*, 34 Via dei Leone, ☎ 0744 58188.

The **Caffè Pazzaglia**, Corso Tacito, has delicious cakes.

Market day on Wednesday (near the stadium).

Annual festival in honour of *St Valentine* (14 February), and Carnival celebrations.

History

The valley was inhabited in the Iron Age as finds from an important necropolis here testify. The city was founded by the Umbri in 672 BC and called *Interamna* from its position between the two streams (*inter amnes*) Nar and Serra. Conquered by the Romans in the 4C–3C, it became an important municipium on the Via Flaminia. The emperor Gallus was murdered here in 253. Just outside the city a basilica was built above the tomb of the martyr St Valentino, beheaded in AD 273. In 1174 Bishop Cristiano di Magonza destroyed much of the city by order of Frederick Barbarossa because it had taken the side of Pope Alexander III. In 1798 the French, under General Lemoine, won a victory here over the Neapolitans.

The centre of the city is **Piazza della Repubblica** and the adjoining **Piazza Europa**, where pedestrian precincts have recently been created near the bright red Palazzo Comunale. In Piazza Europa is the huge **Palazzo Spada** (its main façade is on Via Roma) an unusual fortress-like building of the late 16C, once attributed to Antonio Sangallo the Younger. It was altered in the 17C and 18C. Nearby, raised and surrounded by a little garden, is the church of **San Salvatore**. The 11C–12C façade and nave precede an interesting domed **rotonda**, with a central oculus, once thought to have been a Temple of the Sun. On the site of a Roman house, this was probably built as a little oratory in the 7C. A Roman column supports the altar table and there is a fresco of the Crucifixion. In the adjoining chapel are 14C frescoes (in very bad condition).

Via Roma, the old main street, leads out of Piazza Europa past the façade of Palazzo Spada (see above), the 16C–17C Palazzo Pierfelici, with a good portal, and a tall medieval tower.

On the right the prettily paved **Via dell'Arringo** leads to the charming **Piazza del Duomo**, in a quiet corner of the town.

The **Duomo**, thought to have been founded in the 6C, has an impressive 17C **portico** crowned with a balcony and statues by Corrado Vigni in 1933–37. The main **portal** has a fine frieze dating from the late 12C, and another door was carved in 1439. The **interior** was reconstructed in the 12C, and again in 1570, and decorated in the 17C. On the west wall, is a *Circumcision* painted in 1560 by Livio Agresti. The high altar and tabernacle in precious marbles are by Antonio Minelli (1762). The fine decorations of the **organ** are thought to have been designed by Lorenzo Bernini. The choir is by Domenico Corsi (1559). In the sacristy are fragments of sculptures and a 15C terracotta statue of the *Madonna and Child*. The **crypt** (admission on request) dates from c 1000 and has four ancient columns and a Roman altar with bucrania supports the little altar. The bones of St Anastasia were transferred here in 1904.

In the piazza is a pretty **fountain**, also by Corrado Vigni, and the 16C **Palazzo Bianchini-Riccardi**, formerly Palazzo Rosci (privately owned but admission to the hall and two courtyards sometimes allowed on request).

Just out of the piazza are the overgrown ruins of the **Roman amphitheatre** built in AD 32 by a certain Fausto Tizio Liberale. Part of the wall in opus reticulatum survives. Built at the south-west corner of the Roman city, it could hold up to 10,000 spectators.

Via XI Febbraio leads out of Piazza del Duomo to the Romanesque church of **Sant'Alò**, in the road (left) of the same name, in a peaceful position beside a restored wall fountain and little garden. It has interesting Roman and medieval sculptural fragments on the exterior. The interior, with remains of frescoes, has been closed (for admission ☎ 0744 407148).

Across Via Cavour (where on the right is the 16C Palazzo Mazzancolli), in Via Fratini the 17C Palazzo Fabrizi houses the **Pinacoteca Comunale** (open 10.00–13.00, 16.00–19.00, except Sunday; ☎ 0744 400290). The collection is well labelled. In the first room is L'Alunno's Standard with the *Crucifix and Sts Francis and Bernardine* (1497). In the second room (left) is Benozzo Gozzoli's exquisite small painting of the *Marriage of St Catherine* (signed and dated 1466); a large triptych by Pier Matteo d'Amelia (formerly known as the Master of the Gardner Annunciation) of the *Madonna with four Saints*, complete with predella and painted frame, dated 1485, is a very fine work painted for the church of San Francesco. The triptych of the *Madonna and Child between Sts Peter and Gregory the Great* is attributed to the Maestro della Dormitio di Terni (late 14C). The third room has a standard painted in tempera with the *Madonna of the Misericordia and three bishop saints* by Pietro di Giovanni Ambrosio (of the Sienese school), and two works by Gerolamo Troppa (c 1636–after 1706). The fourth room has an early 18C copy of a *Visitation* by Barocci in Santa Maria in Vallicella in Rome. The fifth room has 18C works, and the last room works by the local painter Orneore Metelli (1872–1938).

At the end of Via Fratini Via Nobili leads left to the church of **San Francesco**, first built in 1265, with an interesting exterior and elegant campanile by Antonio da Orvieto (1345). The interior has beautiful vaulting, and at the end of the south aisle (light on right) is the **Paradisi Chapel** which was frescoed in the mid-15C by Bartolomeo di Tommaso of Foligno with unusual scenes of the *Last Judgement*, inspired by Dante's *La Divina Commedia*. They are among the most interesting works in Umbria of this period (restored in 1988).

In the north aisle is a chapel with a little cupboard preserving reliquaries and church silver, and the sacristy occupies the former Cappella della Croce Santa with remains (high up) of stucco decoration by Sebastiano Fiori (1575). At the west end is an interesting 15C fresco fragment restored in 1997 (showing *Christ* and *God the Father*).

From Piazza della Repubblica (see above) the Corso Vecchio leads north-east. In a little square on the right rises the church of **San Pietro**, rebuilt in 1287 and restored after the Second World War. On the façade is a 15C relief of *Christ blessing*. Among the 14C–15C frescoes inside is a *Transition of the Virgin* (almost totally ruined). In the first niche on the north side is a 14C fresco by a painter from Spoleto. Nearby is **Palazzo Carrara** where part of the archaeological collection of the **Museo Civico** is kept, including local Iron Age finds (open weekdays 08.30–13.00, 16.00–19.00; Sat 08.30–13.00).

The Corso continues past the **Teatro Verdi** built in 1849 by Luigi Poletti with a neo-classical portico (reconstructed after the Second World War) to **San Lorenzo**, with an unusual interior with two naves, one much lower than the other. It has two Roman columns and a painting of the *Martyrdom of St Biagio* (late 16C). To the west is **Corso Tacito**, laid out in the 19C to connect Piazza della Repubblica to the station. Here the *Caffè Pazzaglia*, still famous for its cakes, was opened in 1913.

On the outskirts of the town, across the railway (reached by Viale di Porta Sant'Angelo), in the cemetery, is the church of **Santa Maria del Monumento**, enlarged in 1474, named after a Roman funerary monument (part of which is inserted into the façade). In the interior (open 08.30–09.30), on the south wall, are interesting 15C votive frescoes of uncertain subject matter.

South of the centre, reached by Via Roma, and beyond the River Nera, by Via Mentana, is the 17C basilica of **San Valentino**, on the site of a cemetery with the tomb of the martyr St Valentino, beheaded in AD 273. The first basilica here was probably built in the early 4C, and reconstructed in the 7C. It is usually open 09.00–12.00, 16.00–18.00.

BEYOND TERNI

The environs of Terni are particularly interesting. The Cascate delle Marmore waterfalls are probably the most famous waterfalls in Italy, much visited by Italian tour groups. By contrast the lovely little Lago di Piediluco is relatively unknown and is extremely well preserved. The Abbey of San Pietro in Valle is in a beautiful isolated position and has remarkable 12C frescoes. San Gemini is a pleasant little village, and Palazzo Cesi (unfortunately access is difficult) dominates the attractive village of Acquasparta. The Roman remains of Carsulae, in beautiful countryside, are also of the greatest interest.

Practical information

Information office

IAT del Ternano, Viale Cesare Battisti, Terni, ☎ 0744 423047. The Pro-Loco in San Gemini is closed for structural repairs.

Getting there

By car The **Cascate delle Marmore**, 6km south-east of Terni, are reached by car either by the Rieti road (Via Garibaldi) or the Ferentillo road (Piazza Dante). A bus runs from Piazza Dante in Terni along the Valnerina road (in 10mins).

By rail There is a **station** at Marmore, on the railway line from Rieti (and a path leads from there to the falls).

By bus There are bus services from Terni to Piediluco, San Gemini, and Arrone-Ferentillo (for the abbey of San Pietro in Valle).

Hotels

Stroncone

La Porta del Tempo country house, ☎ 0744 608190.

Piediluco

✩✩✩ *Casalago*, 3 Via Mazzelvetta, ☎ 0744 368421 and ✩✩ *Lido*, 2 Piazza Bonanni, ☎ 0744 368292, with restaurant.

San Gemini ✩✩ *Duomo*, 4 Piazza Duomo, ☎ 0744 630015. In a handsome large late 18C palace with a frescoed *salone*, in a quiet position next to the Duomo. It was opened as a hotel at the beginning of this century and there are spacious public rooms and a terrace and tiny garden. It has 24 rooms and a restaurant open in summer.

San Gemini Fonte

✩ *All'Antica Carsulae*, Via Tiberina, ☎ 0744 630163. A simple hotel with seven pleasant rooms reopened in 1998, with a good restaurant. Unfortunately right on the Via Tiberina, a busy main road.

There are **rooms to let** above **Piediluco** towards Labro at *La Vecchia Osteria*, 9 Valle Spoletina, ☎ 0744 369111, with a restaurant.

Agriturist accommodation

Ferentillo

Abbazia San Pietro in Valle, ☎ 0744 780129. Opened in 1998 in a beautiful well-restored former abbey which is in a very lovely isolated position. Family-run by the owners of the large estate. Twenty-two rooms in the spacious monks' quarters are carefully furnished, some of them overlooking the cloister, very reasonably priced. Breakfast is served in the old vaulted refectory. At present it is only open Apr–Oct, but there are plans to open it all year (there is heating and air-conditioning). There is also a restaurant here, but the set meal provided for guests on half- or full-board terms is rather disappointing. One of the most charming and peaceful spots in Umbria. *Le Due Querce*, 5 Via del Piano, ☎ 0744 780441.

Campsites

✩✩ *I Prati*, ☎ 0744 336200 at **Stroncone** and (open in summer) at the **Cascata delle Marmore** (*Marmore*, ☎ 0744 67198) and **Lago di Piediluco** (*Il Lago*, ☎ 0744 369199).

Restaurants

Stroncone

£££ *Taverna di Portanova*, 1 Via Porta Nuova, ☎ 0744 60496.

Cascate delle Marmore

£££ *Le Marmore*.

Piediluco

Above the lake, towards Labro ££ *La Vecchia Osteria*, 9 Valle Spoletino, see above. In the little resort itself (all ££): *Giosefatta*, 3 Via Gioffi, ☎ 0744 368162; *Grottino*, 59 Corso Salvati, ☎ 0744 368156; and *Lido*, 2 Piazza Bonanni, ☎ 0744 368354.

Arrone

Grottino del Nera, Casteldilago, ☎ 0744 389104 (£££), serving fish.

Polino

££ *La Baita*, Colle Bertone, ☎ 0744 789132.

Ferentillo

£ *Vecchio Ponte*, 3 Via Circonvallazione, ☎ 0744 780333, by the iron bridge across the Nera (pizzas are also served on the weekend); **££** *Abbazia San Pietro in Valle*, see above.

San Gemini

££ *Il Torchio*, Piazza Garibaldi, ☎ 0744 331136; *Duomo*, open in summer only (in the hotel, see above); **£** *Il Colle*, open in summer near the public swimming-pool in the public gardens on Viale Garibaldi.

San Gemini Fonte

££ *All'Antica Carsulae* (see above).

Portaria (near Carsulae) **£** *Pesciaioli*, also a pizzeria which serves a special type of pizza with various fillings (for a full meal at weekends it is best to book, ☎ 0744 931174). It is inconspicuous in the piazza beneath the clock-tower. Next door is the well-signposted **££** *L'Antico Frantoio*, open for dinner only, and outside the village further uphill, **££** *Morettino*.

Annual festivals

At Piediluco the *'Festa delle Acque'* is held at the end of June and beginning of July with fireworks and a procession of illuminated boats after dark. A local festival, the *'Giostra dell'Arme'*, is held at **San Gemini** in late September when two *taverne* are open which offer good meals.

South of Terni

The hill town of **Stroncone** preserves part of its medieval walls and several churches. One kilometre outside is the church of San Francesco with frescoes (one by Tiberio d'Assisi) and a wooden statue of *St Sebastian*.

Collescipoli is an interesting little village, where the church of Santa Maria has a 16C portal, 17C stuccoes and frescoes, and a striking painting of the *Death of St Joseph*, by an unknown 17C painter. Outside, in the cemetery, is the church of Santo Stefano, with a relief of the *Crucifixion* above its portal, and an inscription describing the donation in 1093.

The Cascata delle Marmore

The Cascata delle Marmore, a waterfall, 165m long and on three levels, is one of the most spectacular sites in Italy, and a famous tourist excursion. The falls have been diverted entirely for industrial purposes, but are released to their original channels on certain days throughout the year.

● The opening times tend to change, it is best to check with the IAT del Ternano, ☎ 0744 423047. Normally they can be seen on PH, and for a few hours on weekdays.

The falls are surrounded by poplars, elms, pine trees and ilex woods: a path leads to the best viewpoint. In recent years landslips have threatened the stability of the travertine rock. In great measure the falls are the work of man, for Curius Dentatus, conqueror of the Sabines (271 BC), was the first to cut a channel by which the River Velinus (Velino) was thrown over a precipice into the River Nar, to prevent floods in the plain of Reate (Rieti). Another channel was cut in 1400 and a third (draining the plain of Rieti without flooding Terni) in 1785. Among the many travellers who have admired the falls are Galileo, Charlotte of Brunswick (wife of George IV), Corot and Byron (who stayed here in the Villa Graziani Pressio in 1817 and describes them in *Childe Harold's Pilgrimage*; see also pp. 257 and 196).

Rafting and canoeing are now organised near the falls at the Belvedere

Inferiore (☎ 0330 753420), daily in July and August and at weekends from mid-March to mid-October.

Lago di Piediluco

Piediluco is a charming little resort on the beautiful **Lago di Piediluco**, one of the largest lakes in Umbria (with a perimeter of 17km), the shores of which are very well preserved. The irregular fingers of the lake extend into pretty woods. The attractive long main street of Piediluco runs parallel to the lake past the side of the church of **San Francesco** (open all day), with a fine exterior dating from 1293. It is approached by a wide flight of steps and entered by its side door (the other door, which is bricked up, has a very unusual frieze with a knot design and two lions and the Agnus Dei above). The church contains a stoup made out of an antique capital and (on the north wall) two paintings of prophets (1581). A niche decorated with stuccoes contains a statue of *St John the Baptist*. To the left is a niche with a **Roman statue** of a lady, a remarkable work and an unexpected sight. The frescoes include works by Marcantonio di Antoniazzo.

A lane leads up from the church to the ruins of the **Rocca** (542m), built by Cardinal Albornoz in 1364.

The lower Valnerina with Arrone and San Pietro in Valle

The Valnerina near Terni is rather built up but still heavily wooded with a great variety of trees. It begins to become more attractive around the village of **Arrone**. Here the church of **Santa Maria** (open all day) contains very fine frescoes: to the right of the main altar, the *Madonna of the Misericordia* (1544) is by Jacopo Siculo, and the fresco cycle of the *life of the Virgin* in the main apse (derived from the fresco cycle by Filippo Lippi in the Duomo of Spoleto) is by Vincenzo Tamagni and Giovanni di Spoleto. In the apse to the left of the main altar are three fine terracotta statues of the *Madonna and Child seated* in a niche flanked by two saints. On the left wall is a small painting in a pretty frame which is an early 20C copy of a painting by the school of Perugino, and on the right wall, in a splendid frame, *Supper at Emaus* by the school of Caravaggio.

There is a lovely byroad from Arrone to the Lago di Piediluco and another road ascends through woods to **Polino**, in a spectacular position, above which is Colle Bertone (1232m).

Ferentillo is built on either side of the Valnerina road, and has recently expanded. On one side of the road is the church at Santa Maria (usually closed), which has a tall campanile with a pyramidal top and contains 16C works, and on the other side is the church of **Santo Stefano** (also usually closed), in the crypt of which is a bizarre Museum of Mummies (usually open 09.30–12.30, 14.30–18.00; ☎ 0743 54395). Here are 20 mummified corpses: their exceptional preservation is probably due to the ventilation in the rock and the composition of the earth in which they were buried. The frescoes date from the 15C.

A little further up the valley there are two signposted roads for **San Pietro in Valle**, which is in a wonderful isolated position enclosed by woods and beautiful unspoilt countryside. The abbey is privately owned and was opened as an agriturist hotel and restaurant in 1998. The church, signposted along a path lined by cypresses above the abbey buildings, is opened by a custodian 10.30–13.00, 14.30–17.00 every day (at other times, ☎ 0744 780316).

The domed **church**, founded in the 8C, preserves its triapsidal plan, and contains remarkable though damaged **mural paintings of scriptural scenes** (c 1190). These are among the most important works of this era to have survived in Italy. On the left wall are *Old Testament scenes* and on the right wall *New Testament scenes*. On the west wall and the lower part of the nave walls are later frescoes. Also in the nave are two Roman sarcophagi, one (very damaged) with three ships, and one with remarkable hunting scenes. Near the west door there is an ancient piece of sculpture from a pagan temple. The high altar has a very unusual medieval Lombard altar with decorations in bas-relief signed by 'Ursus', and a panel behind decorated with floral motifs. The mosaic pavement behind the altar is also interesting. The apse frescoes (being restored) include *Christ blessing*, and, below, the *Madonna and Child with angels*, and *Benedictine saints* by the Maestro di Eggi. On the right, set into the presbytery wall, is the so-called sarcophagus of Faroaldo (3C), a Roman work with Dionysiac scenes, and nearby another Roman sarcophagus, with Amore and cupid. In the right apse are fine frescoes by the school of Giotto (the *Madonna with Saints*).

The lovely **campanile** dates from the 12C. From the side door (sometimes opened on request), with two Lombard statuettes on the outer face, the attractive two-tiered **cloister** can be seen.

The **abbey**, beautifully restored, is at present open Apr–Oct, Tues, Fri & Sun 11.00–13.00. The pretty upper Valnerina is described on p. 215.

San Gemini, Carsulae and Acquasparta

San Gemini is a small town famous for its mineral water (see below). There is a large free car-park off the approach road a few metres below **Piazza San Francesco** with a wall fountain below a garden with a large pine tree. Here is Palazzo Comunale with its clock and **San Francesco** with an attractive vaulted interior, and interesting frescoes (15C–17C).

Via Roma, left of the church, leads through the newer part of the town with the 19C **Duomo** next to a large late 18C palace which has been a hotel since the beginning of the 20C. The monumental **gateway** at this end of the town dates from 1723. Off the main road (right) outside the gate, surrounded by a garden, is the well-kept church of **San Nicolò** (privately owned; opened on Fri, Sat & Sun 10.00–13.00, 15.00–17.00) with Roman and medieval remains and a fresco of 1295. The exterior is in very good condition, and there is Roman masonry in the lower part of the walls. The portal has an unusual carved frieze and two lions.

From Piazza San Francesco (see above), **Via Casventino**, a lovely narrow old street, leads through the medieval gateway past fine houses including (no. 22) a beige-coloured palace with details in brick and terracotta rosettes on the cornice. In a little piazza is the 12C **Palazzo del Popolo**, a picturesque small building recently restored (for admission, ☎ 0744 331438), and the side of the oratory of **San Carlo** with frescoes of the 14C–15C in the interior (often closed), including a charming lunette of the Maestà beneath the altar tabernacle.

Via Casventino ends near **San Giovanni** which has two doorways: the one on the right looks on to an attractive little piazza with an arch leading out to a terrace overlooking the valley (disturbed by the superstrada) and towards the hills, and the one on the left near an old gate in the walls, which has a very worn Cosmatesque portal, the mosaics of which have virtually disappeared. The inscription above (now almost invisible) records the date (1199) and architects of the church. The oddly shaped interior has two octagonal pilasters and four gilded wooden altars.

North-east of San Gemini are the spa buildings of **San Gemini Fonte** in a large park where the water can be drunk. Nearby are the extensive Roman remains of **Carsulae** in a beautiful peaceful setting in lovely countryside. It can be reached by two roads, both signposted, off the road between Acquasparta and Cesi. The ruins are unenclosed and explained by maps and signs. This was an important Roman station on the Via Flaminia, on the site of the Umbrian town of Carseoli. It was abandoned after an earthquake.

The little medieval church of **San Damiano** was built from Roman materials. It faces the Via Flaminia, with its ancient paving stones, which formed the cardo maximus of the town. On the side opposite the church is a restored arch near shops which gave access to the forum, once surrounded by public buildings including two temples, the bases of which remain. Via Flaminia leads uphill and winds round to the left to the limit of the town where a beautiful arch, known as the **Arco di San Damiano**, is well preserved. Outside the gate are remains of funerary monuments, one of them a large circular sepulchre and one with a conical roof.

Near the church of San Damiano was the residential district of the Roman town and a basilica, beside which the decumanus maximus leads down towards the amphitheatre, connected to the theatre beyond.

South of San Gemini Fonte is **Cesi**, a little medieval town with the deconsecrated church of Sant'Angelo at the entrance, with an interesting façade. It is sometimes open for concerts. Higher up is the church of Santa Maria (the altarpiece of the *Madonna and Child with saints and angels* of 1308 by an artist, known from this work as the Maestro di Cesi, which shows the influence of the Spoleto school, is no longer on show). Above is Piazza Umberto I with a fine view.

North of San Gemini Fonte is **Portaria** a tiny quiet little village set into the side of a wooded hill surrounded by olives, with several restaurants (see p. 267). On the right of the approach road is a little public fountain still in use as a wash-house. The piazza has a well and postbox of 1674 beneath a tall-clock tower which chimes every quarter of an hour. The stepped street leads up through it and beneath more arches to the church (kept locked) which has an interesting bas-relief of three amphorae on its façade. At the top of the village an old monastery is being restored.

Acquasparta is an attractive little town, north of San Gemini Fonte (market on Thursday). It preserves remains of its walls and in the centre is the fine **Palazzo Cesi** (now owned by the University of Perugia; admission by appointment, ☎ 075/5852222; or enquire at the municipio), built by Giovanni Domenico Bianchi in 1564. Galileo stayed here for a month in 1624 as a guest of Federico Cesi. It has a lovely interior courtyard. In the loggia in the piazza there are interesting Roman cippi and inscriptions. Corso dei Lincei (named to commemorate the refoundation here in 1609 of the Accademia dei Lincei by Federico Cesi) follows the garden wall of the palace.

In the church of **Santa Cecilia** the third south chapel, built with a dome in 1581, contains the tomb of Federico Cesi, and cupboards with reliquaries. The 16C altarpiece of the Crucifixion has recently been restored. Outside the walls is the church of the **Crocifisso** with a façade dating from 1606, and the church of **San Francesco** (kept locked; ask at Santa Cecilia for the key), built in 1290 and containing a 15C Crucifix.

Acquasparta became well known as a spa town after 1908. Its spring water, praised by St Francis, was protected in the 17C by Federico Cesi and is recognised for its curative properties. The mineral water, known as Amerino, is bottled here.

Glossary

Aedicule, small opening framed by two columns and a pediment, originally used in classical architecture

Amphora, antique vase, usually of large dimensions, for oil and other liquids

Ancona, retable or large altarpiece (painted or sculpted) in an architectural frame

Antefix, ornament placed at the lower corners of the tiled roof of a temple to conceal the space between the tiles and the cornice

Antiphonal, choir-book containing a collection of *antiphonae* – verses sung in response by two choirs

Arca, wooden chest with a lid, for sacred or secular use. Also, monumental sarcophagus in stone, used by Christians and pagans

Architrave, lowest part of an entablature, horizontal frame above a door

Archivolt, moulded architrave carried round an arch

Atlantes (or *telamones*), male figures used as supporting columns

Atrium, forecourt, usually of a Byzantine church or a classical Roman house

Attic, topmost storey of a Classical building, hiding the spring of the roof

Badia, *abbazia*, abbey

Baldacchino, canopy supported by columns, usually over an altar

Basilica, originally a Roman building used for public administration; in Christian architecture, an aisled church with a clerestory and apse, and no transepts

Borgo, a suburb; street leading away from the centre of a town

Bottega, the studio of an artist: the pupils who worked under his direction

Bozzetto, sketch for a painting, or a small model for a piece of sculpture

Broccatello, a clouded veined marble from Siena

Bucchero, Etruscan black terracotta ware

Bucranium/a, a form of classical decoration – skulls of oxen garlanded with flowers

Campanile, bell-tower, often detached from the building to which it belongs

Camposanto, cemetery

Canephora, figure bearing a basket, often used as a caryatid

Canopic vase, Egyptian or Etruscan vase enclosing the entrails of the dead

Cantoria, singing-gallery in a church

Cappella, chapel

Cartoon, from *cartone*, meaning large sheet of paper. A full-size preparatory drawing for a painting or fresco

Caryatid, female figure used as a supporting column

Cassoné, a decorated chest, usually a dower chest

Cavea, the part of a theatre or amphitheatre occupied by the rows of seats

Cella, sanctuary of a temple, usually in the centre of the building

Cenacolo, scene of the Last Supper (often in the refectory of a convent)

Chalice, wine cup used in the celebration of Mass

Chiaroscuro, distribution of light and shade, apart from colour, in a painting

Ciborium, casket or tabernacle containing the Host

Cipollino, onion-marble; a greyish marble with streaks of white or green

Cippus, sepulchral monument in the form of an altar

Cista, casket, usually of bronze and cylindrical in shape, to hold jewels, toilet articles, etc., and decorated with mythological subjects

Cloisonné, type of enamel decoration

Columbarium, a building (usually sub-terranean) with niches to hold urns containing the ashes of the dead

Commune, a town or city which adopted a form of independent self-government in the Middle Ages. Municipal government in Italy is called the *Comune*

Condottiere, professional military commander

Confessio, crypt beneath the high altar and raised choir of a church, usually containing the relics of a saint

Corbel, a projecting block, usually of stone

Cupola, dome

Cyclopean, the term applied to walls of unmortared masonry, older than the Etruscan civilisation, and attributed by the ancients to the giant Cyclopes

Diptych, painting or ivory panel in two sections

Dossal, altarpiece

Dosseret, a second block above the capital of a column

Duomo, cathedral

Edicola, *see* aedicule

Exedra, semicircular recess

Ex voto, tablet or small painting expressing gratitude to a saint

Fresco (in Italian, *affresco*), wall-painting using pigments mixed only with water and without the addition of any sort of glue, executed on wet plaster (which acts as a glue). The wall was prepared with a coat of plaster on which a *sinopia* (see below) was often sketched. This was then covered with another coat of fresh plaster only on the area to be painted that day, and the fresco begun. From the 16C onwards a cartoon, a full-size preparatory drawing on a large sheet of paper, was often used instead. It was transferred on to the plaster either by pricking the outline with small holes over which a powder was dusted, or by means of a stylus which left an incised line on the wet plaster. It is possible to detach frescoes, as well as the *sinopie* beneath, from the walls on which they were executed

Giallo antico, red-veined yellow marble from Numidia

Gonfalon, banner of a medieval guild or commune

Graffiti, design on a wall made with an iron tool on a prepared surface, the design showing in white. Also used loosely to describe scratched designs or words on walls

Greek-cross, cross with the arms of equal length

Grisaille, painting in various tones of grey

Grotesque, painted or stucco decoration in the style of the ancient Romans (found during the Renaissance in Nero's Domus Aurea in Rome, then underground, hence the name, from 'grotto'). The delicate ornamental decoration usually includes patterns of flowers, sphynxes, birds, human figures, etc., against a light ground

Herm/ae, quadrangular pillar (or pillars) decreasing in girth towards the ground surmounted by a bust

Hypogeum, subterranean excavation for the burial of the dead (usually Etruscan)

Iconostasis, high balustrade with figures of saints, guarding the sanctuary of a Byzantine church

Impasto, thickly applied oil paint, or early Etruscan ware made of inferior clay

Intarsia (or *tarsia*), inlay of wood, marble, ivory or metal

Intonaco, plaster

Intrados, underside or soffit of an arch

Krater, antique mixing-bowl, conical in shape with rounded base

Kylix, wide shallow vase with two handles and short stem

Latin-cross, cross with a long vertical arm

Lavabo, hand-basin usually outside a refectory or sacristy

Loggia, covered gallery or balcony, usually preceding a larger building

Lunette, semicircular space in a vault or ceiling, or above a door or window, often decorated with a painting or relief

Lustre, iridescent surface used to decorate ceramics made from metallic oxides. Widely used to decorate Islamic pottery, the technique was introduced to Italy in the early 16C by potters working in Umbria in Gubbio and Deruta

Maestà, *Madonna and Child enthroned in majesty*

Maiolica (often called majolica), tin-glazed earthenware, introduced into Italy from Spain in the Renaissance.

Matroneum, gallery reserved for women in early Christian churches

Medallion, large medal; loosely, a circular ornament

Meta, turning-post at either end of a Roman circus

Monochrome, painting or drawing in one colour only

Monolith, single stone

Narthex, vestibule of a Christian basilica

Niello, black substance, usually a compound of sulphur and silver, used in an engraved design on metal surfaces

Nimbus, luminous ring surrounding the heads of saints in paintings; a square nimbus denoted that the person was living at that time

Oculus, round window

Opera (**del Duomo**), the office in charge of the fabric of a building (i.e. the cathedral)

Opus Reticulatum, masonry arranged in squares or diamonds so that the mortar joints make a network pattern

Opus Tessellatum, mosaic formed entirely of square tesserae

Pala, large altarpiece

Palazzo, any dignified and important building

Palombino, fine-grained white marble

Pastiglia, a moulded paste used to decorate small wooden caskets, or furniture

Pavonazzetto, yellow marble blotched with blue

Pax, sacred object used by a priest for the blessing of peace, and offered for the kiss of the faithful. A small plaque or tablet, often circular, engraved, enamelled or painted in a gold or silver frame

Pendentive, concave spandrel beneath a dome

Peristyle, court or garden surrounded by a columned portico

Pietà, group of the Virgin mourning the dead Christ

Pietre dure, hard or semi-precious stones, often used in the form of mosaics to decorate cabinets, table-tops, etc

Pietra serena, fine-grained dark grey sandstone, easy to carve

Pieve, parish church

Piscina, Roman tank; a basin for an officiating priest to wash his hands before Mass

Plaquette, small metal tablet with relief decoration

Pluteus/ei, marble panel (or panels), usually decorated; a series of them used to form a parapet to precede the altar of a church

Podestà, governing magistrate of a city, who was traditionally a foreigner

Polyptych, painting or panel in more than three sections

Porta, gate (or door)

Porta del Morto, in certain old mansions of Umbria and Tuscany, a narrow raised doorway, said to be for the passage of biers of the dead, but more probably for use in troubled times when the main gate would be barred

Predella, small painting or panel, usually in sections, attached below a large altarpiece, illustrating the story of a saint, the life of the Virgin, etc

Presepio, literally, crib or manger. A group of statuary of which the central subject is the Infant Jesus in the manger

Pretura, local magistrates court

Pronaos, porch in front of the cella of a temple

Putto/i, figure of a young boy (or boys) sculpted or painted, usually nude

Quadratura, painted architectural perspectives.

Quatrefoil, four-lobed design

Reredos, decorated screen rising behind an altar

Rhyton, drinking-horn usually ending in an animal's head

Rood-screen, a screen below the rood or Crucifix dividing the nave from the chancel of a church

Scagliola, a material made from selenite and used to imitate marble or pietre dure, often used for altar frontals and columns

Scena, the stage of a Roman theatre

Schiacciato, term used to describe very low relief in sculpture, where there is an emphasis on the delicate line rather than the depth of the panel

Schola cantorum, enclosure for the choristers in the nave of an early Christian church, adjoining the sanctuary

Sinopia, large sketch for a fresco made on the rough wall in a red earth pigment called sinopia (because it originally came from Sinope on the Black Sea). By detaching a fresco it is now possible to see the sinopia beneath and detach that too

Situla, water-bucket

Soffit, underside or intrados of an arch

Spandrel, surface between two arches in an arcade or the triangular space on either side of an arch

Stamnos, big-bellied vase with two small handles at the sides, closed by a lid

Stele, upright stone bearing a monumental inscription

Stemma, coat of arms or heraldic device

Stereobate, basement of a temple or other building

Stoup, vessel for Holy Water, usually near the west door of a church

Stylobate, basement of a columned temple or other building

Tablinum, room in a Roman house with one side opening on to the central courtyard

Telamones, see *atlantes*

Tessera, a small cube of marble, glass, etc., used in mosaic work

Thermae, Roman baths

Tholos, a circular building

Thurible, a censor or vessel for the burning of incense in church

Tondo/i, round painting or bas-relief

Transenna, open grille or screen, usually of marble, in an early Christian church

Travertine, tufa quarried near Tivoli

Triclinium, dining room and reception room of a Roman house

Triptych, painting or panel in three sections

Trompe-l'oeil, literally, a deception of the eye. Used to describe illusionist decoration, painted architectural perspectives, etc

Tufa, porous volcanic rock used as a building stone

Ustrina, a walled area for the cremation of the dead

Villa, country house with its garden

Westwork, west end of a Carolingian or Romanesque church with a massive central tower and, inside, a double storey, with the upper room open to the nave

Index to Italian artists

Index

A